Peace, Discontent, and Constitutional Law

This book offers a multidiscursive analysis of the constitutional foundations for peaceful coexistence, the constitutional background for discontent and the impact of discontent, and the consequences of conflict and revolution on the constitutional order of a democratic society which may lead to its implosion. It explores the capacity of the constitutional order to serve as a reliable framework for peaceful co-existence while allowing for reasonable and legitimate discontent. It outlines the main factors contributing to rising pressure on constitutional order which may produce an implosion of constitutionalism and constitutional democracy as we have come to know it. The collection presents a wide range of views on the ongoing implosion of the liberal-democratic constitutional consensus which predetermined the constitutional axiology, the institutional design, the constitutional mythology and the functioning of the constitutional orders since the last decades of the 20th century. The constitutional perspective is supplemented with perspectives from financial, EU, labour and social security law, administrative law, migration and religious law. Liberal viewpoints encounter radical democratic and critical legal viewpoints. The work thus allows for a plurality of viewpoints, theoretical preferences and thematic discourses offering a pluralist scientific account of the key challenges to peaceful coexistence within the current constitutional framework.

The book provides a valuable resource for academics, researchers and policymakers working in the areas of constitutional law and politics.

Martin Belov is Professor in Constitutional and Comparative Constitutional Law at the University of Sofia 'St. Kliment Ohridski'. He is Vice Dean of the University of Sofia 'St. Kliment Ohridski', Faculty of Law responsible for international relations and digitalization. He has published widely on aspects of comparative constitutional law.

Comparative Constitutional Change

Comparative Constitutional Change has developed into a distinct field of constitutional law. It encompasses the study of constitutions through the way they change and covers a wide scope of topics and methodologies. Books in this series include work on developments in the functions of the constitution, the organization of powers and the protection of rights, as well as research that focuses on formal amendment rules and the relation between constituent and constituted power. The series includes comparative approaches along with books that focus on single jurisdictions, and brings together research monographs and edited collections which allow the expression of different schools of thought. While the focus is primarily on law, where relevant the series may also include political science, historical, philosophical and empirical approaches that explore constitutional change.

Series editors:

Xenophon Contiades is Professor of Public Law, Panteion University, Athens, Greece and Managing Director, Centre for European Constitutional Law, Athens, Greece.

Thomas Fleiner is Emeritus Professor of Law at the University of Fribourg, Switzerland. He teaches and researches in the areas of Federalism, Rule of Law, Multicultural State; Comparative Administrative and Constitutional Law; Political Theory and Philosophy; Swiss Constitutional and Administrative Law; and Legislative Drafting. He has published widely in these and related areas.

Alkmene Fotiadou is Research Associate at the Centre for European Constitutional Law, Athens.

Richard Albert is Professor of Law at the University of Texas at Austin.

Also in the series:

Constitutional Change and Popular Sovereignty
Populism, Politics and the Law in Ireland
Edited by Maria Cahill, Colm Ó Cinnéide, Seán Ó Conaill, and Conor O'Mahony

For more information about this series, please visit: www.routledge.com/Comparative-Constitutional-Change/book-series/COMPCONST

Peace, Discontent and Constitutional Law

Challenges to Constitutional Order and Democracy

Edited by Martin Belov

Routledge
Taylor & Francis Group
LONDON AND NEW YORK

First published 2021
by Routledge
2 Park Square, Milton Park, Abingdon, Oxon OX14 4RN

and by Routledge
52 Vanderbilt Avenue, New York, NY 10017

Routledge is an imprint of the Taylor & Francis Group, an informa business

British Library Cataloguing-in-Publication Data
A catalogue record for this book is available from the British Library

Library of Congress Cataloging-in-Publication Data
Names: Belov, Martin, editor.
Title: Peace, discontent and constitutional law : challenges to constitutional order and democracy / edited by Martin Belov.
Description: Milton Park, Abingdon,
Oxon ; New York, NY : Routledge, 2021. |
Series: Comparative constitutional change |
Includes bibliographical references and index.
Identifiers: LCCN 2020050923 (print) | LCCN 2020050924 (ebook) |
ISBN 9780367539702 (hardback) | ISBN 9781003083894 (ebook)
Subjects: LCSH: Government, Resistance to. | Constitutional law. |
Demonstrations—Law and legislation. | Assembly, Right of.
Classification: LCC K3269 .P43 2021 (print) |
LCC K3269 (ebook) | DDC 342.08/54—dc23
LC record available at https://lccn.loc.gov/2020050923
LC ebook record available at https://lccn.loc.gov/2020050924

ISBN: 978-0-367-53970-2 (hbk)
ISBN: 978-0-367-53972-6 (pbk)
ISBN: 978-1-003-08389-4 (ebk)

Typeset in Galliard
by codeMantra

Contents

About the authors

Martin Belov (editor) is Professor of Constitutional and Comparative Constitutional Law at the University of Sofia 'St. Kliment Ohridski'. He is Vice Dean of the University of Sofia 'St. Kliment Ohridski', Faculty of Law responsible for international relations and digitalization. He has been a visiting professor at University Paris II Panthéon-Assas (2019), University Roma Tre, Rome, Italy (2019), Goethe-University Frankfurt am Main, Germany (2019), University of Girona, Spain (2019), 9 Europa-University Viadrina, Frankfurt (Oder), Germany (2017 and 2018), University of Bari, Italy (2018), European Law and Governance School, Athens (2017–2018), University of Södertorn, Stockholm, Sweden (2017), Scuola Superiore Sant'Anna, Pisa, Italy (2016), University of Warsaw, Poland (2015), University of Lisbon, Portugal (2012), State University of Milan, Italy (2011), University of Cologne, Germany (2007–2009), etc. He has also been a project researcher at the Max-Planck Institute for European Legal History, Frankfurt am Main, Germany (2010–2012) and visiting researcher at the Institute for Federalism, Fribourg, Switzerland (2014). He has undertaken funded research at the University of Oxford (2017), Max-Planck Institute for Comparative Public Law and International Law, Heidelberg, Germany (2009) and many other academic institutions. Martin Belov is member of the European Group of Public Law, International Association of Legislation, the Advisory Board of the Central and Eastern European Forum of Young Legal, Political and Social Theorists, and other scientific and academic organizations. He is member of the scientific boards of many academic journals. He has published 19 books and more than 80 scientific papers.

Enrico Albanesi is an Associate Professor of Constitutional Law at the Department of Law, University of Genoa, and Associate Research Fellow at the Institute of Advanced Legal Studies (IALS), University of London. He wrote a monograph on constitutional pluralism and EU infringement proceedings (2018) and was Visiting Scholar at the College of Europe in Bruges (2016). He gave several presentations overseas (Albania, Algeria, Belgium, Bulgaria, Finland, Iceland, Israel, Japan, Montenegro, Poland, Thailand, the UK, the USA, Spain) and published articles in peer-reviewed international journals (*The Theory and Practice of Legislation*, *European Journal of Law Reform, Statute Law Review*).

Gavin Barrett is a professor in the Sutherland School of Law at University College Dublin, Ireland specialising in EU Law and the sometime Jean Monnet Professor of European Economic and Constitutional Law there. He has written books, book chapters, and articles in leading journals on the Eurozone, the EU and democracy-related subjects. His latest book is *The Evolving Role of National Parliaments in the European Union: Ireland as a Case Study* (Manchester University Press, 2018).

Francesco Bilancia LLB (Hons), PhD Sapienza University – Rome, is a Professor of Public Law and Vice-Director of the Department of Legal and Social Studies at University of Chieti-Pescara (Italy). He is Vice-Director of the journal *Costituzionalismo.it*. He has been a Visiting Research Scholar at the Centre for Socio-Legal Studies in the University of Oxford (2014 and 2016); Professor Convidado at UNISINOS (Rio Grande do Sul, Brazil), 2014. He has led various research groups within national and international projects. His research interests are public and constitutional law to theory of law, fundamental rights, market regulation and social welfare law, EU law, and the European integration process. He has authored, co-authored, and edited about 150 scientific works throughout a 25-year an academic career. He has written a constitutional law handbook (*Corso di diritto costituzionale cedam*, Padua, 2011).

Wojciech Brzozowski is an associate professor at the Faculty of Law and Administration, University of Warsaw, head of the Department of Law and Religion, vice-president of the Polish Association of Law and Religion (PTPW). He also sits on the Committee of Legal Studies of the Polish Academy of Sciences (KNP PAN) and is a member of the International Consortium for Law and Religious Studies (ICLARS). He is also a member of the Advisory Board of the Sofia Legal Science Network (SLSN). His main research areas are constitutional law, law and religion, and international human rights law.

Víctor Manuel Cázares Lira is an independent scholar currently finishing off his intellectual biography of Charles A. Beard. He obtained his doctoral degree in history from the University of Edinburgh after earning a master's degree in history at the University of Uppsala and a bachelor's degree in political science at the National Autonomous University of Mexico. He specialises in the historiography of the founding of America is now researching early Latin American constitutionalism.

Stefano Civitarese Matteucci, LLB (Hons) Bologna University, PhD University of Florence is a professor of public law at the University of Chieti-Pescara (IT) and and an honorary visiting professor at the York Law School (2016–2021). His research interests range from constitutional law to theory of law, administrative law, social welfare law, and EU law. He has authored, co-authored, and edited about 160 scientific works in a25-year academic career. He has led various national and international research projects. In 2017 he co-edited with Simon Halliday *Social Rights in an Age Austerity: European Perspectives* (Routledge). He is the national rapporteur for Italy in He is the national rapporteur for Italy in The Oxford Compendium of National Legal Responses to Covid-19, J. King, O. Ferraz (et. al) (eds), a global project promoted by University College London Faculty of Laws, King's College London Transnational Law Institute, and the Max Planck Institute for Comparative Public Law and International Law.

Marie Diekmann studied law and political science in France and Germany. From 2015 to 2018 she worked on a research project on normative paradoxes in law at the Institute for Social Research in Frankfurt am Main. Since 2019, she has been a research assistant at the Institute for Civil Law and Business Law at the University of Frankfurt. Her research interests are democratic theory, philosophy of law, and labour law.

José Luis Martí is Associate Professor of Law and Political Philosophy at Pompeu Fabra University of Barcelona. He has been Laurance Rockefeller Visiting Fellow at the University Center for Human Values (Princeton University, 2008–2009) and a visiting professor at the University of Richmond (2014). He develops interdisciplinary research on republicanism, global governance, and democratic theory, particularly on deliberative democracy, participatory democracy, collective intelligence and artificial intelligence. He has published dozens of articles and several books, including *La república deliberativa* (Marcial Pons, 2006), *Deliberative Democracy and Its Discontents*, co-edited with Samantha Besson (Ashgate, 2006), *Legal Republicanism*, also co-edited with Samantha Besson (Oxford University Press, 2009), and *A Political Philosophy in Public Life*, co-authored with Philip Pettit (Princeton University Press, 2010). He is currently collaborating on The Governance Lab's CrowdLaw Project researching on how the new technologies may decisively contribute to crowdsourcing law-making and improve its quality as much as its legitimacy on the basis of strong collective intelligence mechanisms.

Teodora Petrova is a researcher within the department of Foreign and International Social Law at the Max-Planck Institute for Social Law and Social Policy and a PhD student at the Ludwig Maximilian University of Munich in Germany. The range of her topics of research include comparative pension law, social and labour rights, as well as trade liberalisation and its reconciliation with international labour standards. Teodora holds a LLM degree from the European Union Institute in Florence, Italy.

Pasquale Viola is a post-doctoral research fellow at the Charles University (Prague, Czech Republic) and holds a PhD in comparative law and processes of integration. His research fields include comparative constitutional law, Asian constitutionalism, environmental and climate change law, political and legal theory. He has been a lecturer and speaker at several international conferences and fora. Among his latest publications: *Costituzionalismo autoctono* (2020), *South Asian Constitutionalism? A Contemporary Pathway Towards an Authentic Constitutional Order* (2020), *The Constitutional Framework of India: Territorial Organization, Political Institutions and Rights* (2020).

Apostolos Vlachogiannis holds a PhD from the University Panthéon-Assas Paris II (*La living constitution: Les juges de la cour suprême des Etats-Unis et la constitution*, Paris: Classiques Garnier, 2014). He works as a legal counsel at the Office of Legal Affairs of the Presidency of the Hellenic Republic and teaches public law at the Hellenic Open University and Panteion University in Athens. His main research interest is comparative constitutional law, constitutional theory, and fundamental rights. He recently published a book (in Greek) entitled *The Constitution in the New European Economic Governance: Trends and Mutations of National Constitutionalism.*

Introduction

Martin Belov

This is a rough book. Its roughness stems from its engagement with the hot topics of the contemporary world and especially with their impact on constitutions, constitutionalism, and constitutional democracy. Thus, the book aims at looking straight in the 'eye of the bull' naturally offering more questions than answers. The contributions to this volume are provocative. They render critical account on the political, economic, social, religious, and cultural challenges to constitutional democracy.

The contributions are unified on two criteria. These are the topical issues of constitutional order, disorder, peace, and discontent discussed in the book and their socio-legal approach to the problems. Nevertheless, the contributors explore a wide range of issues related to multiple fields of constitutionally relevant socio-political relations. They include the constitutional foundations of peace and discontent, an outline of the theory of participatory democracy based on the right to challenge and protest, the main challenges to the 'ordering of orders' and especially of creating a harmonious EU legal order, the key factors for maintenance of the socio-political equilibrium in diverse, pluralist, and even fragmented societies, the outline of the material constitution of the EU, and the topical socio-economic and financial challenges to constitutionalism produced by neoliberal globalisation.

Thus, the contributions to this book provide a multidiscursive account on the factors for the major disruptions in constitutional order. They also explore the main aspects of the issues at stake as well as their most important consequences for keeping the equilibrium of the constitutional order. Indeed, a book on constitutional foundations of order and disorder, of peace and discontent, offering multifaceted debate on the reasons for destabilisation of constitutionalism in these current troubled and transitional times serves as a good point for intellectual and academic reflection, but also raises practical issues with important socio-legal implications.

We are indeed living in rather turbulent times. We are going through a period of deep social, political, and economic change. This change has produced a crisis of capitalism, liberal democracy, and neoliberal globalisation. The crisis has deep impact on societies, economic and financial orders, but also leaves its imprint on constitutionalism and constitutional law as we know it for the last two centuries. In general, it deeply affects Western constitutional civilisation.

Capitalism has been, so far, foundational for democracy. Modern democracy has emerged as a result of the industrial revolution and thus is, to an extent, a product of capitalism. It is, in a sense, a device for pacifying the extremities of capitalism and an institutional device for coordination and mutual cooperation and coexistence of the different strata and forces of the capitalist society. Capitalism has been a precondition for the development of liberal-democratic constitutional order with the institutions of the civil society and the public sphere as their driving force. Non-capitalist democracy has never existed so far with the exception of some very limited experiences with systems loosely resembling democracy as per our contemporary standards in the ancient world and during the late Middle Ages. The experience with Soviet democracies or with other radical forms of detachment of democracy from capitalism shows that non-capitalist democracy has been impossible so far. Hence, from the viewpoint of democracy, capitalism and democracy seem like a couple whose disentanglement usually leads to fictitious authoritarian regimes masqueraded as democracy.

However, it seems that while democracy has been impossible without capitalism, capitalism can be detached from democracy. In this regard, capitalism may be non-democratic. At a certain point, it can suffocate democracy and couple it with authoritarian political and constitutional orders. This puts constitutional democracy in deep danger because history shows that in so far as it cannot exist without capitalism, it may be abandoned by capitalism for the sake of new opportunities which authoritarianism gives for profit maximisation, interest protection, and global expansion. The warnings for the emergence of surveillance capitalism,[1] authoritarian capitalism or even state governed capitalism indicate some of the most important risks stemming from the cross-fertilization between capitalism and authoritarianism. The illiberal democracies[2] can be viewed as product of such hybridization deviating from democracy for the sake of capitalism and trying to provide a model based on political illiberalism awkwardly combined with economic neoliberalism.

Moreover, capitalism is experiencing structural cracks which are the object of intensified research and multiple and rather diverse predictions. There are prophecies foretelling the end of capitalism, or at least the death of its democratic version.[3] There are also discussions of its restructuring and adjustment to the conceptual challenges of the global risk society and the information and technological revolution. Radical and innovative suggestions for the future of

1 Shoshana Zuboff, *The Age of Surveillance Capitalism. The Fight for a Human Future at the New Frontier of Power* (Public Affairs 2019).

2 Fareed Zakaria, *The Future of Freedom: Illiberal Democracy at Home and Abroad* (Norton 2007) 1–304.

3 See Wolfgang Streek, *How Will Capitalism End?* (Verso 2017) 1–272, Thomas Piketty, *Capital in the Twenty-First Century* (Harvard University Press 2017) 1–576 and Paul Mason, *Postcapitalism: A Guide to Our Future* (Penguin 2016) 1–368.

humanity[4] or capitalism[5] are on the rise. Claims for the emergence of surveillance capitalism[6] gain momentum. Nevertheless, while the financial crisis and even the COVID-19 crisis can be defined as manifestations for the crisis of capitalism, it is not clear what will be the future of capitalism and especially its pairing with constitutional democracy. In fact, this is a question which is more important for democracy and constitutionalism than for capitalism. Actually, the most important determinant for the future of capitalism, democracy, and their constitutional dimensions is the ongoing information and technological revolution.

In addition to the crisis of capitalism there is also a crisis of neoliberal globalisation. Globalisation was the most important phenomenon in recent political, economic, and constitutional history. The last and most visible and powerful wave of globalisation has lasted for approximately three decades after the fall of the Berlin Wall. It has profoundly changed the constitutional orders of most parts of the world. It has also produced the emergence of supranational constitutionalism – especially with a view to the EU, and has even triggered the feasible assent of global constitutionalism and global governance. And it has been, maybe temporarily, brought to a standstill by the COVID-19 pandemic.

Brexit, the election of Donald Trump as president of the USA, the rise of illiberal democracies and neo-nationalism and finally the COVID-19 pandemic seem to have deeply challenged the steady trend for neoliberal globalisation. These events may even partially reverse globalisation, bring it to a halt in certain spheres, and replace the project of global constitutionalism with schemes for regional constitutionalism or offer experiments with non-liberal or at least non-neoliberal globalisation. Thus, the project for global post-Westphalian constitutionalism may be replaced by a new vision of regional neo-Westphalian constitutionalism.

In any case, the crisis of neoliberal globalisation has a profound impact on constitutional orders triggering diverse waves of political discontent. Thus, the seemingly stable trend for the establishment of global constitutional order, based on constitutional pluralism and post-Westphalian constitutionalism, may be challenged by neo-Westphalian constitutionalism and a period of global, regional, national, and even subnational constitutional disorder. Consequently, a book exploring the constitutional foundations of peace, order, disorder, and discontent seems to be timely and appropriate. This is so, especially if it provides a critical assessment of the impact of sector-specific disorders and discontents, allocated in the spheres of economy and welfare, maintenance of ethnic, national and religious pluralism and coexistence, and the democratic structures of the society, on constitutionalism and constitutional law.

4 See Yuval Noah Harari, *Homo Deus: A Brief History of Tomorrow* (Vintage 2017), 1–528.
5 See Piketty (2017).
6 See Zuboff (2019).

The crisis of capitalism and neoliberal globalisation is paralleled by a crisis of constitutional democracy. This is simultaneously a crisis of representative democracy, a crisis of party democracy, and a crisis of liberal democracy. Both parts of the concept of representative democracy – representation and democracy – are increasingly contested. All elements of constitutional democracy are being challenged by the ongoing deep shifts in the socio-political context. Party democracy is suffering from the crisis of ideology and from the subsequent crisis of trust and belief. Protest, anti-systemic, and catch-all parties are on the rise while the belief in the feasibility of a party democracy is steadily vanishing. This leads to crisis of representation. In fact, this is a crisis of democratic representation while other non-democratic options such as illiberal, identitarian or overtly autocratic systems are on the rise.

There is an ongoing divorce between liberalism and democracy producing cracks in the fundamental coupling of liberalism with democracy which has been of pivotal importance for constitutional peace and contentment during the twentieth century.[7] Liberal democracy and liberal-democratic constitutionalism were extremely important compromises and very successful formulas for the functioning or Western representative democratic constitutional orders for many decades. Now, their juncture is the object of targeted deconstruction by alternative visions. These are neoliberal globalism and libertarianism, on the one hand, and illiberalism, illiberal democracy, neo-nationalism, and revolutionary constitutionalism,[8] on the other.

The decade 2010–2020 has seen a massive and spectacular clash between these two extreme groups of ideologies. Apart from the intellectual counterposition this clash produces deep tensions also on the political, geopolitical, and financial-economic playgrounds. It has huge, profound, and long-lasting implications for constitutionalism and constitutional law. The most important among them is the replacement of the previous, obviously to a great extent fictitious, consensus for the global spread of constitutional democracy in its liberal-democratic version with waves of constitutional discontent triggering deep constitutional, political, and social disorder.

There are several main reasons for this deep and complex crisis with so diverse and important implications. The first and maybe most important one is the ongoing information and technological revolution. It is in the course of profoundly changing the shape of constitutional orders. New issues are stemming from the information and technology revolution, which is also exposing old discrepancies enshrined in the constitutional orders.[9]

7 See Paul Blokker, 'Populism as a constitutional project' (2019) 17 (2), *International Journal of Constitutional Law*, 536–553 and Paul Blokker, Populist constitutionalism in Carlos de la Torre (ed.) *Routledge Handbook of Global Populism* (Routledge 2018).

8 See Richard Albert, *Revolutionary Constitutionalism. Law, Legitimacy, Power* (Hart 2020) 1–304.

9 See Martin Belov (ed.), *The IT Revolution and its Impact on State, Constitutionalism and Public Law* (Hart 2021), 1–416.

Furthermore, globalisation has reached for the time being some of its limits. It has produced inequalities and asymmetries which require urgent legal and political response. It has opened cracks in constitutional democracy, defined for most of its existence in nationalist terms, which need proper and sincere answers on both national and supranational levels. The emergence of spaces of personal, information and capital flows and especially the migration flows require reconceptualisation of the constitutional schemes used in the last couple of centuries.[10] The thriving financial capitalism escaping from political control, having no visible constitutional framework and detached from the real economy deserves special attention. More precisely, the territorial irresponsibility of financial capital[11] requires urgent political and constitutional answers.

In addition, the constitutional paradigms and the constitutional design that we have inherited from the constitutionalism of the nineteenth and the twentieth centuries are somewhat inadequate for the challenges of the 'world risk society'.[12] The COVID-19 pandemic has shown that we are not well prepared to give an adequate and global response to health and disease related challenges. The same is true for ecological dangers, and the challenges of new technology. They will most likely intensify soon and overburden Western constitutional orders triggering disorder and discontent.

To sum up, there are massive challenges to Western constitutional order on global, regional, national, and subnational levels. The overlap of economic, financial, ecological, health, ethno-religious, and cultural issues, culminating in several recent crises or generating trembling beneath the constitutional surface, produce deep fractures in constitutionalism on conceptual, institutional-normative, and empirical (socio-legal) levels. The deep crisis of liberal-democratic constitutionalism tops the pyramid of concerns related to the adequacy of the constitutional responses to the problems of capitalism, democracy, welfare, and rule of law in the age of the information and technology revolution and the ongoing although disturbed trend towards neoliberal globalisation. The range of the problems is so vast and their importance so huge that we may expect the continuation of the current tendency for the increase of constitutional and political discontent and disorder to the detriment of constitutional peace and order.

We may even predict possible implosion of constitutional democracy resulting in civil disobedience, massive discontent, and true hardship in re-establishing democratic peaceful coexistence based on traditional constitutional axiology and design. The implosion of constitutional democracy will have a durable impact on constitutional civilisation as we know it. It will produce reshaping of the constitutional order, not necessarily in a favourable direction. In any case, this implosion, in conjunction with geopolitical reshuffling of the global political map of power and the rise of the new technologies to new levels with close to

10 See Martin Belov, 'Rule of law in space of flows', in Martin Belov (ed.) *Rule of Law at the Beginning of the Twenty-First Century* (Eleven 2018).

11 Ibid.

12 See Ulrich Beck, *World Risk Society* (Polity 1999).

unprecedented results, will definitely foster the search for new constitutional paradigms better able to master the complexity of the new world (dis)order.

In such a context, the aim of this book is to raise important questions and give some answers to this complex and perplexed set of problems. The book traces the implications of the crisis of constitutional democracy, the stagnation of the supranational constitutionalism of the EU, issues for the establishment of common constitutional coexistence of pluralist and fragmented societies, and the crisis of democratic capitalism. Thus, it adjusts to some of the topical issues challenging the foundations of constitutional democracy.

The overall logic of the book will be presented through an outline of the structure and the main issues discussed by the contributions which are part of it. The core messages of the chapters contribute to the construction of a varied and multidiscursive picture of the current shapes of peace and discontent and their impact on constitutional democracy.

The book is built around two pillars constituting its major object of research interest – the constitutional order and constitutional democracy. They are explored with regard to their ability to ensure peace, coexistence, social equilibrium, and climate of toleration. They are analysed also with a view to their ability to resist disorder, disobedience, and large-scale discontent. The book aims to explore the impact of disorder, disenchantment, economic, financial and sociocultural challenges and crises and political grievances regarding the efficiency and legitimacy of constitutional democracy. It assesses the impact of disorder, the reordering the structure and reforms of the functionality of key concepts and institutions of constitutional law within and beyond statehood[13] on the performance of democratic constitutionalism at the beginning of the twenty-first century.

The book starts with a debate on the constitutional foundations of democratic peace and democratic discontent in times of crisis and transition. The research is inspired by the current crisis of constitutional democracy and the possible transition towards new levels of the constitutional civilisation adjusted to the global information and technology society. However, it explores issues and atempts to outline answers and solutions which have a durable impact also in the context of the traditional constitutional order as it stands at the beginning of the twenty-first century.

In Chapter 1 Martin Belov explores the constitutional framework for democratic peace, coexistence, discontent, and disobedience. He discusses some of the conceptual issues related to the constitutional foundations of order and disorder viewed through the prism of peace and discontent. The chapter starts with explanation of the ordering function of the constitution. Then, he offers an outline of the foundational role of constitutional conflict and constitutional consensus for liberal-democratic constitutionalism. Furthermore, he provides an

13 For constitutionalism beyond statehood see Ulrich Preuss, 'Disconnecting constitutions from statehood: is global constitutionalism a viable concept?' in Petra Dobner and Martin Loughlin (eds) *The Twilight of Constitutionalism?* (Oxford University Press 2010).

epistemological account of the constitutional models of peace and discontent. Finally, he explores the conceptual structure of the constitutional models of peace and discontent. Thus, he offers a systematic outline of the main constitutional models of peace and discontent.

In Chapter 2 José Luis Martí offers the basics of a theory of the right to protest and challenge in a deliberative democracy. He outlines the history of civil disobedience, discontent, political violence, and peaceful contestation. He observes that there is a steady trend towards increasing civic participation, but with definitely diminishing violence used for promotion of civil action and political demands. This fact stimulates Martí to provide a coherent vision on non-violent resistance promoted through the right to protest and challenge.

In that regard, the main theme of the chapter is to explore the nature of the right to protest and challenge, to compare it with existing constitutional rights as well as with non-institutionalised forms of civil discontent, e.g. revolution and civil disobedience, and to offer insights for the need to legally shape such rights due to their important socio-political functions for promoting the expression of discontent in a feasible, but peaceful manner. Hence, Martí allocates the right to protest and challenge in the power grid between peaceful coexistence, the legitimate response to misbehaviour of public power, disobedience, and public discontent.

He traces the historic roots of the right to protest as well as the different forms of peaceful resistance and civil disobedience. He makes a remarkable comparison of these forms stemming from different intellectual and political traditions. He explores the conceptual limits of the right to protest and offers a scaled view allowing for assessment of the proportionality of its use according to the severity of misuse of state power.

José Luis Martí then explores the relationship between democracy, contestation, and the right to protest. He explains the constitutional implications of the right to contestation and protest. Thus, his chapter combines in a very convincing way historical, philosophical, constitutionalist, and socio-legal discourses and reflections on the right to protest as a phenomenon ona the edge between peace and contestation and discontent.

The book continues with critical assessment of the peace and discontent in the EU constitutional order. Part II contains three chapters devoted to the general problem of the 'ordering of the constitutional order'[14] of the EU. It explores the issues stemming from the lack of a proper material constitution of the EU and the problems resulting from the controversies around the concepts of identity and authority in the multilevel constitutional order of the union.

Francesco Bilancia and Stefano Civitarese Matteucci are offering in Chapter 3 an insightful and important analysis of the material constitutional arrangement – or

14 For the concept of 'ordering of constitutional orders' see Evgeni Tanchev, 'The contemporary supranational constitutional pluralism or the ordering of constitutional orders' in Plamen Kirov (ed.) *Constitutional Studies 2012–2013* (St. Kliment Ohridski University Press 2014), 171–198 (in Bulgarian).

the 'material constitution' – of the EU. They are stepping on the concept of material constitution developed by Costantino Mortati and Hans Kelsen and recently revitalised and further developed by Marco Goldoni and Michael Wilkinson.[15]

Francesco Bilancia and Stefano Civitarese Matteucci start with a presentation of their conceptualisation of the constitution as a 'normative-purposive construct' engaging in the broader scientific debate on the normativity of constitutions. They outline their view on the theory of material constitution explaining also the history of the concept. This is done in dialogue with some more classical accounts of the material constitution extracted from the theories of Costantino Mortati and Hans Kelsen. Francesco Bilancia and Stefano Civitarese Matteucci claim that 'constitutions usually are both formal and material and that the former is instrumental in shielding and stabilising the latter'.

Francesco Bilancia and Stefano Civitarese Matteucci apply this thesis to the EU providing a critical assessment of the possibility for defining a material constitution of the EU. The authors believe 'that the EU material constitutional arrangement, only partly formalised, is what at present impedes developing a truly "constitutionalist constitution". In other words, the EU may have a constitutional structure, but still lacks a fundamental political authority which can unify and order an all-purposive set of norms.'

This way Francesco Bilancia and Stefano Civitarese Matteucci contribute to the research on the strategies for stabilisation of the constitutional order, for rendering it stable, authoritative, efficient and legitimate which are of crucial importance for assuring peace and preventing disorder and discontent. In that regard, Chapter 3 relates to both the problems of 'ordering of the EU order', explored by all chapters included in Part II and to the broader issue of establishing constitutional authority and stabilising the societal role of a constitution central to all contributions in this volume.

In Chapter 4 Gavin Barrett provides informative, original, and critical assessment of the recent Weiss decision of the Federal Constitutional Court of Germany. The aim of this chapter is not just to sketch or comment on this very important and somewhat contested decision of the German Constitutional Court but to put it in the context of ordering and adjusting the composite constitutional orders of the EU and its member states. Thus, while discussing a judicial case Barrett actually offers his views on the recent trends in the construction or rather the deconstruction of the EU constitutional order as a bearer of peace, prosperity, and authority in Europe. Hence, while Francesco Bilancia and Stefano Civitarese Matteucci explore in Chapter 3 the issue of authority building from the viewpoint of the material constitution, Barrett does the same but from the perspective of judicial dialogue and legal constitutionalism.[16]

15 See Marco Goldoni and Michael Wilkinson, 'The material constitution' (2018) 81 (4), *The Modern Law Review*, 567–597.

16 See Richard Bellamy, 'Legal constitutionalism', in Richard Bellamy, *Political Constitutionalism: A Republican Defence of the Constitutionality of Democracy* (Cambridge University Press 2007) 13–14.

Gavin Barrett offers his account of why the Weiss judgment of the Federal Constitutional Court of Germany constitutes a counter-revolution to the previous judicial revolution accomplished by the Court of Justice of the EU and what its consequences will be for the composite EU legal order. He contextualises the Weiss judgment explaining it in the light of the case law of the Court of Justice of the EU and the previous case law of the Federal Constitutional Court. He explores the self-assertive stance of the German Federal Constitutional Court and its somewhat nationalist use of interpretation methods which make clear the destabilising potential of the Weiss judgment for the key doctrines of EU law and especially for the principle of its primacy over the national constitutional orders. In Barrett's opinion the German Federal Constitutional Court has considerably endangered the EU constitutional equilibrium and its Weiss judgment is based on flawed reasoning produced in a somewhat unfortunate context. Barrett defines the Weiss judgment as 'a long-threatened volcanic eruption' creating major threats to the EU legal order. Finally, Barrett offers his viewpoint on possible solutions to the constitutional crisis created by Weiss.

A common topic of Gavin Barrett's Chapter 4 and the subsequent Chapter 5, written by Enrico Albanesi, is the issue of constitutional identity, its use and misuse for fostering integration or disintegration, its role for promotion of constitutional nationalism, and its huge destabilising potential for the composite constitutional order of the EU. Albanesi's key thesis is that national identity (under Art. 4(2) TEU) and constitutional identity (as counter-limits) are not the same. He explains the difference between national identity (under Art. 4(2) TEU) and constitutional identity (as counter-limits) on the basis of theoretical reflections as well as through the relevant case law of the national constitutional courts and the Court of Justice of the EU. He explores the jurisprudence of the Court of Justice of the EU in order to show that 'the scope of the identity clause under Art. 4(2) TEU is seen from Luxembourg in a narrower way than that of domestic Constitutional Courts' and that this court applies this clause under a scrutiny of proportionality demonstrating also the legal consequences of such an approach.

Part III offers a debate on the problems of peace, order, and disorder in composite societies. It explores the national, ethnocentric, and religious factors for peace or discontent in the context of the establishment of authoritative and efficient, but at the same time pluralist and legitimate constitutional order. The contributors to Part III analyse the challenges to democratic coexistence in pluralist societies. They emphasise the importance of constitutionalism for framing composite societies and establishing and maintaining the authority and legitimacy of the public order in culturally divided social orders.

Chapter 6 provides a comparative study of the history of establishing constitutional order and peace in foundational moments for composite constitutional orders. Thus, its author – Victor M. Cazares Lira – addresses the problem of authority building and maintenance in times of contestation, discontent, and disorder. He explores how several states with huge importance for comparative constitutional law and comparative constitutional history are building their constitutional orders in times of disorder. More precisely, Cazares Lira focuses on the establishment of constitutional order in crucial moments of disagreement in the United States, Belgium, and Switzerland. The author compares the different strategies for the establishment of authority, identity, and consensus and for the promotion of peace employed by the founding fathers of the United States and the political elites in Latin America and more precisely in Mexico. Thus, the author engages in implicit dialogue with Pasquale Viola, the author of Chapter 7.

Chapter 7 explores the impact of inequality on constitutionally relevant political discontent. The chapter offers comparative study of the models for accommodation of ethno-national diversity in composite, fragmented, and pluralist societies. It provides for comparative constitutional research focused on South Asia and Latin America.

Viola explores the tensions between the socio-cultural and legal fields providing a socio-legal analysis of the impact of national and ethnic diversity on the perspectives for stable constitutional democracy. He focuses on two groups of issues: the cases of subsidiary, hegemonic, and liberal ethnic-based states in Asia and the cases of constitutional acknowledgment of diversity in Latin America. This allows him to come to important conclusions regarding diversity perceived as stigma and stress factor, but also as the founding myth of a state and inspiration for constitutional reform.

Chapter 8, written by Wojciech Brzozowski, polemically and critically assesses the penetration of Islamic law in the European legal orders. The author defines this process as a 'silent revolution'. Thus, this is one of the three chapters in this edited volume devoted to 'silent revolutions'. However, while the chapters of Teodora Petrova and Apostolos Vlachogiannis reflect on 'silent revolutions' in the economic and financial constitutions, Wojciech Brzozowski presents his view on a silent revolution in the sphere of law and religion concerning the secular state and the 'religious constitution' of the European states.

Brzozowski explores the attitude of the Sharia law towards human rights and democracy. He makes a critical juxtaposition between the secular and the Muslim concepts of human rights. In doing so, the author outlines three paths of the Sharia in the European legal space. In his account, these are the open endorsement, the recognition or toleration of extra-legal religious adjudication, and the accommodation of Muslim identity claims. Brzozowski devotes attention also to the interrelation between Islamic religious law and state sovereignty.

The book concludes with Part IV which is devoted to the economic challenges to constitutional peace and order during the crisis of neoliberalism. All the three chapters published in it explore different problems related to the economic and financial foundations of a stable and viable constitutional democracy. They are united by the desire to expose the impact of neoliberal constitutional philosophy on democratic constitutional law and the challenges of transition towards less democratic and less solid economic and financial constitution. The authors aim to show the risks of extreme liberalisation of the economic and financial constitution for the maintenance of a democratic and inclusive constitutional order. This is done in a conceptual and abstract-theoretical way (Diekmann), on the basis of comparative research (Petrova) or via case studies (Vlachogiannis).

In Chapter 9 Marie Diekmann explores the transformative features of law offering some interesting reflections on the possibility for the reconstruction of a radical democratic labour law. The chapter starts with an outline of the main aspects of the crisis of constitutional democracy. This outline is structured around some normative accounts of inclusive democracy featuring a social and democratic labour law as one of its main preconditions. Diekmann confronts us with her account of 'transformation through immanent critique' exposing her view on the 'paradox of liberal law' and the evolution of the labour law and labour movement. Furthermore, the author explores the impact of neoliberal philosophy and neoliberal reforms of labour law on the socio-political equilibrium. She gives some suggestions for reconstruction of a democratic labour law based on an enhanced constitutional approach to labour rights as human rights and the development of a democratic teleology of labour law.

The critical approach of Marie Diekmann is further developed in Chapter 10 by Teodora Petrova. She explores a phenomenon defined by her as 'quiet' revolutions in the pension insurance systems and their constitutional repercussions. Petrova critically assesses the pension reforms inspired by neoliberal philosophy in Eastern Europe. She focuses on three case studies presented in a comparative perspective. These are the cases of Bulgaria, Slovenia, and Latvia. The declared theoretical interest of Petrova is the interrelation between democracies and revolutions in pension insurance. In this context she researches the constitutional foundations of the right to a pension in Bulgaria, Slovenia, and Latvia. The author reflects on the potential of constitutional safeguards' to mitigate quiet revolutions in pension insurance. She explores the limits to constitutional safeguards and the extent of protection for pension rights, the varying depth of constitutional scrutiny, the performance of the constitutional safeguards in the Eastern European climate of public authority mistrust.

The discussion on the constitutional implications of the ongoing profound changes in the economic and financial constitution is concluded by Apostolos Vlachogiannis. The topic of 'silent revolution' in the constitutionally relevant domains of economy and finance is common to Petrova and Vlachogiannis. However, Petrova explores the 'silent revolution' in the pension reforms while Vlachogiannis researches the 'silent revolution' in privatisation during the financial crisis.

In Chapter 11 Vlachogiannis explores the constitutional change in Greece as a result of the financial crisis. More precisely, he focuses on the impact of privatisation in the context of the recent Greek public debt crisis which in his account triggers silent revolution of the economic constitution in Greece. The author explores the stages of privatisation, their results and their impact on the subsequent evolution of the Greek economic constitution. He frames the policy of privatisation in constitutional terms defining it as a constitutional construction.

Vlachogiannis accomplishes his research on the 'living Greek financial constitution' through a descriptive and realist approach embedded also in law and the scientific tradition in economics. He defines his research target as a series of substantial and important changes in the 'living constitution' related to privatisation which have not been integrated in the rather rigid formal Greek constitution. They represent, in Vlachogiannis' view, 'a paradigm shift in the Greek economic constitution, which has undoubtedly moved to a more (neo-)liberal direction in this realm.'

References

Albert, Richard *Revolutionary Constitutionalism. Law, Legitimacy, Power* (Hart 2020)

Beck, Ulrich *World Risk Society* (Polity 1999)

Bellamy, Richard 'Legal constitutionalism' in Richard Bellamy, *Political Constitutionalism: A Republican Defence of the Constitutionality of Democracy* (Cambridge University Press 2007)

Belov, Martin 'Rule of law in space of flows' in Martin Belov (ed.) *Rule of Law at the Beginning of the Twenty-First Century* (Eleven 2018)

Belov, Martin (ed.), *The IT Revolution and its Impact on State, Constitutionalism and Public Law* (Hart 2021)

Blokker, Paul 'Populism as a constitutional project' (2019) 17 (2), *International Journal of Constitutional Law*

Blokker, Paul 'Populist constitutionalism', in Carlos de la Torre (ed.) *Routledge Handbook of Global Populism* (Routledge 2018)

Goldoni Marco and Michael Wilkinson, 'The material constitution' (2018) 81 (4), *The Modern Law Review*

Harari, Yuval Noah *Homo Deus: A Brief History of Tomorrow* (Vintage 2017)

Mason, Paul *Postcapitalism: A Guide to Our Future* (Penguin 2016)

Piketty, Thomas *Capital in the Twenty-First Century* (Harvard University Press 2017)

Preuss, Ulrich 'Disconnecting constitutions from statehood is global constitutionalism a viable concept?' in Petra Dobner and Martin Loughlin (eds) *The Twilight of Constitutionalism?* (Oxford University Press 2010)

Streek, Wolfgang *How Will Capitalism End?* (Verso 2017)

Tanchev, Evgeni 'The contemporary supranational constitutional pluralism or the ordering of constitutional orders' in Plamen Kirov (ed.) *Constitutional Studies 2012–2013* (St. Kliment Ohridski University Press 2014), 171–198 (in Bulgarian)

Zakaria, Fareed *The Future of Freedom: Illiberal Democracy at Home and Abroad* (Norton 2007)

Zuboff, Shoshana *The Age of Surveillance Capitalism. The Fight for a Human Future at the New Frontier of Power* (Public Affairs 2019)

Part I

The constitutional foundations of democratic peace and democratic discontent in times of crisis and transition

1 Constitutional foundations of peace and discontent

Martin Belov

1 Introduction

This chapter aims to provide an outline of some of the conceptual issues related to the constitutional foundations of order and disorder viewed through the prism of peace and discontent.[1] The constitutional shaping of order and disorder is, in fact, a matter of establishing the framework of the range of legally permissible political discontent with its conceptual, institutional, normative, and pragmatic implications.[2] Hence, this chapter will try to present the constitutional strategies and models for safeguarding of obedience and trust as fundamental prerequisites for promotion of peaceful political coexistence and constitutional order. These strategies are subsumed under the overall constitutional models for maintenance of peace and discontent.

One of the key assumptions of this chapter is that constitutions are the main instruments for measuring, framing, and legalising the degrees of public discontent. They also serve as exclusion of forms of disorder due to their constitutionally defined anti-systemic role and potential. The systemic or anti-systemic character of disorder and discontent is a matter of political choice of the constitutional legislator followed by its subsequent constitutional entrenchment. In fact, this is one of the main tasks of the constitutional models of peace and discontent – to define which forms of peace and discontent are systemic and anti-systemic.

Not only discontent, but also peace may be anti-systemic phenomenon. This is the case of the unilaterally imposed peace suffocating political pluralism and legitimate expression of discontent in democratic orders experiencing transition to illiberal democracies and authoritarianism. This problem will be discussed further especially in Section 3 of this chapter.

1 See Azin Tadjdini, 'The Constitutional Dimension of Peace', in Cecilia Marcela Bailliet and Kjetil Mujezinovic Larsen (eds) *Promoting Peace Through International Law* (Oxford University Press 2015), Allen S. Weiner, 'Constitutions as Peace Treaties: A Cautionary Tale for the Arab Spring' (2011) 8 *Stanford Law Review Online* 64.

2 See Michael Sandel *Democracy's Discontent: America in Search of a Public Philosophy* (Harvard University Press 1998) 1–432.

Indeed, it should be admitted that the constitution is only one of the factors for maintenance of peaceful coexistence and satisfaction with the established constitutional order and political regime. Peace and discontent are variables which are dependent also on a range of socio-legal factors contributing to the legality and the legitimacy of the constitutional system and the political establishment. Nevertheless, the constitution is supposed to serve as an institutional channel for expression of discontent and as an instrument for the promotion of peace due to its ordering and legitimation functions. Thus, special attention will be devoted to the ordering function of the constitution as well as to the models for peace and discontent it provides.

Order and disorder are considered as social phenomena with fundamental political importance, which are also entrenched in the constitution and the constitutional law. In addition, they have important implications for the constitutional and political anthropology of societies, for the intellectual apprehension of the permissible or forbidden forms of expression of trust, distrust, anger, or alienation. Conceptually, the constitutional models of peace and disorder also play an educational role for the people and the civil society. In mid- and long term, they form durable attitudes to freedom and its legitimate limits which are gradually being entrenched in the constitutional anthropology of the society. In other words, the constitution serves as an indicator not only for the legal, but also for the legitimate limits of constitutional freedom, the means for its achievement and the instruments for authoritative imposition of order and peace. Thus, the constitution and the overall constitutional tradition serve as determinants for the socially justified frames of consensus and conflict, peace, and discontent.

Hence, peace and discontent are socio-legal categories stretched between the ideal, social, and legal dimensions of constitutionalism. They have projections in the legal mentality, anthropology and consciousness of the people which is based on their socio-political acculturation, education and experience and is framed, thus also being influenced, by the constitutional foundations of peace and discontent. In fact, all three aspects – the ideal, the socio-political, and the legal – have constitutional implications. They altogether form the constitutional foundations of peace and discontent.

Indeed, the constitutions are one of the most important determinants of peace and discontent but are not the ultimate or exclusive factor for the legitimacy of disorder and discontent. They are just the official marker of the borderlines between order and disorder, peace, and discontent. Hence, the constitutions are allocated in the power grid stretched between legality and legitimacy which are the two ultimate criteria for evaluation of the public order, the political order, and the constitutional order.[3]

3 For the conceptual problems of legality and legitimacy, the interrelation and tensions between them see Carl Schmitt, *Legality and Legitimacy* (Duke University Press 2004) 1–212, David Dyzenhaus, *Legality and Legitimacy: Carl Schmitt, Hans Kelsen and Hermann Heller in Weimar* (Oxford University Press 2000) 1–304, Lars Vinx, *Hans Kelsen's Pure Theory of Law. Legality and Legitimacy* (Oxford University Press 2007) 59 and the following and Max Weber, 'Die drei reinen Typen der Legitimen Herrschaft' in Max Weber, *Soziologie. Weltgeschichtliche Analysen. Politik* (Kröner Verlag 1968).

The chapter will start with an outline of the ordering function of the constitution.[4] Then it will explore the foundational role of constitutional conflict and constitutional consensus for liberal-democratic constitutionalism. Special emphasis will be put on the epistemology of the constitutional models for peace and discontent, on their nature, structure, and essential elements.

2 The ordering function of the constitution

The mission of the constitution is to order the society. It must organise socio-political relations making them well-ordered, systematic, predictable, and rational. The constitution has assumed this role after the adoption of the first written constitutions. Before them, states had their political constitution as the durable de facto order of rules for socio-political behaviour. The unwritten constitution was not detachable from its ordering function because it was immediately ordering the society by the very fact of its existence. Thus, the unwritten constitution unites in a simultaneous phenomenon the legal and the socio-political ordering of the society. It is the result of a permanent interaction between content and discontent. It is materialising in itself the fragile equilibrium between political conflict and political consensus. It requires the simultaneous existence of conflict and consensus – the first allowing for evolution and the second granting a degree of stability and predictability.

In the context of unwritten constitutions the constitutional conflict and consensus are merged with the socio-political conflict and consensus. There is no explicit, written model of permissible disorder and conflict detached from the socio-political interaction between the different political players on the ground. The epistemology of order is based on the lack of disorder, but also on the integration of disorder in the official schemes for accomplishment of government and power.

This is not the case with written constitutions. They are the deliberate creation of the human mind resulting in an artificial model of human behaviour imposed on socio-political reality. The written constitution is an abstract model aimed at normative ordering of the socio-political relations conceived as both determinants of this model and as result of it but in any case, as separate from the realm of written constitutional normativity. The written constitution is the result of collective use of intellectual forces for the creation of widely or more narrowly negotiated or imposed rules of the political game. The written constitution rests on the suggestion for improvement of the social world, for its improvement in the name of big ideals and in the light of values, principles, and aims constituting the moral-political foundations of the institutional design. Thus, the written constitution contains a deliberate model of constitutional peace and discontent with its axiological, institutional, and socio-legal implications. It establishes

4 For the ordering function of the constitution see Georg Jellinek, *Allgemeine Staatslehre*, (Springer 1921) 505 and Joachim Detjen 'Verfassung und Werte' in *Die Werteordnung des Grundgesetzes.* (VS Verlag für Sozialwissenschaften 2009), 15. https://doi.org/10.1007/978-3-531-91604-0_2.

constitutional models of desired order and permissible disorder. These models will be outlined later in the chapter.

The very term constitution means to establish something, to create a foundational structure for the society, to give it a durable political form, to shape the mass of facts within a durable and legitimate legal form, to offer official institutional channels for expression of content and discontent, trust and mistrust, agreement, and disagreement. The constitution is called upon to serve as a legal map of the shapes and forms of the state and the political organisation of the society. Thus, by providing the institutional design and the parameters of social and political freedom the constitution is at the core of the processes for social acculturation and socio-political integration.[5] A real, recognised, and efficient constitution must be capable of assuring its place as the central determinant of social peace and obedience and should impose legitimate, proportionate, and just limits to political freedom.

Political freedom is at the core of liberal constitutionalism. The concerns for the full protection of human rights and for establishment of the widest possible sphere for personal liberty is central to it. Thus, liberal constitutionalism is focused on the constitutional frames of liberty and more precisely on the constitutional limitations for public discontent. More radical democratic versions of constitutionalism require an extended frontier for expression of political discontent. Constitutional democracy structured around the concepts of deliberative and participatory democracy presupposes not only traditional liberal tools for expression of discontent and dissatisfaction such as the classic political rights (e.g. freedom of expression, freedom of assembly, freedom of speech etc.), but also more intense forms of disagreement like the right to protest and the right to civil disobedience. In fact, they suggest the need for scaled – proportionate and adequate – responses to illegitimate governmental action. This claim is demonstrated in detail in Chapter 2 of this book by José Luis Martí.

Depending on the context and the concrete political imperatives of the day the constitution performs its ordering function differently. First, the constitution may need to establish order out of disorder. Second, the constitution may be called upon to reshape the existing order replacing it with new order. Finally, the constitution may be adopted to confirm the existing order projecting it into the future.

The constitution should establish order out of disorder in case of radical break down of the previous constitutional and political order. Usually, such disorder is the result of deep and radical ruptures of the constitutional and political system and its underlying political consensus or at least modus vivendi. They may be caused by war, civil conflict, or insurmountable tensions within the society.

5 See Dieter Grimm, 'Integration durch Verfassung' (2004) 32, *Leviathan* 448–463 https://doi.org/10.1007/s11578-004-0031-7 and Gary Schaal, 'Integration durch Verfassung und Verfassungsrechtssprechung? Theoretische Anmerkungen' (2001) 30(2) *Österreichische Zeitschrift für Politikwissenschaft*, 221–232 https://nbnresolving.org/urn:nbn:de:0168-ssoar-59721.

It should be noted that the first written constitutions did not always establish order out of disorder. Indeed, it seems logically reasonable to accept that it is precisely the task of the first written constitution in the history of a particular national constitutional model to establish order out of disorder. In fact, this is one of the most appealing claims of modern written constitutions – to rationalise the world, to impose a systematic power grid on the turbulent and fuzzy socio-political relations.

However, the political history shows that in many cases there has been pre-established order which predates the imposition or negotiation of the first written constitutions. Hence, the first constitutions are acts aimed more or less at radical political reform rather than instruments for creation of order out of disorder. Frequently, they destroy the old order and replace it with a new one. Thus, the ordering function of the first written constitutions has been frequently bound to their disordering and deconstructive function. Ordering and construction has been predetermined and fulfilled in conjunction with deconstruction.

That is why, the constitution is very often called upon to reshape the existing order replacing it with new order. It is a device for reestablishment of the constitutional foundations of peace and discontent, order and disorder, conflict and consensus. In fact, the constitution is always stretched between the societal forces of order and disorder. In that regard, the constitution resembles the Earth. It needs magma, earthquakes, and volcanic eruptions to be alive but it must also try to stabilise the magnetic field and prevent big disasters for life to continue. Thus, the ordering function of the constitution is predestined to maintain the delicate equilibrium between peace and discontent, conflict and consensus since all of them are necessary prerequisites for a viable constitutional order and especially for the establishment and maintenance of constitutional democracy.

Finally, as mentioned above, some constitutions are adopted with the aim to confirm the existing order and to project it into the future. Such 'consolidating constitutions'[6] make the impression of establishing order out of order. However, they are typically used for political or ideological purposes aiming at demonstrating the persistence of peace and consensus while suppressing the discontent and hoping to prevent disorder. Thus, consolidating constitutions are instruments for maintenance and prolongation of the established order suffocating demands for radical change. They are political choice usually detrimental to democracy. Examples are the second wave of communist constitutions which were adopted in the late 1960s and the early 1970is in Central and Eastern Europe aiming to stabilise the Soviet type of constitutionalism and to simulate the advancement to a new stage of communist development while masquerading as the prolongation of the totalitarian regimes.

6 See Evgeni Tanchev, *Introduction in Constitutional Law* (Sibi 2003) 198 (in Bulgarian).

3 The foundational role of constitutional conflict and constitutional consensus for the liberal-democratic constitutionalism

Constitutional conflict and constitutional consensus are central concepts of modern constitutionalism. They are widely discussed in the theory of political pluralism. They play a pivotal role for the constitutional dynamics. Constitutional conflict and constitutional consensus are not categories of valid constitutional law. They are not explicitly regulated by the normative-institutional order. Nevertheless, they are implicitly part of it. This is because the constitution and the constitutional law have a system of legal provisions which shape the permissible frames of constitutional disorder. They also design the model of constitutional order which has been preferred by the constitutional legislator on the establishment of the constitutional system and has been later further developed by the ordinary legislator and the constitutional court.

In fact, constitutional conflict and constitutional consensus are products of several forces – both creative and destructive – enabled to produce the shapes, forms, and institutional design enshrined in the constitutional order and developed in the political process. Ontologically, they are driven by factors and determinants which are either external or internal for the constitutionally framed socio-political order. The external factors are diverse. They include big technological revolutions, geopolitical factors, and large-scale external shocks, e.g. migration, economic stress, etc. The internal factors are the multiple conflicts related to the pluralist structure of the society in terms of social stratification, ethnicity, nationality, race, and religion, gender, and the broad divergence of the philosophic and moral convictions.

Constitutional conflict and constitutional consensus are present in all democratic procedures in the liberal-democratic state. They underlie the electoral process, the parliamentary procedures, and the different procedures for asserting control (e.g. control for legality, control for constitutionality, control for compliance with international and supranational law, parliamentary control, etc.). Conflict and consensus are encoded in all types of democracy – representative, direct, participatory, and deliberative. The political rights provided by the constitution and the rest of the constitutional legislation are tools for legal expression of constitutional conflict and for negotiation of constitutional consensus.

Authoritarian and totalitarian regimes overemphasise the role of order, peace, and discontent. They are based on the presumption of a monolithic structure of the social and political order, the unity of state power, and the homogeneity of society. In such a context, the legality of disorder, socio-political discontent and dissent, and constitutional conflict is excluded per se. Order, consensus and unity are the only possible, legal, and legitimate determinants of the constitutional construction of the totalitarian and authoritarian state.

Authoritarianism and totalitarianism also need conflict. However, they externalise conflict contrasting the ideal of socio-political unity with the threats of internal and external enemies. Thus, conflict is both an anti-systemic phenomenon endangering the proper model of constitutional unity and systemic reason for maintenance of unity against factors of disorder and discontent. This logic – the differentiation between 'friend and enemy' – is well defined by the theory of political decisionism of Carl Schmitt.[7] It is also present in democracy.

Democratic orders also define their enemies[8] and structure their political life on the matrix 'enemy and friend'. However, there are important differences from authoritarian orders. In democratic constitutional systems, the 'enemies' are allowed to participate in the political discourse in so far they are not defined as extremely dangerous for the system and thus as anti-systemic. Democratic constitutional orders allow much wider scope for conflict and legitimate disagreement. They limit only those forms of conflict which are supposed to destroy the very essence of democratic coexistence. The safeguarding of permissible degree and forms of disorder within the overall framework of constitutional order is accomplished on the principle of political pluralism and its constitutional shapes. These shapes are based on the constitutional limitations to political pluralism and their different manifestations such as media pluralism, party pluralism, pluralism of expression and opinion, information pluralism, etc.

Democracy has always been prone to conflicts. In fact, democracy can be viewed as a regime for conflict management. It is a constitutional model that strives at achieving a rather difficult and to an extent controversial purpose. Indeed, democracy rests on conflict. It promotes contestation and public deliberation, exposes and allows for diversity of opinion and mismatch on the strategy and tactics of politics and policy making and even on the ideological and conceptual roots of statehood. Thus, democracy is conflictual per se.

4 Epistemology of the constitutional models of peace and discontent

The models of constitutional peace are enshrined in the constitution. This is done both explicitly and implicitly. They are further developed in the other sources of constitutional law. In most cases, the models of constitutional peace are implicitly provided and are dispersed in the constitutional provisions and the provisions of the other sources of constitutional law. Thus, they need to be reconstructed and exposed via interpretation combining deconstruction, construction, and reconstruction of these models.

Hence, the conceptualisation of constitutional conflict and consensus based on constitutional models for peace and discontent is an invitation for reconstructive interpretation of the constitutional order in general and the constitution in particular. It is a creative intellectual enterprise framed by valid constitutional

7 See Carl Schmitt, *Verfassungslehre* (Duncker & Humblot 1970) 44 and the following.

8 See Tsvetan Todorov, *The Inner Enemies of Democracy* (Polity Press 2014) 1–200 and Ami Pedahzur and Leonard Weinberg 'Modern European Democracy and Its Enemies: The Threat of the Extreme Right' (2001) 2(1) *Politics, Religion and Ideology*, 52–72. DOI: 10.1080/714005438.

law, but open also to the socio-legal determinants of the constitutional and the political order.

Such reconstructive interpretation may be accomplished by the constitutional courts, but this is rather unlikely. The constitutional courts usually pronounce on political rights and democratic procedures. However, they typically relate their reasoning to the principles of popular sovereignty, the rule of law, and democracy but do not subsume the arguments under an explicit and holistic model for maintenance of peace and discontent. This is because the constitutions traditionally work with democracy and political pluralism while discarding peace and discontent as de facto meta-legal and meta-constitutional phenomena. Indeed, peace and discontent do matter, but as a theoretical construct, as products of the political and constitutional philosophy and as phenomena of the socio-political reality.

This attitude is unlikely to change. Democracy and political pluralism are well established concepts which still perform well their normative function. Peace and discontent are concepts which are rather fuzzy, abstract, and theoretical. Nevertheless, they may be particularly useful for shedding additional light on the problems of constitutional conflict and consensus, the foundations of peaceful socio-political coexistence, and the maintenance of order while promoting creative and legitimate disorder.

The ordinary legislator also shapes the models of constitutional peace and discontent. This is done based on acts of Parliament and the normative acts of the government and the ministers which are further developing the values, principles, human rights, and institutions and procedures enshrined in the constitution and serving constitutional foundations of peace and discontent. Nevertheless, the Parliament and the institutions of the executive power are not deliberately shaping holistic and explicit models of constitutional peace and discontent. They are instead following established normative ideologies of fundamental importance for peace and discontent determining the principles of constitutional conflict and constitutional consensus and are pragmatically developing the normative order based on the constitutional framework and with view to socio-political imperatives. Thus, the ordinary legislator is implicitly developing the constitutional model for peace and discontent conceptually established by the constitutional legislator and explained through the prism of the normative ideology developed by the constitutional and political theory, entrenched in the political and constitutional anthropology of the socio-political community and eventually expanded through the interpretative activity of the constitutional courts.

Hence, it is the role of constitutional theory to develop the concepts of constitutional peace and constitutional discontent. The constitutional courts and other authoritative speakers of the community may give important incentives and arguments for theoretical reflection with normative validity in the legal order, but it is the theory which must reconstruct constitutional models of peace and discontent. These models will be able to supplement the constitutional discourse on democracy, political pluralism, and rule of law by offering additional viewpoints and arguments and providing for original complementary theorization.

Naturally, the theoretical models of peace and discontent should be based on valid constitutional law. They must inevitably consider the normative foundations of peace and discontent enshrined in the constitution and further developed by the constitutional courts and the ordinary legislator. The theory of constitutional peace and discontent must be simultaneously descriptive and prescriptive, affirmative and critical. It must describe the parameters of peace and discontent provided by the valid constitutional law and stipulate the key principles and the logic on which they are established thus reaffirming the constitutional model of peace and discontent. At the same time, it must also offer a critical account of the issues of the constitutional model for peace and discontent thus offering insights for its improvement.

The models of constitutional peace are at the same time models of constitutional discontent. This statement is supported by conceptual, logical, and normative reasons. Conceptually both unlimited freedom and overwhelming control and authoritative obedience are impossible. Thus, the imposition of order, the negotiation and maintenance of peace and the expression of discontent by provoking disorder need a common conceptual and legal framework generally supported by the society thus enjoying both legality and legitimacy. Logically, constitutional peace and order are contrary to discontent, disobedience, and disorder. However, both groups of phenomena require their opposites in order to sustain a vital and pluralist society and an efficient, adequate, evolving constitutional and political order.

That is why, normatively, the constitutions must enshrine the constitutional foundations for both expression of constitutional enchantment, consensus, and content and for demonstration of discontent triggering a degree of admissible disorder. Hence, the constitutions simultaneously provide for models of constitutional order and for permissible disorder. Thus, they define the spheres of peace and discontent, of consensus and conflict, of permissible and prohibited conflict. The constitutions, while providing the basis of constitutional peace also delimit the legal shapes of authorised constitutional discontent. Hence, the constitution frames the socio-political conflict by offering a valid model for pacification of discontent or for its due and legal expression in the forms and procedures provided by it.

The mapping of legally permissible political discontent can be defined positively by providing of tools for political disagreement and negatively by prohibiting some of the forms of political discontent. Usually, the constitutions and the other sources of constitutional law do both. They simultaneously shape the framework of permissible conflict by allowing for a range of political rights while also imposing limitations to political freedom serving as safeguards for the maintenance of constitutional peace.

The constitutional model for peace and discontent might be legal, but illegitimate. The tension between legality and legitimacy is a standard dilemma in liberal-democratic constitutionalism. It is itself a result of admitting the fact that in a democratic pluralist society the social and political conflicts are permanent and their intensity, triggering factors, and object might sometimes go well beyond the framework of legality.

In fact, this is the problem of the need to justify or at least theoretically frame those forms of political discontent which expand beyond the legal framework of permissible conflict, but still possess a high degree of legitimacy and are as such constructive for the maintenance of a democratic constitutional order. In other words, there are an increasing number of occasions in which the constitutional model for peace and discontent is rather narrow thus frustrating the society and triggering legitimate extra-legal and illegal discontent. In such cases the narrow legal framework does not ensure the peace but fosters discontent and thus promotes disorder. If the constitutional framework for permissible discontent is designed too narrowly it may trigger and foster discontent instead of promoting peace.

Important examples of phenomena which go beyond the framework of peaceful coexistence but are contextually justified based on axiological reasons such as justice, freedom and equality or pragmatic socio-legal concerns are civil disobedience[9] and the right to revolt against usurpation of the state power.[10] The conceptual foundations of these institutions have been well developed by important authors in political philosophy such as John Locke[11] and Henry David Toreau.[12] The ideology of peaceful disobedience has been promoted also by Mahatma Gandhi and Martin Luther King. Some constitutions and constitutional documents even legalise the right to resistance thus trying to provide some legal grounds for revolutionary disorder in the name of promotion and safeguarding the supreme values of the constitutional order. Here one must point at the US Declaration of Independence legitimising the right to revolt and rebellion against oppression and the so called 'Wehrhafte (Streitbare) Demokratie'[13] or democracy ready for self-defence against usurpation of the democratic constitutional order provided by the German Basic Law. The right to protest as an integrative right including different forms of civil disobedience is discussed in detail by José Luis Martí in Chapter 2 of this book.

9 See Henry David Thoreau, *Civil Disobedience* (CreateSpace Independent Publishing Platform 2014) 1–28, Jennet Kirckpatrick 'Uncivil Disobedience', *Studies in Violence and Democratic Politics* (Princeton University Press 2008), Zawiyah Mohd Zain and Mohammad Agus Yusoff, 'Civil Disobedience: Concept and Practice' (2017) 13 (8) *Asian Social Science*, 129–134.

10 See Harvey Mansfield, 'The Right of Revolution' (1976) 105 (4) *Daedalus*, 151–162. Accessed October 6, 2020. http://www.jstor.org/stable/20024446, Robert Grady, 'Obligation, Consent, and Locke's Right to Revolution: "Who is to Judge?" (1976) 9(2) *Canadian Journal of Political Science*, 277–292. DOI:10.1017/S0008423900043729. John Winfred O'Toole, 'The Right of Revolution' (2011) Boston College, http://hdl.handle.net/2345/1940.

11 See John Locke, *The Second Treatise on Civil Government*, (Prometheus 1986) 1–136.

12 See Henry David Thoreau (2014).

13 See Hans-Jürgen Papier and Wolfgang Durner, 'Streitbare Demokratie', (2003) 128 (3) *Archiv des öffentlichen Rechts*, 340–371. Accessed October 6, 2020. http://www.jstor.org/stable/44316813.

5 Conceptual structure of the constitutional models of peace and discontent

The constitutional models for peace and discontent typically contain several main features. First, they are based on constitutional axiology outlining the system of principles and values that should serve as the conceptual matrix of the constitutionally enshrined variants of peace and discontent. Second, they provide for a specific set of constitutional and more precisely political rights. Third, they are grounded on a particular institutional design of the public power. Fourth, each constitutional model of peace and discontent is framed by a specific variant of constitutional geometry[14] which is structuring its overall outlook. Thus, it is serving as a common visual denominator of the constitutional design of the constitutional axiology and the institutional architecture of the state, the civil society, and human rights.

The differences between the constitutional models of peace and discontent are based on the already mentioned four groups of factors. Typically, these factors act simultaneously as core elements of the constitutional models of peace and discontent. They jointly shape the models while at the same time are determining the differences between them. However, it is not necessary that the constitutional models for peace and discontent differ regarding all four groups of factors which are determining their outlook and design. The difference can concern only some of them. Moreover, there might be a wide range of intermediate options.

Here I will approach the problem of typology of constitutional peace and discontent from two conceptual perspectives. They are not mutually exclusive. They demonstrate different aspects of the constitutional modelling of order and disorder, peace and discontent.

The first one concerns the choice of the constitutional legislator regarding the way political consensus and political conflict must be constitutionally ordered and framed. It is a matter of principal preference what kind of conceptual approach should be used by the constitutional legislator as a framing paradigm regulating the borderlines between peace, permissible and non-permissible discontent. Hence, the first conceptual perspective differentiates between several constitutional models of peace and discontent putting the accent on different variants for organising the process for generating constitutional consensus and channelling of constitutional conflict. It should be stressed that the choice of model is a matter of conceptual, philosophical, and political preference and not just a methodological choice.

According to this first approach the constitutional models for peace and discontent may be organised in three main groups. Thus, we can differentiate

14 See Martin Belov, 'The Challenges to Westphalian Constitutional Geometry in the Age of Supranational Constitutionalism, Global Governance and Information Revolution' in Martin Belov (ed.) *Global Constitutionalism and Its Challenges to Westphalian Constitutional Law* (Hart 2018) 13–38.

between formal-procedural, substantial, and material models of constitutional peace and discontent. Again, it must be considered that these are pure models only in theory while the practice witnesses a range of hybrids using elements from most of them.

The formal-procedural model tries to pacify socio-political discontent by offering instruments, channels, and procedures for its legal expression. Here the legitimacy of constitutional conflict is preconditioned upon the legality of its forms. According to this model constitutional discontent is allowed, but only if expressed via constitutionally provided official formal channels. This model rests on the concept of the pacifying role of proceduralisation of socio-political conflict. It is based on the belief that all socio-political discontent may be transformed into constitutional order and peaceful coexistence after its transformation and collective sublimation through rational constitutional forms and legal procedures.

The substantial model is more demanding. In addition to forms and procedures it also requires a specific outlook of the constitutional axiology that should serve as a safeguard for maintenance of both constitutional consensus and constitutional conflict. In this regard, the constitutional values (e.g. liberty and equality) and constitutional principles promoting substantial democracy spreading beyond representative party democracy and encompassing also wide-ranging forms of direct, participatory, and deliberative democracy are of key importance for the maintenance of appropriate equilibrium between peace and discontent in a democratic and pluralist society.

The material model for constitutional peace and discontent is the most demanding. This is because it requires not only forms and procedures for legal and legitimate expression of content or discontent, not just constitutional axiology and a system of rights and institutions capable of promoting substantial variants of consensus, but also socio-legal, empirical preconditions for peace and discontent. This model is typical for the leftist versions of constitutionalism focusing on the importance of economy, social justice, and de facto equality for pacification or radicalisation of constitutional conflict. The material model for constitutional peace and discontent may be more restrained, e.g. requiring a social market economy and thus socially pacified and socially responsible capitalism. In their extreme versions they aim to establish a class-free society and radical substantial equality.

Actually, the differentiation between formal, substantial, and material versions of constitutional models for peace and discontent mirrors the distinction between formal, substantial, and material constitutionalism. This is not a coincidence since the constitutional models for peace and discontent are central elements of constitutionalism and define its core characteristics. This is because one of the main tasks of constitutionalism is to define the limits of public power and the procedures, shapes, forms, preconditions, and permissible manifestations of human freedom, especially in the political sphere. Hence, the ways and preconditions for generating constitutional consensus and for expressing constitutional conflict are at the centre of constitutionalism perceived as a system of normative ideologies and beliefs, institutional design, and socio-legal practice.

The second approach concerns the choice of a particular constitutional model for peace and discontent. In a sense, this second approach is a result of the choice made regarding the first approach. In other words, the initial choice of formal, substantial, and material versions of constitutional models for peace and discontent predetermines the subsequent and secondary choice of its concrete constitutional design concerning mainly the form of the state, the form of governance, and the constitutional foundations of the political regime.

The second approach comprises the institutional choice for structuring the frame of constitutional order and disorder and for organising the relationship between constitutional conflict and constitutional consensus. Hence, one can differentiate between the following main constitutional models for peace and discontent: the totalitarian model, the authoritarian model, the identitarian illiberal model, the radical democratic model, the liberal-democratic model of representative party democracy, and the polycentric model based on deliberative and participatory democracy. Owing to space constraints these models cannot be discussed in detail here. However, it should be emphasised that they differ mainly based on four criteria: constitutional axiology, system of human rights, constitutional duties and limitations of human rights, institutional design, and constitutional geometry.

Thus, it seems obvious that while the first approach coincides with the main general typology of constitutionalism applied to the problem of ordering constitutional peace and discontent, the second approach follows the link between political regimes and the way they work with, organise, and allow or limit constitutional peace and discontent. Again, it must be taken into account that both approaches are mutually dependent and deeply interrelated.

6 Conclusion

The constitutional models of peace and discontent are not an entirely new phenomenon. They are just another viewpoint allowing for additional conceptualisation and perception of traditional issues of constitutionalism such as constitutional consensus and constitutional conflict, procedures for expression of political satisfaction or dissatisfaction and limits of disagreement and agreement in systems based on political monism, political corporatism, or political pluralism. Thus, the constitutional models of peace and discontent do not aim to replace the traditional typologies of the form of governance or the political regimes behind them. Their main role is to demonstrate the typology of the attitudes of the constitutional legislator towards peace and discontent and to show the main models for structuring of constitutional order and disorder, constitutional consensus, and constitutional conflict.

The focus on the constitutional models of peace and discontent is important not only theoretically, but also for political practice. This is especially true in times of constitutional transition and constitutional reform. The constitution plays a key role in promotion of peace and channelling of discontent. Thus, the institutional design for peaceful coexistence and for legitimate expression of discontent is of pivotal importance for the constitutional management of socio-political order and disorder, particularly in the times of crisis of constitutional democracy in which we are currently living. Thus, the cracks in the constitutional model of democracy and the implosion of constitutional democracy are very much predetermined by the increasing inability of our constitutional models for peace and discontent to cope with the challenges of our times stemming mainly out of globalisation, the information and technological revolution and the exhaustion of our conceptual apparatus that is used to frame the novel socio-political cleavages at the beginning of the twenty-first century.

References

Belov, Martin 'The Challenges to Westphalian Constitutional Geometry in the Age of Supranational Constitutionalism, Global Governance and Information Revolution', in Martin Belov (ed.) *Global Constitutionalism and Its Challenges to Westphalian Constitutional Law* (Hart 2018)

Detjen, Joachim 'Verfassung und Werte' in *Die Werteordnung des Grundgesetzes* (VS Verlag für Sozialwissenschaften 2009)

Dyzenhaus, David *Legality and Legitimacy: Carl Schmitt, Hans Kelsen and Hermann Heller in Weimar* (Oxford University Press 2000)

Grady, Robert 'Obligation, Consent, and Locke's Right to Revolution: "Who is to Judge?"' (1976) 9(2) *Canadian Journal of Political Science*, 277–292. doi:10.1017/S0008423900043729

Grimm, Dieter 'Integration durch Verfassung' (2004) 32, *Leviathan*

Jellinek, Georg *Allgemeine Staatslehre*, (Springer 1921)

Kirckpatrick, Jennet 'Uncivil Disobedience', in *Studies in Violence and Democratic Politics* (Princeton University Press, 2008)

Locke, John *The Second Treatise on Civil Government*, (Prometheus 1986)

Mansfield, Harvey 'The Right of Revolution' (1976) 105 (4) *Daedalus*, 151–162. Accessed October 6, 2020. www.jstor.org/stable/20024446

Mohd Zain, Zawiyah and Yusoff, Mohammad Agus 'Civil Disobedience: Concept and Practice' (2017) 13 (8) *Asian Social Science*

O'Toole, John Winfred 'The Right of Revolution' (2011) Boston College, http://hdl.handle.net/2345/1940

Papier, Hans-Jürgen and Durner, Wolfgang 'Streitbare Demokratie' (2003) 128 (3) *Archiv des öffentlichen Rechts*, 340–371. Accessed October 6, 2020. www.jstor.org/stable/44316813

Pedahzur, Ami and Weinberg, Leonard 'Modern European Democracy and Its Enemies: The Threat of the Extreme Right' (2001) 2(1) *Politics, Religion and Ideology*. DOI: 10.1080/714005438

Sandel, Michael *Democracy's Discontent: America in Search of a Public Philosophy* (Harvard University Press 1998)

Schaal, Gary 'Integration durch Verfassung und Verfassungsrechtssprechung? Theoretische Anmerkungen' (2001) 30(2) *Österreichische Zeitschrift für Politikwissenschaft*

Schmitt, Carl *Verfassungslehre* (Duncker & Humblot 1970)

Schmitt, Carl *Legality and Legitimacy* (Duke University Press 2004)

Tadjdini, Azin 'The Constitutional Dimension of Peace' in Cecilia Marcela Bailliet and Kjetil Mujezinovic Larsen (eds) *Promoting Peace Through International Law* (Oxford University Press 2015)

Tanchev, Evgeni *Introduction in Constitutional Law* (Sibi, 2003) 198 (in Bulgarian)

Thoreau, Henry David *Civil Disobedience*, (CreateSpace Independent Publishing Platform 2014)

Todorov, Tsvetan *The Inner Enemies of Democracy* (Polity Press 2014)

Vinx, Lars *Hans Kelsen's Pure Theory of Law. Legality and Legitimacy* (Oxford University Press 2007)

Weber, Max 'Die drei reinen Typen der Legitimen Herrschaft' in Max Weber, *Soziologie. Weltgeschichtliche Analysen. Politik* (Kröner Verlag 1968)

Weiner, Allen 'Constitutions as Peace Treaties: A Cautionary Tale for the Arab Spring' (2011) 8 *Stanford Law Review Online* 64.

2 The right to protest and contestation in a deliberative democracy

José Luis Martí

1 Introduction

In his recent and controversial book *The Better Angels of Our Nature*, Steven Pinker famously claimed that violence has significantly declined across human history and that today we live in the most peaceful time in human existence (Pinker 2011; see Mann 2018, for a contrasting view). This might be hard to believe, especially if we look at what happened just in the last century (two world wars, the Holocaust and several other genocides, etc.). But there is a clear trend in the history of humankind towards peace and non-violence, and we would be wrong to ignore it. The debate generated around Pinker's view has focused on whether and to what extent violence has, as a matter of fact, effectively declined.

What is claimed in this chapter is something else. It can be assumed that for the last centuries there has been a profound and global cultural shift, an evolution of the most deeply held moral views and attitudes towards positions that are less complacent and less tolerant of violence of any kind, through whatever means, and for whatever reason, with the only exception of self-defence. Despite pervasive important cultural differences, people around the world are less prone today to justify the use of violent means to pursue political aims than ever before.

Just 50 years ago, revolutionary language was omnipresent in political debates all over the world. The processes of decolonisation offered continuity to the two great communist revolutions of the early twentieth century, the Russian and the Chinese, which in turn connected with a number of smaller revolutions, uprisings, and the first wave of decolonisation that took place throughout the nineteenth century. We may see all these phenomena as part of an ongoing historical process that has characterised modernity since its very origins, which were also clearly revolutionary: the Glorious Revolution in Britain in 1688 and, most notably, the American and French Revolutions in 1776 and 1789 respectively. One might claim without much exaggeration that modernity has been characterised by a history of revolutions and uprisings oriented towards democracy and the republican values of liberty, equality and fraternity, that, in a sense, has culminated in the creation and consolidation of constitutional democracies in at least half of the world's states.

We can still find traces of revolutionary language everywhere in the current political landscape: i.e., the Icelandic Pots and Pans Revolution, the Arab Spring Revolution, the Occupy Movement, the Indignados Revolution, the Umbrella Revolution, the Black Lives Matter Revolution, etc. But all these 'revolutions' have something in common that differentiates them from those mentioned in the previous paragraph: all of them have been mostly non-violent. The mythical aura of an armed revolution, that can still be found in the outlook of leftist movements regarding, for instance, the Cuban revolution, has already gone. Violence is no longer an option, perhaps not even against authoritarian, undemocratic governments. Nowadays, democratic revolutions need to be peaceful to be acceptable. And this is not so exclusively based on moral grounds. Non-violent movements seem to be also more successful, that is, more effective in purely practical and strategic terms (Chenoweth and Stephan 2011).

It is not, however, that the practice of political resistance to authority has been ruled out. It has rather significantly mutated into something closer to the democratic right to protest, far from the revolutionary, armed group of class or national liberation (Delmas 2014, Brennan 2018, Schwartzberg 2020). Something changed forever when social democratic protests generalised in Europe and North America in the 1960s and. Those protests were led by wide and diverse social movements who fought for justice and democracy by using mostly non-violent methods and proved to be quite successful. The same pattern has been repeated in many mobilisations in the 1980s and 1990s, such as the anti-globalisation movement, or in the civic protests in Argentina in 2001 caused by the economic crisis, or in the civic revolutions mentioned in the previous paragraph. The same pattern characterises the massive world mobilisations to fight against climate change, or the Black Lives Matter movement in the USA, recently reactivated after the murder of George Floyd. Millions of citizens around the world feel the need to react against injustice, fight for a better world, and try to do it through social protest, assuming that violence is not an acceptable option anymore.

The aim of this chapter is to explore and analyse the scope and the role that contestation and the right to protest may play in a legitimate, constitutional, deliberative democracy. In section 2, I will start by digging into the historical tradition from which this recent trend towards non-violent social protest emerges and will attempt to introduce some conceptual clarity by stipulating a definition of the right to protest and non-violent action and distinguishing them from other areas of the right to resist, such as that of revolution or violent protests.

In section 3, I will develop a normative argument to show that the right to protest is not only linked with personal wellbeing, but also crucial for the legitimacy of a republican deliberative democracy. It is essential, first, for the quality of public deliberation, and second, for the core idea of democracy, which grants that a contestatory citizenry retains the ultimate effective control over public institutions and decisions, as a way to resist public domination – both illegitimacy and injustice – and the ability to impose direction to them.

Finally, in section 4 I will argue that the right to protest should be constitutionally recognised in a direct, explicit form, not as a derivative right covered by other fundamental rights. And I will explore some initial constitutional implications and suggest some preliminary guidelines to help in such constitutionalisation, before concluding the chapter by tacking stock of its main ideas in section 5.

2 Historical and conceptual remarks

The right to protest connects with a very old theme in the history of political philosophy: the right to resistance against tyranny and oppression. This idea – exemplified in the tragic end of Socrates' life – found a clear place in ancient philosophy in the works, for instance, of Plato and Aristotle in the West, and Mozi, Mencius, and Han Feizi, in China and later in medieval and early modern political philosophy and theology, in the works of Aquinas, John of Salisbury, Machiavelli, Mariana, de Vitoria, Suárez, Calvin, Martin Luther, and Hobbes, among others. And a such line of thought is most refined in the modern contractualist tradition, especially in the work of John Locke, who in the last two chapters of the *Two Treatises on Government*, elaborated a whole theory of the conditions that should obtain for citizens to have the right 'to remove [the government] by force' and 'to resume their original liberty', that is, the right to rebel (Locke 1689). For Locke, as much as for most of his predecessors, this was a natural right that every individual possessed to resist arbitrariness and injustice and was not necessarily related to democracy.

Similar ideas can be found, however, in the works of the fathers of modern democratic theory, like Rousseau, Montesquieu, Hamilton, Jefferson, Kant, and Mill. Kant, interestingly, rejected the right of revolution as such, but developed instead a right of criticism, opposition, and objection, that connects also with the right to protest. Not surprisingly, for most of these democratic thinkers, the right of rebellion was granted for citizens only against illegitimate governments, that is, undemocratic, authoritarian ones; while weaker forms of resistance, such as those endorsed by Kant, Jefferson, or Mill, would persist as an unalienable right of citizens, even of those living under a legitimate democratic, regime.

In addition to that, and still from this historical perspective, it is also important to mention that the right of resistance connected in the late nineteenth century and most notably in the twentieth century with the political tradition of pacifism, non-violent action, and civil disobedience, as in the work of Henry D. Thoreau. Thoreau, commonly considered to be the father of civil disobedience, certainly did not invent the idea. This was rooted, in turn, in at least three different older traditions, all of them related in different ways to the right of resistance: i) anarchism, for which any state is illegitimate, and citizens must definitely have a right to resist its existence; ii) certain Christian lines of thought (some rooted in medieval theology, such as the work of Petr Chelchicki in the fifteenth century), such the ones represented by Quakers and other Evangelical churches which developed an abolitionist ideology, for instance, in the works of William Lloyd Garrison and Adin Ballou; and iii) the much older pacifist doctrine of love, that certainly goes back to the religious and political ideas of Jesus, at least as some have interpreted them, but also to certain interpretations of Judaism, Buddhism, Confucianism, Hinduism, or the ideas of Mozi, Lao-Tse, and the even older ones of Zarathustra.

Thoreau's contribution to this tradition is undeniable and significant. But, even more than him, it was Leo Tolstoy's more refined ideas of pacifism, universal love, and what he called 'non-resistance to evil', which was paradoxically the basis for his claim to resist the injustice of states and governments, the ones that resulted being really influential at the beginning of the twentieth century, for instance to Mahatma Gandhi and, through Bayard Rustin, to Martin Luther King, and later on to Nelson Mandela, among other moral heroes of the past century. This all fed the venerable tradition of civil disobedience that in the last few decades has massively attracted the attention of political philosophers, such as John Rawls and Jürgen Habermas, among many others (Rawls 1966; Habermas 1965 and 1982; see also Lefkowitz 2007; Brownlee 2007 and 2012; and Scheuerman 2018). Civil disobedience is definitely not the only form of political protest and resistance that may be acceptable on moral grounds. It has attracted, however, much more attention and discussion than the others, and any attempt to theorise the right to protest may take great inspiration from the debates on civil disobedience, for instance in understanding that certain forms of resistance like protest and even disobedience might be acceptable even in the context of a legitimate state such as a democracy.

The traditional modern view that was implicit in many of the above-mentioned authors was that the right of resistance and rebellion could only be exercised when the government or political authorities were illegitimate or committed gross injustices. The reason was that such a right of resistance was regarded as the reverse of political obligation (Dagger and Lefkowitz 2017). One has the right to resist an authority if and only if one does not have a political obligation to obey such an authority's rules, and vice versa. And you have the duty to obey the rules of any legitimate authority, because this is exactly what having legitimate authority means. This has been called 'the correlativity thesis', since it correlates the right to rule with the duty to obey those rules, and it has been, as mentioned previously, the historically dominant view (Edmundson 2004). But such thesis has been recently problematised, and it is quite common today to see political legitimacy as a correlate to duties other than the duty to obey: for instance, to the duty not to foment a revolution, that is, the duty to use only legal means to change the authority's commands or remove the people in government (Pettit 2012), which do not necessarily come with the duty to obey such commands. As Martin Luther actually anticipated, one thing is having the right to resist the authority in the sense of having the right to rebel, which he denied, and quite a different thing is to have the duty to obey such authority's commands, which is something he thought conditional to the adequacy of such commands to God's (Dagger and Lefkowitz 2017). One might even have the duty to obey minimally legitimate authorities, and still have at the same time the right or even the duty to resist their injustices (Delmas 2014).

The concept of resistance is of course very vague. For some, like Luther, resisting an authority comes close to making a revolution or a coup. In that sense, it is true that the right to resist must be necessarily different and more restrictive than the right to disobey. In contrast, this chapter takes the view that the right of resistance should not be reduced to the right of rebellion or revolution, as the case of civil disobedience perfectly illustrates. Civil disobedience is supposed to be exerted against laws that are regarded as unjust, but in the context of a generally legitimate and minimally just political regime. This is why it is conceived as an exceptional right. Civil disobedience is undoubtedly a form of political resistance, but one that can be exercised only when citizens *do not* have the right to rebel or undertake a revolution. Similarly, many other forms of protest and resistance are equally compatible with the general legitimacy of the government, such as the basic democratic right to criticise or complain about the government, or the right to demonstrate, or boycott, or sit-in, or occupy, etc. But, of course, this depends on how the relevant terms are defined.

All that needs to be shown, for the moment, is that there is huge conceptual unclarity around all these concepts and rights. This is so, partly because the history of political protest and resistance has been very heterogeneous and constantly changing. This chapter has already shown that it is related to very diverse traditions of political and religious thought. There is no unified or shared political theory of all these rights of resistance, and different scholars use different concepts as well as different categories with different meanings. We need a fine-grained sophisticated analytical work that introduces some order and clarity in the concepts of all these rights. Such ambition, however, exceeds the remit of this chapter, since it would require a very complex work of reconstruction and discussion of a wide and complex array of interconnected rights, many of which count already on a consolidated constitutional tradition.

Thus, and to the simple effect of clarifying the normative arguments in the following two sections, a couple of distinctions will be introduced and some basic definitions stipulated here (for an alternative categorisation of the main concepts, see for instance Buchanan 2017).

First of all, since the concept of *resistance* seems to be vague enough to embrace all the other potential rights that are of interest here, let it be taken as the most general category. Thus, it is said that in any political system citizens might enjoy certain *moral rights to resist* the commands and rules enacted by their authorities.[1] Whether this is so, in which forms, through which means,

1 By calling them moral rights, it perhaps ought to be emphasised that their existence does not depend on the concrete recognition by a particular legal system. These are the rights that many authors in the Modern tradition, at least since Locke, and probably under his influence, have called 'natural rights'. Such a label can, however, be misleading, since it might suggest some commitment to the belief in some pre-political natural law. It is obvious to me that these rights are political in nature. They are moral, as has been said, in the sense that they are independent from the actual explicit recognition by some legal system. They belong to the realm of morality that we may identify as political morality. This chapter, as a matter of fact, is supposed to be a contribution to a *normative* constitutional theory that is grounded in such political morality, one that tell us how constitutions should be, and not as an exercise of descriptive or explanatory constitutional theory, but one that simply tells us what constitutions actually say.

and in which conditions these rights might be exerted, this is what a normative political theory must establish. The array of possibilities is wide and vast, and it extends from the right to criticise the government to the right to make a revolution. 'Resistance to an authority', in general, is understood as any action that aims to interfere to certain degree with the activity of such authority, typically with such authority's commands or rules, as a way of showing opposition to it, either in general or regarding one particular command, rule or activity of such authority. Resistance, we may say, then, is an act of opposition that expresses political dissent or even discontent. 'Interfering' does not mean necessarily 'interrupting', even if interrupting the authority's activity or the enforcement of a certain decision or command is certainly a way of resisting it. 'Interfering' might mean 'disturbing' or have a merely expressive character. Again, what it is crucial to understanding is the idea that an act of resistance is always meant to show opposition or dissent, as a way to fight injustice or illegitimacy.

By defining the exercise of the right of resistance as an action, other manifestations of dissent that fall into the category of pure liberty of thought or ideology will not be considered, even if they are also essential to democracy. In a democratic system, nobody can impose a particular ideology or way of thinking. Citizens are free to think whatever they want on any matter, and this includes freedom to disagree with government's rules, no matter how democratic or how majoritarian they are. But disagreeing with, for instance, a decision made by the government is one thing, and resisting it is another. And this is the difference between thinking something or having certain a belief and taking action. However, this taking action does not necessarily imply creating a lot of trouble for the government. Again, taking action for some political purpose is one thing and whether such action has any effect at all is quite a different thing. Taking action might simply consist of 'criticising' the government's decision, understood as an act of uttering or expressing dissent. And such an utterance might end up having no final political effect or relevance. Whether an act of resistance is consequential or not depends on different factors but is not a conceptual requirement of the notion of resistance.

At this point, a distinction between two different categories of rights of resistance needs to be introduced: on the one hand, we can find the rights of rebellion, like the right to make a revolution among others. These rights protect the capacity of trying to remove or overthrow the ruler or those in the government by using illegal means, whether peacefully or violently. And, as previously shown, those rights are commonly regarded as existing only against illegitimate or grossly unjust governments. Citizens under an illegitimate, authoritarian regime have the right to rebel and try to overthrow those in the government, even by making a coup or revolution. The right to rebel, however, does not automatically imply a right to use violent means. If the regime, for instance, is illegitimate but minimally decent, citizens might not have the right to mount a violent coup, but only the right to overthrow the government through peaceful, even if illegal, means, such as helping a foreign country to fight against its own illegal government, or engage in non-violent actions of sabotage (Morkevicius 2013; Buchanan 2017). The right to make and engage in a violent coup or revolution is certainly a very exceptional one.

It is important to make clear, in any case, that citizens who live under a sufficiently legitimate government, typically a democracy, and provided that such government has not committed gross injustices, such as genocide or massive violations of human rights, do not have, following this tradition of thought, the right to rebel, understood as the right to overthrow those in the government by using illegal means. They have the right to try to change or remove those in the government. But they must use the procedures established by the legal system, such as voting for a different party in the next election or activating an impeachment process (Pettit 2012).

Thus, citizens under a legitimate government do not have rights of rebellion. But they may have rights of resistance, defined here as rights of contestation or protest. In fact, in the next section, it will be argued that having such rights is essential for democracy and political legitimacy. And, therefore, if a government deprives its citizens from enjoying those rights of contestation or protest, it becomes illegitimate, and then it triggers the activation of the rights of rebellion.

Let it be stipulated that this second category of rights of resistance defined here as rights to protest covers any right that protects the capacity to act in certain ways aiming at interfering to certain degree with the activity of the authority, as a way of showing opposition to it, when it does not aim at removing or overthrowing such authority through illegal means. In other words, this chapter proposes to define the rights to protest in opposition to the rights of rebellion, in the sense that any right of resistance that is not a right of rebellion is automatically included in the category of the right to protest. Within this wide and heterogeneous category we can find very different concrete rights, such as the right to criticise the government, which is simultaneously an instance of freedom of expression, the right to complain to the administration, the right to demonstrate or march in the streets, which in most constitutional traditions is usually associated with freedom of assembly, the right to participate in sit-ins or occupy public spaces under certain conditions, usually associated to the freedom of movement, the right to boycott certain activities of the authority, etc. In one way or another, constitutional systems already recognise most of these rights. Thus, their exercise, under due conditions, is perfectly legal. That is not the case, though, of civil disobedience, which conceptually requires being illegal. There can be no explicit authorisation by the legal system to disobey the law, even if a person subject to it finds such law unjust. And yet, civil disobedience is conceived as one the most important moral rights to political protest.

Which kinds of actions should be covered by these rights to protest and under which conditions? The answer to this question depends, of course, on the normative theory we endorse, and this is discussed next in the following section.

3 Democracy, contestation, and the right to protest

This section will argue that the right to protest against and dispute the authority's decisions and rules is essential to the idea of democracy and political legitimacy. The exact justification for this claim depends, of course, on the concrete democratic theory that is endorsed. Different theories may give different explanations or arguments for the centrality of that right, or attribute different weight to it. But in general we can say that, like freedom of expression or the liberty of thought, the right to protest should be recognised as a basic democratic right. The line of argument developed in this chapter will be rooted in the idea of deliberative democracy (Bohman and Rehg 1997; Elster 1998; Besson and Martí 2006; Martí 2006; Mansbridge et al. 2010; Mansbridge and Parkinson 2012; Bächtiger et al. 2018; Lafont 2020) and the distinctive republican theory of democratic legitimacy (Pettit 1997; 2012), but much of what will be argued might be equally supported by many other competing democratic theories.

First, a further distinction that became crucial in present political philosophy will be introduced, dividing the field into two realms, and which is very relevant for these purposes: it is the distinction between justice and legitimacy. There are different ways, of course, to draw such distinction. And the most significant democratic theorists, from Rawls to Habermas, and from Pettit to Mansbridge, Christiano, or Lafont, adopt some particular version of it. The simplest form of presenting it is by distinguishing between two different questions (Martí 2017a). The theory of justice tries to answer the question of what we should decide or do (or what a government should decide or do) in a particular situation. It provides us with a normative standard against which we can assess the content of our private or public decisions. Thus, a particular law is unjust if its content does not satisfy the requirements of the correct theory of justice. Whether a law is just or unjust depends, therefore, on which theory of justice is endorsed.

The theory of legitimacy, in turn, tries to answer the interrelated questions of who and how should make a collective decision in the name of the political community. It provides us with a normative standard that allows us to identify who should have the authority to make political decisions and under which conditions such authority should be exerted. If a political authority is legitimate, in that sense, the decisions it makes under the adequate conditions will be legitimate as well, at least in principle, and for content-independent reasons. Thus, we can say that while justice allows us to assess the content of political decisions from the point of view of normative political philosophy, legitimacy allows us to assess whether those decisions, either just or unjust, were made by the adequate person or group of persons, in the right circumstances and following the adequate procedure. These other questions are normatively relevant by themselves, since we are not indifferent to who rules in the name of the community. But this is especially so, for the reason that we disagree greatly about what justice requires.

Under this understanding, it is obvious that justice and legitimacy refer to two separate sets of questions that may well have independent answers. And there is nothing paradoxical in saying that a decision or a law may simultaneously be just but illegitimate, or legitimate but unjust. Both standards, justice and legitimacy, are scalar, not an all-or-nothing matter. So a more precise characterisation would be that a particular political decision might have certain degree of justice or injustice and have at the same time another very different degree of legitimacy. Of course, multiple combinations of different degrees are possible.[2]

Let us return to this topic and explain why this distinction is relevant. The last section stipulated that the general category of rights of resistance might be divided into two kinds of rights: rights of rebellion and rights of contestation or protest. It was also mention, in accordance with a long and well-established tradition, the rights of rebellion are those that citizens may exercise only against illegitimate governments or against governments that have committed gross injustices. When, on the contrary, governments are minimally legitimate, which can be identified as being minimally democratic, the only rights of resistance that are open to their citizens are the rights of contestation or protest. since these rights to protest are focused on in this chapter, what needs to be explained is why it is so important that citizens enjoy some rights of protest in the context of a political regime that we are assuming as minimally legitimate, that is, as democratic. And the most immediate answer should be obvious by now: such a regime may still be not only very imperfect from the point of view of its legitimacy, since all existing democracies are imperfect, but it might make very unjust decisions as well. In other words, citizens may want to resist and express dissent with their government by exercising their rights to protest because they think that some decision or decisions are intolerably unjust, or because they think that the legitimacy of their government or of some decisions should be increased, or for both reasons.

This tells us why protesting might make sense even in a context of minimal political legitimacy. But this does not show yet why citizens should have those rights specifically recognised and protected, instead of seeing them simply as part of a more general liberty. More concretely: why should political protest, such as demonstrating or marching in the streets, or occupying certain public spaces, be especially protected, and going to the beach for a swim should not?

In normal conditions, we are all free to go to the beach and swim, even in winter. This may be understood as an instance of more general freedom of movement. But no constitution in the world recognises and protects the right to go to the beach and swim, and nobody has a specific claim against others to be able to exercise such 'right', other than, again, a general claim to freedom of movement.

2 For many authors, political legitimacy is not entirely independent from justice, in the sense that *pro tanto* legitimate authorities might lose their legitimacy if they commit such gross injustices, such as genocide, war crimes or massive violations of human rights. Being minimally just could be seen, then, as a further requirement for political legitimacy. This is equivalent to saying that certain degrees of injustice produce the loss of legitimacy. However, whether this is so depends of course on the concrete view on political legitimacy that one subscribes, and it is expedient not to go into such detail in this chapter.

It is not only that such a right is not a positive right, in the sense that it does not trigger the obligation of others to provide one with the resources needed to go to the beach and swim. No one definitively has such a positive right. But even if we take it as a negative right, there is no reason why anyone should enjoy such a specific right to the beach to swim, and be granted constitutional protection, other than the generic reasons to preserve general freedom of movement, which may be instantiated in many other ways.

The rest of this section will attempt to provide a reason why the rights of contestation or to protest should be recognised and protected constitutionally as specific rights. A case will be made for why they deserve to be treated like the right to assembly, freedom of expression, liberty of thought, or the right to vote or run in free and periodic elections, and not as the right to go to the beach and swim.

Let us begin with a general argument. Democracy means self-government, that is, the government of the people, by the people and for the people, as Abraham Lincoln popularised. This idea of self-government implies that citizens must be regarded as free and equal, and that they must guide public decision-making as an exercise of their public and private autonomy. Non-autonomous people, for instance, people who are manipulated or constrained by force, are not able to govern themselves. Thus, self-government requires at least some minimal degree of individual and collective autonomy and the capacity of people to guide their representatives on a minimally rational basis. This is why deliberative democracy is not only the dominant view nowadays among democratic theorists, but also the best understanding of democracy.

In a deliberative democracy, political decisions should ideally be the result of an ongoing, open process of deliberation in which free and equal citizens have the capacity to defend their views, exchange arguments to try to rationally convince others, and be moved only by 'the unforced force of the better argument', and not by the argument of mere force (Habermas 1962 and 1996; Bohman and Rehg 1997; Elster 1998; Martí 2006; Besson and Martí 2006; Mansbridge et al. 2010; Lafont 2020). In such ideal process of deliberation, participants aim at achieving a reasonable consensus on certain issues, which should nonetheless be compatible with their plurality of views and pervasive disagreements on many different levels (for a discussion on the role of ideal consensus and its compatibility with democratic pluralism, see Martí 2017b; also Mansbridge et al. 2010). In the end, democracy can be viewed as a special way to deal with disagreements and generate coordinated action around some basic agreements while respecting equal liberty and pluralism.

The idea of a deliberative democracy presupposes that, first, democracy cannot be reduced to electoral representation, majority rule, and the mere aggregation of individual preferences taken as given. Elections are of course needed, because they are the best way to ensure an accountable representation. Voting and the application of majority rule might be necessary as well, since consensus is not a realistic aim for most decisions. But people's preferences are not immutable or already determined. On the contrary, they should be transformed, in the sense of becoming better informed, better grounded, more robust, more enlightened, through public deliberation.

Representative bodies in a deliberative democracy must represent the different views and judgments held by the citizens subject to them and engage in deliberative processes of decision-making. But, with equal importance, citizens themselves should engage in the ongoing informal public deliberation that takes place in the non-institutional public sphere (Habermas 1962), adopting a plurality of forms and shapes in different moments and forums, all of them ideally articulated in what has been called a deliberative system (Mansbridge and Parkinson 2012; see also Lafont 2020). This engagement in public deliberation and in a variety of forms of political participation and activism should help those citizens to develop a personal critical judgment about public issues as much as about the performance of their government. Moreover, we need political dissent expressed through public deliberation because that may be the only way to avoid individual conformity to erroneous majoritarian positions, informational and reputational cascades, and group polarisation (Sunstein 2003). This critical stance of citizens regarding their government and institutions that is strengthened by public deliberation is then essential to the quality of democracy understood as self-government, and ultimately to its legitimacy.

Consequently, freedom of expression should not be merely seen as another civil, individual right that connects with some personal wellbeing, important as this may be. It should also be regarded, as John Stuart Mill did, as a fundamental democratic right that is intrinsically connected with the quality of public debate, and ultimately essential to political legitimacy. No political system can claim to be legitimate if people are deprived of their basic rights to engage in a quality ongoing public deliberation. And this is a reason why in balancing rights and weighing different considerations, constitutional and supreme courts should give very high importance to freedom of expression and always opt for a maximalist interpretation of that right, showing maximum deference to it, even at the expense of other fundamental rights that have no such democratic significance and implications. Recognising, protecting, and promoting freedom of expression, thus, is an essential duty of democratic systems, at the same level of importance than organising free and periodic elections and ensuring a multiplicity of candidates.

Not all manifestations of freedom of expression, however, possess such democratic significance. One has the right to write novels or poems with no political purpose and be still protected by freedom of expression. This might be important for the individual's personal wellbeing, and therefore connect with a fundamental private interest, even if it has no impact in the legitimacy of the government or the wellbeing of others. Many fundamental civil rights, such as the right to life, or to security, or to health, or not to be tortured, have such exclusively private or personal dimensions. Let us be clear on this point. The fact that those rights are exclusively personal does not mean that their protection is not in the public interest or that they are less important. We all share a public interest to live a political community where all those fundamental civil rights are protected. But political rights in a democracy possess an additional value. Depriving someone of the capacity to express her political views and to engage in the public debate does not only damage her personal wellbeing but impoverishes public deliberation in a way that directly affects us all. For that reason, freedom of expression, and more particularly freedom of political expression, deserves special protection in the constitutional systems.

Similarly to what happens to freedom of political expression, the right to protest and contestation plays an essential role in the legitimacy of democracies and deserves maximum protection. In fact, we might regard some manifestations of the right to protest, such as the right to criticise the government or the right to issue a complaint, as instances of freedom of expression itself. At least for those manifestations, the right to protest finds a clear justification in the idea of deliberative democratic legitimacy that was described above. Constitutional systems, it can be said, must give special protection to their citizens' protests because they have an enormous potential to contribute to quality public deliberation.

Some may think that this is not so obvious. Perhaps some kinds of protest do have such potential, as when a government is criticised in the public forum for having committed an injustice. These would precisely be the kinds of protest that overlap with freedom of expression. But the objector might follow. In what sense does a street demonstration, a general strike, a boycott, or occupation of a square, all of them actions that generate, by the way, some cost or harm to others, possess such potential to contribute to public deliberation? It is true that most courts around the world have developed an expansive understanding of freedom of expression that covers actions such as demonstrating, participating in a sit-in, or burning a flag. We may certainly find some expressive meaning in all those actions and see such expression as a contribution to public debate. As the right to protest was defined in the previous section, any action of protest must actually have some expressive meaning, since it is presented as an act of opposition to the government or authority. In any case, something might be lost if we try to reduce all acts of protest to manifestations of freedom of expression. And the best argument to show this is the republican one.

Republicanism is a very old and venerable tradition of political thought that goes back to Aristotle and Cicero, to Machiavelli, Milton and Harrington, to Rousseau, Montesquieu, Kant and Jefferson, among many others. Here the particularly compelling version of the theory that Philip Pettit has recently developed will be exposed (Pettit 1997 and 2012). As it is well known, Pettit characterises republicanism as the political theory based on the basic value of freedom as non-domination. To be free, according to him, does not mean that others refrain from interfering in individuals' courses of action, since individuals might lose their freedom even in the absence of interference, for instance, by simply being exposed to the uncontrolled will of others, or and individual might remain free despite having been interfered by others, insofar as the individual retains effective means of ultimately controlling such interference. What matters for freedom is not interference, but domination. In other words, it is being dominated by others what makes one unfree. But what does being dominated mean?

Domination is defined as the relational property consisting of the potential invasion of choices that the dominating person might exert over the dominated person, so that

> Someone, A, will be dominated in a certain choice by another agent or agency, B, to the extent that B has a power of interfering in the choice that is not itself controlled by A. (...). And when I say that the power of interfering is not controlled by A, I mean that it is not exercised on terms imposed by A: it is not exercised in a direction or according to a pattern that A has the influence to determine.
>
> (Pettit 2012: 50)

This idea of ultimate control, of having the capacity of imposing direction or ultimately dictating the terms in which others are allowed to invade your choices is the key to the republican notion of freedom.

Freedom as non-domination is, according to Pettit, the basic value that defines both republican justice and legitimacy. While social justice 'is a virtue of social institutions that imposes obligations on the horizontal relations between citizens' and seeks 'the promotion of freedom as non-domination on the basis of an equal concern for each citizen' (Pettit 2012: 297 and ch. 2, and 1997), political legitimacy 'is a virtue of political institutions that imposes a demand on the vertical relations between the citizenry and the state' (Pettit 2012: 299–300 and ch. 3).

The main task of the republican idea of political legitimacy is to ensure that 'state coercion of citizens is consistent with their continuing freedom', and the only way to do that is by instituting a democratic regime. Only in a democracy, the people dispose of a system of effective mechanisms that allow them to impose direction to their authorities and representatives. Only in a democracy, can people live 'on the people's terms', and not under the terms dictated by others. For a political system to be democratic, and therefore legitimate, it is required to be under the ultimate control of the people, and such control must be sufficiently individualised, in the sense of granting everyone rights of equal access to such a system of popular influence, unconditioned, in the sense of not falling under the ultimate control of another agent, and efficacious, in the sense that the people need to be able to effectively impose direction to political institutions (Pettit 2012: ch. 3).

This republican idea of democracy as popular control imposes several specific conditions or requirements for political legitimacy. A complete characterisation of it now will take too long. But Pettit, drawing on the old republican tradition, identifies three core elements: i) the equal freedom of citizens (understood, again, as non-domination), ii) the idea of the mixed constitution, which in contemporary terms might be rephrased as a set of constitutional principles and constraints associated to the rule of law and the separation of powers, among others, and iii) a contestatory citizenry, that is, the idea that legitimacy requires vigilant citizens that 'keep the republic to its proper business', for which they need to 'have the collective and individual virtue to track and contest public policies and initiatives: the price of liberty, in the old republican adage, is eternal vigilance' (Pettit 2012: 5). This 'contestatory citizenry' is conceived as the civic complement to constitutionalism: 'it was to be a citizenry committed to interrogating all the elements of government and imposing itself in the determination of law and policy' (Pettit 2012: 5).

This last element is so central to the republican project that Pettit, in his original book of 1997, started calling his democratic theory 'contestatory democracy' (Pettit 1997: chs 6–8). And, even if in his latest works he uses such label less and less, the idea of civic engagement connected to political contestation remains being one of the core elements of his republican view. Contestation, for Pettit, does not only mean having the capacity to criticise political institutions and issue complains. And it is important not only for its expressive dimension. It is a safeguard of the whole system of liberty. And it requires a complex infrastructure, a 'multi-dimensional, multi-centred pattern of contestation' that empowers 'a suitable system of popular influence' (Pettit 2012: 260).

This particular way of understanding contestation has very clear institutional implications. The system must grant i) *full transparency*, 'the capacity of members of the society to know what proposals are under consideration and what measures have passed', ii) *contestability*, 'the opportunity for members to challenge overtures both in advance of legislation and after they have passed into law', and iii) *impartiality*, 'the availability of forums in which challengers can expect an impartial assessment and, ideally, resolution' (Pettit 2012: 215).

Finally, in addition to such institutional implications, the republican theory of democratic legitimacy requires an active and vigilant citizenry, 'a resistive community', as Pettit calls it, 'that is, a community in which, as a matter of fact and/or common belief, people are disposed to resist government, should it ignore popular influence, and government is disposed to avoid triggering resistance. Just the presence of an electoral system, even one that is adjusted in a contestatory way so as to ensure individualised influence, is obviously not enough to guarantee such a resistive culture' (Pettit 2012: 219). What is required, apart from the institutional implications of the idea of the mixed constitution, and in addition to the protection of the 'freedoms of speech, association and travel', is 'a high aggregate level of civic engagement'.

Asking every citizen to be vigilant of every public decision would evidently be too demanding an ideal. What it is needed is 'specialisation and organisation: in short, a division of labour in the exercise of civic vigilance', of the kind that public-interest organisations and bodies represent. 'The engagement that is required to make popular influence robust is rather the activity of the radical social movements that offer an account of common concerns, articulate a suite of popular demands, and challenge government for its failures to recognize or reflect those demands in its policies' (Pettit 2012: 227). Thus, a republic requires a 'contestatory spirit' that 'counts as a form of civic virtue', but one that should be 'readily achievable', not an unrealistic one (Pettit 2012: 228).

Pettit does not explicitly mention the rights to protest. Not surprisingly, he makes reference to the freedom of expression, freedom of association and freedom of movement, as a classic triad. But contestation, as we have seen, is so central an element of his republican theory of democratic legitimacy, that it certainly deserves more constitutional and legal development. He provides a very clear and compelling argument of why contestation is necessary: democracy means ultimate popular control, and periodic elections are not enough to ensure that governments make just decisions that satisfy peoples' demands. This is why we need a complex system of public contestation through which citizens may watch out for, review, criticise, and challenge those public decisions, reflecting the kind of activities in which 'radical social movements' get involved.

This section will conclude by to have showing why constitutional systems should explicitly recognise that the right to protest should be a fundamental democratic right for all citizens. Political protest pays a service to democratic legitimacy in two different ways. In some of its manifestations, it contributes to quality public deliberation, as the one required by deliberative democracy. In all cases, it also contributes to the kind of permanent and active public contestation of political institutions that republican legitimacy also requires. This is why protesting is not like going to the beach. Having the capacity of participating in a protest can certainly have a personal wellbeing dimension, in the same sense as going to the beach, or even, more importantly, as other fundamental civil rights. But political protest possesses an additional value, the central contribution it makes to the legitimacy of democracies (for a less optimistic view, see Stokes 2020). This is why we need an explicit constitutional recognition, protection, and promotion of the right to protest.

4 Some constitutional implications

Democratic constitutions do not usually recognise a right to political protest as a fundamental right (for one of the few legal analyses of that, see El-Haj 2020). Nor it is explicitly included in the Universal Declaration of Human Rights or other transnational conventions on human rights. Most courts have interpreted the freedoms of expression, association, and assembly as protecting certain activities of political protest. Thus, it cannot be said that this right to protest is in no way protected in democracies. But such protection is clearly indirect and suboptimal. Why this right is missing in the main legal instruments of fundamental rights can be conjured as a historical explanation. Most of these constitutions, declarations, and conventions were drafted before the -1960s when social movements and social protests had not achieved the significance that they have now. This might be the reason why many of these instruments recognise a right to form a unionise, sometimes even a right to strike, which was historically truly crucial, and not a general right to political protest.

In the previous section, however, it has been argued that having protected the capacity to exert political protest is not only important for personal wellbeing, but also crucial for democratic legitimacy. It is as fundamental as having the right to vote in free and periodic elections. For that reason, the right to protest should not only be constitutionally protected, but institutionally safeguarded and promoted. This section will first discuss why the current, indirect constitutional protection is insufficient and, why it deserves explicit recognition and protection, and second, some broad guidelines will be given about how such a constitutionally explicit right to protest should be understood. However, elaborating a complete theory of the right to protest exceeds the parameters of this chapter.

The section will start with the question of why we need an explicit recognition of the right to protest and having it covered through the freedoms of expression, assembly, association and movement is not enough. Do we lose anything if we reduce the acts of protest to exercises of the freedoms of expression, association, assembly and movement? Yes, we do. It is true that all actions of protest possess an expressive dimension, and that many of them are performed collectively through some kind of coordinated action, in assembly with others, quite often, although not always, requiring some movement. But this does not mean that they might be sufficiently protected by the freedoms of expression, association, assembly, or movement. Voting possesses an undoubtedly expressive dimension, and it is certainly something that we do collectively, through coordinated action, and travelling to the polling station. But we do not think that the fundamental democratic interest in having the right to vote in a free election could be sufficiently protected from a constitutional point of view, if it were covered only by the freedom of expression, assembly, and movement.

The reason is that what is essential to voting is neither the mere expressive act, nor the movements that we need to take, or the fact that our action is coordinated with others and sometimes we assemble with them. All this might be important, but it is not the essential purpose of voting. What is essential in enjoying voting rights is the fact of having the capacity to exert equal influence in the direction of government. This is why we need a specific constitutional protection of those rights, as much as a whole institutional system that articulates the exercise of the rights. And the same argument applies to the right to protest. What is essential to the actions of protest or contestation is not only the expression of opinions, or the movements or the assembly of protesters, as such. What is essential is the capacity of remaining vigilant of the government's decisions and actions, contributing to a quality public deliberation that may improve and empower every citizen's political judgment, and contributing to the denunciation of injustices when they occur. All this is vital for democratic legitimacy and deserves its own central place in the legal and constitutional instruments of protection of fundamental rights.

Now, how should we protect the right to protest? Important as this right is, it is obviously not limitless. As any other fundamental right, it must be limited by the protection of the rights of others. There exists, for instance, a well-established tradition already mentioned above that draws a line between violent and non-violent protests, under the assumption that only non-violent protests should be protected by this right, as it happens, for instance, with the debate on civil disobedience (Brownlee 2007 and 2012; Lefkowitz 2007; Scheuerman 2018). There are, however, several conceptual difficulties around such distinction (Weinstein 2007; Buchanan 2017; Mantena 2020). First of all, the meaning of violence itself is far from clear (on how its meaning has actually changed across history, see Mantena 2020). Should it refer to *physical* violence, only, or include *psychological* violence? Does such violence need to be *actual* violence, whether physical or psychological, or it may be *potential*, as in a threat of the use of force? Does it apply to violence against human beings, only, or should it include violence against inanimate things? It is not obvious why slapping a police officer in the face or pinching him slightly in his arm should be immediately ruled out and burning the whole parliament or destroying an airport without any violence on people should not. All these are complicated questions, and there is no space hereto pay due attention to them here. Perhaps we should phrase the right to protest in its simplest terms and in the most economical way, and leave the task of interpreting, balancing, and weighing different considerations to courts, a task they may perform in a particularistic form.

This chapter began by claiming that violence is increasingly seen as morally impermissible. The kinds of incidents in which violent actions are regarded as morally acceptable or justified are more and more exceptional. It is convincing that much in our understanding of the right to protest depends crucially on being able to appreciate the enormous importance of non-violent actions, pacifism, and the idea of passive resistance for current social movements and protests. Perhaps the presence or absence of violence in political protests is of undoubted moral relevance. And it is right, for instance, when the International Covenant on Civil and Political Rights recognises the right of assembly (article 21) only when it is 'peaceful', but then interprets it in a maximalist way, with very few limits. But at the same time we all know that any social protest may easily result in some acts of violence, at least against certain objects, like breaking traffic lights or shop windows, and it is not obvious to why this should make that protest totally impermissible and unprotected from a constitutional point of view. At the same time, and as mentioned in in the previous paragraph, it is not obvious to me why the relevant criterion should be that of violence against human beings, so excluding actions that cause obvious and massive harm to the community as a whole and the public interest. This is why, as it happens with most other rights, only a particularistic balancing of rights and weighing of considerations may allow us to identify the correct solution for each case.

One final consideration needs to be added. Having the right to protest constitutionally recognised and protected, as has been defended here, is probably not enough. Its centrality for democratic legitimacy, which is comparable only to voting rights and the right to run for office, makes this right something that governments should not only respect, but actively protect, designing specific and sophisticated safeguards, and also actively promote, for instance by teaching young people in schools how to become engaged citizens in possession possess adequate civic virtues and know how to exert their role as safeguards of justice and vigilant peaceful and civic protesters. Democracies should significantly improve the way democracy and democratic values are being taught in schools, which also includes some explicit teaching about political and social protests. But, again, elaborating this point would exceed the limits of this chapter.

5 Conclusion

This chapter has been a preliminary attempt to develop the grounds of a theory of the democratic right to protest. Despite the enormous and growing literature that social and democratic movements and protests are generating, this chapter has shown that there is very little conceptual clarity regarding the different rights concerning the more general category of rights of resistance, and some preliminary conceptual remarks have been developed in order to introduce some clarity, even if much more analytical work needs to be done. Despite the important role that those democratic movements and social protests play nowadays in democracies in the promotion of justice, which will quite likely be even more important in the future, constitutions, international declarations and conventions, and other legal instruments do not usually recognise and explicitly protect a right to protest. This chapter has attempted to show why this absence implies a serious deficit from the perspective of democratic legitimacy, a gap that should be filled in as soon as possible. Finally, it has been argued that the right to protest should be explicitly constitutionalised, and have suggested some initial implications and general guidelines about how to do it have been suggested.

Martin Luther King, one of the heroes of social movements and protest in defence of civil rights, non-violent action, and civil disobedience in the twentieth century, is believed to have said that 'the arc of the moral universe is long but bends towards justice'. The truth is that Dr King borrowed that quote from the abolitionist minister Theodore Parker, who made that claim in 1853 in one of his sermons. This brings us back to the rich, venerable and millenary tradition of pacifism, the doctrine of love, and resistance to injustice. Theodore Parker and Dr King might have been right when they said that the arc of moral universe bends towards justice, but the reasoning is not one of historical or moral necessity. The promotion of justice depends on the efforts of thousands, hundreds of thousands, millions of citizens who, across history, and mostly anonymously, have stood up and protested against what they regarded as intolerable injustice. Because the world continues unjust and quite illegitimate, we still desperately need these people. And, if we want to prove Parker and King right, we would need to do better by giving them adequate instruments for their acts of civic heroism: that is, recognising, protecting, and promoting their right to protest.

References

Bächtiger, André et al. (eds), 2018: *The Oxford Handbook on Deliberative Democracy*, Oxford: Oxford University Press.

Besson, Samantha and José Luis Martí (eds), 2006: *Deliberative Democracy and Its Discontents*, London: Ashgate.

Bohman, James and William Rehg (eds), 1997: *Deliberative Democracy. Essays on Reason and Politics*, Cambridge (Mass.): MIT Press.

Brennan, Jason, 2018: *When All Else Fails. The Ethics of Resistance to State Injustice*, Princeton (NJ): Princeton University Press.

Brownlee, Kimberley, [2007] revised in 2013: 'Civil Disobedience', *Stanford Encyclopedia of Philosophy*: https://plato.stanford.edu/entries/civil-disobedience/

Brownlee, Kimberley, 2012: *Conscience and Conviction. The Case for Civil Disobedience*, Oxford: Oxford University Press.

Buchanan, Allen, 2017: 'Revolution', *Stanford Encyclopedia of Philosophy:* https://plato.stanford.edu/entries/revolution/

Chenoweth, Erica and Maria Stephan, 2011: *Why Civil Resistance Works. The Strategic Logic of Nonviolent Action*, New York: Columbia University Press.

Dagger, Richard and David Lefkowitz, 2017 [2014]: "Political Obligation", *Stanford Encyclopedia of Philosophy*: https://plato.stanford.edu/entries/political-obligation/

Delmas, Candice, 2014: 'Political Resistance: A Matter of Fairness', *Law and Philosophy*, 33(4): 465–488.

Edmundson, David, 2004: 'State of the Art: The Duty to Obey the Law', *Legal Theory*, 10: 215–259.

El-Haj, Tabatha Abu, 2020: 'Defining Nonviolence as a Matter of Law and Politics', in M. Schwartzberg (ed), *Nomos. LXII. Protest and Dissent*, New York: New York University Press.

Elster, Jon (ed.), 1998: *Deliberative Democracy*, Cambridge: Cambridge University Press.

Habermas, Jürgen, [1962] 1989: *The Structural Transformations of the Public Sphere*, Cambridge (Mass.): MIT Press.

Habermas, Jürgen, 1985: 'Civil Disobedience: Litmus Test for the Democratic Constitutional State', *Berkeley Journal of Sociology*, 30: 95–116.

Habermas, Jürgen, 1996: *Between Facts and Norms*, Cambridge (Mass.): MIT Press.

Lafont, Cristina, 2020: *Democracy Without Shortcuts: A Participatory Conception of Deliberative Democracy*, Oxford: Oxford University Press.

Lefkowitz, David, 2007: 'On a Moral Right to Civil Disobedience', *Ethics*, 117: 202–233.

Locke, John, [1689] 1965: *Two Treatises on Government*, ed. by Peter Laslett, New York: Mentor.

Mann, Michael, 2018: 'Have Wars and Violence Declined?', *Theory and Society*, 47, 37–60: https://doi.org/10.1007/s11186-018-9305-y

Mansbridge, Jane, et al., 2010: 'The Place of Self-interest and the Role of Power in Deliberative Democracy', *Journal of Political Philosophy*, 18(1), 64–100.

Mansbridge, Jane and John Parkinson, 2012: *Deliberative Systems*, Cambridge: Cambridge University Press.

Mantena, Karuna, 2020: 'Competing Theories of Nonviolent Politics', in M. Schwartzberg (ed.), *Nomos. LXII. Protest and Dissent*, New York: New York University Press.

Martí, José Luis, 2006: *La república deliberative. Una teoría de la democracia*, Madrid: Marcial Pons.

Martí, José Luis, 2017a: 'Democratic Legitimacy and the Sources of International Law', in Samantha Besson and Jean d'Aspremont (eds), *The Oxford Handbook on the Sources of International Law*, Oxford: Oxford University Press, 724–745.

Martí, José Luis, 2017b: 'Pluralism and Consensus in Deliberative Democracy', *Critical Review of International Social and Political Philosophy*, 20(5): 556–579.

Morkevicius, Valerie, 2013: "Why We Need a Just Rebellion Theory?", *Ethics and International Affairs*, 27(4): 401–411.

Pettit, Philip, 1997: *Republicanism. A Theory of Freedom and Government*, Cambridge: Cambridge University Press.
Pettit, Philip, 2012: *On the People's Terms. A Republican Theory and Model of Democracy*, Cambridge: Cambridge University Press.
Pinker, Steven, 2011: *The Better Angels of Our Nature. Why Violence Has Declined*, London: Viking.
Rawls, John, 1966: 'The Justification of Civil Disobedience', in Hugo Bedau (ed.), *Civil Disobedience. Theory and Practice*, Indianapolis: Bobbs Merrill.
Schwartzberg, Melissa (ed.), 2020: *Nomos. LXII. Protest and Dissent*, New York: New York University Press.
Scheuerman, William, 2018: *Civil Disobedience*, London: Polity.
Stokes, Susan, 2020: 'Are Protests Good or Bad for Democracy?', in M. Schwartzberg (ed.), *Nomos. LXII. Protest and Dissent*, New York: New York University Press.
Sunstein, Cass, 2003: *Why Societies Need Dissent*, Cambridge (Mass.): Harvard University Press.
Weinstein, Jeremy, 2007: *Inside Rebellion. The Politics of Insurgent Violence*, Cambridge: Cambridge University Press.

Part II

Peace and discontent in the EU constitutional order

3 The material constitutional arrangement of the European Union

Francesco Bilancia and Stefano Civitarese Matteucci

1 Introduction

In this chapter, we address two exceedingly grand questions: in which sense, can we speak of a material constitution of the EU? And, can the pandemic we have been living through, bring about constitutional change that is constituent power regarding the EU? The vastness of such issues suggests delimiting the scope of the chapter, which we narrow in two respects. First, we limit ourselves to sowing the seeds for possible further research. Our aim, indeed, is to offer some conceptual clarification about the notions evoked in the questions thereof, mainly on how to conceive of the 'material constitution', a notion that has recently been revamped in constitutional theory discourse. Second, we avoid considering all the overwhelming literature dealing with such questions and engage selectively with what is strictly necessary to sketch out our argument.

We structure the chapter as follows. In section 2, we present our view regarding the constitution as a normative-purposive construct based on a conception which can be defined 'neo-classical'. In sections 3 and 4 we take on the notion of the material constitution, mainly by discussing the theories of Costantino Mortati and Hans Kelsen, to cast light on the connection between the material constitution and the rule of recognition of a legal system. We purport that constitutions usually are both formal and material and that the former is instrumental in shielding and stabilising the latter. In section 5, we use the findings of these two sections to discuss the issue of the EU (material) constitution. Section 6 concludes. Our fundamental claim is that the EU material constitutional arrangement, only partly formalised, is what at present impedes developing a truly 'constitutionalist constitution'. In other words, the EU may have a constitutional structure, but still lacks a fundamental political authority which can unify and order an all-purposive set of norms.

2 The normativity of constitutions

The first question presented in the introduction encompasses two controversial concepts. The idea of an EU constitution and that regarding the 'material constitution'. A sizeable part of this chapter will revolve around the latter. We assume the correlative/opposite notion of 'material' is 'formal'. Thus, in this context, the material Constitution is countered with the formal Constitution. This is the correlation/opposition that Constantino Mortati uses at the beginning of his monograph on 'The Constitution in a Material Sense',[1] where he observes that by deducing the content of the Constitution from the same constitutional text one is led to absorb the material determination into the formal.

The distinction between the Constitution in the material and the formal sense is made by Hans Kelsen too. He explains that 'the Constitution in the material sense must be distinguished from the constitution in the formal sense, namely, a document called 'constitution', which, as a written constitution, may contain not only norms regulating the creation of general norms (that is, legislation) but also norms concerning other politically important subjects'.[2]

We shall come back in the next two sections to the approaches of these two authors. We note here that by 'formal' they both mean written/textual. Given this assumption, we purport in what follows that the formal should not be intended in contradiction with the material.[3] To clarify, they are also dimensions both essential to the notion of the Constitution as a legal artefact. To meet this end, we need to clarify in what sense we refer to the Constitution, first, and then what we mean by the material constitution, in the following two sections.

The main feature of modern constitutionalism is the claim to establish legitimate government through a law which is superior to ordinary law.[4] The set of legal norms which made up the Constitution emanates from a process of political decision. This process deals somehow with constituent power, which in turn can bring about a revolutionary event in establishing a new constitutional regime. This latter point is possibly the most controversial and elusive, involving the role of the people and their relationship with the institutions of government once

1 Costantino Mortati, *La Costituzione in senso materiale* (Giuffrè 1940) 7. From now on CMS.

2 Hans Kelsen, *Pure Theory of Law* (University of California Press 1967) 222.

3 Our understanding of such terms is largely, but not completely, coincident with what John E Fossum and Agustin J Menendez, *The Constitution's Gift* (Rowman & Littlefield, 2011) 19–26, explain regarding the three notions of the formal, material, and normative Constitution. They expose that the formal Constitution is written as well as 'singular', 'the constitution has to be made one in the social practice of referring to the constitutional canon or constitutional book as the constitution' (20). For them, the material constitution in the legal sense (as opposed to the sociological one) has two characters in that it is composed of legal norms rather than of other normative systems, and such norms concern the 'institutional structure, the decision-making processes, and the basic entitlements that the subjects of law acknowledge to one another'. In this way, though, the material constitution ends up becoming mingled with the rule of recognition. Indeed, the authors write that 'European law has constituted an autonomous legal order from its very inception to the extent that it contained a distinct and proper rule of recognition, that is, to the extent that the metanorms, or norms which grounded the validity of European norms, were not external but internal to the European legal order' (23). See below Section 4.

4 Dieter Grimm, 'Types of Constitutions' in Michel Rosenfeld and Andràs Sajò (eds), *The Oxford Handbook of Comparative Constitutional Law* (Oxford University Press 2012) 103.

established.[5] By saying that the establishment and exercise of public power are legitimate because they originate from the people as the source of power, one may refer to an array of conceptions to make sense of constituent power. Just think of the different instantiation of the people as the true bearer of the Constitution in the US tradition, a component of the idea of sovereignty in Germany and Italy, the spiritualised embodiment of the Nation in France.

We do not indulge in this chapter in reassessing the meaning of the relationship between people, democracy and constitutionalism.[6] Taking for granted that any kind of relationship must exist,[7] we limit ourselves to observing that by constituent power, we do not mean necessarily a single constitutional moment or event.[8] There is a possibility of conceiving it, and the material constitution, as having an evolutionary rather than only revolutionary pattern.[9]

Emmanuel Sieyès, the first theorist of the *pouvoir constituant* as rooted in a popular democratic process, used to say that the Nation is always in the 'state of nature'. It is from this standpoint that Carl Schmitt elaborates his powerful idea of the impossibility of a logically construed notion of constituent power: 'The theory of the pouvoir constituant is incomprehensible simply as a form of mechanistic rationalism. The people, the Nation, the primordial force of any state – these always constitute new organs. From the infinite, incomprehensible

5 See Martin Loughlin and Neil Walker, 'Introduction', in (eds), *The Paradox of Constitutionalism: Constituent Power and Constitutional Form* (Oxford University Press 2007) 1–9.

6 Emmanuel Sieyès saw the Nation (people) as 'the origin of everything [...] the law itself' – Emmanuel Sieyès, *Qu'est-ce que le tiers-état?* 2nd ed. (Arnold 1979) 79. In the recent literature on constitutionalism, the way of reconceptualising and 'relocating' the role of the people in constitution-making processes have been the subject of an important discussion. It has started by the assumption, advanced by constitutional sociology, that the people are not a unitary or collective agent, but a communicative device, which assumes a specific function in relating the political to the legal system and the other way around (see Kolja Möller, 'From constituent to destituent power beyond the state' (2018) 9 *Transnational Legal Theory* 32–55).

7 As Nico Krisch, 'Pouvoir constituant and pouvoir irritant in the postnational order' (2016) 14 *International Journal of Constitutional Law* 657–679 puts it, 'Contemporary constitutions cannot do without a reference to their grounding in a decision by 'the people,' even if their creation may not actually have involved the people in a meaningful role'.

8 A type of constitution-making which does not require a traumatic event has been characterised as 'post-sovereign', in that it focuses on the exclusion of any single agency, institution or individual that claims to embody the sovereign power and authority of 'the constituent people.' At the same time, it is also 'post-revolutionary' for radical changes are accomplished beyond the antinomy reform-revolution – Andrew Arato, *Post Sovereign Constitution Making: Learning and Legitimacy* (Oxford University Press 2016) 16. A deeper antinomy is that between the idea of the immanence of constituent power (Hans R Lindahl, 'Constituent power and reflexive identity: towards an ontology of collective selfhood'; Emilios Christodoulidis, 'Against substitution: the constitutional thinking of dissensus', 189) and the idea of the complete disappearance of constituent power once absorbed in the constituted power. Against such an antinomy is to theorise a third way in which the constituent power and 'revolutionary spirit' must survive in an institutional form as a space for political action and participation in government, Hannah Arendt, *On Revolution* (Viking 1963) 125.

9 Andrew Arato, *The Adventures of the Constituent Power. Beyond Revolutions?* (Cambridge University Press 2017) 3.

abyss of the force [Macht] of the pouvoir constituant, new forms emerge incessantly, which it can destroy at any time and in which its power is never limited for good'.[10] One way of trying to harness this 'Macht' is by developing a concept of the material constitution which does not reduce it to mere facts, but it is somehow legal.

Finally, a modern constitution must be normative,[11] meaning that the political process takes place within the constraints that the Constitution has laid down. As Dieter Grimm puts it, 'Constitution… turned from a descriptive into a prescriptive notion'.[12] As we articulate in the next section, this normativity entails a purposive aspect too, as long as it is linked to the political arrangement on which the Constitution rests. This point is crucial, as one may want to refer to the Constitution either in the descriptive 'former' meaning – that is the basic rules through which government works – or in the modern normative meaning. Our quest for an EU constitution points to the latter. In turn, the regulation of political power and related goals must be 'comprehensive in the sense that no pre- or extra-constitutional bearers of public power and pre- or extra-constitutional means to exercise this power are recognised'.[13]

We need to remind ourselves that historically, the emergence of the modern state in continental Europe – or government in Britain – was the precondition of the modern Constitution. Does this mean that there is a necessary correlation between statehood and constitutionalism? Probably not, even though, as for every vague concept (state, Constitution), when one moves towards the fringe, the borders become blurred.[14] Let us stress that by not linking the Constitution necessarily to the state does not follow that a constitution of the EU exists.[15] As has been noted, not every structure that fulfils constitutional functions is a constitution.[16] On another note, the notion of 'constitution' applied to international organisations – let alone to a supposed 'global polity' – is highly debatable. As has been remarked, 'amidst all of the talk about constitutions on the international plane, it is sometimes difficult to see how the constitutional analysis bears conceptual fruit'.[17]

10 Carl Schmitt, *Dictatorship. From the Origin of the Modern Concept of Sovereignty to Proletarian Class Struggle* (Polity 2014), 123.

11 As opposed both to a nominal and semantic constitution. See Karl Lowenstein, *Political Power and the Governmental Process* (University of Chicago Press 1957) 147.

12 Dieter Grimm (n 4) 103 A: 2012.

13 Ibid. 104.

14 Christoph Mollers, 'Pouvoir constituant – constitution – constitutionalisation' in Armin von Bogdandy and Juergen Bast (eds), *Principles of European Constitutional Law* (Hart/Beck 2006) 195, denies the idea of Constitution must be limited to the state.

15 The 'European Union does not have a formal constitution' neither does it 'have a constitution in a normative sense' John E Fossum and Agustín J Menéndez (n 3) 22, 26.

16 Christoph Mollers (n 14) 197.

17 Julian Arato, 'Constitutionality and constitutionalism beyond the state: two perspectives on the material Constitution of the United Nations' (2012) 10 *International Journal of Constitutional Law* 627–659.

Be it as it may, transnationalism is the main competitor of the conception of the Constitution sketched above, which has been defined neo-classical.[18] The existence of different bodies of transnational norms, in particular those promoting rights, administered by a network of national, supranational and international courts challenges at the core the very idea of a "single constitutionally organised polity, which immediately expresses the principle of collective/volitional self-legislation inscribed in constituent power".[19] Among them, the role of the EU is ambiguously twofold. As we will see in section 5, the EU is a robust junction of such a transnational network as well as the most effective weapon against the dangers of globalisation and the allure of neoliberal pan-constitutionalism. A character of the said transnational arrangement would be that the constituent power could no longer be conceived as a political force, for it has been legalised via transnational legal norms, especially when the said comprehensiveness in regulating public power is put into question. However, this kind of challenge to constituent power seems to overshoot the mark by presenting it in terms of pure autonomous political will, truly original.[20] For this chapter's sake, we take aside the puzzling epistemological status of the constituent power as well as the empirical restraints that globalisation poses to it. We claim there must be a normative stance to support a republican idea of constituent power. As has been noted, this notion is undoubtedly more complex nowadays than it was in the eighteenth century. Yet 'with its emphasis on agency – and in democratic terms, popular collective agency – it provides a very distinctive foundation for a legal and political order'. In other words, the concept, in the domain of justificatory discourse, still constitutes a powerful weapon to counter neoliberal pan-constitutionalism by raising the question of the legitimacy of a constitutional settlement.

3 The idea of the material constitution

The material constitution has been recently depicted as a theory about the ordering forces (political, economic, geopolitical) which set up and underpin the Constitution.[21] As has been argued, it challenges in the first place the idea that the Constitution is something we can reduce to the application of principles and norms by constitutional courts.[22] In this respect, it looks akin to political constitutionalism. However, it wants to supplement the 'political' approach by 'grappling with the deeper societal context in which formal constitutional development is embedded'.[23] Hence, one cannot grasp the material constitution

18 Chris Thornhill, 'Contemporary Constitutionalism and the Dialectic of Constituent Power' (2012) 1 *Global Constitutionalism* 369–404, 373.

19 Ibid.

20 Ibid.

21 Marco Goldoni and Michael A Wilkinson, 'The material constitution' (2018) 81 *The Modern Law Review* 567–597, 580.

22 Ibid., 569.

23 Ibid.

merely by enhancing judicial with political analysis and exposing the dynamic regarding the relationships between the legislature and the executive in the governing arrangements of the polity.

One of the threads upon which this approach is based,[24] leads us back to the theory of the Italian constitutional law scholar Costantino Mortati revealed in *La Costituzione in senso materiale* (1940). Mortati was critical that law could be described in terms of legal provisions all inferior to a formally posited constitution. Neither did he agree with Santi Romano, the most influential figure in Italian public law scholarship at the beginning of twentieth century, that every legal system is necessarily made of 'institutions' as the prior organisational, legal factor. Before and above the formal Constitution, the existence of an 'original constitution' should have been acknowledged. One that consists of two elements: *a fundamental goal* and a *political party* as the means to achieve the first. The goal had to be comprehensive enough to include in unity the various interests which the state contemplates.

In Mortati's view, this 'original' or 'material' constitution was not the sociological basis of the formal Constitution. He purported it was as legal as the latter, for it constituted the criterion to confer legal energy to any other act by which the system evolves. Mortati thought that by contrasting a 'true constitution', grounded on material forces, with a 'legal constitution' one would cleave any communication between the two, thereby denying legitimacy to the latter. Only by acknowledging the legal value of the 'material constitution' could one see its reverberation into the formal Constitution. The latter, in turn, would stabilise and guarantee the political equilibrium and goals of which the material Constitution was made of, even though it would not wholly and definitively absorb the 'ideology of the dominant political forces'. The latter could always guide the evolution of the Constitution irrespective of the promotion of written amendments. In other words, for Mortati, there should have been embeddedness between the two meanings of the Constitution. They are, respectively, to imbue the supreme national institutions with fundamental constitutive goals through the dominant party and stabilise and guarantee such goals as much as possible. By combining such functions, one could grasp the diachronic meaning of the Constitution beyond its birth as well as its claim to persist over time. For Mortati, the purposive factor which pervades the formal Constitution as something immanent to politics, in its organised party form, lets the Constitution advance happily its claim to last. Such a purpose is the criterion by which to assess the relationship between stability and change. It is also a means to reach an equilibrium between them. How the dominant political party has come to determine the form of state and government is not outside the legal domain.

24 There are several other intellectual roots of the idea with different nuances. See Marco Goldoni and Michael A Wilkinson (n 21) and Marco Goldoni, 'The Material Constitution', in Richard Bellamy and Jeff King (eds), *The Cambridge Handbook of Constitutional Theory* (Cambridge University Press, forthcoming 2021).

Thus, a legal scholar must study the process of 'legalisation' of politics, starting from the constituent power.

Let us make it clear at this point to what extent we deem possible to employ a notion that when it was first conceived had ideological implications. It is plausible to interpret Mortati's *Constitution in a material sense* as an attempt to make the fascist regime legitimate. Hence, any operation of extracting 'value' from this theory must go along with the caution that too much insistence on the political force as pursuing unity[25] risks undermining the other idea which is intimately connected to constituent power. That is the polity who infuses democratic legitimation to the constituent process. The idea of a political value or purpose taken as the founding principle of a legal order, in Mortati's view, carries a normative force which ends up prevailing over the (formal) Constitution and informs the political process of material integration, steered by the dominating party into the material constitution.[26] This part of the theory, which is unsuitable for dealing with the pluralistic nature of societies and political systems, betrays an intent, despite the descriptive stance it purports. The intent is to give theoretical poise to the ambition of the dominating political forces to shape the Constitution and the legal system around a set of values and goals rather than the formal Constitution. This artificial unity is also acted against any other different material entity, to neutralise and absorb any pluralistic and conflicting instance. Nevertheless, we can treasure from Mortati's theory the emphasis on the necessity of considering the political dimension of a constitutional order as well as the 'forces' and diverse 'values' which structure it.

On the other hand, it has been noted that the reference to party politics must not be necessarily traced to totalitarian regimes. Mortati had possibly in mind the Gramscian concept of the party as the new Prince,[27] getting along with a long tradition of politics as the art of governing by elites.[28] The idea of the

25 The political party, Costantino Mortati argues, is 'the active factor of the original institution, [the party] is necessary for the institution to assume political form. Hence, there must be only one party, since one is the principle of any political form' (CMS 73).

26 CMS 73.

27 Sergio Bartole, 'Costituzione materiale e ragionamento giuridico' (1982) *Diritto e Società* 610, from the perspective of constitutional interpretation. Walter L Adamson, *Hegemony and Revolution: Antonio Gramsci's Political and Cultural Theory* (University of California Press 1980) 207, discusses Antonio Gramsci's approach in developing a theory of proletarian political organisation in the *Notebooks*. Although Gramsci took the Machiavellian theme of political leadership as a starting point, unlike Machiavelli he rejected the Renaissance myth of the 'great legislator'. Adamson quotes the following phrase from the *Notebooks*. The modern prince 'cannot be a real person, a concrete individual. It can only be an organism, a complex element in society in which a collective will, which has already been recognised and has, to some extent asserted itself in action, begins to take concrete form. History has already provided this organism. And it is the political party – the first cell in which there come together germs of a collective will be tending to become universal and total'.

28 Hannah Arendt (n 8) 35.

material constitution, in this vein, was also a challenge to the agnosticism of the liberal concept of the state towards the phenomenon of party politics.[29]

The relationship between the state and the polity was a real concern to Mortati. The problem he sensed was how to reconcile the unity of the state, which is not to be found in the array of posited legal norms, with societal differences. Yet, he failed – but it is possibly due to his ideological bias – to recognise the political role of social pluralism. That unity must be rooted in a substantive unifying principle. From this point of view, the role of the material constitution is to lay down insuperable barriers to constitutional amendments in the name of such a unifying principle. For this being conceivable, Mortati claims, it is necessary to 'demonstrate' that such limits spring from legal sources which are subject to the law (are law) at the very moment in which they create the constitutional order.[30]

In the years following the birth of the Italian Republic (as a member of the constituent assembly), Mortati, dealing with the vexed question about the distinction between rules and principles, argued that principles have normative traction in that they bind those who are expected to apply the law in their interpretive effort. Besides, when a constitutional review is contemplated, principles can be used to invalidate conflicting statutory law. One of the main functions of the material constitution is in fact to guarantee the immutability of the 'constitutional core', which in turn coincides with the ends which it consists of from a substantive perspective.

Over the years, the idea of the material constitution has been somewhat incorporated into the Italian constitutional discourse, albeit in a twisted way. In Mortati's view – or at least by adopting a charitable interpretation of it – the function of the material constitution was to keep the formal 'alive and well' by resorting to the constitutive ends as embodied by the political parties. However, in the Italian constitutional scholarship, it was reduced to a view that pointed either to the collective of the political forces which upheld the formal Constitution or the 'de facto' powers (economic or social) however capable of influencing the functioning of democratic institutions.

Thereby, the idea of the material constitution has often been equalled to that of effectiveness as the guiding principle of institutional dynamics. A leading Italian constitutional scholar, Cesare Pinelli,[31] purports, however, that the kernel of the material constitution would have somehow been interiorised in the same concept of the formal Constitution through the doctrine of unwritten

29 A prominent advocate of this hostility towards parties had been Vittorio Emanuele Orlando, another prominent Italian public law scholar and politician during the first half of the last century of liberal orientation.

30 CMS 205. After the collapse of the fascist regime, Costantino Mortati reasserted the fundamental tenets of his theory, especially in a book about the constituent assembly called *La Costituente. La teoria. La storia. Il problema italiano* (Darsena 1945). However, here the resistance parties replaced the fascist party as the driving constituent force.

31 Cesare Pinelli, 'Costituzione formale-costituzione materiale' (2010) *Enciclopedia Treccani Dizionario di Storia* www.treccani.it/enciclopedia/costituzione-formale-costituzione-materiale_(Dizionario-di-Storia)/.

limits to constitutional amendments. The latter is the doctrine expressed by the Italian Constitutional Court (ICC) in the decision n. 1146 of 1988 about the interpretation of the prohibition from amending the Constitution to change the republican form of the state provided for in article 139 of the Constitution. While a pure originalist interpretation of this clause would limit its scope to the prohibition from going back to a monarchic form, the ICC – and a vast body of literature – includes in the term 'republican form' the supreme principles of the Republic as laid down in the first part of the Constitution. In other words, the republican form contains the same elements that in the theory of the material constitution embodied its teleological component. The practical effect of this doctrine is that substantive (material) norms (such as those guaranteeing democracy, equality, free speech and other fundamental rights) trump (formal) secondary rules of change and bind political power. Moreover, these supreme constitutional principles can be used by the ICC to strike down legislation if the court finds the latter in conflict with the former.

Our problem is that this notion of an unamendable 'fundamental core' of the Constitution is still conceptually dependent on the dichotomy between constituted and constituent power where the latter is only authorised to make a change in so far as it does not affect the former. Thus, the issues remain regarding, on the one hand, how one conceptualises constituent power, and on the other, who decides what are the 'supreme principles', how are they detected and, in the end, what are they? The divide between the political and legal Constitution seems to lie upon these questions.[32]

4 The material constitution as the subject of a social practice

By developing and actualising Mortati's approach, Marco Goldoni and Michael Wilkinson[33] have recently pointed out four ordering factors which instantiate the material Constitution: (1) formation of legal and political unity; (2) an effective governing activity; (3) political subjects that link social organisation and the governing activity by pursuing (4) a set of purposive norms (which can take, among others, the form of principles, aims or values). We assume that the primary factors – to which somehow the other two can be traced – are political unity, which requires an authority (political subject) as the 'bearer' who creates and maintains the material Constitution,[34] and purposive norms. It is somewhat intuitive that they must have a material dimension.[35]

32 Along this line, one of the major objections to the material constitution has been raised by Sergio Bartole (n 25) 605, from the perspective of constitutional interpretation.

33 Marco Goldoni and Michael A. Wilkinson (n 21) and (n 24).

34 Marco Goldoni (n 24).

35 Principles can be written down of course, but their structure entails a reference to some substance which is beyond the entrenchment in a document.

First, a question arises about how to handle these factors. The theory of the material constitution appears *prima facie* to be a descriptive concept to embody the fundamental political decision on the arrangement of the polity. The point of the material constitution is that it lays down the legal bases of the entire legal order. The material constitution at the same time buttresses the formal Constitution, and it is stabilised by the latter (see below). In other words, such legal bases are the said 'ordering factors'. They are linked with the constituent power and as such, determine the core principles of the Constitution.

In this sense, one can describe them in the same way as one can describe, say, article 1 of the German Basic Law by explaining that it reads that 'human dignity shall be inviolable. To respect and protect it shall be the duty of all state authority'. This is a descriptive statement about norms. By this point, we mean that the material constitution if it must be a legal artefact, as the theory purports, must have a normative nature as well. This implies that one must always look at the past to discover what the material constitution looks like, precisely at the moment in time when the constituent power reached an (albeit temporary) 'state of rest'. This observation helps mark the difference both with the idea of the 'living constitution' and the assumption that the Constitution is equalled to how political power is actually exerted at any given moment in time.[36]

This prompts us to be clear on what one means by correctly purporting that the study of the material constitution is an exercise in constitutional understanding.[37] If it is that one necessitates grasping somehow what is the content of the material constitution, then it does not contradict the above normative tenet. If, however, by such a descriptive stance one means that the Constitution ends up being something traceable to the pre-modern idea of the Constitution, then we face a problem. Either it becomes another way of disregarding the fundamental normative nature of the legal system by attributing the label of 'legality' to any set of facts that can be described as wielding political power over communities, or it is only a methodological device. As for this latter hypothesis, it may sound strange, though, to use a term normally associated with a substantive notion to refer to methodology. Let us think of the statement 'the material constitution is a methodology to understand what the material constitution is'. One can use criteria to understand how the material constitution can be conceptualised – and by that it can beclaimed that the material constitution is composed of different ordering factors – but one must be able to point out what those who are subject to the Constitution ought to do.

To be fair, and take on board our epistemological presupposition, we believe that even in 'describing' institutions and norms, one cannot avoid some normative commitment. Behind the apparent objective stance of the study of the material constitution, an intent emerges. It is to confer stability to a constitutional

36 'Political constitutionalism' – which is often described as akin to ancient constitutionalism – is normative too. See Richard Bellamy, *Political Constitutionalism: A Republican Defence of the Constitutionality of Democracy* (Cambridge University Press 2007) 5.

37 Marco Goldoni, ibid.

order by detecting its social and political roots. The risk of such an endeavour, then, is to stick with an ever-changing subjective description of what constitutes the material driving forces of a society with no counterfactual function of the Constitution whatsoever. With this, we are back to the question of how to identify the factors which shape the material constitution, as society evolves, and contemporary polities must face manifold pluralistic tensions.

We believe that the route to follow for grasping the concept of the material constitution is to resort to the notion of the rule of recognition of a legal system. Only by doing this, can one combine the notion of a political constitution and the detection of the ordering forces which shape the constitutional structures of a given community without giving up the 'formal' and 'normative' requirements of normative constitutionalism.

In his book, Mortati criticises Hans Kelsen's *Grundnorm* by making the well-known argument about its fictitious nature and purporting that the 'first constitution' is nothing less than the Constitution in the material sense.[38] He completely overlooks that Kelsen, in turn, theorises the existence of a 'constitution in the material sense'. In the *Pure Theory of Law* Kelsen explains that

> 'The Constitution represents the highest level of positive law. 'Constitution' is understood here in its material sense, that is, we understand by Constitution the positive norm or norms which regulate the creation of general legal norms. The Constitution may be created by custom of a specific act performed by one or several individuals, that is, by a legislative act. In the latter case it is always formulated in a document and hence called a 'written' constitution, in contradistinction to the 'unwritten' Constitution brought about by custom. The material constitution may consist partly of norms of written and partly of unwritten law. The unwritten norms of Constitution may be codified; and if this codification is the work of a law creating organ and therefore acquires binding force, it becomes a written constitution'.[39]

As has been noted, then, what makes the material constitution material, in this account, is its function, not any content.[40] Kelsen does not clarify whether the material constitution must have procedural content only. He is almost exclusively interested in the mechanism through which the rules governing legislation receive a specific formal constitutional form and, besides, a device for a constitutional amendment is entrenched. In this way, it is the formal Constitution which underpins and stabilises the material Constitution, not the reverse.[41] From this, some authors have purported that by adopting Kelsen's perspective, one cannot claim that the material constitution may also have any substantive 'political'

38 CMS, 21–27.
39 Hans Kelsen (n 2) 222.
40 Lars Vinx, *Hans Kelsen's Pure Theory of Law* (Oxford University Press 2007) 158.
41 For Vinx (n 40) 158, the Constitution in the formal sense is the beginning of 'constitutionalism'.

content.[42] The fact that Kelsen refers to this possibility by speaking of the formal written Constitution, though, does not imply that it cannot be the case for the material constitution as well. Especially if we supplement the meta-reflexive nature of the 'rules that regulate the creation of general legal norms' with the concept of secondary rules introduced by Hart, whose principal token is the rule of recognition, we can think of substantive rules, as part of the rule of recognition of a legal system. They 'regulate the creation of general legal norms' by assuming a set of fundamental principles and some form of political unity by the identification of the bearer – the political authority[43] – of the Constitution.[44] Given that the rule of recognition is rooted in social practice, it is by assuming that the latter includes such fundamental norms as the ones setting up the purposive norms and the organising principles of political authority that one can make sense of the material constitution *qua* legal notion. The most promising way in which the rule of recognition, which encompasses the material Constitution, may be thought is by conceiving it in terms of a constitutive rule grounded on social conventions.[45]

In brief, there is no contradiction between the formal and material Constitution. Constitutions are normally both formal and material at the same time. The material ordering factors which constitute the kernel of the Constitution become truly 'constitutional' through the entrenchment of the documentary (formal) constitution. At the same time, if a highly ranked written document is ordinarily necessary for having a (formal) constitution, it is not sufficient. The documentary constitution must have codified the ordering forces of the Constitution. On the other hand, without such a codification, the material constitution cannot acquire those characters of certainty and stability, which are typical of law in modern societies.

It remains, of course, an area of vagueness regarding the amendable/non-amendable parts of the Constitution given to possible controversy about the ordering factors that have been stabilised. The relationship between the material and formal constitutions, then, is highly significant. When the phenomenon of strengthening the material constitution by the formal does not occur, we should

42 Marco Goldoni and Michael A Wilkinson (n 21) 570; Andrew Arato (n 9) 4.

43 This leads us back to Mortati's theoretical insight on the 'real subject who makes the constitution and keeps it alive'... a political entity assumed as real, concrete, factual power, acting as a material foundation, or source of the legal order'.

44 As reported by Andrew Arato (n 42) 5, Dieter Grimm, in *Die Zukunft der Verfassung* (Suhrkamp 1991), identifies Constitution as that 'complex of norms which fundamentally regulates the setting up and exercise of state power and the relationship of state and society' [11] thus linking fundamental rights with political institutions. Yet, he does not disregard the distinction between secondary and primary rules. In fact, Grimm speaks of 'a group of basic norms for the making of political decisions, aiming at the possessors of power, and a group of politically generated norms aiming at its subjects' [14]. The Constitution is thus differentiated from ordinary law by the fact that 'it has the highest power itself as its object.'

45 Marco Goldoni (n 24), Andrei Marmor, *Social Conventions. From Language to Law* (Princeton University Press 2009) 155.

speak of 'non-constitutionalist or minimally constitutionalist constitutions. Many formal constitutions are made for ideological reasons and sometimes primarily for external consumption. But if there is a significant overlap between the formal and material constitution, the latter is indeed strengthened and stabilised by becoming public and is potentially enforceable. When the material structure that is formalised includes limitations on the holders of the most important powers of government, we can speak of constitutionalism in more than a minimal sense'.[46]

5 The EU 'constitutional progress'

We can now finally sketch out an answer to the question presented at the start regarding in what sense we can speak of a material constitution of the EU. By applying the tenets of the material constitution to the European Union, Marco Goldoni has recently argued that the EU has a material constitution indeed, although a relatively fragile one. The main clue would be the existence of a form of political unity, whose bearers are national governments, with some fundamental goals attached revolving around the creation of the single market and financial stability.

We doubt, though, that the EU has either a 'formal' or a 'material' *modern* Constitution with the meaning specified above. We argue that it does have a material constitutional arrangement, partly formalised, which is precisely what at present impedes developing a 'constitutionalist constitution'. In other words, the EU may have a constitutional structure, but still lacks a fundamental political authority which can unify and order an all-purposive set of norms.

There are of course written documents, the Treaties, which allegedly had the effect of constituting a new legal order. A well-known strand of scholarship purports that the EU also possesses a constitution after the 'constitutionalisation' of the Treaties operated by the CJEU.[47] Does it amount to a formalisation of the Constitution in a material sense, as such part of the rule of recognition of the EU legal order? And, on the other hand, does it have the character of comprehensiveness to the extent that it 'excludes extra-constitutional power-holders and unconstitutional ways and means of exercising power'[48] and that can pursue the 'general interest' of the polity by handling political conflicts within the European society?

If we start by looking at the alleged documentary constitution, the Treaties, we find in the TEU a solemn proclamation of general goals which seem to refer to the wider regulation of state power and the relationship between state and society. Just consider articles 2 and 3 that read, respectively, that 'the Union is

46 Andrew Arato (n 42) 6.

47 Christopher Thornhill, 'The European Constitution and the pouvoir constituant – no longer, or never, Sui Generis?' in Jiří Přibáň (ed), *Self-Constitution of European Society: Beyond EU Politics, Law and Governance* (Routledge 2016) 13–36, 16.

48 Dieter Grimm (n 4) 109.

founded on the values of respect for human dignity, freedom, democracy, equality, the rule of law and respect for human rights, including the rights of persons belonging to minorities …' and that 'the Union's aim is to promote peace, its values and the well-being of its peoples'. They are, though, completely deprived of any performative function by the provisions of TFEU, which instead expresses the truly operational and ordering factors of the European Union.

Throughout the TFEU, we do not find any room for political goals except for those that national governments have entrenched in the TFEU. There is no room for manoeuvring which has been left in the hands of the EU institutions out of the political compromise reached by the contracting States. It has solidified political energy and values which have been built around the interests of private companies,[49] sociologically the real driving force of European integration and the primary addressees of EU legal rules.[50] One can easily recognise that the incorporation of such interests within the Treaties, as fundamental political decisions, aims to legalise the material power of the markets.[51] Tellingly, the European Commission has been given the task of drafting all the EU legislation precisely to preserve such a compromise and guarantee that regulation stays within those limits. Then, while we can speak of a substantial overlapping between the formal 'constitutional sources' and the material constitutional dimension for the TFEU, as for the TEU we can rightly speak of a constitutional-like document made for ideological reasons with no linkages with the material ordering forces.

Alternative ideas and political views regarding the process of integration cannot make their way through any legal process able to affect EU legislation.[52] Hence, any transformative capacity of the (constitutional) law to build a different narrative and give different form to diverse political objectives is hollowed out. The correspondence between material and formal regarding the TFEU, in the end, concerns the lack among the EU institutions of any political autonomy from State Governments. They are the only in charge of the creation of what we may call 'political law' throughout 'the legal system building process, in which the most important moment while achieving political unity must be the "translation of the political decision in fundamental legal norms'.[53]

49 Temistocle Martines, *Contributo ad una teoria giuridica delle forze politiche* (Giuffrè 1957), uses the term 'forze politiche' (political forces). See also Carlo Esposito, *La validità delle leggi. Studio sui limiti della potestà legislativa, i vizi degli atti legislativi e il controllo giurisdizionale* (Giuffrè 1934) 230.

50 In this sense already Costantino Mortati, 'Costituzione (dottrine generali)' (1962) *XI Enciclopedia del diritto* 167.

51 See Gianni Ferrara, 'I diritti politici nell'ordinamento europeo', in *AIC Annuario* 1999 (Cedam 2000) 480, about the lack of effective political rights within a legal system which does not even recognise a 'right to politics'.

52 It is what Vezio Crisafulli 'Per una teoria giuridica dell'indirizzo politico' (1939) *Studi urbinati* 45, claims.

53 Ibid. 46, nt. 18.

The bearers of this material constitutional arrangement are national governments, the Masters of the Treaties,[54] but it is questionable that they encompass *legitimate* political unity. Let us consider, for example, what is the actual content of fundamental principles in their relationship with the rule of law and the protection of individual rights.[55] The material arrangement codified in the TFEU twists from the start the role of such principles.[56] The narrow content given to equality is a case in point. It is no longer, as in many of the constitutional traditions of the Member States, a fundamental political value for pursuing equal access to life opportunities and redistributive policies. It has become a mere benchmark to tackle 'legal' discrimination. The highly debated legitimacy problem comes here centre stage, especially if we compare the EU legal order with the 'traditional' constitutions of the Member States. The material, and partly formal, constitutional arrangement of the EU, based on market and financial regulation, completely displaced natural aspirations, needs and expectations of 'ordinary people'.

By resorting to Mortati's categories, this asymmetry reminds us of the 'relations between legal order in a formal sense…and the material order which is the expression of the law "implied (assumed)" by its own foundations'. By matching this insight with the evolutionary approach that a conventionalist idea of the rule of recognition brings about, we can see that the fundamental structure of the legal system is not stationary and unamendable over time. It relies on the substantial economic, social and political interests that were given to it by the "real foundation", the concrete substratum which defined the sense and substance of it. In doing so, it becomes easier to see how many traditional constitutional values have been betrayed or exploited.[57] Ultimately, the issue revolves around political unity as an ordering factor, which implies legal and political authority. The lack of a European political central power is, in turn, responsible for the legitimacy issue, for there is no political authority to take up individual rights and social needs. This is, by the way, one of the main reasons why populism is spreading out across Europe.

54 See Markus Patberg, 'Challenging the masters of the treaties: emerging narratives of constituent power in the European Union' (2018) 7 *Global Constitutionalism* 263–293, where four alternative public narratives of constituent power in the EU are discussed.

55 'Versteht man unter "Gesetz" jeden Befehl, der von einer bestimmten Stelle ausgeht oder in einem bestimmten Verfahren zustande kommt, so ist das Prinzip der Gesetzmässigkeit reiner Absolutismus', Carl Schmitt, cit., 200, 211 on the relationship between the principle of equality and the rule of law.

56 Carl Schmitt, 'Grundrechte und Grundpflichten' (1932), in C Schmitt, 'Verfassungsrechtliche Aufsätze aus den Jahren 1924–1954: Materialien zu einer Verfassungslehre' (Duncker & Humblot 1958) 181, particularly 190 referring to the law and its substantial meaning postulated in the second part of the Weimar Constitution in defining the nature of the fundamental rights. 'Vielmehr hat jede konkrete Art Staat ihre ganz spezifischen Grundrechte. Die "Fundamentalrechte" z.B. einer feudalen oder ständischen Monarchie sind nicht nur inhaltlich, sondern auch in ihrer rechtslogischen Struktur anders geartet als die Freiheitsrechte eines liberalen Rechtsstaates…und wiederum anders als die Grundrechte des werktätigen und ausgebeuteten Volkes in einem sozialistischen Klassenstaat' (190).

57 Costantino Mortati (n 50) 155, 158, 162 f., 167. See also Ferdinand Lassalle, 'Uber Verfassungswesen' in 2 Gesammalte Reden Und Schriften 38 (Cassirer ed, 1920). See at least Costantino Mortati, CMS, particularly at 64 and Id (n 50) 155, 162 f., 168 f.

A normative commitment towards a 'constitutionalist constitution' calls for change. How to change the material framework of the EU is not for us to say here. Yet, we would like to briefly point out some, albeit contradictory, signs of development and its possible (or desirable) direction. Putting it bluntly, is it possible – and desirable – to devise, in the immediate future, a project of political unification built around common and homogeneous values on which the European demos can converge? Or the compass of the dominant ideas is still firmly pointing to the regulatory framework of the common market and the economic and monetary union?

While the lack of federal authority in Europe, as well as that of a federal-like power to balance the dominance of the States, are barely disputable,[58] the creation of an autonomous constitutional federal dimension to equilibrate such hard asymmetries as, particularly, those generated by monetary distribution policy, must be problematised. One way is to postulate a shared EU citizenship substantiated by political rights and redistributive policies. The precondition of this 'movement', irrespective of any directionality or functionalistic approach,[59] is to change an entity that works out policies into one that deals with politics. Politics needs a political community, though. However, without making risk-sharing and redistribution – both among citizens and the Member States – a topic of democratic debate and decision-making, there is no political community.[60]

One could be tempted to interpret as a movement towards such a direction the so-called Next Generation EU Recovery Plan. It is the decision by the Member States, within the European Council, to pass a special investment programme[61]

58 In this sense Roger D Kelemen, *The Rules of Federalism. Institutions and Regulatory Politics in the EU and Beyond* (Harvard University Press 2004) 1, 23, 160. See, also, Giandomenico Majone, *Rethinking the Union of Europe post Crisis. Has Integration Gone Too Far?* (Cambridge University Press 2014).

59 It means to overcome the very idea of a 'project' steered by any elitist instance. This approach cripples the still important democratic narrative of 'popular sovereignty'. The challenge is to show European citizens that Europe can be a space where to change collectively their common fortunes rather than an entity perceived as dominated by unchangeable, inherited political and social hierarchies (see Marija Bartl, 'From Europe-as-project to a Real Political Community' at www.socialeurope.eu/from-europe-as-project).

60 See Marija Bartl, 'Hayek upside-down: on the democratic effects of transnational lists' (2020) 21 *German Law Journal* 57–62, 59, who rightly notes that 'Questions of EU-wide solidarity and risk-sharing have also remained anathema in political discourses across national public spheres. The lack of a shared European public sphere made it difficult not only to develop a sense of belonging between EU citizens that would ground solidarity, but also prevented the emergence of pan-European political programs that would have to tackle the questions of distributive justice across the EU, and which would have to be discussed and defended as such at both European and national levels'.

61 See the Conclusions of the Special meeting of the European Council of 17, 18, 19, 20 and 21 July 2020, Brussels 21 July 2020, available at www.consilium.europa.eu/media/45109/210720-euco-final-conclusions-en.pdf: 'the emphasis is now shifting to mitigating the socio-economic damage. This requires an unprecedented effort and an innovative approach, fostering convergence, resilience and transformation in the European Union. At the request of the Heads of State or Government, the Commission presented at the end of May a very wide-ranging package combining the future Multiannual Financial Framework (MFF) and a specific Recovery effort under Next Generation EU (NGEU)', emphasis added.

for increasing Member States' spending capacity in the face of the harsh economic consequences of the pandemic caused by COVID-19. Thanks to the multiple financing lines established by this programme, *'the Commission will be authorised to borrow funds on behalf of the Union on the capital markets. The proceeds will be transferred to Union programmes in accordance with NGEU.'*

An innovative feature of the programme is the redistributive character of some of the measures as well as the emphasis on the European Social Pillar and the reduction of the gender gap. Still, there are conditions attached to guarantee the financial interests of the EU and States are expected to balance their books by 2021.[62]

We should not overestimate the political and institutional significance and scope of this 'historical decision' as symptoms of a new institutional approach.[63] Nonetheless, by reading Part II of the Conclusions of the Special meeting of the European Council,[64] titled 'expenditure', we hardly escape the impression of a change in the traditional system of financial relations between the EU, the markets and the Member States. There is, for example, an explicit mention of 'supporting investment, job creation and growth, helping reduce economic, social and territorial disparities within the Member States and across Europe'.[65] It is an instance of 'Financial Authority Migration' from the Member States to EU institutions, which only a few months ago would have been unthinkable.[66] Pandemic aside, which was undoubtedly the proximate generating factor of such a sudden change, this decision reveals at least that a political-constitutional struggle has been set in motion. Hints of the elusive insurgence of constituent power cannot be denied.

The conflict is between two opposite views about the present stage of the process of European integration. On the one hand, the notion – which can be derived from very different inputs and political venues and that accommodates a variety of political ideals – of a Union rooted in solidarity, which implies among other things the idea of mutualised debt as a necessary condition for European unity. On the other hand, there is an (often) unarticulated vision of the EU as 'business as usual', which hinges on the long-standing functionalist

62 See www.consilium.europa.eu/en/press/press-releases/2020/06/11/eurogroup-statement-on-greece-of-11-june-2020/.

63 For healthy scepticism regarding the EU Recovery Plan, see Varoufakis, 'The EU coronavirus fund will take Europe another step towards disintegration': www.theguardian.com/world/commentisfree/2020/jul/24/eu-coronavirus-fund-europe-recovery-package.

64 17 in the English version.

65 See the measures at Heading 2, 'Cohesion, resilience and values' 21, aimed at 'contributing to reducing disparities between the levels of development of the various regions and the backwardness of the least favoured regions'.

66 The coronavirus has made politically thinkable many things that were unthinkable before. Primarily, the assumption that markets are self-sufficient problem-solving entities (see, for example, the discussion on 'Just Transition' at www.socialeurope.eu/focus/just-transition) and the neoliberal obsession for debasing government action. See Mariana Mazzucato and Giulio Quaggiotto, 'The big failure of small government', www.project-syndicate.org/commentary/small-governments-big-failure-covid19-by-mariana-mazzucato-and-giulio-quaggiotto-2020-05?barrier=accesspaylog.

interpretation of the EU trajectory.[67] The paradox of the latter view is that, by professing the virtues of the status quo, it seems to accelerate the prospect of Europe's disintegration.

It is, finally, interesting to place within this struggle the *Weiss* judgment by the German Constitutional Court, which has famously ruled that the European Central Bank's mass bond-buying, to stabilise the Eurozone partly violates the German Constitution.[68] The Constitutional Court in Karlsruhe said there is not enough German political oversight in the purchases. It reasserted the sovereignty of the Member States over the EU institutions about fiscal policies by claiming that democratically legitimate political bodies must decide it.

The point of contention was about the allegedly disproportionate use by the ECB of monetary policy, thereby impinging on political economy. The most common reaction to this ruling has been either to stress the erroneous stance of the GCC regarding the competence of the CJEU to decide on the remit of European institutions or to reprimand the German judges for their selfish attitude towards the EBC 'whatever it takes' policy.

Others have indulged in commenting, once more, on the never-ending saga of judicial dialogue/conflict boosted by the predominant narrative about constitutional pluralism in the European constitutional landscape.[69] By zooming out from the most evident legal dispute between the two courts, we can see that the stake was much higher than that. It was precisely about – as has been pointedly noted – the unsustainability of keeping to 'muddling through'.[70] That is to say, not to face the 'existential' issue of monetary policy to ease States' financial and economic problems (sitting along with the objective of 'sound public finance') with no fiscal capacity to meet the challenge of solidarity reconstruction and transformation of the economy as well as a central bank capable of acting as buyer and lender of last resort under the supervision of politically responsible democratic institutions.

67 Along this fault line sits, for example, the division between 'the frugal four' and 'the irresponsible South' Member States (Luiza Bialasiewicz, 'National stereotypes in times of COVID-19: the 'frugal four' and the 'irresponsible South', www.opendemocracy.net/en/can-europe-make-it/national-stereotypes-in-times-of-covid-19-the-frugal-four-and-the-irresponsible-south/, which cuts across different political families). There is, of course, the third view represented by sovreignist and populist movements, which as long as is sincerely (and not opportunistically) expressed calls itself out of the struggle about the future of Europe as a political institution.

68 BVerGe, Second Senate, 5 May 2020, 2 BvR 859/15, 2 BvR 1651/15, 2 BvR 2006/15, 2 BvR 980/16.

69 Daniel Sarmiento and Joseph H Weiler, 'The EU judiciary after Weiss: proposing a new mixed chamber of the Court of Justice' 2020/6/02 VerfBlog, https://verfassungsblog.de/the-eu-judiciary-after-weiss/, DOI: https://doi.org/10.17176/20200602-133615-0. See Roger D Kelemen, Piet Eeckhout, Federico Fabbrini, Laurent Pech and Renata Uitz, 'National courts cannot override CJEU judgments: a joint statement in defense of the EU legal order' 2020/5/26 VerfBlog https://verfassungsblog.de/national-courts-cannot-override-cjeu-judgments/, DOI: https://doi.org/10.17176/20200527-013240-0.

70 Marco Dani, Joana Mendes, Agustín J Menéndez, Michael A Wilkinson, Harm Schepel and Edoardo Chiti, 'At the end of the law: a moment of truth for the Eurozone and the EU', 2020/5/15 VerfBlog https://verfassungsblog.de/at-the-end-of-the-law/.

Therefore, it may be the case that the bold stance by the GCC is among the factors that triggered the response by the European Council, which led to the Recovery Plan. This response is unprecedented also because it formally shifts the decision to partly mutualise public debt (which is what the GCC claims the so-called quantitative easing by the ECB amounts to do) from a technical to a political site.

In other words, the confrontation between the two most powerful courts in Europe cuts across the ongoing conflict regarding the future of the EU. The asymmetric and fragmented mode of the EU constitutional arrangement makes the Weiss judgment in turn paradoxical. It is barely deniable that the GCC is advocating (all instrumental motivations aside) democratic legitimacy versus technocratic decision-making. At the same time, the main effect of such a stance is to jeopardise a disposition of solidarity and unity among the Member States. The point is that solidarity, in this case, is only the exterior output of a policy of financial stability rather than a substantive purposive norm of the European material constitution. This is yet another proof about the 'true' nature of the constitutional arrangement of the EU as well as the inadequacy of the courts to 'constitutionalise' the political process.

6 Conclusion

We have claimed that constitutions normally have both a formal and a material part. Counterintuitive as it may sound, it is the former which shields and stabilises the latter. In so far as it happens, the entrenchment of the ordering forces of 'real political power' may reveal particularly strong resistance to change. Our fundamental claim is that the EU material constitutional arrangement, only partly formalised, is what at present impedes developing a truly 'constitutionalist constitution'. At present, the EU lacks a fundamental political authority which can unify and order an all-purposive set of norms.

A normative constitution needs concrete and substantial political consent as a basis for its legitimacy. The category of the *Constitution in a material sense* is useful for understanding decision-making processes, powers, forms of expression of legal rules. Hence, if we want to figure out an EU constitutional dimension, we must focus on what Ferdinand Lassalle used to call the 'real constitution',[71] to yield 'so strong and efficient a political power' as to impose itself to any real political actor within the system. This notion embodies the necessity of providing for a central political authority capable of being recognisable as minded to the needs and aspiration of the people, and thereby legitimate. Only this form of identification will determine 'people acquiescence' in a new legal system rooted in political constitutionalism. The making of a morally and legally legitimised EU *authority* is the crucial challenge of the next future, the revolutionary path that the Europeans need.[72]

71 Ferdinand Lassalle (n 57) 7.

72 Massimo Fichera, *The foundations of the EU as a polity* (Edward Elgar Pub 2018); Massimo Fichera, Sakari Hänninen and Kaarlo Tuori (eds), *Polity and Crisis. Reflections on the European Odyssey* (Routledge 2016).

References

Adamson WL, *Hegemony and Revolution: Antonio Gramsci's Political and Cultural Theory* (University of California Press 1980)

Arato A, *Post Sovereign Constitution Making: Learning and Legitimacy* (Oxford University Press 2016)

Arato A, *The Adventures of the Constituent Power. Beyond Revolutions?* (Cambridge University Press 2017)

Arato J, 'Constitutionality and constitutionalism beyond the state: two perspectives on the material constitution of the United Nations' (2012) 10 *International Journal of Constitutional Law* 627–659

Arendt H, *On Revolution* (Viking 1963)

Bartl M, 'From Europe-as-project to a real political community', www.socialeurope.eu/from-europe-as-project (24 April 2019).

Bartl M, 'Hayek upside-down: on the democratic effects of transnational lists' (2020) 21 *German Law Journal* 57–62

Bartole S, 'Costituzione materiale e ragionamento giuridico' (1982) *Diritto e Società* 610

Bellamy R, *Political Constitutionalism: A Republican Defence of the Constitutionality of Democracy* (Cambridge University Press 2007)

Bialasiewicz L, 'National stereotypes in times of COVID-19: the "frugal four" and the "irresponsible" South', www.opendemocracy.net/en/can-europe-make-it/national-stereotypes-in-times-of-covid-19-the-frugal-four-and-the-irresponsible-south/

Crisafulli V, 'Per una teoria giuridica dell'indirizzo politico' (1939) *Studi urbinati*

Christodoulidis E, 'Against substitution: the constitutional thinking of dissensus', in M Loughlin and N Walker (eds), *The Paradox of Constitutionalism: Constituent Power and Constitutional Form* (Oxford University Press 2007)

Dani M, Mendes J, Menendez AJ, Wilkinson MA, Schepel H and Chiti E, 'At the end of the law: a moment of truth for the Eurozone and the EU', 15 May 2020 VerfBlog

Esposito C, *La validità delle leggi. Studio sui limiti della potestà legislativa, i vizi degli atti legislativi e il controllo giurisdizionale* (Giuffrè 1934)

Ferrara G, 'I diritti politici nell'ordinamento europeo', in *AIC Annuario 1999* (Cedam 2000)

Fichera M, Hänninen S and Tuori K (eds), *Polity and Crisis. Reflections on the European Odyssey* (Routledge 2016)

Fichera M, *The Foundations of the EU as a Polity* (Edward Elgar Publishing 2018)

Fossum JE and Menendez AJ, *The Constitution's Gift* (Rowman & Littlefield, 2011)

Goldoni M, 'The material constitution', in R Bellamy and J King (eds), *The Cambridge Handbook of Constitutional Theory* (Cambridge University Press, forthcoming)

Goldoni M and Wilkinson MA, 'The material constitution' (2018) 81 *The Modern Law Review* 567–597

Grimm D, *Die Zukunft der Verfassung* (Suhrkamp 1991)

Grimm D, 'Types of constitutions' in M Rosenfeld and A Sajò (eds), *The Oxford Handbook of Comparative Constitutional Law* (Oxford University Press 2012)

Kelemen RD, *The Rules of Federalism. Institutions and Regulatory Politics in the EU and Beyond* (Harvard University Press 2004)

Kelemen RD, Eeckhout P, Fabbrini F, Pech L and Uitz R, 'National courts cannot override CJEU judgments: a joint statement in defense of the EU Legal Order' 26 May 2020 VerfBlog

Kelsen H, *Pure Theory of Law* (University of California Press 1967)

Krisch N, 'Pouvoir constituant and pouvoir irritant in the postnational order' (2016) 14 *International Journal of Constitutional Law* 657–679

Lassalle F, 'Uber Verfassungswesen' in 2 Gesammalte Reden Und Schriften 38 (Cassirer ed, 1920)

Lindahl HR, 'Constituent power and reflexive identity: towards an ontology of collective selfhood' in M Loughlin and N Walker (eds), *The Paradox of Constitutionalism: Constituent Power and Constitutional Form* (Oxford University Press 2007)

Loughlin M and Walker N, 'Introduction', in M Loughlin and N Walker (eds), *The Paradox of Constitutionalism: Constituent Power and Constitutional Form* (Oxford University Press 2007)

Lowenstein K, *Political Power and the Governmental Process* (University of Chicago Press 1957)

Majone G, *Rethinking the Union of Europe post Crisis. Has Integration Gone Too Far?* (Cambridge University Press 2014)

Marmor A, *Social Conventions. From Language to Law* (Princeton University Press 2009)

Martines T, *Contributo ad una teoria giuridica delle forze politiche* (Giuffrè 1957)

Mazzucato M and Quaggiotto G, 'The big failure of small government', www.project-syndicate.org/commentary/small-governments-big-failure-covid19-by-mariana-mazzucato-and-giulio-quaggiotto-2020-05?barrier=accesspaylog

Möller K, 'From constituent to destituent power beyond the state' (2018) 9 *Transnational Legal Theory* 32–55

Mollers C, 'Pouvoir constituant–constitution–constitutionalisation' in A von Bogdandy and J Bast (eds), *Principles of European Constitutional Law* (Hart/Beck 2006)

Mortati C, 'Costituzione (dottrine generali)' (1962) *XI Enciclopedia del diritto*

Mortati C, *La Costituente. La teoria. La storia. Il problema italiano* (Darsena 1945)

Mortati C, *La Costituzione in senso materiale* (Giuffrè 1940)

Patberg M, 'Challenging the masters of the treaties: emerging narratives of constituent power in the European Union' (2018) 7 *Global Constitutionalism* 263–293

Pinelli C, 'Costituzione formale-costituzione materiale', (2010) *Enciclopedia Treccani Dizionario di Storia*

Sarmiento D and Weiler JH, 'The EU judiciary after Weiss: proposing a new mixed chamber of the court of justice' 2020/6/02 VerfBlog

Schmitt C, 'Grundrechte und Grundpflichten' (1932), in C Schmitt, 'Verfassungsrechtliche Aufsätze aus den Jahren 1924–1954: Materialien zu einer Verfassungslehre' (Duncker & Humblot 1958)

Schmitt C, *Dictatorship. From the Origin of the Modern Concept of Sovereignty to Proletarian Class Struggle* (Polity Press 2014)

Sieyès E, *Qu'est-ce que le tiers-état?* 2nd ed. (Arnold 1979)

Thornhill C, 'Contemporary constitutionalism and the dialectic of constituent power' (2012) 1 *Global Constitutionalism* 369–404

Thornhill C, 'The European constitution and the pouvoir constituant – No longer, or never, sui generis?' in J Přibáň (ed), *Self-Constitution of European Society: Beyond EU Politics, Law and Governance* (Routledge 2016) 13–36

Varoufakis Y, 'The EU coronavirus fund will take Europe another step towards disintegration', www.theguardian.com/world/commentisfree/2020/jul/24/eu-coronavirus-fund-europe-recovery-package

Vinx L, *Hans Kelsen's Pure Theory of Law* (Oxford University Press 2007)

4 'Don't you know they're talkin' 'bout a revolution? (It sounds like a whisper)'

The *Bundesverfassungsgericht* ruling in *Weiss*

Gavin Barrett[1]

By contrast with ordinary international treaties, the EEC Treaty has created its own legal system which, on the entry into force of the Treaty, became an integral part of the legal systems of the Member States and which their courts are bound to apply.

By creating a Community of unlimited duration, having its own institutions, its own personality, its own legal capacity and capacity of representation on the international plane and, more particularly, real powers stemming from a limitation of sovereignty or a transfer of powers from the states to the Community, the Member States have limited their sovereign rights and have thus created a body of law which binds both their nationals and themselves.

The integration into the laws of each Member State of provisions which derive from the Community and more generally the terms and the spirit of the Treaty, make it impossible for the states, as a corollary, to accord precedence to a unilateral and subsequent measure over a legal system accepted by them on a basis of reciprocity. Such a measure cannot therefore be inconsistent with that legal system. The law stemming from the Treaty, an independent source of law, could not because of its special and original nature, be overridden by domestic legal provisions, however framed, without being deprived of its character as Community law and without the legal basis of the Community itself being called into question.

1 Introduction – in the beginning was revolution

The above words – among the most famous ever to have emanated from the European Court of Justice – can be credited as having given form to a true legal revolution. They are the words of the European Court of Justice in *Costa v ENEL*[2] in which that Court established the doctrine of supremacy. This is the idea that in the event of a collision between EEC (now European Union) law on the one hand and national law on the other within a field of EEC (now EU)

1 Professor, Sutherland School of Law, University College Dublin.

2 *Flaminio Costa v. ENEL* ECLI:EU:C:1964:66.

competence, European law would prevail, and – as was revealed in later case law – would render the relevant national law domestically inapplicable to the extent of its inconsistency with European law.[3] *Costa* was a case which itself followed hard on the heels of the Court's own earlier ruling in *Van Gend en Loos*[4] in which it had established the doctrine of direct effect,[5] the idea that European Union law confers on individuals rights which national courts must enforce.

We may mention in passing that both *Costa* and *Van Gend en Loos* explicitly also enunciated – by way of a stepping stone to their more famous findings – the doctrine of the autonomy of EEC (now European Union) law, which is the idea that EEC law was neither public international law nor a form of domestic law but rather that the EEC Treaty system on its entry into force created its own legal system.[6] Implicitly of course that liberated the Court to determine the characteristics of the legal system in terms of questions like supremacy, direct effect, and some other issues. It is worth pausing here to make if only briefly a number of further points.

The first is that in both *Costa* and *Van Gend en Loos,* the Court of Justice asserted implicitly or otherwise at least three things:

(a) it decided that it was for European Union law and the Court of Justice to identify the Court and the legal system that has power to answer the direct effect and supremacy questions. The Court's doing this is commonly called its assertion of *Kompetenz Kompetenz* – the Court saying that it gets to appoint the referee. It gets to decide, in other words, on who will adjudicate on direct effect and supremacy.
(b) the Court then made that adjudication in favour of itself (and the system of EU law). In other words, it appointed itself the referee. It held that it, the ECJ itself (and EU law) could provide the answer to the direct effect and supremacy questions. Another way of putting this is that it adjudicated that it, the European Court of Justice had *Kompetenz*; and
(c) the Court then decided the main issue in each case – that Community law was directly effective in *Van Gend en Loos* and that it was supreme in *Costa v ENEL.*

The facts of *Costa v. ENEL* involved an electricity bill for an amount of far less than a euro. Those of *Van Gend en Loos* concerned the rather technical issue of the legality of a taxation reclassification under Dutch law of an obscure chemical called ureaformaldehyde. Such factual backgrounds may have concealed the colossal revolution in the constitutional legal order in Europe which these rulings

3 *Amministrazione delle Finanze dello Stato v. Simmenthal SpA* ECLI:EU:C:1978:49.

4 *NV Algemene Transport- en Expeditie Onderneming van Gend & Loos v. Netherlands Inland Revenue Administration* ECLI:EU:C:1963:1.

5 And implicitly also supremacy, although the Court did not address this issue in its ruling, so that that doctrine is usually regarded as having originated in *Costa v. ENEL.*

6 See in this regard for example the words quoted at the beginning of this chapter.

asserted had taken place on the entry into force of the Treaty of Rome. The two rulings are correctly regarded as foundation stones in the creation of what has become the world's first truly supranational international legal order.

The European Union has come to be regarded as a powerful entity on the international stage and it is. But it is frequently unappreciated, at least outside the legal world – and more than occasionally inside it – just how dependent economic and political power is on the law. With no army, a miniscule budget compared to any national federation, the integration process in the EU is to a huge extent integration through law. As such, it hangs almost entirely on one slim thread – the willingness of national courts to follow the lead of the European Court of Justice. If that thread breaks, the mighty economic and soft power that is the European Union in the modern world crumbles to insignificance, losing most of the influence it has. That power is not to be underestimated since it seemingly includes the ability to ensure peace in a continent formerly ravaged for centuries by interminable violent conflicts – thus constituting a revolution of its own kind.[7]

The revolutionary regime envisaged in *Costa v. ENEL* is thus a fragile one. Like any revolution – indeed any system of government – it depends for its effectiveness on the consent of those meant to be governed by it. Crucially, in the case of the judicial doctrine of supremacy, the consent required includes that of national constitutional courts. As Weiler has written

> the revolutionary nature of the doctrine of supremacy is necessarily bi-dimensional. One dimension is the elaboration of the parameters of the doctrine by the European Court. But its full reception, the second dimension, depends on its incorporation into the constitutional orders of the Member States and its affirmation by their supreme courts. It is relatively easy to trace the evolution of the Community dimension of the doctrine…
>
> As regards the second dimension, the evolutionary character of the process is more complicated. It should be remembered that in respect of the original Member States there was no specific constitutional preparation for this European Court-inspired development.[8]

For any state that joined with or after the first enlargement of the then Communities in 1973, there can be less excuse for judicial claims of non-acceptance of these core Community doctrines. They were, after all, well established by the time the first enlargement took place. Such claims can be made with more purported justification by courts in the original six Member States. Returning to our three-part assertion by the European Court of Justice (i.e., (a) *Kompetenz Kompetenz*, (b) *Kompetenz* and (c) the supremacy/direct effect of EU law), in practice, when matters have come before national courts, national courts have

7 See for one account of these, B. Simms, *Europe – The Struggle for Supremacy – 1453 to the Present* (Penguin, London, 2014).

8 J. Weiler, 'The Community System: The Dual Character of Supranationalism' (1981) YEL 267 at 275–276.

only ever really agreed to the third assertion – and sometimes, as we shall see, not even to that. Few have ever agreed to what we have identified as the first and second implicit assertions of the Court in *Costa* and *Van Gend en Loos* – *Kompetenz Kompetenz* and *Kompetenz*.

2 Counter-revolution

The BVG has over many years earned a deserved reputation as the national court 'against whose decisions there is no judicial remedy under national law' (to use the language of Article 267 TFEU) that is simultaneously (a) least likely to engage in its obligation to make references under Article 267 to the European Court of Justice and (b) most likely to qualify its own acceptance of the doctrine of supremacy as enunciated in *Costa v. ENEL*. In its entire existence it has made two Article 267 references – and on each occasion, probably only because it was forced into this step by its own ruling in *Honeywell*.[9] One such reference was its extraordinarily aggressive reference in the *Gauweiler* case, the second the reference which the BVG made in *Weiss* – where Karlsruhe responded to the opinion proffered to it by the Court of Justice by rejecting it, and without ever supplying the opportunity (which both the interests of judicial dialogue and EU law required it to give) to the Luxembourg Court to pronounce again.[10]

Craig and de Búrca have formulated a set of questions which can be deployed as a useful four-part test of the extent national courts' acceptance of supremacy. One is whether a Member State's court accepts the supremacy of EU law within the field of EU competence (something they generally do). A second is its conceptual basis for doing so: is it because of the reasoning offered in *Costa* or on the basis of national legal provisions? (Generally, it is the latter.). A third issue is whether the national court accepts the implicit claim by the European Court of Justice of *Kompetenz Kompetenz* (something virtually none of them does).[11] A fourth is whether a national court places limits on its acceptance of supremacy (on grounds such as human rights, *ultra vires* concerns, or questions of constitutional identity).

Surveying briefly the pre-*Weiss* jurisprudence of the European Court of Justice, it is plain, first, that the German courts do accept the supremacy – or as they would have it the primacy – of European law – as an effective functional necessity of the integration process: as the BVG has put it, '*the primacy of application* follows from Union law because the Union could not exist as a legal community if the uniform effectiveness of Union law were not safeguarded in the Member States.'[12]

9 2 BvR 2661/06 6 July 2010.

10 Contrast the approach of the Italian Constitutional Court in *Taricco* (mentioned in the text below), although that Court's approach was also not without the capacity to create difficulties. See also C. Amalfitano and O. Pollicino, 'Two Courts, Two Languages? The Taricco Saga Ends on a Worrying Note', Verfassungsblog, 5 June 2018.

11 See P. Craig and G. de Burca *EU Law – Text, Cases and Materials* (sixth edition, 2015) at p. 279 ff.

12 See Honeywell ruling of the BVG, BVerfG, 2 BvR 2661/06, 6 July 2010 at para. 53 thereof. Emphasis added.

Second, the reasons why the BVG accepts the supremacy of EU law are founded – apart from the functional concerns which actually form much of the basis of the reasoning in *Costa* – solidly on the text of the German Constitution, rather than on the text of the TEU or the TFEU: specifically, Art. 23.1 of the *Grundgesetz* which provides, *inter alia* that

> with a view to establishing a united Europe, the Federal Republic of Germany shall participate in the development of the European Union that is committed to democratic, social and federal principles, to the rule of law and to the principle of subsidiarity and that guarantees a level of protection of basic rights essentially comparable to that afforded by this Basic Law. To this end the Federation may transfer sovereign powers by a law with the consent of the Bundesrat...[13]

The third litmus test of the degree of acceptance of supremacy of EU law – *i.e.*, whether the national court accepts the implicit claim by the European Court of Justice of *Kompetenz Kompetenz* – has clearly been rejected by the *Bundesverfassungsgericht*. In *Weiss* itself the BVG was to be at its clearest on this point (although this merely reflected earlier case law).[14] It asserted explicitly in defiance of the implicit foundation of both *Van Gend en Loos* and *Costa v. ENEL* that

> the Basic Law does not authorise German state organs to transfer sovereign powers to the European Union in such a way that the European Union were authorised, in the independent exercise of its powers, to create new competences for itself. *It prohibits conferring upon the European Union the competence to decide on its own competences.*[15]

The most interesting part of our test of the degree of acceptance of the supremacy doctrine for present purposes, however, is the fourth: the limits to supremacy that the BVG has insisted on over time. The first came in its 1974 *Solange* case

13 *Bundesverfassung* translated by C. Tomuschat, D. Currie, D. Kommers, and R Kerr, in cooperation with the Language Service of the German *Bundestag* and available online at www.gesetze-im-internet.de/englisch_gg/englisch_gg.html#p0127.

14 Sufficient evidence for this could also be seen in the *Brunner/Maastricht* case in which the BVG asserted that 'the validity and application of European law in Germany depend on the application-of-law instruction of the Accession Act. Germany thus preserves the quality of a sovereign State in its own right...' (Para. 55). It will be immediately seen that this involves not just a claim of *Kompetenz Kompetenz* but of *Kompetenz* as well: the BVG not alone implied that it should appoint the referee, but also appointed the German legal system and therefore itself to this role. The rejection of any *Kompetenz Kompetenz* for the Court of Justice was also reflected in the *Honeywell* judgment in which the BVG observed, 'if... the Member States were to completely forgo *ultra vires* review, disposal of the treaty basis *would be transferred to the Union bodies alone,* even if their understanding of the law led in the practical outcome to an amendment of a Treaty or to an expansion of competences' (Para. 57 of the ruling of the Court). Emphasis added.) This, it was clearly implied, could not be.

15 Para. 102 of the ruling.

law. In *Solange I* – which was in effect the BVG's response to the European Court of Justice ruling in *Internationale Handesgesellschaft* asserting the supremacy of EU law even over a conflicting provision of fundamental rights guarantees in the German Constitution – the BVG conditionalised its acceptance of that ECJ ruling, holding that 'provisionally…in the hypothetical case of a conflict between Community law and…the guarantees of fundamental rights in the Constitution…the guarantee of fundamental rights in the Constitution prevails as long as the competent organs of the Community have not removed the conflict of norms in accordance with the Treaty mechanism.' Perhaps encouraged by the development of fundamental rights as a general principle of Community law, the BVG softened its approach in *Solange II,* in which it held that

> In view of these developments, it must be held that, so long as the European Communities (*Solange die Europäischen Gemeinschaften…*) and in particular the case law of the European Court, generally ensure an effective protection of fundamental rights as against the sovereign powers of the Communities which is to be regarded as substantially similar to the protection of fundamental rights required unconditionally by the Constitution, and in so far as they generally safeguard the essential content of fundamental rights, the Federal Constitutional Court will no longer exercise its jurisdiction to decide on the applicability of secondary Community legislation cited as the legal basis for any acts of German civil courts or authorities within the sovereign jurisdiction of the Federal Republic of Germany, and it will no longer review such legislation by the standard of the fundamental rights contained in the Constitution.[16]

A second limitation emerged in the *Brunner* case (also known as the Maastricht judgment in which the BVG asserted that there were competence limits to the extent of Germany's submission to primacy). The language of the Court in *Brunner* is worth contemplating. It was uncomprisingly statist and intergovernmental, stressing the language of national sovereignty and asserting the position of the States as '*die Herren der Verträge*'. If we can deem *Costa v. ENEL* a revolution in pursuance of a supranational Europe as the only possible way to guarantee a functioning common market (such a market being itself a tool in pursuit of a higher ideal of lasting peace) then *Brunner* launched an unsympathetic conservative counter-revolution belatedly seeking to strangle the notion of a revolutionary new European legal system at birth, and countenancing nothing less than the maintenance of nation states in all their Westphalian grandeur as masters who would brook no rival:

16 Re *Wünsche Handelsgesellschaft* (2 BvR 197/83). See para. 48 of the ruling of the Court, which is reproduced at [1987] 3 CMLR 225 (see p. 264 thereof).

> The Federal Republic of Germany, therefore, even after the Union Treaty comes into force, will remain a member of a federation of States, the common authority of which is derived from the member-States and can only have binding effects within the German sovereign sphere by virtue of the German instruction that its law be applied. Germany is one of the 'Masters of the Treaties', which have established their adherence to the Union Treaty concluded 'for an unlimited period'... with the intention of long-term membership but could also ultimately revoke that adherence by a contrary act. The validity and application of European law in Germany depend on the application-of-law instruction of the Accession Act. Germany thus preserves the quality of a sovereign State in its own right...[17]

The Court did not shrink from issuing a warning:

> in future it will have to be noted as regards interpretation of enabling provisions by Community institutions and agencies that the Union Treaty as a matter of principle distinguishes between the exercise of a sovereign power conferred for limited purposes and the amending of the Treaty, so that its interpretation may not have effects that are equivalent to an extension of the Treaty. *Such an interpretation of enabling rules would not produce any binding effects for Germany.*[18]

The stakes of the competence review were there for all to see. A Germany whose courts felt competence bounds were being overstepped would regard itself as legally exempted from any binding effects, thus threatening the stability of the whole EU law edifice, both economically and as a united legal endeavour.

The *Banana Import* cases saw *ultra vires* counter-revolutionism further pursued.[19] Later, however, the BVG withdrew – just as it had in relation to the fundamental rights case law – to a more conciliatory position (even if, in the light of very recent developments, this subsequent withdrawal now seems to have been temporary in nature). Thus in *Honeywell*, the BVG continued to maintain

17 Para. 55.

18 Para. 99 of the ruling. Emphasis added.

19 See Case C-280/93 *Federal Republic of Germany v. Council of the European Union* ECLI:EU:C:1994:367; and C-466/93 – *Atlanta Fruchthandelsgesellschaft and Others (II) v. Bundesamt für Ernährung und Forstwirtschaft* ECLI:EU:C:1995:370. See further N. Reich, *'Judge-made Europe à la carte: Some Remarks on Recent Conflicts between European and German Constitutional Law Provoked by the Banana Litigation'* (1996) 7 *European Journal of International Law* 103; and the now rather prophetic-looking article by U. Everling, *'Will Europe Slip on Bananas – The Bananas Judgment of the Court of Justice and National Courts'* (1996) 33 *Common Market Law Review* 401. See for interesting contemporaneous overviews of the law in this area, J. Weiler, U. Haltern, 'The Autonomy of the Community Legal Order-Through the Looking Glass' (1996) 37 *Harvard International Law Journal* 411 and M Aziz, *Sovereignty Lost, Sovereignty Regained? The European Integration Project and the Bundesverfassungsgericht*, EUI Working Paper, RSC 2001/31, Robert Schuman Center for Advanced Studies, 2001.

its right to apply *ultra vires* review, but nonetheless couched it in far gentler language, observing that:

> the applicable principle is that of conferral (Article 5.1 sentence 1 and Article 5.2 sentence 1 TEU). The Federal Constitutional Court is hence empowered and obliged to review acts on the part of the European bodies and institutions with regard to whether they take place on the basis of *manifest transgressions of competence* or on the basis of the exercise of competence in the area of constitutional identity which is not assignable (Article 79.3 in conjunction with Article 1 and Article 20 of the Basic Law)… and where appropriate to declare the inapplicability of acts for the German legal system which exceed competences.

The BVG now indicated appeared to want to stress that the *Brunner* limits would be broadly drawn, holding for example that '*ultra vires* review may only be exercised in a manner which is open towards European law'[20] and that '*ultra vires* review by the Federal Constitutional Court can… only be considered if it is *manifest* that acts of the European bodies and institutions have taken place outside the transferred competences'.[21] As will be seen however, this latter promise of moderation in *ultra vires* review was to be reneged upon in *Weiss*, where the form rather than the substance of *Honeywell* remained in evidence.

In its 2009 *Lisbon* ruling, the BVG also deployed the doctrine of national constitutional identity as a third limit on its acceptance of the doctrine of supremacy – i.e., the notion that there is a core content to a national constitutional order that is inviolable, or as the Court has put it, 'European unification on the basis of a treaty union of sovereign states may…not be achieved in such a way that not sufficient space is left to the Member States for the political formation of the economic, cultural and social living conditions.'[22]

The BVG declared that identity review 'ensures that the primacy of application of Union law only applies by virtue and in the context of the constitutional empowerment that continues in effect'.[23] In the German context, identity review made it possible, according to the Court, to examine whether, due to the action of European institutions, the principles under Article 1 (i.e. human dignity, human rights, and the legally binding force of basic rights) and Article 20 of the Basic Law (i.e., constitutional principles including the democratic nature of the state and the binding nature of the constitutional order), declared inviolable in Article 79.3 of the Basic Law, (i.e., the famous eternity clause) have been violated.'[24] The Court however went further than this and produced a long list of

20 Para. 58.
21 Para. 61. Emphasis added.
22 BVG 2 BvE 2/08 30 June 2009 at para. 249 of the ruling.
23 2 BvE 2/08 30 June 2009. Para. 240 of the ruling.
24 Ibid.

Staatsaufgaben – necessary tasks a state must fulfil.[25] Its ruling has been rightly excoriated since it provided no theory or system whatsoever for this list: to quote Halberstam and Myers, 'the "theory" of the Court [was] a *post hoc* argument in support of a preordained result.'[26] The BVG, it appears, wanted limitations on European integration. This approach gave it those limits.

What else is there to say before we get to the *Weiss* decision itself? Two points that may be made are that over the years since *Solange* was decided in 1974, the BVG has engaged in an extraordinary amount of conditionalising of European integration and some very ominous-sounding warnings. (In the latter respect, one need only think of the *Brunner/Maastricht* ruling.) If one keeps saying one will only accept something '*solange*' – as long as an ever-lengthening series of conditions is met – there is a very real danger that one will eventually paint oneself into a corner. In cases like *Solange II* and *Honeywell*, the Court managed to wipe away some of the conditionality it had painted around itself, and yet there are risks if one continues to engage in such conditionalised acceptance of change that such an escape will not always be so easily effected.

Second, implicit threats of the kind that the BVG has been making since at least *Brunner* come at a risk to the party making them. If the party follows through, the consequences (which in *Brunner* and subsequent such cases involve effectively threatening that the German legal order will break away from the EU legal order) may be devastating for the future of Europe, since they involve abandoning a system that has protected peace and prosperity for over six decades. Yet if the Court do not follow through, they will be accused of crying wolf and thereby lose face. It is hard to believe that the BVG in *Gauweiler* did not feel some humiliation in swallowing hard and then rather meekly accepting the ruling of the European Court of Justice having first sent it an initial highly aggressively reasoned reference.[27] And yet it was the BVG which had put itself in this awkward situation in the first place.

Apart from noting the conditionalised nature of BVG acceptance of European integration, also worthy of note is that prominent members of the Constitutional Court – including its now-retired president – Andreas Voßkuhle – have for long rejected any idea of a hierarchy in the European judicial order. In this vision, instead of their being a hierarchy in European Union law, with the European Court of Justice sitting at the top, there is what he refers to as multilevel cooperation.[28] The vision which is put forward is that rather like a mobile hanging over a child's cot in which every element balances every other element so that

25 The list is long, but covers in particular the areas of substantive and formal criminal law, social welfare ('living conditions in a social state'), culturally important decisions (including some on religion), fundamental fiscal decisions taxation and expenditure and the use of force inside and outside the state. See paras. 249 to 260, and in particular para. 252 of the ruling.

26 D. Halberstam and C. Möllers, 'The German Constitutional Court says "Ja zu Deutschland!"' (2009) *German Law Journal* 1219 at 1250.

27 BVerfG, Order of the Second Senate of 14 January 2014 – 2 BvR 2728/13 – paras. 1–24, available in English at www.bverfg.de/e/rs20140114_2bvr272813en.html.

28 See e.g., A. Voßkuhle, *Multilevel Cooperation of the European Constitutional Courts: Der Europaische Verfassungsgerichtverbund* (2010) EUConst 175.

the whole structure remains in harmony.[29] This 'mobile' vision is reflected in the *Weiss* ruling where the Court asserts that

> in principle, certain tensions are thus inherent in the design of the European Union; they must be resolved in a cooperative manner, in keeping with the spirit of European integration, and mitigated through mutual respect and understanding. This reflects the nature of the European Union as a union based on the multilevel cooperation of sovereign states, constitutions, administrations and courts.[30]

The vision has its attractions, especially for those who have concerns about the rather unlimited nature of the power which the European Court of Justice enjoys at the centre of the European integration process, which is admittedly a weakness in the design of the European legal system. The difficulty with the BVG solution however – and one never adequately answered by Voßkuhle – is that it is alternatively unworkable or undemocratic. Hence if every constitutional/Supreme Court in Europe adopts this approach, the model overbalances. The European Court of Justice cannot possibly respond to the legal demands of 27 different legal systems, each establishing conditions of its own on the operation of the supremacy doctrine. The BVG in *Weiss* openly acknowledges the danger but effectively moves on from it with a metaphorical shrug of its shoulders, and an assertion – belied by the reasoning and outcome in *Weiss* itself – that collisions will be rare.

> If any Member State could readily invoke the authority to decide, through its own courts, on the validity of EU acts, this could undermine the precedence of application accorded to EU law and jeopardise its uniform application. Yet if the Member States were to completely refrain from conducting any kind of *ultra vires* review, they would grant EU organs exclusive authority over the Treaties even in cases where the EU adopts a legal interpretation that would essentially amount to a treaty amendment or an expansion of its competences. Though cases in which institutions, bodies, offices and agencies of the European Union exceed their competences are exceptionally possible, it is to be expected that these instances remain rare due to the institutional and procedural safeguards enshrined in EU law. Nevertheless, where they do occur, the constitutional perspective might not perfectly match the perspective of EU law given that, even under the Lisbon Treaty, the Member States remain the 'Masters of the Treaties' and the EU has not evolved into a federal state.[31]

29 The mobile metaphor has been used on multiple occasions by Voßkuhle himself. See e.g., A. Voßkuhle 'Pyramid or Mobile? – Human Rights Protection by the European Constitutional Courts', paper delivered at opening of the judicial year 2014, European Court of Human Rights, Strasbourg, 31 January 2014.

30 Para. 111.

31 See para. 111 of the Court's reasoning.

If on the other hand, this balancing exercise is only carried out by some constitutional or supreme courts, then the question of legitimacy rears its head. Who appointed the *Bundesverfassungsgericht* to carry out this role on behalf of all of the national legal systems? Why should the European legal system bend to the demands of a German court and the German legal system rather than that of others? The model simply fails to convince.

Another objection to it is that as applied by the BVG, the model looks rather less like the Voßkuhle-postulated balanced-'mobile'-type multilevel-cooperation-in-revolt-against-the-idea-of-a-European-law-hierarchy-with-the-European-Court-of-Justice-at-the-top than the creation of *another* European law hierarchy – but this time with the BVG itself at the apex. (In this context, it was interesting to note factors such as the seeming surprise of the BVG that the ECB had not agreed to participate in the oral hearing.[32] The failure of the BVG – unlike its Italian counterpart – to re-refer what turned out to be dramatic conclusions on EU law to the European Court of Justice, in order to give the latter Court the chance to express its views, was also notable. The BVG's notion of dialogue seems rather focused on giving the ECJ the opportunity to listen to *it* and not *vice versa,* and its supposedly cooperative relationship with the European Court of Justice appears strikingly hierarchical.) With these thoughts in mind, let us turn to the *Weiss* case itself.

3 The *Weiss* case prior to the May 2020 BVG ruling

The *Bundesverfassungsgericht*'s *Weiss* decision of 5 May 2020 was in effect its answer to the December 2018 preliminary ruling of the European Court of Justice in the same case.[33] Since we are focusing on the BVG ruling rather than the ECJ decision, only some particularly significant aspects and findings of the Court of Justice ruling need be adverted to here.

As already noted, just like the reference in the earlier *Gauweiler* case (which involved the ECB's OMT programme),[34] the reference in *Weiss*[35] was effectively forced on the *Bundesverfassungsgericht* by its own earlier reasoning in the *Honeywell*

32 See para. 83. The BVG's characterisation of the Opinion under Article 267 as a submission to the German court also had a curious ring to it See para. 223, where the BVG observed that 'the CJEU submits that…'. In fairness, this phrase is found only in the English translation, not the original German version.

33 *Case C-493/17 Weiss and others* ECLI:EU:C:2018:1000. See H. Hofmann, *Controlling the Powers of the ECB: Delegation, Discretion, Reasoning and Care – What Gauweiler, Weiss and others can teach us*, Ademu Working Paper Series WP 2018/107, Barcelona, 2018) and more recently M. Dawson and A. Bobic, 'Quantitative Easing at the Court of Justice – Doing Whatever it Takes to Save the Euro' (2019) 56 *Common Market Law Review* 1005.

34 See *Peter Gauweiler and Others v. Deutscher Bundestag*, Judgment of the Court (Grand Chamber) of 16 June 2015 ECLI:EU:C:2015:400. The OMT programme was the ECB's Outright Monetary Transactions programme for purchases in secondary sovereign bond markets.

35 See for the reference in Weiss, BVerfG, Order of the Second Senate of 18 July 2017–2 BvR 859/15.

case.[36] *Weiss* was a challenge brought before the German Court regarding the 'Public Sector Purchase Programme' (PSPP), [37] which in turn is the main element of the ECB's framework quantitative easing programme, the 'Expanded Asset Purchase Programme' (EAPP). Unlike the OMT programme which had been at issue in *Gauweiler*, which has never been implemented,[38] the Expanded Asset Purchase Programme *has* been implemented – and the figures involved are extremely large. The accumulated stock of EAPP bonds stood at €2.86 *trillion* at the end of May 2020.[39] Of this, €2.32 trillion – over 81% – was due to purchases under the PSPP.

The Court of Justice in *Weiss* (a 15-judge Grand Chamber, rather than a plenary Court as in *Gauweiler* and *Pringle* expressly reaffirmed the approach already taken by it in *Pringle* [40] and *Gauweiler* that 'in order to determine whether a measure falls within the area of monetary policy it is appropriate to refer principally to the objectives of that measure. The instruments which the measure employs in order to attain those objectives are also relevant.'[41] The Court confirmed that the PSPP programme involved monetary policy, noting that it was apparent from the decision's recital that its purpose:

> is to contribute to a return of inflation rates to levels below, but close to, 2% over the medium term.
>
> In that regard, it is important to point out that the authors of the Treaties chose to define the primary objective of the Union's monetary policy – namely the maintenance of price stability – in a general and abstract manner, but did not spell out precisely how that objective was to be given concrete expression in quantitative terms. [42]

The Court of Justice also reaffirmed the view previously expressed in *Gauweiler* that a monetary policy measure could not be treated as equivalent to an economic policy measure for the sole reason that it might have indirect effects that can also

36 Under the reasoning in *Honeywell*,

> 'prior to the acceptance of an *ultra vires* act on the part of the European bodies and institutions, the Court of Justice is…to be afforded the opportunity to interpret the Treaties, as well as to rule on the validity and interpretation of the legal acts in question, in the context of preliminary ruling proceedings according to Article 267 TFEU,

(See BVerfG, Order of the Second Senate of 06 July 2010 – 2 BvR 2661/06 at para. 60).

37 The case involved various constitutional challenges before the ECB involving the participation of the German Central Bank (the *Bundesbank*) in decisions of the ECB and the alleged failures of the *Bundesbank*, German Federal Government and German Parliament regarding those decisions (see para. 13 of the ruling of the Court of Justice).

38 It remains to date therefore more a market-restraining threat than an actual programme.

39 See European Central Bank, 'Asset purchase programmes', available online at www.ecb.europa.eu/mopo/implement/omt/html/index.en.html.

40 *Pringle v. Government of Ireland and Others* Judgment of the Court of 27 November 2012 ECLI:EU:C:2012:756.

41 Para. 53 of the ruling of the Court.

42 Paras. 54–55 of the ruling of the Court.

be sought in the context of economic policy.[43] It expressly declined to concur in the *Bundesverfassungsgericht*'s view that 'that any effects of an open-market operations programme that were knowingly accepted and definitely foreseeable by the ESCB when the programme was set up should not be regarded as 'indirect effects' of the programme.'[44]

The Court thus sought to maintain control over the crucial borderline between monetary and economic policy[45] – as well as control of the other crucial battle line regarding the legality of the PSPP: a limited view was taken of the monetary financing prohibition by the Court, just as it had been in *Gauweiler*.[46] According to the Court of Justice, the relevant PSPP decisions did not violate the Article 123 monetary financing prohibition. The Court conceded that the ESCB's intervention would have been incompatible with Article 123 only if potential purchasers of government bonds on the primary markets knew *for certain* that the ESCB was going to purchase those bonds within a certain period and under conditions allowing them to act, *de facto*, as intermediaries for the ESCB for the direct purchase of those bonds from public authorities and bodies.[47] But it denied that such certainty existed here, although it admitted that private operators had been enabled 'to foresee, to some extent, significant aspects of the ESCB's future actions on the secondary markets.'[48] *Certainty* was avoided by various safeguards (such as blackout periods of uncertain duration when no bonds would be purchased) and avoidance of advance specification of purchase volumes.[49] The Court of Justice further refused to consider arguments relating to the decision's provisions on the sharing of losses, arguing that this would involve 'an advisory opinion on a problem which is, at this stage, hypothetical'.[50]

The Luxembourg Court's ruling in *Weiss* – rather like its earlier ruling in *Gauweiler* – saw the Court of Justice decline to see the law frustrate what, if it is not a revolution in Economic and Monetary Union has at least been a major evolution – a shift away from the original rule-based EMU to a more policy-based approach involving (a) a much more discretionary and interventionist role for institutions like the ECB and for the European Stability Mechanism and (b) less trust in the efficacy of a rigidly literal approach to rules to safeguard the continued existence of the Eurozone; as Hinarejos terms it, 'a different EMU

43 Para. 61 of the ruling of the Court citing para. 52 of *Gauweiler* and para. 56 of *Pringle*.
44 Para. 62 of the ruling of the Court.
45 In this regard, the programme of purchases at issue in *Weiss* was clearly easier territory to defend as monetary policy than the OMT programme at issue in *Gauweiler* had been.
46 And just as a limited view had been taken of the no-bailout rule in *Pringle*.
47 Para. 110 of the ruling of the Court.
48 Para. 112 of the ruling of the Court.
49 See para. 113 *et seq.* of the ruling of the Court.
50 Cf. however the Court's ruling in *Case C-621/18 Wightman and others* ECLI:EU:C:2018:999 regarding the prospect of the UK withdrawing its Art. 50 Brexit notice. At the time that case was decided, this was a hypothetical prospect, but one in relation to which the Court was content to make a ruling. Note also that the Court rejected (as it had in *Gauweiler*) any contention that the policy at issue in *Weiss* was disproportionate (see paras. 71–100 of the ruling of the Court).

with a new overarching objective (the safeguarding of the stability of the euro area) that demands managerialism and policy-making'.[51] The ECJ was not the *source* of the developments in EMU's structures and functioning. These were decided upon by the Member States inside and outside the EU's political institutions. But the permissive approach adopted by the Court was key in allowing this evolutionary/revolutionary approach to continue, and for things to change in order that they may remain the same.[52] Since the alternative approach might well have marked the end of EMU, it is perhaps not surprising that the Court of Justice has adopted the approach it has. The Court has a certain level of form here – its policy of non-interventionism in a politically highly controversial area has a long history dating back to before the time of crisis. Nonetheless, it had to tread nimbly in order to avoid rules from an earlier phase of EMU frustrating the construction and functioning of initiatives only latterly revealed to be needed to buttress and prevent the collapse of the EMU edifice, constructed as this was in that earlier era.[53]

4 The BVG judgment in *Weiss*: a bombshell ruling in a raiment of moderation

The BVG ruling of 5 May 2020 in response to the Court of Justice ruling came as something of a bombshell. The ruling itself may be summarised briefly. In the operative part, the BVG held that the German Federal Government and *Bundestag* had violated Germany's *Grundgesetz* (Basic Law) by failing to take suitable steps challenging the failure of the ECB's Governing Council to assess or substantiate whether the PSPP measures satisfied the principle of proportionality.[54]

The finding in the case was thus not directed at any European institution but rather at the German Federal Government and the *Bundestag*. Furthermore, the BVG was holding there to have been a violation of the German Constitution

51 Hinarejos 2015, p. 143. Note also Fabbrini 2014, pp. 70-71 and in particular his entirely accurate observation that the 'mechanisms of financial stabilization represent an entirely new addition to the architecture of the EMU constitution' constructed in the wake of the discovery 'that it was actually much easier on paper than in reality to let a country of the Eurozone default without this producing a systemic effect on the stability of the Eurozone as a whole'.

52 See G. di Lampedusa, *Il Gattopardo* (Feltrinelli, Milan, 2013).

53 The giving of the Court's *imprimatur* to the crisis-era evolution of the economic and monetary union has not of course been entirely uncontroversial. See for a critical perspective, M. Everson and C. Joerges, 'Who is the Guardian for Constitutionalism in Europe After the Financial Crisis?' in S. Kröger (Ed.), *Political Representation in the European Union: Still Democratic in Times of Crisis?* (Abingdon, Routledge, 2014) at 400. See generally for some valuable reflections concerning the restrained approach of the Court regarding all three categories of case to come before it in the crisis era, Hinarejos 2015, pp. 140–144 and 152–153. Among the challenges here, as she points out, 'is to elucidate those cases where the Court may be asked to review changes to the constitutional underpinnings of EMU that are not the result of the appropriate political process and that are too significant to be 'ratified' by a court' (Ibid., 152.)

54 See paras. 3 to 4.

rather than EU law. All this seems legitimate. However, it is crucial to recall that depending on how tightly the provisions of the German Constitution relevant to European integration are interpreted, what in form is an interpretation of German law becomes very quickly in effect an interpretation of European law. What is very striking about the BVG reasoning in *Weiss* is just how much of the ruling actually consisted of interpretation of EU law principles and rules, with the *Bundesverfassungsgericht* taking over the role of an allegedly misfiring Court of Justice. The BVG of course could fall safely back on the assertion that it was confining itself to interpreting the scope of the German authorisation to join the EU, rather than EU law itself, but the difference in the *Weiss* case was vanishingly small.[55]

Similarly, the BVG can claim that it does not seek to invalidate European Union legal norms but merely to control the actions of German constitutional institutions. This is also true. But Germany's population size and economic might make it a key player – sometimes *the* key player – in European integration. If the effect of a BVG ruling was to end German participation in any European policy area, this would be likely to cripple the European policy in question and destroy its chances of success (particularly in matters concerning EMU, in which only a 19-strong subset of EU states participates). It seems curiously ironic that in a ruling in which the BVG berated the ECJ for its neglect of the indirect economic effects of monetary policies, the BVG itself paid so little regard to the indirect effect of its own rulings, which affect all European

55 Note in this regard para. 164 of the reasoning in which the Court opined:

> 'The determination under constitutional law whether the Federal Government and the *Bundestag* discharged their responsibility with regard to European integration (*Integrationsverantwortung*) hinges on the preliminary question whether the ESCB's actions in terms of adopting and implementing the PSPP remain within the competences conferred upon it. Given that...the Federal Constitutional Court cannot rely on the *Weiss* Judgment of the CJEU in this regard, it must conduct its own review to decide this preliminary question. Based on its own review, the Second Senate concludes that, due to the lack of sufficient proportionality considerations, [the various decisions concerning the PSPP] are neither covered by the monetary policy competence of the ECB (Art. 127(1) first sentence TFEU) nor by its merely supporting competence regarding the Member States' economic policies (Art. 127(1) second sentence TFEU).'

The Court also substituted its own interpretation of the Art 123 TFEU prohibition on monetary financing for that of the Court of Justice, proffering its own interpretations on the significance under Article 123 e.g., of a blackout period in making purchases (paras. 187-191) (while damning the approach of the Court of Justice on this issue as 'manifestly unsuitable'); e.g., of holding securities to maturity (para. 192 ff.); e.g., of the need for purchase volumes to be determined in advance and subject to limits (para. 201 ff.); e.g., of the need for a binding exit strategy for ending the programme (para. 212). The BVG did not shrink from informing the ECJ of what was required by 'a proper application' of the latter Court's own criteria for judging a breach of Article 123 involved, although in this case it reached its own conclusion that no manifest circumvention of Article 123(1) TFEU was ascertainable (the presence of a manifest transgression being required as a review standard by the BVG's own case-law in *Honeywell* 2 BvR 2661/06, 6 July 2010. (see para. 55 of reasoning in that case).

states, and not just Germany.[56] Indeed, the German-centric approach of the BVG in *Weiss* was quite striking. All of the expert third parties that were heard by the BVG were German.[57] Moreover, the economic interests which the Court berated the ECJ for not having taken into account in a proportionality review were those which had attained particular prominence in recent German public criticisms of ECB action.[58]

As already noted, it was to the *Bundestag* and the German Federal Government that the BVG addressed its expectations. According to the Court, these constitutional organs could only discharge their lasting responsibility with regard to European integration if they continuously monitored the execution of the European integration agenda. According to the Court, where measures taken by EU institutions, bodies, offices and agencies exceeded the limits of the European integration agenda in a manifest and structurally significant manner, it was incumbent upon the Federal Government and the Bundestag to actively address the question how the order of competences could be restored.[59]

The BVG acknowledged the duty of moderation imposed on it under its own earlier jurisprudence, the effect of which was that holding an EU act to have violated the principal of conferral required 'that the act manifestly exceeds EU competences, resulting in a structurally significant shift in the division of competences to the detriment of the Member States.'[60] Any expectation that this would lead to a *Honeywell*-style moderate approach by the BVG in *Weiss* was quickly dissipated, however.

5 The BVG's opening salvoes: the deployment of the *ultra vires* doctrine against the ECJ

Remarkably, the BVG now made plain that it was prepared to deploy its *ultra vires* review against the European Court of Justice *itself* rather than just the ECB, basing its approach on how the latter court had supposedly misapplied its interpretive function. The BVG asserted 'the [ECJ] mandate conferred in Art. 19(1) second sentence TEU would be exceeded where the traditional European methods of interpretation or, more broadly, the general legal principles that are common to the laws of Member States are manifestly disregarded.'[61] If the ECJ crossed that limit, then, as far as the *Bundesverfassungsgericht* was concerned, its actions would no longer be

56 See for such criticism of the Court of Justice e.g., paras. 122–123 of the Court's reasoning.

57 See para. 82. The Court did take the time to note icily that 'the ECB chose not to participate in the oral hearing' however (Para. 83).

58 Hence the BVG pointed out the relevance of 'taking into account, in the proportionality assessment pursuant to Art. 5(1) second sentence and Art. 5(4) TEU, the effects that a programme for the purchase of government bonds has on, for example, public debt, personal savings, pension and retirement schemes, real estate prices and the keeping afloat of economically unviable companies...' (see para. 139).

59 Paras. 108–109.

60 See para. 110 (echoing the language of the BVG's earlier *Honeywell* ruling). This would generally be the case if the exercise of the competence at EU level were to require a treaty amendment in accordance with EU law, according to the Court.

61 Para. 112.

covered by the mandate conferred in Art. 19(1) second sentence TEU [62] – and thus 'at least in relation to Germany, its decision then lacks the minimum of democratic legitimation necessary under [the European clause of the *Grundgesetz*]'[63]

The BVG quickly qualified the ECB Governing Council's decisions on the PSPP as *ultra vires* (for reasons we shall return to in this chapter).[64] It acknowledged that the 'the CJEU [had] expressed a different view and that the interpretation put forward by the CJEU is, in principle, binding upon the Federal Constitutional Court'. However, the BVG asserted that in this case 'the delimitation of competences undertaken by the CJEU is simply untenable'.[65] In effect, what was being seen here therefore was reliance on the ultra vires doctrine to engage in open defiance of an Article 267 ruling by the European Court of Justice. According to the Court,

> Where an *ultra vires* review or an identity review raises questions regarding the validity or interpretation of a measure taken by institutions, bodies, offices and agencies of the European Union, the Federal Constitutional Court, in principle, bases its review on the understanding and the assessment of such a measure as put forward by the CJEU. *However, this no longer applies where the interpretation of the Treaties is simply not comprehensible and thus objectively arbitrary.* [66]

The BVG explained

> in its [December 2018 Weiss ruling], the CJEU held that the Decision of the ECB Governing Council on the PSPP and its subsequent amendments were still within the ambit of the ECB's competences…This view manifestly fails to give consideration to the importance and scope of the principle of proportionality (Art. 5(1) second sentence and Art. 5(4) TEU), which also applies to the division of competences, and is no longer tenable from a methodological perspective given that it completely disregards the actual effects of the PSPP… Therefore, the Judgment of the CJEU of 11 December 2018 manifestly exceeds the mandate conferred upon it in Art. 19(1) second sentence TEU, resulting in a structurally significant shift in the order of competences to the detriment of the Member States. To this extent, the CJEU Judgment itself constitutes an *ultra vires* act and thus has no binding effect [in Germany][67]

62 Read in conjunction with Germany's domestic Act of Approval.
63 Para. 113.
64 Para. 117.
65 Ibid.
66 Para. 118.
67 Para. 119.

The BVG made plain its view that the CJEU should have taken into account the economic effects of the PSPP decisions, doing so in excoriating language:

> The CJEU's approach to disregard the actual effects of the PSPP for the purposes of assessing the measure's proportionality...and to refrain from conducting an overall assessment and appraisal in this regard...does not satisfy the requirements of a *comprehensible review* as to whether the ESCB and the ECB observe the limits of their monetary policy mandate. Applied in this manner, the principle of proportionality cannot fulfil its corrective function for the purposes of safeguarding the competences of the Member States.[68]

Again,

> the specific manner in which the CJEU applies the principle of proportionality in the case at hand renders that principle *meaningless* for the purposes of distinguishing, in relation to the PSPP, between monetary policy and economic policy, i.e. between the exclusive monetary policy competence conferred upon the EU... and the limited conferral upon the EU of the competence to coordinate general economic policies...[69]

Further,

> when applied in this manner, as undertaken by the CJEU, the principle of proportionality enshrined in Art. 5(1) second sentence and Art. 5(4) TEU cannot fulfil its corrective function for the purposes of safeguarding the competences of the Member States. *The complete disregard of the PSPP's economic policy effects means that already the determination of the ESCB's objectives is not comprehensible from a methodological perspective...*[70]

The BVG insisted on its own – strict – standard of scrutiny in interpreting EU competences:

> where fundamental interests of the Member States are affected, *as is generally the case when interpreting the competences conferred upon the European Union as such* and its democratically legitimated European integration agenda (*Integrationsprogramm*), judicial review may not simply accept positions asserted by the ECB without closer scrutiny..."[71]

68 Para 123. Emphasis added.

69 Para. 127. Emphasis added.

70 Para. 133. Emphasis added. The BVG asserted that the methodological approach of the Court of Justice was different from that in virtually all other areas of EU law (see para. 133 ff.).

71 Para. 142. Emphasis added. Elsewhere in its ruling, the BVG claimed that the principle of conferral was 'one of the fundamental principles of the European Union', but almost in the same

The BVG's conclusion was that because of the Luxembourg Court's misinterpretation of the principle of proportionality, it had exceeded the judicial mandate conferred upon it by Article 19 TEU: its judgment was an *ultra vires* act not binding upon the BVG.[72]

According to the BVG, the abandonment by the Court of Justice of the distinction between economic policy and monetary policy which was involved in its faulty approach to proportionality had allowed 'the ESCB to pursue an economic policy agenda by means of bonds purchases', adding that 'this has no basis in primary law.'[73] The CJEU having thus acted *ultra vires,* its judgment had in this respect, the BVG asserted, 'no binding force in Germany'.[74]

6 Taking over the ECJ's role regarding the ECB: the BVG on proportionality, monetary financing and constitutional identity

The BVG promptly took over *itself* the role of deciding whether the PSPP was *ultra vires* the powers of the ESCB, observing that 'given that, for the reasons set out above, the Federal Constitutional Court cannot rely on the *Weiss* Judgment of the CJEU in this regard, it must conduct its own review to decide this preliminary question'.[75]

According to the BVG's substitute analysis, proportionality required that the PSPP 'constitute a suitable and necessary means for achieving the aim pursued'.[76] It further required 'that the programme's monetary policy objective and its economic policy effects be identified, weighed and balanced against one another.'[77] It was not however ascertainable that this had been done. For this lack of balancing and lack of stating the reasons informing such balancing', the ECB decisions were, the BVG held, *ultra vires* the monetary policy mandate of the ECB.[78]

The BVG – not content with replacing the ECJ's analysis with its own insofar as concerns proportionality analysis – also set out in very considerable detail its own views of what the monetary financing prohibition in Article 123 TFEU required – at the one time both second-guessing and differing in important respects from what the ECJ in *Weiss* had deemed this Article to require. (Thus for example, the BVG opined that 'the criterion of a blackout period, as interpreted and applied by the CJEU, is manifestly unsuitable for preventing a circumvention of Art. 123(1) TFEU.'[79]) However, in contrast to the BVG's conclusion regarding proportionality, it concluded that, based on a proper application – meaning,

breath that it was 'not solely a principle of EU law but also incorporates constitutional principles from the Member States' (see para. 158).

72 Para. 154.

73 Para. 162.

74 Para. 163.

75 Para. 164.

76 Para. 165.

77 Ibid.

78 Para. 177.

79 Para.191 and see generally regarding Article 123, paras.180–221 of the BVG's reasoning.

naturally, the BVG's *own* application – of the criteria set out by the CJEU, and on the basis of an overall assessment, that it was not ascertainable that the purchases under the PSPP *manifestly* circumvented the prohibition of monetary financing.[80] (The criterion of manifest breach had been the standard established for *ultra vires* review under the BVG's earlier *Honeywell* ruling.)[81]

The judgment also involved the application of the Court's constitutional identity doctrine, elucidated upon previously in considerable (if rather systemically unconvincing)[82] detail by the Court in its *Lisbon* ruling. The Court noted that the PSPP did not provide for a risk-sharing regime (entailing redistribution of losses resulting from open-market operations carried out by national central banks). The Court observed that 'the adoption of such a risk-sharing regime is not intended and would in any case be prohibited under primary law...Against this backdrop, it can be ruled out that the PSPP affects the constitutional identity of the Basic Law.'[83]

Notwithstanding the dramatic nature of its findings regarding both the Court of Justice and the ECB, the BVG limited the direct consequences thereof, holding that

> as the PSPP constitutes an *ultra vires* act, given the ECB's failure to substantiate that the programme is proportionate, their responsibility with regard to European integration... requires the Federal Government and the *Bundestag* to take steps seeking to ensure that the ECB conducts a proportionality assessment in relation to the PSPP.[84]

80 See paras. 213–216 in particular.

81 Elsewhere in its ruling, the BVG seemed to indicate there had been no breach *at all* of Art. 123. Hence at para. 116, it held, somewhat disdainfully, that

> 'even though certain details of the CJEU's arguments raise considerable concerns, the interpretation of Art. 123 TFEU undertaken by the CJEU can still be considered tenable from a methodological perspective. On this basis, the ECB decisions at issue *cannot be found to violate the prohibition of monetary financing* ... It essentially follows from the replies of the CJEU... that the PSPP does not pose a risk to the overall budgetary responsibility of the *Bundestag*' (emphasis added).

82 See especially in this regard, Halberstam and Möllers (n 26).

83 Para. 228. See generally paras. 222 to 228.

84 Para. 232 of the Court's reasoning. More specifically, the BVG required that the Federal Government and the *Bundestag* clearly communicate their legal view to the ECB or take other steps to ensure that conformity with the Treaties is restored. See also summary of the outcome of the BVG *Weiss* judgment insofar as concerns the ECB at para.116 et seq., where the Court held

> '...the Federal Government and the German *Bundestag* violated the rights of the complainants ... by failing to take suitable steps challenging that the ECB... neither assessed nor substantiated that the measures provided for in these decisions satisfy the principle of proportionality. In light of this [the relevant decisions] constitute a qualified, i.e. manifest and structurally significant, exceeding of the competences assigned to the ECB...'

i.e., in Art. 119 and Art. 127 ff. TFEU and in Art. 17 ff. of the ESCB Statute. As already seen in the text above, the differing view of the legality of the ECB's actions that the CJEU set out in its Judgment of 11 December 2018 was dismissed as 'not [meriting] a different conclusion, given that on this point, the judgment is simply not comprehensible so that, to this extent, the judgment was rendered *ultra vires*.'

The Court gave teeth to its findings by decreeing that, following a three-month transitional period,[85] (a) the *Bundesbank* could no longer participate in the implementation and execution of decisions concerning the PSPP; and (b) the *Bundesbank* would have to ensure that the bonds already purchased under the PSPP and held in its portfolio were sold – in both cases unless the ECB Governing Council adopted a new decision demonstrating that the monetary policy objectives pursued by the ECB were not disproportionate to the economic and fiscal policy effects resulting from the programme.[86]

7 Long threatened and not unprecedented – but still the most serious defiance of the ECJ in its entire history

The BVG ruling in *Weiss* has been the latest strike in an ongoing counter-revolution. Yet in the same way in which the technical nature of the legal issues at stake in *Costa v. ENEL* may have obscured at EU level the extent of the revolution which had taken place, repeated outbreaks of assertiveness over the years on the part of the BVG followed by repeated subsequent episodes of readiness to be conciliatory may have concealed for many the extent of the counter-revolution going on in Karlsruhe. Unlike *Costa v. ENEL* and *Van Gend en Loos*, the *Weiss* case ruling by the BVG has not been a one-or-two-case uprising subsequently honed in later case-law. It is the last and most dangerous eruption of a volcano which has rumbled for years, spitting out occasional defiance before quietening down and has only now exploded, revealing to a heretofore rather inattentive world, its true revolutionary – or rather counter-revolutionary – impact.

Weiss and its impact on the European Union have variously been likened to 'a nuclear bomb',[87] a (judicial) 'direct declaration of war [88] and a 'spectre' which, unresolved, will 'hover and threaten the integrity of the EU',[89] and it has been described by eminent scholars as having raised 'justified laments'.[90] In constitutional terms, *Weiss* raises issues for the EU constitutional system not dissimilar to those raised for the United States by the South Carolina nullification crisis of 1832–1833.[91] The fact that the BVG had built towards this point in some of its earlier rulings has not detracted from the dismay the ruling has generated.

85 To permit coordination with the ESCB.

86 Para. 235. The BVG envisaged coordination with the ESCB in both respects.

87 M. Avbelj, 'The Right Question about the FCC Ultra Vires Decision', Verfassungsblog, 6 May 2020. A similar metaphor is used in D. Sarmiento 'An Infringement Action Against Germany After its Constitutional Court's Ruling in Weiss? The Long Term and the Short Term' *EU Law Live*, 12 May 2020.

88 CF, between the BVG and the ECJ. See A. Thiele, 'Das BVerfG und die Büchse der ultra-vires-Pandora – Das Urteil in Sachen Anleihenkaufprogramm der EZB', Verfassungsblog, 5 May 2020.

89 J. Weiler and D. Sarmiento, 'The EU Judiciary After Weiss – Proposing a New Mixed Chamber of the Court of Justice', *EU Law Live*, 1 June 2020.

90 Ibid.

91 This occurred when South Carolina adopted an Ordinance of Nullification declaring tariffs which had been imposed by the US federal law in 1828 and 1832 to have been unconstitutional

Although described by many as an unprecedented judicial decision, the case has in fact had several precedents in other Member States of the EU – a point seized upon by both the reputed main judicial architects of the *Weiss* ruling in subsequent media interviews.[92] Hence the Czech Constitutional Court in the 2012 case of *Landtovà* had already declared an ECJ ruling on social security to be *ultra vires*. The Danish Supreme Court held in *Ajos* that judge-made principles of EU law concerning the general principle of non-discrimination on grounds of age to lack binding force when confronted with contrary national legislation. In *MAS*, the Italian Constitutional Court threatened to defy the ECJ ruling in *Taricco* concerning limitation periods applicable to criminal offences in relation to VAT. And in *Melloni*, the Spanish Constitutional Court appeared to imply it was not bound by the ECJ ruling in the same case, even if it ended up adopting similar reasoning in the end.[93]

The *Weiss* ruling clearly, nevertheless, stands out on its own as 'the most serious defiance of the ECJ's authority in the European Union's history'.[94] It matters that the constitutional court is that of Germany, economically and politically the most important state of the EU and of the Eurozone – and moreover, a court so highly respected. Apart from its significance for Germany and therefore for the EU, *Weiss* has greatly increased the danger that the deployment of the *ultra vires* doctrine by national constitutional courts generally in relation to decisions of EU institutions will now become normalised, with all the damaging consequences for the unity of the EU legal order which this could entail.

In *Weiss*, the BVG engaged in outright defiance of the European Court of Justice, undermining the role of the Court of Justice both as the authentic interpreter of EU law *and* as the reviewer of the actions of EU institutions for compliance with EU law and seeking to supplant the ECJ's voice as the last word on the meaning of EU standards. The BVG not alone tried to define the mandate of the ECB in a manner different from that stipulated by the Luxembourg court, but also sought to determine the very methodology the Court of Justice

---

and unenforceable in South Carolina. Congress responded to both with legislation authorising the use of military force against South Carolina and legislation reducing the objected-to tariff and the Ordinance was repealed, although the issue of states' rights remained live and would lead to the Civil War. South Carolina was the first state to secede in 1860. See generally W. Freehling, *Prelude to Civil War: The Nullification Controversy in South Carolina 1816-1836* (Harper and Row, New York, 1965). (See also F. Fabbrini and R. D. Keleman, 'With One Court Decision, Germany May Be Plunging Europe into a Constitutional Crisis', *Washington Post*, 7 May 2020).

92 See G. di Lorenzo and H. Wefing, 'Erfolg ist Eher Kalt', *Die Zeit*, 14 May 2020 (an interview with BVG President Voßkuhle) and R. Müller, 'Das Urteil war zwingend', *Frankfurter Allgemeine Zeitung*, 13 May, 2020 (an interview with Judge Huber).

93 See in relation to these rulings, D. Sarmiento, 'Requiem for Judicial Dialogue – the German Federal Constitutional Court's Judgment in the Weiss Case and its European Implications', *EU Law Live* 16 (9 May 2020) 9 at 13.

94 F. Fabbrini and R. Keleman (n. 91).

should use in its own reasoning. This is a serious matter – the European Union, to adapt Stalin's mocking question about the pope, has no divisions – the role of its legal order and its key doctrines and respect for the Court of Justice play an outsize role in holding it together and its effectiveness. Viewed in this light, the BVG's brushing aside of a judgment of the Court of Justice involved an assault on the very core of the Union and an attack on what holds the Union together.

Moreover, by neglecting to refer the issues it deemed to have been raised back to the Court of Justice, the BVG showed little real interest in any judicial dialogue with Luxembourg.[95] It was not for nothing that one media report of the decision was entitled *'German Court Lays Down EU Law'*.[96] As Sauer observed

> in the end, the BVerfG [engaged] in this case as if it were the Supreme Court of the EU while ostensibly worrying about German democracy. Even in a constitutional order of pluralism this is hard to justify. [97]

Beyond the substance of what the BVG did, the ruling is remarkable for its harsh tone and, specifically, for the disrespect it showed for the Luxembourg court's reasoning. The astonishing language of the BVG regarding the ECJ's reasoning was probably driven for the most part by the BVG's need to demonstrate compliance with the strict standard for *ultra vires* review laid down by the German court in its earlier *Honeywell* case (which, one is reminded, required the court, before declaring any EU act to be *ultra vires*, to make an Article 267 reference to the Court of Justice and to arrive, in the light of this, at the conclusion that there had been a structurally significant shift of competences contrary to the principle of conferral). Indeed, this was subsequently expressly acknowledged to have been a factor by one of the main architects of the *Weiss* judgment (Huber J.) and implicitly by the other (Voßkuhle P.).[98] However, if one is to draw consolation from that, it can only be at the expense of acknowledging the – even more inappropriate – deployment of (*Lisbon*-style) result-based reasoning in *Weiss*.[99]

95 Cf. BVG President Voßkuhle who, in a subsequent interview, and without apparent irony, termed the ruling 'a contribution to the dialogue' between the BVG and the ECJ (di Lorenzo and Wefing (n 92)).

96 M. Karnitschnig, 'German court lays down EU law', *Politico*, 5 May 2020. Similarly, see H. Sauer, 'Substantive EU Law Review Beyond the Veil of Democracy: the German Federal Constitutional Court Ultimately Acts as Supreme Court of the EU' *EU Law Live* 16 (9 May 2020).

97 Ibid., 8.

98 See Müller (n 92) where J. Huber is recorded as saying

> 'Die Begriffe 'schlechterdings nicht mehr nochvollziehbar' und "willkürlich" klingen hart. Sie sind es aber nicht, weil sie es dem Bundesverfassungsgericht überhaupt erst ermöglichen, in eine 'Ultra vires'-Kontrolle einzutreten.'

Similarly BVG President Voßkuhle observed of the *Weiss* ruling that 'einige Formulierungen darin, das Wort "willkürlich" etwa, mögen dem Laien schroff erscheinen, Juristen wissen sie richtig einzuschätzen' (di Lorenzo and Wefing (n 92)).

99 Note Sauer's not-unrelated caustic observation that 'in the end, 'whatever it takes' seems to have outweighed the 'within our mandate' caveat (Sauer (n 96) at 8).

In fairness to the Karlsruhe court, there really is, as has already been adverted to, a 'who watches the watchman' lacuna in the EU legal order, given the absence of any control over the ECJ's rulings in the matter of competence combined with the difficulty in amending the Treaties. As we have seen, the BVG provided its own answer to this – in effect that it should be for a court – and more specifically, the BVG itself – to control the ECJ, at least as far as Germany was concerned. This approach is supposedly based on the idea of supranational and national jurisdictions balancing each other out, in the manner of a mobile hanging over a child's cot (although in reality seems to translate more into a hierarchical model with the expected position of the BVG and the ECJ reversed). As already noted, the model suffers both from legitimacy and from workability problems, however. No one (other than themselves) has given national courts this controlling role.

There is, furthermore, an issue of competence here. National constitutional courts – including the BVG – are not specialised European courts and their expertise in European law issues can be limited. Moreover, if fewer than the full complement of the constitutional courts of *all* EU Member States exercise this function, legitimacy issues are raised: why should the BVG alone, or else the constitutional courts of Germany and some other states alone be given this function, thus amplifying the voice of these courts and legal systems above that of others? Such a situation is both undemocratic and unlikely to be politically acceptable to the excluded Member States. If, on the other hand, the constitutional courts of *all* EU Member States give themselves such a control function, the system breaks down, as the Court of Justice cannot possibly modify its approach to answer to the demands of 27 different national constitutional courts and their respective legal systems. Both legitimacy and efficiency considerations would thus seem to suggest that much the wiser course would be to leave to Luxembourg that which is Luxembourg's and to Karlsruhe that which is Karlsruhe's.

8 Two threats to the existing EU legal order

Respectively, the *Weiss* ruling can be said to involve two major threats to the existing EU legal order. The first threat is to the operation of the doctrine of supremacy (or primacy, as the BVG would have it). At one level, *Weiss* came as no surprise in this respect. As we have seen, the BVG has been waging a form of judicial guerrilla warfare for decades – and more specifically, at least since its ruling in the *Kloppenburg* and *Maastricht* judgments of 1987 and 1993 respectively (with the latter case in particular introducing the *ultra vires* doctrine to the Court's pronouncements in this field) – in its revolt against the understanding of European law expounded in cases beginning with *Costa* and *Van Gend en Loos*. To some extent the rulings in these BVG cases and other rulings that followed them were merely operationalised by *Weiss,* albeit in a strikingly aggressive manner: there have been competing visions of primacy/supremacy for decades. The difficulty is that such a pluralist approach to primacy can work – if at all – only if combined with considerable judicial modesty in approach. Yet this was a quality striking for its absence in the *Weiss* ruling.

From the time of the *Maastricht* judgment, a deeper, more fundamental difference between the approach of Karlsruhe and that of Luxembourg has also been evident. The BVG's approach sees the EU as state-based and lacking in possibilities for legitimation other than through the States, who remain, according to Karlsruhe's binary vision, the *Herren der Verträge*.[100] This state-based vision – involving what one observer has termed 'legal nationalism'[101] – contrasts with the quasi-federal vision of the European Union of itself.[102]

The second threat *Weiss* involved was to the independence of the ECB. The ruling effectively threw a sizeable measure of grit into the engine of this institution. The ruling's immediate economic effects may not be very far-reaching. Indeed, they have been described as trivial.[103] The PSPP programme under attack in *Weiss* had already completed most of whatever good it would do by the time the ruling was delivered (as, the BVG must have been aware). The ruling actually poses a greater threat to the ECB's more recent and more extensive €750 billion Pandemic Emergency Purchase Programme (PEPP). Some of the reasoning of the BVG concerning the PSPP seems inimical with this, since the BVG appeared to regard PSPP compliance with the Article 123 TFEU prohibition of monetary financing as having been conditional on a list of conditions that happen to have been met by the PSPP but were not met by the more recent programme.[104] Yet here again the time taken for cases to come before the BVG again may prevent serious damage being done.

Weiss is nonetheless a veritable spoke in the works of the ECB, since it is likely to interfere with *future* EU monetary policy. As Enderlein has observed, the BVG ruling puts the ECB under a constant threat, with the probable intention of the Karlsruhe court having been to get the Bank to internalise BVG thinking so that no ex-post BVG ruling will ever actually become necessary. The effect of this threat is to weaken the Bank politically and in the eyes of the markets.[105] Tighter scrutiny by the Court of Justice of the ECB seems in any case impractical. Courts are ill-fitted to play an active role in the market-moving, shadow-boxing world of central banks, and the ECB cannot be expected to dance in that

100 Hence the observation by Coeuré that 'beyond monetary policy, this is a discussion on whether the EU is a group of sovereign nations deferring competences to common institutions, or a partial federation' (Tweeted from @BCoeure, 6 May 2020.)

101 See thread tweeted by H. Enderlein (@henrikenderlein) on 5 May 2020.

102 The domestic political context of the ruling is perhaps worthy of note. Quite apart from the criticisms raised when the BVG failed to follow through on its initially aggressive stance in *Gauweiler*, a growth in the level of scepticism expressed towards European integration has been visible. German politicians – like those of many other countries – frequently remain silent when it comes to acknowledging the benefits of European integration, 'allowing the hijacking of public debate in the last decade by voices framing the EU and the euro in particular – as an expensive act of charity Germany can increasingly ill afford' (D. Scally, 'Germany needs to hear truth about benefits of euro', *Irish Times*, 7 May 2020).

103 Weiler and Sarmiento (n 89).

104 M. Poiares Maduro, 'Some Preliminary Remarks on the PSPP Decision of the German Constitutional Court', Verfassungsblog, 6 May 2020 at para. 3 thereof.

105 See in this regard the thread tweeted by H. Enderlein (@henrikenderlein) on 5 May 2020.

ring effectively carrying the BVG on its back shouting into its ear an amorphous set of conditions it must meet if Germany is not to walk out.

9 Flawed reasoning in an unfortunate context

Overall, the reasoning deployed by the German Federal Constitutional Court appears unconvincing in quite a number of respects. Among the most serious criticisms have been:

(a) *the BVG's poorly reasoned assertion that the Court of Justice acted ultra vires.* As Sauer has pointed out, even assuming the Court did not sufficiently adhere to the principle of conferral with regard to the ECB and even ignoring the very good reasons that exist for according the ECB a wide margin of appreciation, 'accusing the CJEU of exceeding its mandate when it is too generous in its judicial review of the other EU organs is simply not coherent.' At worst, this might have been a substantive EU law violation – but not an *ultra vires* decision;[106]

(b) *the BVG's impractical idea of strict ongoing judicial scrutiny of the ECB's monetary policy.* This topic is returned to in the text below. Suffice it to add here that, apart from its sheer impracticability, the idea that the independence of the ECB requires strict scrutiny to avoid transgressions of national democracy has also been criticised as an inappropriate legal transplant from German constitutional law straight into EU *ultra vires* standards – in other words, a blurring by the BVG of German constitutional law and EU law;[107]

(c) *the BVG's advocacy of the idea that the ECB should balance anticipated monetary advantages of its decisions against their economic disadvantages.* This extraordinary proposal has been variously described as 'impossible to comply with',[108] 'naïve' [109] and 'economically illiterate'.[110] Moreover, it arguably flies in the face of the explicit wording of Article 127 TFEU, which stipulates that 'the *primary objective* of the European System of Central Banks is to maintain price stability' and that it is

106 Sauer (n 96) at 5–6.

107 Ibid., 6–7.

108 In other words, given the absence of any common denominator with which to balance the effects of economic and monetary policy and the absence further even of any definition of economic or monetary policy (see P. Nicolaides, 'The Judgment of the Federal Constitutional Court of Germany on the Public Sector Asset Purchase Programme of the European Central Bank: Setting an Impossible and Contradictory Test of Proportionality', *EU Law Live No.* 17 (15 May 2020).

109 See in this regard the thread tweeted by H. Enderlein (@henrikenderlein) on 5 May 2020.

110 The description of Sandbu, who has pointed out that 'as the ECJ understood, but the German court seems not to, any loosening of financial conditions will have [the objected-to economic] effects; it is precisely through them that monetary policy affects inflation' (M. Sandbu, 'German Court Has Set a Bomb Under the EU Legal Order', *Financial Times*, 5 May 2020).

'*without prejudice to the objective of price stability*' that the ESCB is to support the general economic policies in the Union.[111]

There was no explanation why the Court's proportionality test only took account of economic costs of decisions without also requiring attention to be paid to economic benefits.[112] At one level, it was particularly surprising that such reasoning emanate from Germany of all places, which has been the European homeland of independent central bank monetary policy. At another level, it was not: the kind of factors explicitly mentioned by the Court as meriting being taken into account by the ECB look suspiciously like the factors for long highlighted by conservative German economic commentators.[113]

(d) *the BVG's suggestion that failure to state reasons can constitute grounds for declaring an act of an EU institution ultra vires.* Sauer has pointed out that even in German law, failure to state reasons does not mean a decision has been made without competence but merely unlawfully (because it prevents judicial review).[114]

The strained and unconvincing quality of the BVG's unflattering descriptions of the reasoning of the Court of Justice in the *Weiss* case has already been noted, as has its probable origins in the need to impress the (unconvincing) view that the *Honeywell* standard for *ultra vires* review had been met. However, this is far from the only way in which the ruling in *Weiss* appears strained. Addressing its conclusions to the Bundesbank also seems a stretch: the Bundesbank is an administrative authority, not a constitutional organ. (For this reason, the BVG ruling deemed the legal claims challenging the Bundesbank's participation in PSPP not to be admissible.) The BVG's call on the Bundesbank towards the end of its reasoning not to participate in the PSPP without evidence of its proportionality thus had a distinctly anomalous ring.[115]

111 Emphasis added. See also Nicolaides (n 108).

112 See Poiares Maduro (n 104) at para. 2 thereof.

113 Hence Sandbu's observation that 'the 'economic policy effects' that worry the court are the one-sided litany well known from the conservative fringe of German monetary politics: by lowering interest rates, QE helps governments, hurts 'savers or insurance policyholders' and 'allows economically unviable companies to stay on the market'' (see Sandbu (n 110)).

114 Sauer (n 96) at 7. How a violation of Article 123 TFEU by the ECB – investigated by the BVG, but held not to have been 'manifest' – might have involved an *ultra vires* act was similarly not explained by the BVG.

115 Strikingly, it was not repeated in the operative part of its judgment. See more generally N. de Arabia-Sellier, 'Between Karlsruhe and Luxembourg lies Frankfurt? The Bundesbank and the Bundesverfassungsgericht's PSPP decision', *EU Law Live* (No. 17) (15 May 2020) at 3 notes that 'it is likely that the constitutional organs [i.e., the Federal Government and the *Bundestag*], rather than the *Bundesbank* will be in charge of evaluating the proportionate character of the PSPP. Not only did the *Bundesverfassungsgericht* refrain from directly ordering the *Bundesbank* to withdraw its participation in the PSPP but it also did not rule on the *Bundesbank's* participation in any other, present or future, similar monetary policy programmes' (Ibid., p. 3).

If *Weiss* saw the BVG stretch the law in several respects, it followed in a well-established tradition, since the very origins of the deployment of *ultra vires* review in *Kloppenburg/Maastricht* involved stretching the pre-existing law[116] and the *Lisbon* ruling's expansive view of the requirements of democracy and of the constitutional identity of a state. Furthermore, an extraordinarily liberal view of standing has continued to be taken by the BVG right up to and including in *Weiss*.[117]

The *Weiss* ruling also had an unfortunate context – that of a rule of law crisis in Hungary and Poland. Although BVG President Voßkuhle claimed the ruling as a victory for the rule of law, its effect in practice to date seems to have been to encourage those working to undermine the rule of law.[118] As was acknowledged by Voßkuhle the ruling's publication saw the wrong people cheering, including the Polish government, who clearly felt it provided encouragement for them.[119] This was only to be expected: what the BVG demands as sauce for a German goose can hardly be expected to be barred from the menu for a Polish gander: whether the BVG like it or not, the *Weiss* ruling clearly buttresses the spurious claims of Europe's autocrats of the legitimacy of their pick and mix approach to EU law.

10 What is the solution to the crisis created by *Weiss*?

The greatest difficulty with *Weiss* is deciding how to cope with its destabilising implications, or, as Sarmiento has put it, 'to heal the wound so irresponsibly inflicted by the Bundesverfassungsgericht'.[120]

The immediate reaction of both the ECB and the ECJ was to express defiance. The Court issued a press release which included a reminder of the Court's case law according to which a preliminary ruling is binding on a national court for the purposes of the decision to be given in the proceedings occasioning the reference, and warning that in order to ensure that EU law is applied uniformly, it is the Court of Justice alone – which was created for that purpose by the Member States – that has jurisdiction to rule that an act of an EU institution was contrary

116 *Ultra vires* review for European Union law began with Kloppenburg and Maastricht rulings. See P. Craig, 'The ECJ and Ultra Vires Action: A Conceptual Analysis' (2011) 48 *CMLRev* 395.

117 The net effect of these is that individual actions can frequently be brought challenging EU law actions that do not affect individual rights – exactly the situation in *Weiss* – where they could not be brought outside the context of European integration (see Sauer (n 96) at 4).

118 See di Lorenzo and Wefing (n 92). See also K. Matussek and S. Bodoni, 'German Judges Strike Back, Say ECB Isn't Master of Universe', Bloomberg, 12 May 2020.

119 Not that BVG President Voßkuhle seemed unduly troubled by this. His rather laconic observation on the point (beyond denying both the validity of comparisons between the Polish and German approaches and the relevance of the Polish reaction to legal reasoning) was that 'die Polen tun, was sie tun, unabhängig davon, was wir tun' (see di Lorenzo and Wefing (n 92)).

120 D. Sarmiento, 'Requiem for Judicial Dialogue – the German Federal Constitutional Court's Judgment in the Weiss Case and its European Implications' *EU Law Live* 16 (9 May 2020) 9 at 20.

to EU law.[121] The ECB President expressed the intention to continue 'undeterred' to do whatever was needed to deliver on its mandate.

The Bank quickly hedged its position, however. Apart from engaging in contingency planning for the eventuality that Bundesbank participation in PSPP purchases would have to stop (possibly to be accompanied by legal action in respect of the Bundesbank's failure to fulfil its bond-buying obligations as a member of the Eurosystem of central banks),[122] it also sought to meet the BVG's demands by making extensive reference in the minutes of the June monetary policy meeting of the Governing Council (themselves the longest ever such minutes) to the respective costs and benefits of policy decisions past (like the PSPP) and future (like the PEPP) and in particular (repeatedly) to proportionality.[123] Unpublished documents providing justifications for decisions were also provided to the Bundesbank for presentation to the Bundestag and German Government. For their part all German institutions involved also cooperated (the Bundestag and German Government reputedly approving the relevant decisions within one day and four days respectively of the relevant communications).[124] In early August, the Bundesbank pronounced itself satisfied that the concerns expressed by the BVG had been dealt with.[125]

One issue in this regard will be for the Commission to decide if Germany should be prosecuted under Article 258 for the transgressions of the BVG against the EU legal order, a possibility highlighted with the finding in *Köbler* that the actions of national judiciaries could even give rise to state liability in certain circumstances. Various reasons have been suggested as to why such a prosecution should occur.[126] One is that it would be invidious *not* to prosecute since the Commission has done so in relation to Poland's refusal to comply with ECJ rulings.[127] (As opposed to this, there has been a dearth of prosecutions of other states whose constitutional tribunals have revolted against aspects of the EU legal order.) Other reasons that have been advanced have been that such a prosecution would compel the reactivation of the dialogue spurned by the BVG when it delivered its ruling without referring the matter back to the Court of

121 Court of Justice of the European Union Press release following the judgment of the German Constitutional Court of 5 May 2020 (Press Release No 58/20 Luxembourg, 8 May 2020).

122 F. Canepa and B. Koranyi, 'Exclusive: ECB Prepares for the Worst – Life Without the Bundesbank', Reuters.com, 26 May 2020.

123 See 'Account of the Monetary Policy Meeting of the Governing Council of the European Central Bank held in Frankfurt am Main on Wednesday and Thursday, 3-4 June 2020', and published online at www.ecb.europa.eu/press/accounts/2020/html/ecb.mg200625~fd97330d5f.en.html

124 B. Koranyi and F. Canepa, 'ECB to Release Documents to Defuse German Court Challenge' Reuters.com, 24 June, 2020. For a good account of the chain of events involved, see the lengthy twitter thread by C. Marsh under the name of @GeneralTheorist, 31 July 2020.

125 A. Weber, 'Bundesbank Will Continue Bond Buying as German Court Spat Ends', Bloomberg 3 August, 2020.

126 See generally in this regard, F. Fabbrini, 'Suing the BverfG', Verfassungsblog, 13 May 2020.

127 Sarmiento (n 93) at 18.

Justice;[128] or that it would clarify the law;[129] or that it would be a necessary and powerful symbol.[130] Other voices have counselled caution however,[131] noting that prosecutions in respect of judicial behaviour are rare[132] and likely to be counter-productive, and would be pointless if the German Government cannot do anything to remedy the breach in question.[133]

If things really must change in order to stay the same, what changes are needed? Suggestions have been made of the need for constitutional change within Germany or Treaty change at European level, or indeed both. As regards German constitutional change, to the extent that some of the reasoning was based on the BVG concept of German democracy (protected as this is by the operation of the eternity clause), it should be noted that a constitutional amendment would be of little value.

As regards Treaty reform, BVG case law has also imposed limits, with the *Weiss* ruling for example, underlining how the BVG sees debt mutualisation as impinging on German democracy because it leaves the German people liable for debts incurred by others. This effectively creates constitutional limits (both through parliamentary approval and conditionality) which Treaty amendments cannot alter.[134] Ideas for various potentially useful Treaty amendments have nonetheless been made. One such suggestion has been the express broadening of the ECB mandate. Another is the creation of a Constitutional Chamber to which European Court of Justice decisions about the scope of EU law competences can be appealed against, thereby ending the admittedly anomalous situation in which the Court of Justice enjoys largely unreviewed and untrammelled jurisdiction in this field.[135] It may turn out to be a lucky coincidence in this regard that the Conference on the Future of Europe – which seeks to reflect on the medium-to-long-term future of the EU and on the question of what reforms should be made to its institutions and policies – is expected to begin soon.

It has been speculated that one result of the ruling in *Weiss* might be to increase the incentive to develop Europe as a fiscal union, thereby reducing the role of unelected central bankers in running the Eurozone. Matej has argued that 'if the EU fiscal union existed and if it was based on a meaningful EU budget, legitimated by a vibrant EU democracy, there would be no, or much less, need of ECB venturing with its monetary mechanisms into fiscal and democratic domains.' [136] Too much should not be hoped for in this regard, however, given

128 See M. Arnold, G. Chazan and S. Fleming, 'How Can Europe Solve the Crisis Created by Germany's Highest Court?' *Financial Times*, 5 May 2020.

129 Ibid.

130 Weiler and Sarmiento (n 89).

131 Sarmiento (n 87) (moderating the author's earlier call for an infringement action in the immediate aftermath of the BVG ruling).

132 Ibid.

133 Ibid.

134 See Poiares Maduro (n 104) at para. 4 thereof.

135 See Weiler and Sarmiento (n 89).

136 Avbelj (n 87).

that the various challenged activities heretofore engaged in by the European Central Bank have by now become the norm for central banks even in federal entities with far more power centralised fiscal authorities.

Another linked idea – which would escape what the BVG sees as German constitutional debt mutualisation limits – has been that of developing the concept of EU 'own resources'.[137] It may not have been entirely coincidental that the ultimately decisive U-turn by Germany towards advocacy (with France) of what came to be known as the new temporary recovery instrument Next Generation EU, with financial firepower of €750 billion (of which €390 million would be in the form of grants) financed by long-term EU borrowing began very shortly after the *Weiss* ruling.

The immediate reaction of Chancellor Merkel to the ruling itself had been to seek to avoid any danger that the crisis might be escalated by EU institutions and to advise that the ECB ought to use the bridge offered by the BVG in terms of establishing that the PSPP decisions were indeed proportionate.[138] The danger of this however is that such a position might crystallise into acceptance of an unacceptable BVG ruling.[139] The idea of treading water may nonetheless possibly be the right one, however, for the reason that it gives the BVG the opportunity of backing down from a position in many respects seems untenable. The likelihood of this happening has perhaps been increased by the departure from the Court of President Voßkuhle, one of two judges in the Court associated with a hard line towards the European Union.[140]

If this does not happen, yet another possibility would be for the other Eurozone states to proceed with quantitative easing without Germany (given that the BVG ruling binds only that state)[141] but – given the outsize importance of that country to the 19-member Eurozone (proportionally even greater than Germany's major importance to the EU as a whole) – this would clearly be a suboptimal result and might well have negative market implications.

Overall, the *Bundesverfassungsgericht* may fairly be said to have dug Europe into a hole with its ruling in *Weiss*. Yet only time will determine the true importance of the ruling. As, Sarmiento has noted, *Weiss*

137 Maduro (n 104) at para. 4.

138 See M. Arnold, G. Chazan and S. Fleming, 'How Can Europe Solve the Crisis Created by Germany's Highest Court?' *Financial Times*, 5 May 2020.

139 It was remarkable to see how quickly conservative German opinion moved to siding with the BVG's demands (see e.g., R. Müller, 'Eine Union des Guten Willens', *Frankfurter Allgemeine Zeitung*, 14 May 2020.)

140 Interestingly in this regard, on 15 June, the BVG dismissed a challenge to the ECB's Corporate Sector Purchase Programme (CSPP) on procedural grounds of a kind that might possibly have been used in the PSPP case, had the BVG been so inclined. (Decision of the Second Chamber of the Second Senate, 15 June 2020. (2 BvR 71/20, Rn. 1–30) ECLI:DE:BVerfG:2020:rk20200615.2bvr007120).

141 Fabbrini and Keleman (n 91).

> might be its most significant ruling in its more than 70-year long history. It could be one of the key moments of European integration. Or it could be just an unfortunate anecdote, a sinister chapter in the EU's long road towards a more perfect union…an error stemming from parochial views of parochial lawyers unable to understand…the lethal consequences of their lack of vision.[142]

Viewed from the present, *Weiss* appears to be a ruling which suffers (in exchange for whatever limited benefits it may have) from various defects. It may ultimately be remembered as a case in which the BVG pressed the nuclear button on rather frivolous terms, and then failed to engage constructively in a judicial dialogue requiring mutual respect and sensitivity.[143] The ruling arguably championed an inappropriate level of judicial interference in a field in which courts are not sufficiently expert. It has also risked generating divisions along a number of axes – between the Commission and Germany, between the Bundesbank and the European Central Bank but most importantly and enduringly, between national courts and the European Court of Justice.

If the final consequences of the case remain to be seen, certainly neither the reasoning nor the outcome of the case provide much by way of evidence of any benefits to having 'self-empowered and unelected national courts turning themselves (with no clear legal basis to do so under EU law), into the ultimate interpreters of EU law itself'.[144] If Europe needs some kind of revolution, there nonetheless seems to be little need for this kind. If Europe needs a fiscal revolution, one can only hope that perhaps the spider's web of difficulties created by the *Weiss* ruling for ECB action may constitute some kind of spur to this happening sooner rather than later.

References

Amalfitano C and Pollicino O, 'Two Courts, Two Languages? The Taricco Saga Ends on a Worrying Note', Verfassungsblog, 5 June 2018

Arnold M, Chazan G and Fleming S, 'How Can Europe Solve the Crisis Created by Germany's Highest Court?' *Financial Times*, 5 May 2020.

Avbelj M, 'The Right Question about the FCC Ultra Vires Decision', Verfassungsblog, 6 May 2020

Aziz M, *Sovereignty Lost, Sovereignty Regained? The European Integration Project and the Bundesverfassungsgericht*, EUI Working Paper, RSC 2001/31, Robert Schuman Centre for Advanced Studies, 2001

Canepa F and Koranyi B, 'Exclusive: ECB Prepares for the Worst – Life Without the Bundesbank', Reuters.com, 26 May 2020

142 Sarmiento (n 93) at 9.

143 Ibid., 18.

144 Ibid., 19.

Court of Justice of the European Union, Press release following the judgment of the German *Constitutional Court of 5 May 2020* (Press Release No 58/20 Luxembourg, 8 May 2020)

Craig P 'The ECJ and Ultra Vires Action: A Conceptual Analysis' (2011) 48 *Common Market Law Review* 395

Craig P and de Burca G, *EU Law – Text, Cases and Materials* (sixth edition, OUP, 2015)

Dawson M and Bobic A, 'Quantitative Easing at the Court of Justice – Doing Whatever it Takes to Save the Euro' (2019) 56 *Common Market Law Review* 1005

de Arabia-Sellier N, 'Between Karlsruhe and Luxembourg lies Frankfurt? The Bundesbank and the Bundesverfassungsgericht's PSPP decision' *EU Law Live* (No. 17) (15 May 2020)

di Lampedusa G, *Il Gattopardo* (Feltrinelli, Milan, 2013).

di Lorenzo G and Wefing H, 'Erfolg ist Eher Kalt', *Die Zeit*, 14 May 2020

European Central Bank, *Account of the monetary policy meeting of the Governing Council of the European Central Bank held in Frankfurt am Main on Wednesday and Thursday, 3–4 June 2020* published online at www.ecb.europa.eu/press/accounts/2020/html/ecb.mg200625~fd97330d5f.en.html

European Central Bank, *Asset purchase programmes*, available online at www.ecb.europa.eu/mopo/implement/omt/html/index.en.html

Everling U, 'Will Europe Slip on Bananas – The Bananas Judgment of the Court of Justice and National Courts' (1996) 33 *Common Market Law Review* 401

Everson M & Joerges C, 'Who is the Guardian for Constitutionalism in Europe After the Financial Crisis?' in Kröger S (Ed.), *Political Representation in the European Union: Still Democratic in Times of Crisis?* (Routledge, Abingdon, 2014) 400

Fabbrini F, 'The Euro-Crisis and the Courts: Judicial Review and the Political Process in Comparative Perspective', (2014) 32 *Berkeley J. Int'l Law* 64

Fabbrini F, 'Suing the BverfG', Verfassungsblog, 13 May 2020

Fabbrini F and Keleman RD, 'With One Court Decision, Germany May Be Plunging Europe into a Constitutional Crisis', *Washington Post*, 7 May 2020

Freehling W, *Prelude to Civil War: The Nullification Controversy in South Carolina 1816–1836* (Harper and Row, New York, 1965)

Halberstam D and Möllers C, 'The German Constitutional Court says "Ja zu Deutschland!"' (2009) *German Law Journal* 1219

Hinarejos A, *The Euro Area Crisis in Constitutional Perspective* (Oxford University Press 2015)

Hofmann H, *Controlling the Powers of the ECB: Delegation, Discretion, Reasoning and Care – What Gauweiler, Weiss and others can teach us*, Ademu Working Paper Series WP 2018/107, Barcelona, 2018

Jestaedt M, Lepsius O, Möllers C and Schönberger C, *Das entgrenzte Gericht* (Suhrkamp, Berlin, 2011)

Karnitschnig M, 'German Court Lays Down EU law', *Politico*, 5 May 2020

Koranyi B and Canepa F 'ECB to Release Documents to Defuse German Court Challenge' Reuters.com, 24 June 2020

Matussek K and Bodoni S, 'German Judges Strike Back, Say ECB Isn't Master of Universe', Bloomberg, 12 May 2020

Müller R, 'Das Urteil war zwingend', *Frankfurter Allgemeine Zeitung*, 13 May 2020

Müller R, 'Eine Union des Guten Willens', *Frankfurter Allgemeine Zeitung*, 14 May 2020

Nicolaides P, 'The Judgment of the Federal Constitutional Court of Germany on the Public Sector Asset Purchase Programme of the European Central Bank: Setting an Impossible and Contradictory Test of Proportionality', *EU Law Live* 17, 15 May 2020

Poiares Maduro M, 'Some Preliminary Remarks on the PSPP Decision of the German Constitutional Court', Verfassungsblog, 6 May 2020

Reich N, 'Judge-made Europe à la carte: Some Remarks on Recent Conflicts between European and German Constitutional Law Provoked by the Banana Litigation' (1996) 7 *European Journal of International Law* 103

Sandbu M, 'German Court Has Set a Bomb Under the EU Legal Order', *Financial Times*, 5 May 2020

Sarmiento D, 'An Infringement Action Against Germany After its Constitutional Court's Ruling in Weiss? The Long Term and the Short Term', *EU Law Live*, 12 May 2020

Sarmiento D, 'Requiem for Judicial Dialogue – the German Federal Constitutional Court's Judgment in the Weiss Case and its European Implications' *EU Law Live* 16, 9 May 2020

Sauer H, 'Substantive EU Law Review Beyond the Veil of Democracy: the German Federal Constitutional Court Ultimately Acts as Supreme Court of the EU' *EU Law Live* No. 16, 9 May 2020

Scally D, 'Germany Needs to Hear Truth about Benefits of Euro', *Irish Times*, 7 May 2020

Simms B, *Europe – The Struggle for Supremacy – 1453 to the Present* (Penguin 2014)

Thiele A, 'Das BVerfG und die Büchse der ultra-vires-Pandora – Das Urteil in Sachen Anleihenkaufprogramm der EZB', Verfassungsblog, 5 May 2020

Voßkuhle A, 'Multilevel Cooperation of the European Constitutional Courts: Der Europäische Verfassungsgerichtverbund' (2010) *European Constitutional Law Review* 175

Voßkuhle A, 'Pyramid or Mobile? – Human Rights Protection by the European Constitutional Courts', paper delivered at opening of the judicial year 2014, European Court of Human Rights, Strasbourg, 31 January 2014

Weber A, 'Bundesbank Will Continue Bond Buying as German Court Spat Ends', Bloomberg 3 August 2020.

Weiler J, 'The Community System: The Dual Character of Supranationalism' (1981) YEL 267

Weiler J and Haltern U, 'The Autonomy of the Community Legal Order-Through the Looking Glass' (1996) 37 *Harvard International Law Journal* 411

Weiler J and Sarmiento D, 'The EU Judiciary After Weiss – Proposing a New Mixed Chamber of the Court of Justice', *EU Law Live*, 1 June 2020

5 National identity (under Art. 4(2) TEU) and constitutional identity (as counter-limits) are not the same

Enrico Albanesi

1 Introduction: protecting constitutional orders from a constitutional revolution coming from the EU

In constitutional orders, constitutional identity is seen as the ultimate limit beyond which any constitutional amendment would be considered unconstitutional.[1]

When it comes to the relationship between EU Member States and EU law, from a domestic perspective such a limit is best known under the etiquette of 'counter-limits', i.e. the limits to the self-limitation to their own sovereignty that Member States allowed in favour of the EU.[2] In other words, the limits to protect the domestic constitutional order from a constitutional revolution coming from the EU itself:[3] a red line which has been seen by some scholars as part of a 'third wave' of judicial review, compare a context where domestic jurisdictions prefer their own conception of fundamental rights to that required by international norms.[4]

1 Michel Rosenfeld, *The Identity of the Constitutional Subject. Selfhood, Citizenship, Culture, and Community* (Routledge 2010) 30–33 and Gary J Jacobsohn, *Constitutional Identity* (Harvard University Press 2010) 6 and 70–71 (one should bear in mind that according to Jacobsohn, a constitutional text is not coterminous with its constitutional identity, anyway). See also Yaniv Roznai, *Unconstitutional Constitutional Amendments. The Limits of Amendment Powers* (Oxford University Press 2019) 141 and 148–150, who speaks of a 'set of basic constitutional principles that form the constitutional identity' (but also uses other expressions such as 'state's basic constitutional principles', 'primary constitutive values of the constitutional order', 'basic principles', 'basic structure', 'basic features' or 'fundamental principles' of the constitution) and Richard Albert, *Constitutional Amendments. Making, Breaking, and Changing Constitutions* (Oxford University Press 2019) 84–92 and 150 (who bases his theory of constitutional dismemberment, as distinct from constitutional amendment, among other features, on a dismemberment of a constitution's identity).

2 The expression was first used by the Italian scholar Paolo Barile. See Paolo Barile, *Scritti di diritto costituzionale* (Cedam 1967) 701–720. The Italian Constitutional Court used this concept in 1973 (see Corte costituzionale, sent. 27 December 1973, n. 183, para. 9 *Considerato in diritto*) and the German Constitutional Tribunal in 1974 (see BVerfGE 37, 271).

3 Yaniv Roznai and Gary J Jacobsohn, *Constitutional Revolution* (Yale University Press 2020) Chapter 4 and their critical analysis of the German Constitutional Tribunal case law.

4 Doreen Lustig and Joseph H Weiler, 'Judicial review in the contemporary world – Retrospective and prospective' (2018) *I•CON* 16 158.

Under Art. 4(2) TEU, as amended by the Treaty of Lisbon,[5] the EU 'shall respect the equality of Member States before the Treaties as well as their national identities, inherent in their fundamental structures, political and constitutional, inclusive of regional and local self-government'. As has been noted, the EU has self-limited the primacy of EU law,[6] thus its legal order,[7] in favour of Member States' identities, provided that they respect fundamental values under Art. 2 TEU.[8]

As will be noted, such an identity clause under Art. 4(2) TEU has been regarded by many scholars[9] and many Member States' Constitutional Courts[10] as a transposition of counter-limits into EU law. In other words, according to these views, the EU would self-limit its own legal order in favour of Member States' counter-limits.

On the contrary, the chapter will demonstrate that: (i) from a theoretical perspective, the legal nature of the aforementioned concepts, cf. national identity (under Art. 4(2) TEU) and constitutional identity (as counter-limits), cannot be the same, although their contents might partially overlap: counter-limits are a limit to a self-limitation of their sovereignty by Member States under their domestic constitution, whereas national identity is a self-limitation to its sovereignty by the EU under the Treaties; (ii) actually, in the European Court of Justice (ECJ) case-law, the scope of the identity clause under Art. 4(2) TEU is seen in a narrower way than that of domestic Constitutional Courts: that is, at least in the specific judgments issued so far, as something concerning cultural and structural elements, which might partially overlap constitutional identity,

5 However, on Art. 4(2) TEU as 'the apex of a 'crescendo', see Giuseppe Martinico, *The Tangled Complexity of the EU Constitutional Process. The Frustrating Knot of Europe* (Routledge 2013) 92.

6 See, among others, Oreste Pollicino, *Allargamento dell'Europa a est e rapporti tra Corti costituzionali e Corti europee. Verso una teoria generale dell'impatto interordinamentale del diritto sovranazionale?* (Giuffrè 2010) 176.

7 See, among others, Mautizio Pedrazza Gorlero, 'Alla ricerca della forma "condizionante". Introduzione ai rapporti fra Corti costituzionali nazionali e Corti Europee dopo il Trattato di Lisbona' in Maurizio Pedrazza Gorlero (ed), *Corti costituzionali e Corti europee dopo il Trattato di Lisbona* (Edizioni scientifiche italiane 2010) 1–24.

8 See, among others, Armin von Bogdandy and Stephan Schill, 'Overcoming Absolute Primacy: Respect for National Identity under the Lisbon Treaty' (2011) *Common Market Law Review* 4 1430 and Stelio Mangiameli, 'The Union's Homogeneity and Its Common Values in the Treaty of the European Union' in Hermann-Josef Blanke and Stelio Mangiameli (eds), *The European Union after Lisbon. Constitutional Basis, Economic Order and External Action* (Springer Verlag 2012) 35. On the tools to protect fundamental values under Art. 2 TEU, see Enrico Albanesi, 'The use of the EU infringement procedures to protect *de facto* the rule of law via the development of the parameter: from obligations under the Treaties to the Charter of Fundamental Rights' in Martin Belov (ed.), *Courts, Politics and Constitutional Law. Judicialization of Politics and Politicization of the Judiciary* (Routledge 2020) 228–246.

9 Among others, Antonio Ruggeri, 'Le fonti del diritto europunitario ed i loro rapporti con le fonti nazionali' in Pasquale Costanzo, Luca Mezzetti, and Antonio Ruggeri, *Lineamenti di diritto costituzionale dell'Unione europea* (Giappichelli 2019) 329–332.

10 See below Section 3.

although this has never been pointed out by the ECJ; (iii) moreover, the way the ECJ applies the identity clause under Art. 4(2) TEU (i.e. under the proportionality test), differs from the way Constitutional Courts look at counter-limits (i.e. as a rigid limit to the EU law).

Such a view brings the risk of a lacuna in the relations between the EU and Member States, that is unavoidable, though, when it comes to counter-limits which are applied domestically by Constitutional Courts and which cannot be connected with the identity clause under Art. 4(2) TEU, in its narrow sense, which emerges from the ECJ case-law.

This is the reason why, as will be argued here, the EU and Member States should do their best to shape their action to the principle of sincere cooperation under Art. 4(3) TEU, when it comes to Art. 4(2) TEU.

On the one hand, Member States should do their best not to bring under the etiquette of 'national identity', interests they consider counter-limits but fall outside the scope of 'national identity' under Art. 4(2) TEU, in its narrow sense. They should also check whether a principle they consider as a part of their counter-limits could be found in EU constitutional law (e.g. the Charter of Fundamental Rights of the European Union – CFREU) or could be brought under the etiquette of 'constitutional traditions common to the Member States' (as happened in the *Taricco* case),[11] which constitute general principles of EU law.

On the other hand, the ECJ should do its best to consider as national identity only the interests that Member States point out as such. However, Member States would be helped in doing so, only if the ECJ framed the concept of national identity under Art. 4(2) TEU in a clearer way than it has done so far.

The chapter will proceed as follows. First, it will be demonstrated the difference between national identity (under Art. 4(2) TEU) and constitutional identity (as counter-limits) from a theoretical perspective (Section 2). Second, case-law of Constitutional Courts in Member States will be analysed, in order to show that, from their perspective, the identity clause under Art. 4(2) TEU is seen as a transposition of counter-limits into EU law (Section 3). Third, the ECJ case-law will be similarly examined, so as to show that the scope of the identity clause under Art. 4(2) TEU is seen from Luxembourg in a narrower way than that of domestic Constitutional Courts. Moreover, it will be shown that the ECJ applies that clause under a scrutiny of proportionality (Section 4). Finally, the chapter will focus on the legal consequences of such a view.

The role that the principle of sincere cooperation under Art. 4(3) TEU should play in this context will be explored: as for Member States, when they deal with an interest that they consider one of their counter-limits; as for the ECJ, when it shapes the concept of national identity under Art. 4(2) TEU, in its narrow sense (Section 5). It will be then argued that the use of the principle of sincere cooperation could reduce to the bare minimum the risk of a clash between EU and its Member States when it comes to national identity and counter-limits.

11 See Sections 3 and 5.

The risk of a clash still exists, though. However, as will be concluded, such a lacuna in the relationships between the EU and Member States is unavoidable (Conclusions).

2 The different legal nature of national identity (under Art. 4(2) TEU) and constitutional identity (as counter-limits)

From a theoretical perspective, the legal nature of the national identity clause (under Art. 4(2) TEU) and of constitutional identity, as counter-limits, is different.

If we assume that every legal order lies on a rule of recognition which sets the criteria of validity of its own norms (thus, the criteria of validity of other legal orders' norm within itself), according to Hart's view,[12] the conclusion we can draw is that also domestic and EU legal orders rest on their own rule of recognition.

This was clearly pointed out by MacCormick in developing his idea of constitutional pluralism. According to MacCormick, demonstrating how the controversial issue of sovereignty can be dealt with when it comes to the relationship between such two legal orders that are *both* sovereign, it is necessary to guard against a monocular view of things.[13] It is just that legal concept, namely Hart's rule of recognition, that allows MacCormick to draw the conclusion that sovereignty can be seen as divided between the EU and Member States.[14]

The concept of constitutional pluralism with regard to the relationship between the EU and Member States has been developed and shaped under different perspectives by other scholars, such as Walker[15] and Maduro,[16] among others.[17] All these views, however, rest on Hart's concept of the rule of recognition. Such theories could run the risk of seeming to be 'poetry',[18] if one does not reflect on and point out the actual rule(s) of recognition of the EU and Member States. In other words, those rules under which the EU, on the one hand, and each Member State, on the other, self-limited their own sovereignty in favour of the other.[19]

12 Herbert L A Hart, *The Concept of Law* (3rd edn, Oxford University Press 2012) 94.

13 Neil MacCormick, 'Beyond the sovereign state' (1993) *The Modern Law Review* 56 1–18.

14 Neil MacCormick, *Questioning Sovereignty. Law, State, and Nation in the European Commonwealth* (Oxford University Press 1999) 113–136.

15 Neil Walker, 'The idea of constitutional pluralism' (2002) *The Modern Law Review* 65 317–359.

16 Miguel P Maduro, 'Contrapunctual law: Europe's constitutional pluralism in Action' in Neil Walker (ed.), *Sovereignty in Transition* (Hart 2003) 501–537.

17 For a comprehensive overview, see Klemen Jaklic, *Constitutional Pluralism in the EU* (Oxford University Press 2014) and Matej Avbelj and Jan Komárek (eds), *Constitutional Pluralism in the European Union and Beyond* (Hart 2012).

18 As noted by Willem T Eijsbouts and Leonard F M Besselink, '"The law of laws" – overcoming pluralism' (2008) *European Constitutional Law Review* 396.

19 Giovanni Guzzetta, *La contaminazione costituzionale del diritto europeo. Interrogativi su un ordinamento in divenire* (Giappichelli 2015) 23.

As for the rule of recognition within each Member State's legal order, it is embedded in those clauses (usually set in their Constitutions) under which every State has self-limited their own sovereignty in favour of the EU, *save the respect of the counter-limits*. For example, this is the case of Art. 11 of the Italian Constitution or Art. 24 of the Basic Law for the Federal Republic of Germany, to be read, as for the counter-limits, in connection with, respectively, the case-law of the Italian Constitutional Court and of the German Constitutional Tribunal.[20] *Mutatis mutandis*, this is also true with regards to the United Kingdom.[21]

As for the rule of recognition within the EU legal order, such a clause seems to be Art. 4(2) TEU. As already noted above,[22] *the EU has self-limited its own legal order in favour of national identities*, provided that they respect fundamental values under Art. 2 TEU.

All that said, the different nature of the identity clause (under Art. 4(2) TEU) and of constitutional identity, as counter-limits, should be now clear. On the one hand, counter-limits are the limits of self-limitation to their sovereignty by Member States under their domestic constitution. On the other hand, national identity is a self-limitation by the EU under the Treaties. Moreover, one should bear in mind that counter-limits are set under domestic case-law whereas the identity clause is a provision under the Treaty, i.e. it is a provision under EU law, which is applied by the ECJ, with the legal consequences which will be set out below.[23]

3 Constitutional Courts case-law: Art. 4(2) TEU as a transposition of counter-limits into EU law

Once the different legal nature of identity clause (under Art. 4(2) TEU) and constitutional identity (as counter-limits) has been demonstrated, the way the scope of the identity clause is seen and the way the clause is applied by the ECJ, should be analysed. This will show that for the ECJ, the identity clause under Art. 4(2) TEU, as for its scope and as for the way it is applied, is something narrower and more flexible than what the counter-limits are for the Constitutional Courts of Member States. However, if one looks at the ECJ case-law, they can infer that these two concepts might overlap, although this has never been pointed out by the ECJ.

Before carrying out such an analysis in the following two Sections, the case-law of some of the Constitutional Courts of EU Member States should be examined, in order to show that, on the contrary, Art. 4(2) TEU is seen by them as a transposition of counter-limits into EU law. Such a view is shared by many scholars[24] (but criticised by others).[25] However, according to such a scholarly

20 See note 2.
21 MacCormick (n 13) 1–18.
22 See Section 1.
23 See Section 4.
24 See, among others, Ruggeri (n 9) 329.
25 See Section 4.

view, the antinomies between EU law and counter-limits in the light of Art. 4(2) TEU are wisely seen at least as a matter of balance between the principle of EU law primacy and counter-limits.[26] In other words, according to such theories, EU law primacy and counter-limits are not to be seen as two armies lined up one in front of another.[27] That is not the opinion of national Constitutional Courts though, which never mention techniques of balancing norms, when it comes to Art. 4(2) TEU.

It should be also mentioned that case-law examined here concerns potential (see the Latvian and the German cases) or concrete (see the Italian and the Hungarian cases) controversies regarding the *ultra vires* control carried out by Constitutional Courts, i.e. the ***domestic*** control of the compatibility of EU law with the counter-limits. Notwithstanding this, it is significant that, in order to strengthen their arguments, Constitutional Courts mention the identity clause under Art. 4(2) TEU as it was a transposition of counter-limits *into EU law*.

In 2009 the Constitutional Court of the Republic of Latvia examined the case of the conformity of the Treaty of Lisbon to the Latvian Constitution. On that occasion it noted that under Art. 4(2)TEU, 'the TEU *expressis verbis* provides for identity of the Member States and respect to sovereignty thereof, which is even more emphasized than in other effective treaties' and that 'this norm in particular guarantees that henceforth there shall exist states and their fundamental constitutional structures, as well as their values, principles, and basic rights that cannot be lost by establishing a supranational organization'.[28]

This view was even more openly expressed by the German Constitutional Tribunal in the famous *Lissabon-Urteil*, issued on 30 June 2009.

When reaffirming the *ultra vires* review that can be carried out when the EU transgresses the boundaries of its competences to see whether 'the inviolable core of the constitutional identity of the Basic Law [...] is respected' (i.e. counter-limits), the German Constitutional Tribunal stated that

> otherwise, with progressing integration, the fundamental political and constitutional structures of sovereign Member States, which are recognised by Article 4.2 first sentence Lisbon TEU, cannot be safeguarded in any other way. In this respect, the guarantee of national constitutional identity under constitutional and Union law go hand in hand in the European legal area. The identity review makes it possible to examine whether due to any action of European institutions, the principles under Article 1 and Article 20 of the Basic Law, declared inviolable in Article 79.3 of the Basic Law, have been violated.[29]

26 Antonio Ruggeri, 'Dimensione europea della tutela dei diritti fondamentali e tecniche interpretative' (2010) *Il diritto dell'Unione europea* 125–147. See also Pietro Faraguna, *Ai confini della Costituzione. Principi supremi e identità costituzionale* (FrancoAngeli 2015) 151–188.

27 Antonio Ruggeri, 'Primato del diritto sovranazionale *versus* identità costituzionale? (Alla ricerca dell'araba fenice costituzionale: i "controlimiti")' (2016) *Lo Stato* 47–69.

28 Constitutional Court of the Republic of Latvia, Judgment 7 April 2009, Case No. 2008-35-01, para. 16.2.

29 BVerfGE 123, 267, para. 240.

In another part of the judgment, the German Constitutional Tribunal stated that '[German] constitutional identity, which is inviolable under Article 79.3 of the Basic Law [i.e. counter-limits] is also respected by European treaty law, namely Article 4.2 first sentence Lisbon TEU'. [30] Clearly, for the German Constitutional Tribunal, constitutional identity (as counter-limits) and national identity (under Art. 4(2) TEU) are the same.

It is worth mentioning that in 2017, in its reference for a preliminary ruling concerning the validity of the decisions of the European Central Bank on the Public Sector Purchase Programme (PSPP), the German Constitutional Tribunal asked whether it was compatible with Art. 4(2) TEU for a decision of the European Central Bank

> to provide for the entirety of the losses that might be sustained by one of the central banks following a potential default by a Member State to be shared between the central banks of the Member States, in a context in which the scale of those losses would make it necessary to recapitalise that central bank.

However, the ECJ found that question to be inadmissible, as it concerned a problem which was, at that stage, hypothetical.[31] On 5 May 2020 the German Constitutional Tribunal, carrying out an *ultra vires* and identity review, ruled that the PSPP affects German constitutional identity (however, this time Art. 4(2) TEU was not mentioned).[32]

The same view has been expressed, even more explicitly, by the Polish Constitutional Tribunal when in 2010 scrutinised the conformity of the Treaty of Lisbon with the Polish Constitution. After stating that constitutional identity is a concept which determines the scope of excluding – from the competence to confer competences – the matters which constitute the heart of the matter, the Polish Constitutional Tribunal held that 'an equivalent of the concept of constitutional identity in the primary EU law is the concept of national identity' under Art. 4(2) TEU and that 'the constitutional identity remains in a close relation with the concept of national identity, which also includes traditions and culture'.[33]

The Italian Constitutional Court mentioned, at least indirectly, Art. 4(2) TEU in the famous *Taricco* case, between 2017 and 2019.

On the one hand, the referral for a preliminary ruling submitted by the Italian Constitutional Court in 2017 mentioned the Italian supreme values (i.e. counter-limits). In the third question of the referral, the Italian Constitutional Court asked the ECJ whether the *Taricco* judgment should be interpreted as requiring the criminal court to apply Art. 325 TFEU; and to not apply national legislation even where such a disapplication is at variance with the overriding principles of the constitution of the Member State concerned or with the inalienable rights of the individual conferred by its constitution, thus the counter-limits (in that

30 BVerfGE 123, 267, para. 339.
31 Judgment 11 December 2018 in Case 493/17, Weiss and others [2018], paras. 159–167.
32 2 BvR 859/15, 2 BvR 1651/15, 2 BvR 2006/15, 2 BvR 980/16, para 228.
33 Polish Constitutional Tribunal K 32/09, 24 November 2010, para. III.2.1.

controversy, the relevant constitutional principle was that offences and penalties must be defined by laws).

However, it should also be noted that the Italian Constitutional Court acted in a very cooperative way:[34] as someone noted, it simply explained but did not oppose the Italian counter-limits[35] to the ECJ, and it connected the principle of legality with the constitutional traditions common to the Member States under Art. 6(3) TEU, which constitute general principles of the Union's law. As is well known, this is the path that the ECJ then followed in its decision on the preliminary ruling:[36] the ECJ did not make any reference to either national identity nor to Art. 4(2) TUE but, as suggested by the Italian Constitutional Court, it took the principle that offences and penalties must be defined by laws, under the etiquette of 'constitutional traditions common to the Member States'. A path which allowed the ECJ to avoid a clash with the Italian Constitutional Court. I will return to this solution later.[37]

On the other hand, in the 2017 referral mentioned above, the Italian Constitutional Court clearly mentioned the identity clause under Art. 4(2) TEU, although only when setting the scene of its referral.[38] Moreover, in the 2018 judgment subsequent to the ECJ preliminary ruling, although not mentioning Art. 4(2) TEU, the Italian Constitutional Court referred to the principle that offences and penalties must be defined by laws, as part of the Italian 'constitutional identity',[39] when mentioning the re-interpretation of Art. 325 TFEU made by the ECJ in its decision on the preliminary ruling. This choice has been criticised because, once the ECJ decided to follow the cooperative path suggested by the Constitutional Court itself (that of constitutional traditions common to the Member States), mentioning constitutional identity again appeared to be unfair and not dialogue oriented.[40]

In 2016 the Hungarian Constitutional Court, focusing on the *ultra vires* control to be carried out on EU law, expressly mentioned the identity clause under Art. 4(2) TEU as referred to Hungary's constitutional self-identity, highlighting

34 Barbara Guastaferro, '*Derubricare* i conflitti costituzionali per risolverli: sezionando il caso *Taricco*' (2018) *Quaderni costituzionali* 441–461.

35 Antonio Ruggeri, 'Ultimatum della Consulta alla Corte di giustizia su Taricco, in una pronuncia che *espone*, ma non ancora *oppone*, i controlimiti (A margine di Corte cost. n. 24 del 2017)' in Alessandro Bernardi and Cristiano Cupelli (eds), *Il caso* Taricco *e il dialogo tra le Corti. L'ordinanza 24/2017 della Corte costituzionale* (Jovene 2017) 393–404.

36 Judgment 5 December 2017 in Case C-42/17, M.A.S. [2017], para. 53.

37 See Section 5.

38 Corte costituzionale, ord. 26 January 2017, n. 24. This is noted by Roberto Mastroianni, 'La Corte costituzionale si rivolge alla Corte di Giustizia in tema di "controlimiti" costituzionali: è un vero dialogo?' in Bernardi and Cupelli (n 35) 291–295.

39 Corte costituzionale, sent. 3 May 2018, n. 115.

40 Antonio Ruggeri, 'Taricco, amaro finale di partita' (2018) *Consulta online* 494–499 and Federico Fabbrini and Oreste Pollicino, 'Constitutional identity in Italy. Institutional disagreement at a time of political change' in Christian Calliess and Gerhard van der Schyff (eds), *Constitutional Identity in a Europe of Multilevel Constitutionalism* (Cambridge University Press 2020) 213–221.

as examples: freedoms, the division of powers, republic as the form of government, respect of autonomies under public law, the freedom of religion, exercising lawful authority, parliamentarism, the equality of rights, acknowledging judicial power, the protection of the nationalities.[41]

However, such a decision has been strongly criticised by some scholars. On the one hand, because, with regard to the concrete controversy (concerning the quota decision of the European Council based on which some asylum seekers would be located from Greece and Italy to other Member States), there was no fundamental interest of the society to be legitimately protected under the shield of the Hungarian constitutional self-identity; but only the will of the Hungarian government not to have any refugees in Hungary.[42] On the other hand, because the Hungarian constitutional self-identity was shaped by the Hungarian Constitutional Court under an ambiguous concept, namely its historical constitution.[43] An interpretation of the constitutional identity which has been seen as inconsistent with the values under Art. 2 TEU: 'an unconstitutional national constitutional identity', thus, as has been noted.[44]

4 ECJ case-law: a narrower view of the scope of the national identity clause under Art. 4(2) TEU and its application under the principle of proportionality

It is now time to examine the ECJ case-law on the identity clause under Art. 4(2) TEU, so as to show, on the one hand, that its scope is seen in a narrower way by the ECJ; and on the other hand, that the ECJ applies the clause under proportionality test.

The decisions, which have been issued by the ECJ since the entry into force of the Treaty of Lisbon in 2009,[45] can be divided into four types: (i) the ECJ recognised the relevance of an underpinning interest of a Member State, as connected to its national identity under Art. 4(2) TEU; (ii) the ECJ recognised an underpinning interest of a Member State, as connected to its national identity under Art. 4(2) TEU, but denied the relevance of such an interest in the concrete controversy, in the light of a scrutiny of proportionality; (iii) the ECJ stated that no violation of national identity under Art. 4(2) TEU could be actually found in the controversy concerned but it did not explain the reason why, at least in theory, national identity could come to the fore in the fields concerned; (iv) the ECJ, at least implicitly, refused to recognise an underpinning interest of a Member State as connected to its national identity under Art. 4(2) TEU.

41 Hungarian Constitutional Court, Decision 22/2016 (XII. 5.) AB, paras 61–65.

42 Gábor Halmai, 'The Hungarian National(ist) Constitutional Identity' (2017) *Quaderni costituzionali* 1 154.

43 Ibid., 154.

44 Ibid., 154.

45 In detail, until 2014, see Giacomo Di Federico, 'Identifying national identities in the case law of the Court of Justice of the European Union' (2014) *Il Diritto dell'Unione europea* 769–802.

As for the first group of decisions, in recognising the relevance of an underpinning interest of a Member State, as connected to its national identity under Art. 4(2) TEU, it becomes clear that the ECJ's view is narrower than that of Constitutional Courts, when it comes to the scope of the identity clause. However, if one looks at the ECJ case-law, they can infer that the two concepts (national identity and counter-limits) might overlap, although this has never been pointed out by the ECJ.

As has been noted, the reference by the ECJ is more to the preservation of *cultural* elements of national identity,[46] such as 'the status of the State as a Republic',[47] the 'protection and promotion of a language'[48] or 'one or more official languages' of a Member State,[49] the 'institution of [traditional] marriage'.[50]

When the ECJ refers to interests which go beyond cultural elements of national identity, such interests are always strictly 'inherent in the[...] *fundamental structures*, political and constitutional' (emphasis added) of the relevant Member State, as Art. 4(2)TEU literally reads: such as 'the division of competences between the *Länder*' or 'within a Member State',[51] 'the manner in which the transposition [of a directive] was to be achieved' in that Member State (i.e. *via* State's or Autonomous Community's action),[52] 'constitutional self-governance' of Overseas Countries and Territories.[53]

As for the second group of decisions, the ECJ has recognised an underpinning interest of a Member State, as connected to its national identity under Art. 4(2) TEU but denied the relevance of such an interest in the concrete controversy, in the light of a scrutiny of proportionality.

For example, the ECJ admitted that the respect for 'the history, cultural, tradition and national identity' is a legitimate aim under Art. 4(2) TEU but also noted that such an interest could be 'effectively safeguarded otherwise' than by

46 Monica Claes, 'Negotiating constitutional identity or whose identity is it anyway?' in Monica Claes, Maartje de Visser, Patricia Popelier, and Catherine Van De Hening (eds), *Constitutional Conversations in Europe* (Intersentia 2012) 229.

47 Judgment 22 December 2010 in Case C-208/09, Sayn-Wittgenstein [2010], para. 92 and Judgment 2 June 2016 in Case C-438/14, Bogendorff [2016], para. 73.

48 Judgment 11 May 2011 in Case C-391/09, Runevič-Vardyn [2011], para. 85.

49 Judgment 16 April 2013 in Case C-202/11, Anton Las [2013], para. 26.

50 Judgment 5 June 2018 in Case C-673/16, Coman [2018], paras. 45–46.

51 Judgment 12 June 2014 in Case C-156/13, Digibet [2014], para. 34 and Judgment 21 December 2016 in Case C-51/15, Remondis [2016], para. 40.

52 Judgment 24 October 2013 in Case C-151/12, *Commission v. Kingdom of Spain* [2013], para. 37.

53 Judgment 31 October 2019, in Case C-391/17, *Commission v. United Kingdom of Great Britain and Northern Ireland* [2019], para. 91 and Judgment 31 October 2019, in Case C-395/17, *Commission v. Kingdom of the Netherlands* [2019], para. 93. However, the ECJ did not accept the argument, relating to the OCT's constitutional self-governance (concerning, respectively Anguilla's, on the one hand, and Curaçao's and Aruba's, on the other hand), in so far as the two Member States do not 'state how the liability of a Member State for the actions of its OCTs, which is without prejudice to the tasks entrusted to them by the OCT Decision, could undermine their self-governance'.

imposing a nationality condition for access to profession of civil-law notary.[54] In other words, the measure issued by the Member State was found by the ECJ as disproportionate to the aim achieved.

It is interesting to note that the same argument has been recently used by Poland and Hungary to argue that Art. 4(2) TEU entitled them to disapply the 2015 Relocation Decisions, in order to ensure social and cultural cohesion, as well as to avoid potential ethnic and religious conflicts, which the relocation of applicants for international protection in their territories would provoke. In her Opinion on 31 October 2019 the Advocate General at the ECJ rejected this argument and noted that the 'Member States' legitimate interest in preserving social and cultural cohesion may be safeguarded effectively by other and less restrictive means than a unilateral and complete refusal to fulfil their obligations under EU law'.[55] The ECJ basically agreed with the Advocate General on this point.[56]

In another controversy, even if *not explicitly*, the ECJ recognised also the competitive selection process (as the general rule for the entry of a citizen in the civil service) as part of the national identity under Art. 4(2) TEU. Once again, the ECJ, in applying that article, balanced it with other values: it stated that 'that provision cannot be interpreted so as to deprive a worker of the protection granted to [them] by the Union law in force in that area'.[57]

As for the third group of decisions, the ECJ stated that no violation of national identity under Art. 4(2) TEU could actually be found in those controversies. However, it did not explain the reason why, at least in theory, national identity could come to the fore in those fields.

For example, the ECJ stated that EU law on fixed-term works could not affect the fundamental structure of Member States, as the EU law gives to them the discretionary power of regulating the public sector in a different way from in the private sector.[58] In another controversy, the ECJ argued that the application to the Judiciary of the European law concerning part-time workers could not affect national identity of the Member State, because the aim of EU law is merely the extension to judges of the scope of the principle of equal treatment and their protection against discrimination as compared with full-time workers.[59]

However, as said, the ECJ did not explain why national identity could be relevant and what national identity would mean in those fields. Someone noted that the principle of the impartiality of Public Administration and the principle

54 Judgment 24 May 2011 in Case C-51/08, *Commission v. Grand Duchy of Luxembourg* [2011], para. 124.

55 Opinion of Advocate General 31 October 2019 in Case C-715/17, C-718/17 and C-719/17, *Commission v. Republic of Poland, Republic of Hungary and Czech Republic*, para. 227.

56 Judgment 2 April 2020 in Case C-715/17, C-718/17 and C-719/17, *Commission v. Republic of Poland, Republic of Hungary and Czech Republic*, para. 170.

57 Judgment 13 June 2019 in Case C-317/18, Correia Moreira [2019], paras 61–62.

58 Judgment 1 October 2010 in Case C-3/10, Affatato [2010], paras 40–41.

59 Judgment 1 March 2012 in Case C-393/10, O'Brien [2012], para. 49.

of independence of the Judiciary should be respectively considered as the values underpinning national identity in those two decisions.[60]

As for the fourth group of decisions, the ECJ has implicitly refused to recognise an underpinning interest of a Member State as connected to its national identity under Art. 4(2) TEU.

That was the case of a Member State (Slovak Republic) that assumed the protection of its sovereignty (when prohibiting the entry to its territory of the then Hungarian President of the Republic) as an interest to be protected under the identity clause.[61] The ECJ noted that Art. 21 TFEU did not oblige the Slovak Republic to guarantee access to its territory to the President of Hungary: the fact that a Union citizen performs the duties of a Head of State is such as to justify a limitation, based on international law, on the exercise of the right of free movement conferred on that person by Art. 21 TFEU.[62] Such an argument allowed the ECJ not to deal expressly with the nature of the protection of sovereignty, whether it could be considered as part of national identity under Art. 4(2) TEU or not.

In another case, a Member State used the argument of Art. 4(2) TEU in an action for annulment of a directive on control of weapons: the prohibition of the possession of certain semi-automatic firearms was seen by the State not in compliance with Art. 4(2) TEU, 'pursuant to which Member States are solely responsible for national security in their territory and must have the possibility of maintaining law and order in that territory'.[63]

It seems that in these two judgments the ECJ has implicitly refused to recognise the protection of sovereignty as such, as an interest to be protected under the identity clause.[64]

All that said, although the ECJ developed its view concerning Art. 4(2) TEU on a case-based approach and without *explicitly* stating that national identity is something different from the counter-limits, although an overlap is always possible,[65] the conclusion which could be drawn from this analysis is the following.

First, as for the scope of the identity clause, the ECJ's view is narrower than that of the Constitutional Courts, as it tends to include under Art. 4(2) TEU mainly those interests which are connected with the protection of *cultural* elements of national identity[66] and, when it goes beyond that, only those interests

60 Giacomo Di Federico, 'Il ruolo dell'art. 4, par. 2, TUE nella soluzione dei conflitti interordinamentali' (2019) *Quaderni costituzionali* 342–343.

61 Judgment 16 October 2012 in Case C-364/10, *Hungary v. Slovak Republic* [2012], para. 35.

62 Ibid., para. 51.

63 Judgment 3 December 2019 in Case C-482/17, Action of annulment brought by the Czech Republic [2019], para. 23.

64 On constitutional identity as 'an alternative to holistic sovereignty', see Martin Belov, 'The Functions of Constitutional Identity Performed in the Context of Constitutionalization of the EU Order and Europeanization of the Legal Orders of EU Member States' (2017) *Perspective on Federalism* 9 74–75 and 81–86.

65 Di Federico (n 60) 343–344.

66 Claes (n 46) 229. See also Barbara Guastaferro, 'Beyond the *exceptionalism* of constitutional conflicts: the *Ordinary* Functions of the Identity Clause' (2012) *Yearbook of European Law* 31 311.

which are connected with the protection of *fundamental structures*, political and constitutional, of Member States.[67] After all, Art. 4(2) TEU does not refer to *constitutional* identity but to *national* identity.[68]

It remains open as to whether national identity should be something which differentiates Member States from one another[69] and, thus, does not overlap with constitutional traditions common to the Member States.[70] Surely, most of the interests which have been explicitly considered by the ECJ as part of national identity (such as the status of the State as a Republic, the protection and promotion of a specific official language or the institution of traditional marriage) are shared by *some* Member States but are not common to all of them.

Second, when the ECJ recognises an underpinning interest of a Member State, as connected to its national identity under Art. 4(2) TEU, it applies this article under a proportionality test.[71]

Third, sovereignty, as such, has been (at least implicitly) excluded by the ECJ from the scope of the national identity clause.[72]

On the contrary, as seen above,[73] when it comes to Art. 4(2) TEU, Constitutional Courts tend to see national identity as the inviolable core of their domestic constitution. Moreover, they never mention techniques of balancing this core with EU norms.

Obviously, national identity (under Art. 4(2) TEU) and constitutional identity (as counter-limits) can partially overlap. However, as has been noted, Art. 4(2) TEU 'should *not* be read as intending to allow the national (constitutional) court to unilaterally refuse to apply EU law, on the grounds that they are protecting national constitutional identity'.[74] In other words, Constitutional Courts cannot rely upon Art. 4(2) TEU in order to state the protection of counter-limits domestically.[75]

5 The principle of sincere cooperation revised (also in the light of the *Taricco* case)

Many scholars have underlined the role that can be played against this background by the principle of sincere cooperation under Art. 4(3) TEU. It has been

67 Von Bogdandy and Schill (n 8) 1430–1431.

68 Elke Cloots, *National Identity in EU Law* (Oxford University Press 2015) 166. In general, on the distinction between constitutional and national identity, see Rosenfeld (n 1) 10–12, 18, 73–75 and 100 and Jacobsohn (n 1) 8–10.

69 Leonard F M Besselink, *A Composite European Constitution* (Europa Law Publishing 2007).

70 Leonard F M Besselink, 'National and constitutional identity before and after Lisbon' (2010) *Utrecht Law Review* 47.

71 Von Bogdandy and Schill (n 8) 1441–1442. Critically Simona Polimeni, *Controlimiti e identità costituzionale nazionale. Contributo per una ricostruzione del "dialogo" tra le Corti* (Editoriale scientifica 2018) 252–256.

72 Von Bogdandy and Schill (n 8) 1425.

73 See Section 3.

74 Claes (n 46) 221.

75 Guastaferro (n 66) 310–311.

noted that the ECJ and Constitutional Courts can be viewed 'as complimentary parts of European composite constitutional adjudication [that] requires strategies of mutual conflict prevention by both the ECJ and the domestic constitutional courts'.[76]

Such a mutual cooperation has been essentially shaped by scholars as follows. On the one hand, the ECJ cannot determine the content of a Member State's national identity itself. On the other hand, as Art. 4(2) TEU is subject to the interpretation and control of the ECJ, the Court is not bound by the views of a domestic Constitutional Court on the effect the invocation of national identity should have.[77] In other words, someone described this as a 'mirroring mechanism';[78] others underlined that the State has an absolute monopoly over the definition of national identity (the 'what'), whereas the power to determine the compatibility of legitimate interests with EU obligations (the 'how') is vested in the ECJ.[79]

I, personally, do agree with these views.[80] However, I would try to focus on the role which can be played in this context by a principle of sincere cooperation revised.

In the light of what has been noted above, that is national identity (under Art. 4(2) TEU) and constitutional identity (as counter-limits) *cannot be*[81] and *are not seen* by the ECJ[82] as the same, although they can partially overlap, the principle of sincere cooperation under Art. 4(3) TEU should be interpreted as follows. As for Member States, they should do their best not to bring under the etiquette of 'national identity', interests that they consider counter-limits but fall outside the scope of 'national identity' under Art. 4(2) TEU, as narrowly framed by the ECJ. In other words, as already noted above,[83] Constitutional Courts should not rely upon Art. 4(2) TEU in order to state the protection of counter-limits domestically.

Beside this, Member States should do their best to see whether a principle they consider as part of their counter-limits, could be also found in EU constitutional law (e.g. in the CFREU) or could be brought under the etiquette of 'constitutional traditions common to the Member States'.[84] Such a choice would also get

76 Von Bogdandy and Schill (n 8) 1447–1448.

77 Ibid., 1448. See also Besselink (n 70) 45, Pedrazza Gorlero (n 7) 20–24, Cloots (n 68) 146 and Di Federico (n 60) 350. See also Pietro Faraguna, 'Constitutional identity in the EU – a shield or a sword?' (2017) *German Law Journal* 18 1637.

78 Claes (n. 46) 221.

79 Theodore Konstadinides, 'Constitutional identity as a shield and as a sword: the European legal order within the framework of national constitutional settlement' (2011) *Cambridge Yearbook of European Legal Studies* 13 216.

80 E. Albanesi, *Pluralismo costituzionale e procedura d'infrazione dell'Unione europea* (Giappichelli 2018) 87.

81 See Section 2.

82 See Section 4.

83 See Section 4.

84 As has been noted, 'the overwhelming majority of the cases where constitutional identity is at stake do not involve specific characters of a single Member State constitutional tradition. On the contrary, constitutional identity is often called into question in connection with fundamental

the ECJ off the hook, if the issue was brought before it: thus, the ECJ would not be obliged to deal with counter-limits (which, as such, are not of its competences under Art. 4(2) TEU) and would not be obliged to declare that those interests cannot be brought within the scope of national identity under Art. 4(2) TEU, in its narrow sense. Moreover, this would allow the ECJ to make a balance between EU provisions (once again, one should bear in mind that constitutional traditions common to the Member States constitute general principles of *the Union's law*) and avoid a clash. Clearly, this will be the fruit of the judicial dialogue with the Member State concerned.[85]

In the *Taricco* case the Italian Constitutional Court followed this path only partially. As already mentioned above,[86] on the one hand, it mentioned the Italian supreme values, i.e. counter-limits: in the third question of the referral, the Italian Constitutional Court asked to the ECJ whether the *Taricco* judgment should be applied even where such an application is at variance with them. Although only when setting the scene of its referral, it also mentioned Art. 4(2) TEU. However, the EJC could not answer that question (and it did not) because, as already said, counter-limits are not of its competences under Art. 4(2) TEU. In any case, in the *Taricco* case the interest mentioned by the Italian Constitutional Court (i.e. the principle that offences and penalties must be defined by laws) fell outside the scope of national identity under Art. 4(2) TEU, in its narrow sense, which emerges from ECJ case-law.

On the other hand, very wisely, the Italian Constitutional Court did its best to interpret the interest concerned from the perspective of constitutional traditions common to the Member States and show this path to the ECJ. This allowed the ECJ to balance different EU provisions (the original *Taricco* rule and constitutional traditions common to the Member States, as general principles of the Union's law) and thus avoid a conflict.

From the perspective which has been held here, the first part of the Italian Constitutional Court's legal reasoning (i.e. mentioning counter-limits before the ECJ and invoking Art. 4(2) TEU out of turn) was not in compliance with the principle of sincere cooperation; on the contrary, the second part (i.e. doing its best to connect the interest concerned to constitutional traditions common to the Member States) was.

As for the ECJ, as already said, it should do its best to consider as national identity only the interests that Member States point out as such. However, Member States would be helped in doing so, only if the ECJ framed the narrow

principles [...] that are deeply rooted in the European tradition of constitutionalism'. Therefore, 'a substantial agreement seems to emerge when a bundle of constitutional principles [...] are considered'. See Faraguna (n 77) 1638–1639.

85 'Nonetheless, once one focuses on concrete constitutional questions connected to the application of these principles, disagreements emerge again. In these cases, the so-called judicial dialogue is not only useful, but also necessary'. See Faraguna (n 77) 1639.

86 See Section 3.

concept of national identity under Art. 4(2) TEU in a clearer way, as already seen above,[87] than it has so far done.[88]

6 Conclusions: an unavoidable lacuna

As demonstrated here, in the light of the principle of sincere cooperation, on the one hand, Member States should refrain from bringing under the etiquette of 'national identity' interests that they consider counter-limits but fall outside the scope of 'national identity' under Art. 4(2) TEU, as narrowly framed by the ECJ. They should also do their best to check whether a principle they consider as a part of their counter-limits, could be also found in EU constitutional law (e.g. in the CFREU) or could be brought under the etiquette of 'constitutional traditions common to the Member States'. This would allow the ECJ to strike a balance between various EU provisions (namely, EU constitutional law or constitutional traditions common to the Member States) so avoiding a clash.

It is worth noting that the Italian Constitutional Court in 2019, in its first referral for a preliminary ruling[89] after the conclusion of the *Taricco* case, acted in a very cooperative way.[90] First, just because, as in the *Taricco case*, it referred for a preliminary ruling. Second, it did not mention Art. 4(2) TEU but it took the interest at stake (the right to silence, as a corollary of the right of defence) under the etiquette of 'constitutional traditions common to the Member States', other than the CFREU and the European Convention on Human Rights.[91] However, once again according to its view, it did not lose the opportunity also to point out that the right to silence (as a corollary to the right of defence), being a fundamental right, is typical of the Italian constitutional identity.[92]

On the other hand, the ECJ should frame the narrow concept of national identity under Art. 4(2) TEU in a clearer way than it has done so far: this would help Member States in pointing out the interests which fall within the scope of national identity under Art. 4(2) TEU, in its narrow sense.

The risk of a clash still exists, though,[93] but such a lacuna in the relationships between the EU and Member States is unavoidable because, as demonstrated here, from a theoretical perspective the legal nature of the identity clause and

87 See Section 4 and Di Federico (n 60) 343–344. See also Anita Schnettger, 'Article 4(2) TEU as a Vehicle for National Constitutional Identity in the Shared European Legal System' in Calliess and van der Schyff (n 40) 10 and 35–36 who noted that the ECJ did not put forward a clear directive regarding the interpretation and application of Art. 4(2) TEU.

88 Against this view, Pietro Faraguna, 'Taking constitutional identities away from the courts' (2016) *Brooklyn Journal of International Law* 41 521.

89 See Case C-481/19.

90 Enrico Albanesi, 'Che cosa il caso *Taricco* ha insegnato alla Corte costituzionale. Un nuovo rinvio pregiudiziale a fronte dei controlimiti' (2020) *Giurisprudenza costituzionale* 1 425–444.

91 See Corte costituzionale, ord. 10 May 2019, n. 117, para. 10.2 *Considerato in diritto*.

92 See Corte costituzionale, ord. 10 May 2019, n. 117, para. 7.1 *Considerato in diritto*.

93 As has been noted, optimistically, by von Bogdandy and Schill (n 8) 1449 and, pessimistically, by Martinico (n 5) 94.

counter-limits is different.[94] When an interest can be connected neither with EU constitutional law/constitutional traditions common to Member States, nor with national identity under Art. 4(2) TEU, in its narrow sense, Member States could still domestically consider EU law to not be in compliance with their counter-limits.

However, the principle of sincere cooperation revised should reduce to the bare minimum the risk of a clash between the EU and its Member States when it comes to national identity and counter-limits.

References

Enrico Albanesi, *Pluralismo costituzionale e procedura d'infrazione dell'Unione europea* (Giappichelli 2018).

Enrico Albanesi, 'The use of the EU infringement procedures to protect *de facto* the rule of law via the development of the parameter: from obligations under the Treaties to the Charter of Fundamental Rights' in Martin Belov (ed.), *Courts, Politics and Constitutional Law. Judicialization of Politics and Politicization of the Judiciary* (Routledge 2020) 228–246.

Enrico Albanesi, 'Che cosa il caso *Taricco* ha insegnato alla Corte costituzionale. Un nuovo rinvio pregiudiziale a fronte dei controlimiti' (2020) *Giurisprudenza costituzionale* 1 425–444.

Richard Albert, *Constitutional Amendments. Making, Breaking, and Changing Constitutions* (Oxford University Press 2019).

Matej Avbelj and Jan Komárek (eds), *Constitutional Pluralism in the European Union and Beyond* (Hart 2012).

Paolo Barile, *Scritti di diritto costituzionale* (Cedam 1967) 701–720.

Martin Belov (ed), 'The functions of constitutional identity performed in the context of constitutionalization of the EU order and Europeanization of the legal orders of EU member States' (2017) *Perspective on Federalism* 9 72–97.

Martin Belov (ed), *Courts, Politics and Constitutional Law. Judicialization of Politics and Politicization of the Judiciary* (Routledge 2020).

Alessandro Bernardi and Cristiano Cupelli (eds), *Il caso* Taricco *e il dialogo tra le Corti. L'ordinanza 24/2017 della Corte costituzionale* (Jovene 2017).

Leonard F M Besselink, *A Composite European Constitution* (Europa Law Publishing 2007).

Leonard F M Besselink, 'National and constitutional identity before and after Lisbon' (2010) *Utrecht Law Review* 36–49.

Hermann-Josef Blanke and Stelio Mangiameli (eds), *The European Union after Lisbon. Constitutional Basis, Economic Order and External Action* (Springer Verlag 2012).

Christian Calliess and Gerhard van der Schyff (eds), *Constitutional Identity in a Europe of Multilevel Constitutionalism* (Cambridge University Press 2020).

Monica Claes, 'Negotiating constitutional identity or whose identity is it anyway?' in Monica Claes, Maartje de Visser, Patricia Popelier and Catherine Van de Hening (eds), *Constitutional Conversations in Europe* (Intersentia 2012) 205–233.

Monica Claes, Maartje de Visser, Patricia Popelier and Catherine Van de Hening (eds), *Constitutional Conversations in Europe* (Intersentia 2012).

94 See Section 2.

Elke Cloots, *National Identity in EU Law* (Oxford University Press 2015).

Pasquale Costanzo, Luca Mezzetti and Antonio Ruggeri, *Lineamenti di diritto costituzionale dell'Unione europea* (Giappichelli 2019).

Barbara Guastaferro, 'Beyond the *exceptionalism* of constitutional conflicts: the *Ordinary* functions of the identity clause' (2012) *Yearbook of European Law* 31 263–318.

Barbara Guastaferro, '*Derubricare* i conflitti costituzionali per risolverli: sezionando il caso *Taricco*' (2018) *Quaderni costituzionali* 441–61.

Giacomo Di Federico, 'Identifying national identities in the case law of the Court of Justice of the European Union' (2014) *Il Diritto dell'Unione europea* 769–802.

Giacomo Di Federico, 'Il ruolo dell'art. 4, par. 2, TUE nella soluzione dei conflitti interordinamentali' (2019) *Quaderni costituzionali* 333–356.

Willem T Eijsbouts and Leonard F M Besselink, '"The Law of Laws" – Overcoming Pluralism' (2008) *European Constitutional Law Review* 395–398.

Federico Fabbrini and Oreste Pollicino, 'Constitutional identity in Italy. Institutional disagreement at a time of political change' in Christian Calliess and Gerhard van der Schyff (eds), *Constitutional Identity in a Europe of Multilevel Constitutionalism* (Cambridge University Press 2020) 201–221.

Pietro Faraguna, *Ai confini della Costituzione. Principi supremi e identità costituzionale* (FrancoAngeli 2015).

Pietro Faraguna, 'Taking constitutional identities away from the courts' (2016) *Brooklyn Journal of International Law* 41 491–578.

Pietro Faraguna, 'Constitutional identity in the EU – a shield or a sword?' (2017) *German Law Journal* 18 1617–1640.

Giovanni Guzzetta, *La contaminazione costituzionale del diritto europeo. Interrogativi su un ordinamento in divenire* (Giappichelli 2015).

Gábor Halmai, 'The Hungarian national(ist) constitutional identity' (2017) *Quaderni costituzionali* 1 151–154.

Herbert L A Hart, *The Concept of Law* (3rd edn, Oxford University Press 2012).

Gary J Jacobsohn, *Constitutional Identity* (Harvard University Press 2010).

Klemen Jaklic, *Constitutional Pluralism in the EU* (Oxford University Press 2014).

Theodore Konstadinides, 'Constitutional identity as a shield and as a sword: the European legal order within the framework of national constitutional settlement' (2011) *Cambridge Yearbook of European Legal Studies* 13 195–218.

Doreen Lustig and Joseph H Weiler, 'Judicial review in the contemporary world – retrospective and prospective' (2018) *I•CON* 16 315–172.

Miguel P Maduro, 'Contrapunctual law: Europe's constitutional pluralism in action' in Neil Walker (ed), *Sovereignty in Transition* (Hart 2003) 501–537.

Neil MacCormick, 'Beyond the sovereign state' (1993) *The Modern Law Review* 56 1–18.

Neil MacCormick, *Questioning Sovereignty. Law, State, and Nation in the European Commonwealth* (Oxford University Press 1999).

Stelio Mangiameli, 'The union's homogeneity and its common values in the treaty of the European Union' in Hermann-Josef Blanke and Stelio Mangiameli (eds), *The European Union after Lisbon. Constitutional Basis, Economic Order and External Action* (Springer/Verlag 2012) 21–46.

Giuseppe Martinico, *The Tangled Complexity of the EU Constitutional Process. The Frustrating Knot of Europe* (Routledge 2013).

Roberto Mastroianni, 'La Corte costituzionale si rivolge alla Corte di Giustizia in tema di "controlimiti" costituzionali: è un vero dialogo?' in Alessandro Bernardi and Cristiano Cupelli (eds), *Il caso* Taricco *e il dialogo tra le Corti. L'ordinanza 24/2017 della Corte costituzionale* (Jovene 2017) 291–95.

Maurizio Pedrazza Gorlero (ed), *Corti costituzionali e Corti europee dopo il Trattato di Lisbona* (Edizioni scientifiche italiane 2010).

Maurizio Pedrazza Gorlero, 'Alla ricerca della forma "condizionante". Introduzione ai rapporti fra Corti costituzionali nazionali e Corti Europee dopo il Trattato di Lisbona' in Maurizio Pedrazza Gorlero (ed.), *Corti costituzionali e Corti europee dopo il Trattato di Lisbona* (Edizioni scientifiche italiane 2010) 1–24.

Simona Polimeni, *Controlimiti e identità costituzionale nazionale. Contributo per una ricostruzione del "dialogo" tra le Corti* (Editoriale scientifica 2018).

Oreste Pollicino, *Allargamento dell'Europa a est e rapporti tra Corti costituzionali e Corti europee. Verso una teoria generale dell'impatto interordinamentale del diritto sovranazionale?* (Giuffrè 2010).

Michel Rosenfeld, *The Identity of the Constitutional Subject. Selfhood, Citizenship, Culture, and Community* (Routledge 2010).

Yaniv Roznai, *Unconstitutional Constitutional Amendments. The Limits of Amendment Powers* (Oxford University Press 2019).

Yianiv Roznai and Gary J Jacobsohn, *Constitutional Revolution* (Yale University Press 2020).

Antonio Ruggeri, 'Dimensione europea della tutela dei diritti fondamentali e tecniche interpretative' (2010) *Il diritto dell'Unione europea* 125–147.

Antonio Ruggeri, 'Primato del diritto sovranazionale *versus* identità costituzionale? (Alla ricerca dell'araba fenice costituzionale: i "controlimiti")' (2016) *Lo Stato* 47–69.

Antonio Ruggeri, 'Ultimatum della Consulta alla Corte di giustizia su Taricco, in una pronuncia che *espone*, ma non ancora *oppone*, i controlimiti (A margine di Corte cost. n. 24 del 2017)' in Alessandro Bernardi and Cristiano Cupelli (eds), *Il caso* Taricco *e il dialogo tra le Corti. L'ordinanza 24/2017 della Corte costituzionale* (Jovene 2017) 393–404.

Antonio Ruggeri, 'Taricco, amaro finale di partita' (2018) *Consulta online* 494–499.

Antonio Ruggeri, 'Le fonti del diritto europunitario ed i loro rapporti con le fonti nazionali' in Pasquale Costanzo, Luca Mezzetti and Antonio Ruggeri, *Lineamenti di diritto costituzionale dell'Unione europea* (Giappichelli 2019) 274–332.

Anita Schnettger, 'Article 4(2) TEU as a vehicle for national constitutional identity in the shared European legal system' in Christian Calliess and Gerhard van der Schyff (eds), *Constitutional Identity in a Europe of Multilevel Constitutionalism* (Cambridge University Press 2020) 9–37.

Armin von Bogdandy and Stephan Schill, 'Overcoming absolute primacy: respect for national identity under the Lisbon Treaty' (2011) *Common Market Law Review* 4 1417–1453.

Neil Walker, 'The idea of constitutional pluralism' (2002) *The Modern Law Review* 65 317–359.

Part III

Peace, order, and disorder in composite societies

National, ethnocentric, and religious factors for peace or discontent

6 Building order in age of revolutions

A transnational history of constitution making: 1787–1867

Víctor Manuel Cázares Lira

1 Introduction

Constitutions have always enjoyed a highly regarded place in both contemporary politics and liberal political thought. Traditionally, constitutions have been put on a pedestal as the protectors of the ideals of law and justice beyond the reach of ordinary politics. Considering the increasing aversion towards traditional politics and the rise of populism around the world, constitutional government has become the last institutional resort for tackling complex social and economic issues. Constitutions are widely seen as impartial mechanisms for processing conflicts and securing individual rights; they embody the very essence of the rule of law, register noble national aspirations, and stand like certificates of good political behaviour in the international arena. Also, constitutions have been thought of as legal devices aiming to represent people's values, to organise political institutions, to set limits to governments and to enshrine rights for citizens.[1] Finally, constitutions often appear as the standard recipe for establishing democracy, peace, and justice around the world.[2] In fact, the idea of constitutionalism has been constantly regarded as a synonym for democratic government.[3]

The expanding reputation of constitutionalism, however, has often come in tandem with great disappointments and greater conceptual ambiguity. Lurking behind the diagnosis of the maladies of contemporary constitutional democracies there is a sense that current democratic governments have been overwhelmed with increasing problems and new tasks, while lacking state capacities to tackle them effectively.[4] Constitutional democracies, a leading constitu-

1 Dario Castiglione, 'The Political Theory of the Constitution' in Richard Bellamy and Dario Castiglione (eds), *Constitutionalism in Transformation: European and Theoretical Perspectives* (Blackwell 1996) 5–23.

2 Christine Bell, 'Introduction: Bargaining on constitutions: Political Settlements and Constitutional State-building' (2017) 6 *Global Constitutionalism* 13, Walter F. Murphy, *Constitutional Democracy: Creating and Maintaining a Just Political Order* (Johns Hopkins University Press 2007).

3 Richard Bellamy (ed), *Constitutionalism and Democracy* (Routledge 2016).

4 Mark A. Graber, Sanford Levinson and Mark Tushnet (eds), *Constitutional Democracy in Crisis?* (Oxford University Press 2018).

tional scholar has argued, worked better in polities with lower populations, less cultural diversity and less complicated histories.[5] One of the aims of this chapter is to show that constitutionalism, even in its early years, has always faced similar problems concerning the governance of diverse polities, but it also seeks to address conceptual problems related to the centrality of democracy in our political discourse. As the political scientist Jens Bartelson has pointed out, the more central and important a concept becomes, the more meanings it acquires, rendering it less intelligible and turning conceptual analysis into a political battleground.[6] As the political scientist Giovanni Sartori put it, the failure of constitutions often stems from problems in constitutional theory.[7] It is precisely in how we think about constitutions that the rollercoaster of illusions and delusions begins. In a way, the more we reaffirm the value of constitutions as the embodiment of social aspirations and individual rights, the less we can see the full range of things that constitutions have been done in history. In a nutshell, this chapter explores an everlasting problem in thinking about constitutions as tools for liberalism that has cast a long shadow over how they have been instruments for imperialism.

Today, the idea of a constitution presupposes the core principles of liberalism, denoting a normative program for designing governments with limited powers along with a sacred list of universal individual rights. Thus, constitutionalism has been deeply fused with liberalism and democracy.[8] The origins of this combination between natural law theory and written constitutions are often traced back to Philadelphia in 1787. Sartori argued that the very concept of a constitution changed after the adoption of the US Constitution, acquiring its modern connotation as a tool for the protection of liberty instead of being a mere description of the organisation of government. As a legal scholar recently put it, the US Constitution of 1787 marked the beginnings of classical liberal constitutionalism in America.[9]

Based on the latest scholarship on the field of Early American History, this chapter compares and reviews the failures and successes of different constitutional designs in the Americas and Europe as a way of grasping what constitutions have done in terms of internal security and territorial expansion. Also, this chapter touches upon the relevance of constitutional design for explaining political development in Latin America during the nineteenth century. This has been an eternal puzzle since, in theory, most of the sister republics in South America tried to replicate parts of the US constitutional model without success.[10]

5 Martin Loughlin, 'The Contemporary Crisis of Constitutional Democracy' (2019) 29 *Oxford Journal of Legal Studies* 435, 439.

6 Jens Bartelson, *A Genealogy of Sovereignty* (Cambridge University Press 1995) 49.

7 Giovanni Sartori, *Comparative Constitutional Engineering: An Inquiry into Structures, Incentives and Outcomes* (Macmillan 1994) 199.

8 Russell Harding, *Liberalism, Constitutionalism and Democracy* (Oxford University Press 1999).

9 Richard A. Epstein, *The Classical Liberal Constitution: The Uncertain Quest for Limited Government* (Harvard University Press 2014).

10 Caitlin Fitz, *Our Sister Republics: The United States in an Age of American Revolutions* (Norton 2016).

In this regard, the constitutional experience of Mexico is relevant because since its independence, its intellectual and political elite adopted an unwavering liberal program aiming to achieve the progress they saw in the US political system.[11]

Yet, as this chapter will show, the US Constitution was less concerned with liberalism than with forging a government able to compete with European empires in the international arena. Firstly, I unpack key works and ideas shaping the contemporary studies on the American Revolution and the US Constitution, explaining the relevance of the concept of empire for understanding the period. Then, I analyse the failure of the Confederate constitutional project and the relevance of the US Civil War for the constitutional history of Canada. Then I explore briefly the emergence and development of constitutionalism in Europe by comparing and analysing the cases of Switzerland and Belgium. Finally, I explore the constitutional history of Mexico during the nineteenth century.

2 The independence of the United States of America

The collapse of European empires in the Americas came along with a vast process of redistribution and reorganisation of political power that, far from embracing democracy, tried to recompose the former imperial methods for the new sovereign states which often aimed to expand and control new territories and indigenous peoples.[12] The rise of written constitutions took place in the context of restructuring social and political relations between provinces, native peoples, economic groups, and former imperial authorities.[13] 'Enthusiasm for employing new written constitutions as engines of improvement and enhanced rights', asserted historian Linda Colley, 'could easily become entangled with the ambition to deploy these instruments in order to manage, shape and even invade others'.[14] In fact, the leaders of the American Revolution faced an overwhelming dilemma because the lofty ideological aspirations that guided their revolt against the British Empire were at odds with the kind of structure of power they needed to survive in an adverse geopolitical environment. 'The paradox of that the new republic', historian J. G. A. Pocock noted, 'born of the revolt against empire, had a commitment to empire – and to empire of settlement – built into its structure'.[15]

11 Jaime E. Rodríguez O (ed), *The Divine Charter: Constitutionalism and Liberalism in Nineteenth-Century Mexico* (Rowman and Littlefield 2005); Charles A. Hale, *The Transformation of Liberalism in Late Nineteenth-Century Mexico* (Princeton University Press 1989).

12 Jeremy Adelman, 'An Age of Imperial Revolutions' (2008) 13 *The American Historical Review* 319.

13 Lauren Benton, 'Constitutions and Empires'; (2006) 31 *Law and Social Inquiry* 473; Bartolomé Clavero, 'Constitucionalismo y colonialismo en las américas: el paradigma perdido en la historia constitucional' (2017) 53 *Revista de historia del derecho* 23.

14 Linda Colley, 'Empires of Writing: Britain, America and Constitutions, 1776–1848' (2014) 23 *Law and History Review* 237, 254.

15 J. G. A. Pocock, *Virtue, Commerce and History* (Cambridge University Press 1985) 86.

Although the concept of empire often conveys negative connotations, it has become an analytical alternative to the idea of nation-state that allows scholars to look at the different ways of governing large territories comprised of different peoples and regions.[16] Unlike the concept of nation that often leads us to think of law, power, and society as homogenous entities, the idea of empire provides wider lenses to look at the many ways political authority is exercised across different territories, over several societies, and through a multiplicity of laws. The imperial rule was not predicated on a horizontal and totalitarian government but grounded on allowing and creating different degrees of sovereignty and different spheres of autonomy, thus making uneven polities which liberal elites across the globe would try hard to transform into states connected by a common culture and single markets.[17] Indeed, while liberal constitutionalism has been focused on the relations between the state and individuals, imperial constitutionalism looks now at the many forms of relations among groups, regions and peoples. Although constitutionalism and imperialism look like incompatible concepts in theory, in practice the connections between both were closer than previously assumed and were part of a global process of reordering the world.[18]

Initially, the early American state endured several hurdles and obstacles in its forging of a stable government. French diplomats looked at the United States 'like the small nations of Europe, as an object to be manipulated to their own ends'.[19] Before the ink of the Declaration of Independence could dry, the revolutionary leaders discovered its perils. Just as Latin America would experience in the post-independence period, the new nation underwent hyperinflation, devaluation, fiscal problems, debt crises, and commercial conflicts among its regions. The economic prosperity they associated with free trade did not yield results and the many attempts to regulate the markets were not enough to stabilise the economy.[20] Most economic problems emerged from a lack of institutional tools to harmonise fiscal and monetary policies. To tackle the situation, many states tried to stop issuing paper money, to privatise the monetary policies, and to apply harsh tax collection measures, but such methods only deepened the crisis causing widespread popular revolts which eventually forced local politicians to adopt

16 James Muldoon, *Empire and Order: The Concept of Empire, 800–1800* (Macmillan 1999) 138.

17 Anthony Pagden, *Lords of all the World: Ideologies of Empire in Spain, Britain and France c.1500–c.1800* (Yale University Press 1995) 178–200; Duncan Bell, *Reordering the World* (Princeton University Press 2016); C. A. Bayly, *The Birth of the Modern World, 1870–1914: Global Connections and Comparisons* (Blackwell 2004) 247–283.

18 Jennifer Pitts, 'Political Theory of Empire and Imperialism', in Sankar Muthu (ed.), *Empire and Modern Political Thought* (Cambridge University Press 2012); Lauren Benton and Lisa Ford, *Rage for Order: the British Empire and the Origins of International Law, 1800–1850* (Harvard University Press 2016).

19 George Herring, *From Colony to Superpower: U.S. Foreign Relations since 1776* (Oxford University Press 2008) 21.

20 Cathy D. Matson and Peter Onuf, *A Union of Interests: Political Economic Thought in Revolutionary America* (University Press of Kansas, 1990) 31–49.

a more flexible approach, thus angering national and international creditors.[21] Remarkably, the scenario in Latin America was rather similar: weak states failed to levy taxes and to tame popular revolts or local magnates.[22] Thus, the political elites in Latin America and the United States considered repression and coercion as methods for enforcing taxation but these strategies failed. In fact, there were rumours of establishing a dictatorial regime, which Washington promptly placated, and even the president of the Congress, Nathaniel Gorham, tried to lure the Prince of Prussia to restore a monarchical government in North America.[23]

Facing problems of internal cooperation, fiscal and financial crisis and lacking a uniform foreign policy, many revolutionary leaders began to explore other ideas beyond classical liberalism or republicanism, abandoning traditional ways of thinking about confederations with weak executives and strong states.[24] Sailing against those ideological trends was as hard for the promoters of a new constitution as it has been difficult for historians trying to make sense of the origins of the US Constitution. As historian Gordon S. Wood put it, by

> attempting to confront and retard the thrust of the Revolution, with the rhetoric of the Revolution, the Federalists fixed the terms for the future discussion of American politics. Thus, they brought the ideology of the Revolution to consummation and created a distinctively American political theory only at the cost of eventually impoverishing later American political thought.[25]

In other words, in the framing of the Constitution, the needs for a stronger government were mixed with and justified in the popular ideological terms of the period, thus coalescing republicanism, liberalism and imperialism in a bewildering fashion. However, it was understood that 'the violations of traditional republicanism were necessary to achieve American's shared longstanding goal of developing an expansive empire'.[26]

Rather than determining if the early American state was going to be liberal or republican, the thorniest questions after independence revolved around managing effectively relations among member states and with foreign states. The

21 Terry Bouton, 'The Trials of the Confederation' in Jane Kamensky (ed), *The Oxford Handbook of the American Revolution* (Oxford University Press 2012).

22 Fernando López-Alves, *State Formation and Democracy in Latin America, 1810–1900* (Duke University Press 2000) 18–20.

23 George Washington. 'Officers of the Army' (Speech at Head Quarters Newburgh, 15 March 1783). https://founders.archives.gov/documents/Washington/99-01-02-10840 accessed 24 August 2020; Richard Krauel, 'Prince Henry of Prussia and the Regency of the United States, 1786' (1911) 17 *The American Historical Review* 44.

24 Peter Onuf, *The Origins of the Federal Republic: Jurisdictional Controversies in the United States 1775–1787* (University of Pennsylvania Press, 1983) 179.

25 Gordon S. Wood, *The Creation of the American Republic, 1776–1787* (University of North Carolina Press 1969) 562.

26 Christopher Flanagan, 'A Revolution for Empire: Ideas and the Making of the Constitution, 1787–8', (2018) 8 *Journal of Early American History* 153, 157.

political history of the post-independence era, wrote historian Drew R. McCoy, was 'less a story of ideological controversy (…) than it is a reflection of the daunting challenge of fashioning political coherence from the recalcitrant materials of a regionally differentiated colonial past'.[27] In fact, the revolutionary leaders faced the same complicated political problem that had always vexed the British Empire: how to balance power and authority between a centre and the peripheries.[28] To preserve their independence, revolutionary leaders,

> began to consider different modes of power sharing among entities at a single level of government (the legislature, the judiciary and the executive) as a means of carrying out their larger commitments to power sharing between a national centre and a peripheral constellation of states.[29]

Rather than debating liberalism and republicanism, most delegates debated two visions of federalism: one pushing for national supremacy and the other championing state sovereignty. However, as historian Jack Rakove aptly noted, the final federal structure represented a fusion of positions full of nuances, uncertainties, and deviations that still baffles modern commentators.[30]

Historian Max Edling has argued that the US Constitution of 1787 did not radically change the relationship between the federal government and the states the Articles of Confederation had envisioned but provided the latter with the means to execute its powers without resorting to the states. One of the strategies employed for this was shifting the idea of state representation in Congress for people's representation with a mechanism for proportional representation of citizens. The consequences of this small change consumed most energy of the delegates at Philadelphia, leaving details about the specific national powers of the new government. The second strategy implied the supremacy of constitutional law over state legislation implicit in the idea of judicial review. The third approach implied the use of military force against individuals not against states.

However, securing the monopoly of coercion was closely connected to many other aspects of government, particularly to financial matters such as public debt and taxation. The idea of establishing a well-financed army was extremely controversial since standing armies were seen as the main enemies of republican freedoms.[31] The Federalists assuaged their critics' fears by arguing that

27 Drew R. McCoy, 'James Madison and Visions of American Nationality in the Confederation Period. A Regional Perspective', in Richard Beeman, Stephen Botein, and Edward C. Carter II (eds), *Beyond Confederation: Origins of the Constitution and American National Identity* (University of North Carolina Press 1987) 229.

28 Jack P. Green, *Peripheries and Center: Constitutional Development in the Extended Polities of the British Empire and the United States, 1607–1788* (Norton 1986).

29 Alison L. LaCroix, *The Ideological Origins of American Federalism* (Cambridge University Press 2010) 9.

30 Jack N. Rakove, *Original Meanings: Politics and Ideas in the Making of the Constitution* (Vintage 1997) 372–343.

31 Lawrence Cress, 'Republican Liberty and National Security: American Military Policy as an Ideological Problem, 1783 to 1789', (1981) 38 *The William and Mary Quarterly* 73.

the best way to protect international commerce and to guarantee economic prosperity was by strengthening the country's military power.[32] It is worth noting that unlike most early Latin American constitutions, the constitution of 1787 centralised most powers related to war-making and devised a sound system to finance the subsequent wars the United States was bound to fight since it was still surrounded by European empires (Spain still had Florida and Britain still controlled the territories that would become Canada) and native peoples who were also consolidating military powers through federations such as Tecumseh's Confederacy and the Creek Confederacy. In contrast, the new Latin American states did not face great military threats and engaged in limited wars that required fewer resources, which, according to Miguel Angel Centeno, explains why the state capacity in the south of the continent remained underdeveloped.[33]

The centralisation of fiscal and military powers helped the United States not only to re-establish its public credit but more importantly it took the country away from the pattern of political instability and territorial disintegration that came to dominate the rest of the continent during the nineteenth century. In fact, the United States was the first undeveloped nation that could effectively assert its sovereignty in a war-ridden international context by providing the central government with key infrastructural powers.[34] After all, as Alexander Hamilton argued during the process of ratification, without providing the central government with proper troops and funding, the United States would have not been able to resist foreign interference.[35] Public finance and war-making were inevitably connected and strengthening the latter required streamlining the former. Hamilton tried to adopt the British system of war-making by restructuring public debt as a way of getting loans in the international market at low-interest rates, but such a plan required an independent fiscal apparatus and stopping states from acquiring public debt and issuing paper money.[36]

In this regard, the Federalists sought to replace the requisition system to collect taxes with unlimited federal powers for taxation. Both measures, Edling argues, aimed to successfully mobilise the country's resources not only to properly fund war-making activities but also to secure a better reputation in the international bond market.[37] State leaders feared that by relinquishing the power to tax they could lose their sovereignty and become the target of exacting taxes. The Federalists replied arguing that state's taxes would drop since the central government would absorb all the financial burdens related to war-making and public debts that would be financed mainly through indirect taxes and taxes on

32 Max Edling, *A Revolution in Favor of Government: Origins of the U.S. Constitution and the Making of the American State* (Oxford University Press 2003) 83–84.

33 Miguel Angel Centeno, *Blood and Debt: War and the Nation-State in Latin America* (The Pennsylvania State University Press 2002).

34 Daniel J. Hulsebosch, 'Being Like a State: How Americans (and Britons Built the Constitutional Infrastructure of a Developing Nation' (2018) 59 *William and Mary Law Review* 1239.

35 Jacob E. Cooke (ed), *The Federalist* (Wesleyan University Press 1961) 91–92.

36 Max Edling, '"So Immense Power in the Affairs of War': Alexander Hamilton and the Restoration of Public Credit', (2007) 64 *The William and Mary Quarterly* 287.

37 Edling (n 32) 163–174.

imported goods, leaving to the states the option of raising direct taxes yet without delegating the right to collect them in case the central government needed extra resources.[38] The unlimited federal right to levy direct taxes has rarely been questioned, only the methods to determine them fairly considering each state's population have triggered great constitutional debates and has become an absurd hurdle for many fiscal reforms in the United States.[39] Many of the odd aspects of the fiscal structure that emerged with the Constitution of 1787 as well as the many inequalities in terms of political representation (including the Electoral College and the infamous Three-Fifths Compromise) came from slave owners who saw in the unlimited power to tax as an imminent threat to slavery.[40] As historian Robin Einhorn has argued, the anti-government rhetoric of the early republic was not grounded on liberalism but in the protection of slavery.[41] Although the Constitution did not explicitly intend to protect slavery, its original design was filled with compromises designed to lure slave owners who saw in the federal army a mighty shield against slave insurrections.[42] As the previous case shows, the Constitution was not really designed to protect minorities or individual rights, but was as Madison said, a way of forming a union among states to protect themselves against powerful neighbouring states.[43] In terms of international security, the Constitution succeeded greatly and after 1812 the United States garnered enough military and political power to assert its unquestionable dominion over its territories and beyond the Appalachian Mountains marking the beginnings of its imperial expansion over the continent.[44]

3 The independence of Switzerland and the dependence of Belgium

While the nation building process in Latin America was remarkably chaotic during the nineteenth century, in Europe, after the French Revolution several

38 Ibid. 175–205.

39 Calvin H. Johnson, 'Fixing the Constitutional Absurdity of the Apportionment of Direct Tax' (2004) 21 *Constitutional Commentary* 295; Bruce Ackerman, 'Taxation and the Constitution' (1999) 99 *Columbia Law Review* 1.

40 Robin Einhorn, 'Patrick Henry's case Against the Constitution: The Structural Problem with Slavery', (2002) 22 *Journal of the Early Republic* 549.

41 Robin Einhorn, 'Tax Aversion and the Legacy of Slavery' (2006) www.press.uchicago.edu/Misc/Chicago/194876.html accessed 24 August 2020.

42 Paul Finkelman, 'Slavery and the Constitutional Convention: Making a Covenant with Death', in Richard Beeman, Stephen Botein, and Edward C. Carter II (eds) (n 27) 188–225; David Waldstreicher, *Slavery's Constitution: From Revolution to Ratification* (Hill and Wang 2009); George William Van Cleve, *A Slaveholders' Union: Slavery, Politics and the Constitution in the Early American Republic* (University of Chicago Press 2010).

43 James Madison, 'Preface to Debates in the Convention of 1787,' (1787) www.consource.org/document/james-madison-preface-to-debates-in-the-convention-of-1787/, accessed 24 August 2020.

44 Fred Anderson and Andrew Cayton, *The Dominion of War: Empire and Liberty in North America, 1500–2000* (Viking 2005) 229.

conflicts marked the rise of modern nations.[45] European nations were also shaped by a great social, demographic and cultural diversity and the articulation of uniform polities even on a smaller scale represented a deeply contested process. Indeed, lurking behind most European polities were not latent nations but composite monarchies comprised of 'a myriad smaller territorial and jurisdictional units jealously guarding their independent status'.[46]

Recent scholarship in Latin America has unearthed the thorny and complex system of administration and different levels of government that made the region a labyrinth of sovereignties. Constitutions on both sides of the Atlantic stood at the core of a process of knitting together societies via federal arrangements. Doing it effectively remains today as the global promise of federalism and the highest aspiration of the European Union.

Yet the road towards integration has always met unsurmountable challenges. In his grand imperial vision, Napoleon tried to integrate Europe via written constitutions as a means to governing more effectively his expanding empire, by framing homogeneous administrative units.[47] Once again, we should really reconsider and think about the origins of constitutions less as social pacts among equal citizens of homogenous polities, and more as pragmatic agreements to effectively govern over diverse peoples and territories. This brief account of the political development in Switzerland and Belgium can shed light upon the dynamics of constitutionalism in the making of nation states in Europe.[48]

James Madison noted that Switzerland until 1787 had been one of the few confederations where the principle of two sovereignties had not generated a civil war and he attributed such peaceful political life to geographical and demographical factors and the country's irrelevance in international affairs.[49] This mythical oasis ended when Napoleon invaded it and created the Helvetic Republic in 1798, in the first attempt to make Switzerland a unitary state working under the premises of modern representative democracy.[50] However, Switzerland quickly faced profound divisions and experienced chronic political instability, forcing the French to intervene again to restore the former federal system of sovereign cantons.[51]

The new constitution, the Act of Mediation of 1803, drafted by Napoleon against the principles of the French Revolution, was a bold political move aiming to keep Switzerland within the sphere of influence of the French empire and to

45 Andreas Wimmer and Yuval Feinstein, 'The Rise of the Nation-State across the World, 1816 to 2001', (2010) 75 *American Sociological Review* 764.

46 J. H. Elliott, 'A Europe of Composite Monarchies', (1992) 137 *Past and Present* 48, 51.

47 Stuart Woolf, *Napoleon's Integration of Europe* (Routledge 1991) 125–127.

48 Ute Planert (ed.), *Napoleon Empire: European Politics in Global Perspective* (Palgrave 2016).

49 Cooke (n 35) 122–123.

50 Robert R. Palmer, *The Age of Democratic Revolution* (first published 1959, Princeton University Press 2014) 680.

51 Oliver Zimmer, *A Contested Nation: History, Memory and Nationalism in Switzerland* (Cambridge University Press 2003) 82.

address the ongoing crisis.[52] For a while, the nation enjoyed a relatively peaceful political life until Napoleon lost the battle of Leipzig in 1813, thus creating a vacuum of power and again stirring political and regional divisions which led to the restoration of the pre-1798 constitutional order.

During the 1830s, political instability mixed with religious questions produced violent clashes across the country, reaching a particularly bloody and chilling climax in 1847.[53] In 1848, de Tocqueville who had previously praised Americans for – according to him – developing a weak federal state, called for the creation of a stronger central government in Switzerland as the only way of stopping the spiral of violence and chaos.[54] Two constitutional reforms, in 1848 and 1874, helped to create a federal state in line with the US Constitution of 1787 centralising powers over war affairs and international relations free from cantonal intervention, developing an independent judiciary, and furthering the formation of a national and functional market.[55] The centralisation of financial powers took longer but after the reform of 1881, the Swiss state could finally develop a uniform and independent monetary policy, thus making a country without any wealth in metals an important player in the global financial system.[56]

At the end of the nineteenth century, a gradual process of centralisation of fiscal, commercial and military powers in Switzerland, underpinned not only the basis for its incredible economic growth but also the grounds for its political independence and territorial integrity, even during the wars that troubled twentieth-century Europe.[57] However, a romantic vision of Swiss federalism recreating the myth of free and sovereign cantons where public decisions come directly from the people voting under a clear sky still lies at the heart of Swiss national identity.[58] In the liberal mythology, the constitution of 1848 stands as another episode in the long history of Switzerland's struggle for achieving individual rights and local autonomy,[59] casting a long shadow upon the process of centralisation

52 Oliver Beaud, 'Federation and Empire: About a Conceptual Distinction of Political Forms' in Amnon Lev (ed), *The Federal Idea: Public Law Between Governance and Political Life* (Hart Publishing, 2017) 63–66.

53 Clive H. Church, *A Concise History of Switzerland* (Cambridge University Press 2013) 155–161.

54 Aurelian Craiutu and Jeremy Jennings, *Tocqueville on America after 1840: Letters and Other Writings* (Cambridge University Press 2009) 354–369.

55 Giovanni Biagini, 'Switzerland', in Dawn Oliver and Carlo Fusaroc (eds), *How Constitutions Change: A Comparative Study* (Hart Publishing 2011) 304–308; James H. Hutson, *The Sister Republics: Switzerland and the United States from 1776 to the Present* (Library of Congress 1991) 32–41.

56 Ernest Baltensperger and Peter Kugler, *Swiss Monetary History Since the Early 19th Century* (Cambridge University Press 2017) 7–53.

57 Church (n 53) 132–161; Clive H. Church and Paolo Darnaelli, 'The Dynamics of Confederalism and Federalism: Comparing Switzerland and the EU', (2005)15 *Regional and Federal Studies* 163.

58 Beatrice Eugster and Oliver Strijbis, 'The Swiss: A Political Nation?' (2011) 17 *Swiss Political Science Review* 397; Clive H. Church, *The Politics and Government of Switzerland* (Macmillan 2004) 11–22; Carol L. Schmid, *Conflict and Consensus in Switzerland* (University of California Press 1981) 1–14.

59 Marc H. Lerner, *A Laboratory of Liberty: The Transformation of Political Culture in Republican Switzerland, 1750–1848* (Brill 2012) 322–325.

of key infrastructural powers by which the country acquired the state capacity to control internal conflicts and effectively manage international relations.

Belgium provides an example that should make us further examine the early influence of American constitutionalism in Europe. In October of 1789, a revolution against the emperor Joseph II attempted to form a new nation called the United States of Belgium.[60] However, the revolutionary leaders, inspired by the Articles of Confederation of 1781, instituted a weak central government delegating many powers to the regions prompting the collapse of the first attempt to forge an independent Belgium. The country achieved its independence from the Kingdom of the Netherlands after an international arrangement between Great Britain and France in 1830 as a way of creating a buffer state between them.[61] A year later, Belgium adopted a new constitution that has been constantly showcased as the lodestar of liberal constitutionalism in Europe despite keeping a monarch and many restrictions on the popular vote. In fact, rather than liberalism, a pragmatic conservatism pulses at its heart.[62] Even though the Belgian Constitution of 1831 has been widely praised, it has not been correctly analysed,[63] but we know that most fiscal, monetary, and foreign relations affairs were centralised giving the new nation relative stability and securing its independence. Notwithstanding, Belgium faced fewer external pressures since it was under international protection from 1830 to 1914.[64] Recently, after key constitutional reforms, Belgium again adopted a decentralised system delegating many powers (particularly fiscal) to its regions, generating an incredible level of political instability, leaving the country without a government for more than 589 days and awakening fears about disintegration.[65]

4 Constitutional history of North America

The Civil War (1861–1865) in the United States was not an isolated event but part of a larger global phenomenon of political violence that reshaped the internal

60 Jane Judge, *The United States of Belgium: The Story of the First Belgium Revolution* (Leuven University Press 2018).

61 Els Witte, Jan Craeybeckx, and Alain Meyen, *Political History of Belgium: From 1830 onwards* (VUB University Press 2000) 24.

62 A de Dijn, 'A Pragmatic Conservatism: Montesquieu and The Framing of the Belgian Constitution (1830–1831)' (2002) 38 *History of European Ideas* 227.

63 Brecht Desaure, Raf Geenens, Christophe Maes, Stefan Sottiaux, 'The Belgian Constitution: Modern Constitutionalism's Greatest Triumph?' (2018) 35 *Journal of Constitutional History* 17.

64 John Fritzmaurice, *The Politics of Belgium: A Unique Federalism* (Hurst and Company 1996) 253.

65 Jean Beaufays, 'Belgium: A Dualist Political System?' (1988) 18 *Publius* 63; Willi Leibritz, 'Fiscal Federalism in Belgium: Main Challenges and Considerations for Reform' (OECD Economics Department Working Papers 2009); Kris Deschouwer, *The Politics of Belgium: Governing a Divided Society* (Macmillan 2009) 18–41; Samuel Henry, 'Belgium's Survival at Risk in French-Dutch Split' *Edmonton Journal* (Alberta, 23 April 2010); Ljubisa Despotovic and Dorde Stojanovic, 'Belgian Consociative Democracy, An Outline for a Portrait of 'Unsuccessful' federalism' (2011) 8 *Megatrend Review* 89.

and external borders of the constitutional regimes in North America.[66] The war was the greatest test for the US Constitution since its ratification, revealing the strength and flaws of the American system of government. Unhappy about the prospects of slavery under the Lincoln's administration, the Confederate States seceded from the United States and immediately adopted a new constitution setting up a weak central government and robust state rights. Marshall L. DeRosa has argued that the Confederate Constitution did not represent an abrupt departure with the American constitutional tradition nor a legal disguise to protect slavery, but a return to the spirit of the Articles of Confederation.[67] Yet that was precisely the problem that explains the failure of the Confederacy to keep its independence. They, in fact, adopted again a system of requisitions to fund its central government with catastrophic consequences for the war effort. 'The entire experience', Currie argues, 'serves as a grim reminder why the central government was given the power to raise and support armies'.[68] Southern leaders assumed that their lucrative industries – in this case, cotton – would be enough to pay for the troops and obtain credit on the international market.[69] 'King Cotton' strategy of 1861–2', historian Jay Sexton argued, 'effectively prevented the Confederacy from implementing a coherent policy of international finance until it was too late. When Southern agents finally succeeded in floating the only foreign loan of the war, the Erlanger scheme of 1863, mismanagement bungled the operation and contributed to its demise'.[70] In the end, rather than looking at the failure of the Confederacy, Max Edling has suggested that the victory of Lincoln was grounded on the powers the US Constitution granted to the federal government to wage wars effectively. [71]

At the end of the Civil War, the United States considered annexing Canada[72] but the British quickly reorganised its territories in North America to unify them under a new federal state with the Constitution of 1867. With a new constitution, the British tried not only to stop the expansion of the United States,

66 Williams L. Morton, 'British North America and a Continent in Dissolution, 1861–71', (1962) 47 *History* 139; Patrick J. Kelly, 'The European Revolutions of 1848 and the Trasnational Turn in Civil War History' (2014) 4 *The Journal of the Civil War Era* 431; Don H. Doyle *American Civil Wars: The United States, Latin America, Europe and the Crisis of 1860s* (University of North Carolina Press 2017).

67 Marshall L. DeRosa, *The Confederate Constitution of 1861: An Inquiry into American Constitutionalism* (University of Missouri Press 1991).

68 David P. Currie, 'Through the Looking-Glass: The Confederate Constitution in Congress, 1861–1865' (2004) 90 *Virginia Law Review* 1257, 1275.

69 Eugene R. Dattel, 'Cotton and the Civil War' (2008) *Mississippi History Now* http://mshistorynow.mdah.state.ms.us/articles/291/cotton-and-the-civil-war> accessed 24 August 2020; Jay Sexton, *Debtor Diplomacy: Finance and American Foreign Relations in the Civil War Era* (Oxford University Press 2005) 134–189.

70 Ibid. 247.

71 Max Edling, *A Hercules in the Cradle: War, Money and the American State, 1783–1867* (University of Chicago Press, 2014) 178–221.

72 David E. Shi, 'Sward's Attempt to Annex British Columbia, 1865–1869' (1978) 47 *Pacific Historical Review* 217.

but also to underpin Canada's later territorial expansion. [73] The founders of Canada followed the recipe for success by centralising important fiscal aspects and securing 'the unrestricted taxing rights and residuary legislative power of the federal parliament'.[74] They considered that the theory of state's rights had produced the Civil War in the United States and wanted to avoid such a model at all costs, adopting instead a highly centralised system that scholars described as *subordinated federalism.*[75] The general population and many regional groups resisted such increases in the authority of the central government, particularly regarding taxation, couching their opposition in liberal terms while the proponents of the constitution argued in favour of a more interventionist state. [76] In the end, the more centralised vision, which Hamilton inspired, prevailed.[77] The ghost of Hamilton also inspired a banking reform that helped Canada to prevent the fragmentation of its banking system just in time to avoid the worse consequences of the financial crisis of 1871.[78] Once Canada consolidated its central government and financial system, its Western expansion was secured. The active engagement of the central government in the expansion and administration of new territories continues today as a testimony of the lasting legacy of imperial constitutionalism in Canada.[79] After all, imperialism, as historian Carl Berger has recently shown, was latent not only in the Constitution of 1867 but also, and more importantly, it impregnated the entire political culture of the age.[80]

Mexico was born as a vast empire stretching from Oregon to Costa Rica, making it the largest country in the continent. Since Mexico began the war for independence in 1810 the process of fragmentation of power and authority began as many regions and towns stopped paying taxes to the Spanish imperial

73 Phillip Buckner, 'The Creation of the Dominion of Canada', in Phillip Buckner (ed), *Canada and the British Empire* (Oxford University Press 2010); E. A. Heaman, *A Short History of the State in Canada* (Toronto University Press 2015) 111.

74 G. P. Browne, *Documents on the Confederation of British North America* (McGill Queen's University Press 2009) xxiv.

75 *Parliamentary debates on the subject of the confederation of the British North American provinces*, 3rd session, 8th Provincial Parliament of Canada (Parliamentary Printers 1865) 29–45; Bruce W. Hodgins, 'The Canadian Political Elite Attitude's Towards the Nature of the Plan of Union', in W.H. Heick (ed), *Federalism in Canada and Australia: The Early Years* (Wilfrid Laurier University Press 1978).

76 Andrew Smith, 'Toryism, Classical Liberalism and Capitalism: The Politics of Taxation and the Struggle for Canadian Confederation' (2008) 89 *The Canadian Historical Review* 1; E. A. Heaman, *Tax, Order, and Good Government: A New Political History of Canada, 1867–1917* (McGill Queen's University Press 2005) 21–182.

77 Frederick Vaughan, *The Canadian Federalist Experiment: From Defiant Monarchy to Reluctant Republic* (McGill Queen's University Press 2003) 106–112.

78 Andrew Smith, 'Continental Divided: The Canadian Banking and Currency Laws of 1871 in the Mirror of the United States' (2012) 13 *Entreprise and Society* 455.

79 David E. Smith, *The Invisible Crown: The First Principle of Canadian Government* (first published 1995, Toronto University Press 2013) 162.

80 Carl Berger, *The Sense of Power: Studies In the Ideas of Canadian Imperialism, 1867–1914* (University of Toronto Press 2013).

authorities. The making of the Constitution of 1824 marked the beginning of a process of rearticulating social, political, and economic relations of the country. Under the mantle of liberalism, Mexico built up a weak central government, a poor administrative state, and raised a tiny army, making the country easy prey for internal and external threats during the nineteenth century.[81] Unsurprisingly, 'the Constitution of 1824, with its weak executive, strong legislature, and mass political participation, failed to meet the challenges of the first decade of independent life. The charter not only granted authority to the states but also empowered the pueblos campesinos, the former Indian repúblicas'.[82] With this highly decentralised system, the early Mexican state not only failed to monopolise violence but also, and more importantly, it promoted the proliferation of regional armies at the service of local elites engaged in the private exploitation of the country's vast natural resources.[83] During the 1830s, the political and liberal elites noted and tried to tackle the situation. The ghost of Hamilton, embodied it in the idea of a strong central government with large fiscal powers, floated across the country yet the spectre of a strong executive remained a deeper fear.[84]

In 1836 the Congress tried to impose a centralised regime by issuing a new constitution called Seven Laws but without modifying the decentralisation of fiscal and military powers.[85] The constitution assigned more responsibilities to the executive power but without giving it any means to achieve them. Even worse, it decentralised tax collection even more.[86]

In this context, Mexico's favourite villain, Antonio López de Santa Anna, tried to centralise everything by instituting a dictatorship via the Constitution of 1843. Yet absolute power without taxes and armies remained powerless, so the new regime ended up resorting to brutal and disorganised repression that fed a cycle of endless rebellions.[87]

81 Marcello Carmagnani, 'Finanzas y estado en México, 1820–1880' (1983) 9 Ibero-Amerikanisches Archiv 279; Josefina Z. Vazquéz, 'Un viejo tema: el federalismo y el centralismo', (1993) 42 *Historia Mexicana* 621, 624; David Pantoja Morán, *Bases del constitucionalismo mexicano: La Constitución de 1824 y la teoría constitucional* (Fondo de Cultura Económica 2017).

82 Rodríguez (n 11) 22.

83 Antonio Annino, ´Soberanías en lucha' in Antonio Annino and François-Xavier Guerra (eds), *Inventando la nación: Iberoamérica siglo XIX* (Fondo de Cultura Económica 2003) 182; Stephen Neufeld, 'Military and Nation in Mexico, 1821–1916' in William H. Beezley (ed), *A Companion to Mexican History and Culture* (Blackwell 2011) 390–403.

84 Catherine Andrews, 'Reformar la Constitución de 1824: planes, proyectos y constituciones, 1824–1847' in Cecilia Noriega and Alicia Salmeron (eds) *México: Un siglo de historia constitucional, 1808–1917* (Instituto Mora 2009) 73–96; Joshua Simon, *The Ideology of Creole Revolution: Imperialism and Independence in American and Latin American Political Thought* (Cambridge University Press 2017) 128–167.

85 Michael Costeloe, *The Central Republic in Mexico, 1835–1846* (Cambridge University Press 1993) 303–306.

86 Barbara A. Tenenbaum, *The Politics of Penury: Debts and Taxes in Mexico, 1821–1856* (University of New Mexico Press) 43.

87 Will Fowler, *Malcontents, Rebels, and Pronunciados: The Politics of Insurrection in Nineteenth-Century Mexico* (University of Nebraska Press, 2012).

On the eve of the war with the United States, Mexico not only lacked an army but also, and more importantly, had several unconnected regional armed forces unwilling to participate in the defence of national security.[88] Of course, Mexicans fought furiously against the United States and there is large evidence of commitment to the war effort across the country, but they needed better institutional means to cooperate and to organise human and financial resources.[89] In fact, in the middle of the war with the United States, Mexico re-established the constitutional order framed in 1824, thus hampering the chance of better channelling Mexico's military powers. In the end, Mexico was defeated in 1848, losing more than half of its territory.

Yet we should not look at the war between Mexico and the United States as a conflict between two nations but more as a confrontation of two constitutional models. The victory of the United States, Max Edling has argued, only showed the relevance of constitutions as mechanisms to better coordinate state relations within a federation and to more effectively mobilise the nation's resources.[90] In fact, Edling suggests that taking into account Mexico's vast natural resources, the country just needed a better constitutional system to stop America's expansion[91] as Canada did. Arguably, in Mexico, the triumph of liberal constitutionalism brought down the Mexican state.

In 1853, Santa Anna returned to Mexico from his exile in Colombia and tried, again, to impose a central authority with wide powers over fiscal and military affairs. Indeed, Santa Anna tried every trick up his sleeve to make the government work: he borrowed extensively, raised taxes and even sold territory. Yet Santa Anna's rule was, in the end, a personal government unresponsive to social groups, regional elites or even generals. Without a proper way of channelling the growing social discomfort or political institutions to gather support from, his personal rule was doomed.[92] The rebellion of 1855 against Santa Anna not only showed the high level of social resentment but also the many economic groups, even indigenous peoples, and regional elites who still supported a liberal system that promised them a small parcel of power to do as they please.[93]

88 Brian R. Hamnett, 'Early Liberalism, and the Regional Politics of Oaxaca, 1828–1853' (1991) 10 *Bulletin of Latin American Research* 3, 9–10; José Antonio Serrano Ortega, 'Sobre la centralización de la república: estructura militar y sistema político en Guanajuato, 1835–1847' (2012) 83 *Secuencia*; Josefina Zoraida Vázquez, 'Reflexiones sobre el ejército mexicano y la fundación del estado mexicano' in Juan Ortiz Escamilla (ed.), *Fuerzas militares en Iberoamérica siglos XVIII y XIX* (El Colegio de México 2015) 219–232.

89 Peter Guardino, *The Dead March: A History of the Mexican-American War* (Harvard University Press 2017).

90 Max Edling, 'En historia om tva republiker: Finansieringen av det Mexikanska kriget' in Max Edling and Patrik Winton (eds) *Ett nödvändigt ont. Statsskuld och politik i Förenta Staterna och Sverige 1780–1870* (Opuscula Historica Upsaliensia 2009); Max Edling, 'When Johnny Comes Marching Home … from the Bank' (2008) 9 *Common Place* www.common-place-archives.org/vol-09/no-01/edling/> accessed 24 August 2020.

91 Edling (n71) 168–174.

92 Will Fowler, *Santa Anna of Mexico* (University of Nebraska Press 2007) 289–316.

93 Guy P. Thomson, 'Bulwarks of Patriotic Liberalism: National Guard, Philharmonic Corps and Patriotic Juntas in Mexico, 1847–88' (1990) 22 *Journal of Latin American Studies* 31;

Mexican liberal constitutionalism witnessed its most significant victory with the Constitution of 1857, which continues to occupy a very special place in the pantheon of national mythology as the legal source of contemporary individual liberties.[94] However, without reforming the fiscal, financial, and military structure of the state, Mexico was once again easy prey of another foreign adversary – France invaded in 1861 – and fell back to the hands of an authoritarian general, Porfirio Díaz, who imposed his personal rule on a country that apparently could not rule itself. Díaz managed to attract foreign investors, fix internal relations among states, boost the formation of a truly national market, repair international relations with the United States and Europe, and to dimly improve the standard of living of the expanding population who experienced for the first time two decades of relative political stability, all without abolishing the Constitution of 1857, which became a dead letter throughout his mandate.[95]

At the end of the nineteenth century, many countries in Latin America, like Mexico, developed more integrated economic systems oriented towards the international market, yet, internally political liberties were halted. This liberal-conservative constitutional model, argued historian Roberto Gargarella, 'favored the consolidation of an extremely unfair distribution of resources' and limited 'the possibilities of politically resisting that situation'.[96] In other words, the liberal constitutionalism of the age, not only encouraged a dictatorship as the only method for political stability, as the jurist Emilio Rabasa noted, but also forced the opposition to revolution as the only method for resistance.[97] Perhaps we should start to rethink the origins of the so-called *caudillismo* in Latin America less in terms of a political culture keen on strong men and more as a desperate attempt to bring order when constitutions fail to provide central governments with basic infrastructural powers.[98]

5 Constitutional imperialism

If we set aside the classical conception of constitutionalism as charters of moral rights[99] and we pay closer attention to the origins and functions of written con-

Guy P. Thomson, 'Popular Aspects of Liberalism in Mexico, 1848–1888' (1991) 10 *Bulletin of Latin American Research* 265; Peter F. Guardino, *Peasants, Politics, and the Formation of Mexico's National State: Guerrero, 1800–1857* (Stanford University Press. 1996) 178–210.

94 Imer B. Flores, 'La Constitución de 1857 y sus reformas: A 150 años de su promulgación', in Diego Valadés and Miguel Carbonell (eds), *El proceso constituyente mexicano: a 150 años de la Constitución de 1857 y 90 de la constitución de 1917* (Instituto de Investigaciones Jurídicas, UNAM 2007) 285–324.

95 Friedrich Katz', The Liberal Republic and the Porfiriato, 1867–1910' in Leslie Bethell (ed.), *Mexico since Independence* (Cambridge University Press 2012) 49–124.

96 Roberto Gargarella, *Latin American Constitutionalism, 1810–2010: The Engine Room of the Constitution* (Oxford University Press 2013) 199.

97 Emilio Rabasa, *La constitución y la dictadura* (first published 1912 Porrúa 1976).

98 Pedro Castro, 'Caudillismo in Latin America, yesterday and today' (2007) 27 *Política y Cultura* 9.

99 Larry Alexander, 'What Are Constitutions, and What Should (and Can) They Do?' (2011) 28 *Social Philosophy and Policy* 1.

stitutions, as historian Linda Colley has suggested, we can envisage their role as tools for administrating diverse territories and peoples. In fact, the liberal conception of constitutionalism has prevented historians from studying the impact of constitutions in key areas of political and economic development such as fiscal, military, and financial affairs.[100]

Finally, the framers of the US Constitution of 1787 recognised that to secure a stable government it was more important to make compromises than try to impose a moral vision onto a large and diverse society. Even the incorporation of the Bill of Rights, which is often confused with the spirit of the constitution, was part of a compromise with large sections of the population.[101] In the end, very few were fully satisfied with the final document. However, as Charles A. Beard once pointed out, the major interest groups of the country were involved in the constitution-making process, thus securing, not a democracy, but a stable government.[102] Successful constitutions, Beard argued, were not a product of theories of government but of a process of adjusting the powers of the government to its immediate historical problems.

Hamilton was a true hero in Beard's account; he embodied the ideal of statesmanship Beard admired. Beard often suggested the need to 'study the life of Alexander Hamilton, that great realist and constructor of political power', because Hamilton knew the 'fine art' of manipulating interests to back up his policies'. Alexander Hamilton's national vision, Beard said 'was much above a great many of the men who were operating around him, but he used them, played one group over against another, in the realization of a larger program which he had in mind. I think statesmen do that, can do that'.[103]

As Stephen Holmes has recently put it, the primary goal of constitutions 'was not to limit pre-existing power but to create power out of powerlessness. The legendary constitution-makers of Great Legislators of antiquity were worshiped as religious figures not because they protected minority rights but because they organise their communities for military defence and conquest'. Their almost mystical status came from knowing how 'to turn a disorganized rabble into a fighting machine'. Constitutions, Holmes concludes, 'meant to help struggling

100 Today we know that the creation of unitary fiscal states helped pre-modern states to better face external and internal threats, to professionalize public administration and to devote more resources to economic development. Patrick K. O'Brien, 'Reflections on Fiscal Foundations and Contexts for the Formation of Economically Effective Eurasian States from the Rise of Venice to the Opium War' in Yun-Casalilla and Patrick K. O'Brien (eds), *The Rise of Fiscal States: A Global History 1500–1914* (Cambridge University Press 2012) 443.

101 Richard Labunski, *James Madison and the Struggle for the Bill of Rights* (Oxford University Press 2006).

102 Charles A. Beard, *An Economic Interpretation of the United States* Constitution (first published 1913 Free Press 1941).

103 Charles A. Beard to George E. Sokolsky, 21 Nov. 1930, Box 22, George E. Sokolsky Papers, Coll.: 59004, Hoover Institution Archives; John Braeman, 'Charles A. Beard at Mid-Career: Reflections' (1987) 2 *International Journal of Social Education* 60, 83.

communities to maintain their borders, coherence and resilience in a dangerous world'.[104]

Rather than thinking about constitutions in terms of political philosophies or national aspirations, we should try looking at their multiple functions and compromises and the social and historical moments in which they emerged in a way that can illuminate the problems they were meant to serve and the problems they can resolve today.[105] The art of politics and government, as the philosopher Margalit Avishai has said, is not easy and most of it lies in the capacity to make compromises that respect human dignity and address the pressing problems of today.[106] Perhaps the only problem with liberal constitutionalism lies in the innocuous premise that makes us think that a weak government constitutes the only way of protecting individual freedoms, making citizens turn away from other more substantive conceptions of liberty and better conceptions of government.[107]

References

Parliamentary debates on the subject of the confederation of the British North American provinces, 3rd session, 8th Provincial Parliament of Canada (Parliamentary Printers 1865)

Ackerman B, 'Taxation and the Constitution' (1999) 99 *Columbia Law Review* 1

Adelman J, 'An Age of Imperial Revolutions' (2008) 13 *The American Historical Review* 319

Alexander L, 'What Are Constitutions, and What Should (and can) They do?' (2011) 28 *Social Philosophy and Policy* 1

Anderson F and Cayton A, *The Dominion of War: Empire and Liberty in North America, 1500–2000* (Viking 2005)

Andrews C, 'Reformar la constitución de 1824: planes, proyectos y constituciones, 1824–1847', in Cecilia Noriega and Alicia Salmeron (eds) *Mexico: Un siglo de historia constitucional, 1808–1917* (Instituto Mora 2009)

Annino A, 'Soberanías en lucha' in Antonio Annino and François-Xavier Guerra (eds), *Inventando la nación: Iberoamérica siglo XIX* (Fondo de Cultura Económica 2003)

Avishai M, *On Compromise and Rotten Compromises* (Princeton University Press 2009)

Baltensperger E and Kugler P, *Swiss Monetary History Since the Early 19th Century* (Cambridge University Press 2017)

Bayly CA, *The Birth of the Modern World, 1870–1914: Global Connections and Comparisons* (Blackwell 2004)

Bartelson J, *A Genealogy of Sovereignty* (Cambridge University Press 1995)

104 Stephen Holmes, 'Constitutions and Constitutionalism' in Michel Rosenfeld and András Sajó (eds), *The Oxford Handbook of Comparative Constitutional Law* (Oxford University Press 2012).

105 Sanford Levinson, 'Compromise and Constitutionalism' (2011) 38 *Pepperdine Law Review* 821; Kim Scheppele 'Aspirational and aversive constitutionalism: The case for studying cross-constitutional influence through negative models' (2003) 1 *International Journal of Constitutional Law* 296.

106 Margalit Avishai, *On Compromise and Rotten Compromises* (Princeton University Press 2009).

107 Philippe Van Parijs, *Real Freedom for All: What (if Anything) Can Justify Capitalism?* (Oxford University Press 2003).

Beard C, *An Economic Interpretation of the United States Constitution* (first published 1913 Free Press 1941)

Beaud O, 'Federation and Empire: About a Conceptual Distinction of Political Forms' in Amnon Lev (ed.), *The Federal Idea: Public Law Between Governance and Political Life* (Hart Publishing 2017)

Beaufays J, 'Belgium: A Dualist Political System?' (1988) 18 *Publius* 63

Bell C, 'Introduction: Bargaining on Constitutions: Political Settlements and Constitutional State-building' (2017) 6 *Global Constitutionalism* 13

Bell D, *Reordering the World* (Princeton University Press 2016)

Bellamy R, (ed.), *Constitutionalism and Democracy* (Routledge 2016)

Benton L, 'Constitutions and Empires' (2006) 31 *Law and Social Inquiry* 473

Benton L and Ford L, *Rage for Order: the British Empire and the Origins of International Law, 1800–1850* (Harvard University Press 2016)

Berger C, *The Sense of Power: Studies in the Ideas of Canadian Imperialism, 1867–1914* (University of Toronto Press 2013)

Biagini G, 'Switzerland' in Dawn Oliver and Carlo Fusaroc (eds), *How Constitutions Change: A Comparative Study* (Hart Publishing 2011)

Bouton T, 'The Trials of the Confederation' in Jane Kamensky (ed), *The Oxford Handbook of the American Revolution* (Oxford University Press 2012)

Braeman J, 'Charles A. Beard at Mid-Career: Reflections' (1987) 2 *International Journal of Social Education* 60.

Browne GP, *Documents on the Confederation of British North America* (McGill Queen's University Press 2009)

Buckner P, 'The Creation of the Dominion of Canada', in Phillip Buckner (ed), *Canada and the British Empire* (Oxford University Press 2010)

Castiglione D, 'The Political Theory of the Constitution' in Richard Bellamy and Dario Castiglione (eds), *Constitutionalism in Transformation: European and Theoretical Perspectives* (Blackwell 1996)

Carmagnani M, 'Finanzas y estado en México, 1820–1880', (1983) 9 *Ibero-Amerikanisches Archiv* 279

Castro P, 'Caudillismo in Latin America, Yesterday and Today' (2007) 27 *Política y Cultura* 9

Centeno M, *Blood and Debt: War and the Nation-State in Latin America* (The Pennsylvania State University Press 2002)

Church CH, *The Politics and Government of Switzerland* (Macmillan 2004)

Church CH, *A Concise History of Switzerland* (CUP 2013)

Church CH and Darnaelli P, 'The Dynamics of Confederalism and Federalism: Comparing Switzerland and the EU' (2005)15 *Regional and Federal Studies* 163

Clavero B, 'Constitucionalismo y colonialismo en las américas: El paradigma perdido en la historia constitucional' (2017) 53 *Revista de Historia del Derecho* 23

Cleve Van W, *A Slaveholders' Union: Slavery, Politics and the Constitution in the Early American Republic* (University of Chicago Press 2010)

Colley L, 'Empires of Writing: Britain, America and Constitutions, 1776–1848' (2014) 23 *Law and History Review* 237

Cooke J, (ed), *The Federalist* (Wesleyan University Press 1961)

Costeloe M, *The Central Republic in Mexico, 1835–1846* (Cambridge University Press 1993),

Craiutu A and Jennings J, *Tocqueville on America after 1840: Letters and Other Writings* (Cambridge University Press 2009)

Cress L, 'Republican Liberty and National Security: American Military Policy as an Ideological Problem, 1783 to 1789' (1981) 38 *The William and Mary Quarterly* 73
Currie D, 'Through the Looking-Glass: The Confederate Constitution in Congress, 1861–1865' (2004) 90 *Virginia Law Review* 1257
Dattel E, 'Cotton and the Civil War' (2008) *Mississippi History Now* http://mshistorynow.mdah.state.ms.us/articles/291/cotton-and-the-civil-war
DeRosa M, *The Confederate Constitution of 1861: An Inquiry into American Constitutionalism* (University of Missouri Press 1991)
Desaure B, Geenens R, Maes C and Sottiaux S, 'The Belgian Constitution: Modern Constitutionalism's Greatest Triumph?' (2018) 35 *Journal of Constitutional History* 17
Deschouwer K, *The Politics of Belgium: Governing a Divided Society* (Macmillan 2009)
Despotovic L and Stojanovic D, 'Belgian Consociative Democracy, An Outline for a Portrait of "Unsuccessful' federalism" (2011) 8 *Megatrend Review* 89
Dijn A, 'A Pragmatic Conservatism: Montesquieu and the framing of the Belgian Constitution (1830–1831)' (2002) 38 *History of European Ideas* 227
Doyle D, *American Civil Wars: The United States, Latin America, Europe and the Crisis of 1860s* (University of North Carolina Press 2017)
Edling M, *A Revolution in Favor of Government: Origins of the U.S. Constitution and the Making of the American State* (Oxford University Press 2003)
Edling M, '"So Immense Power in the Affairs of War": Alexander Hamilton and the Restoration of Public Credit' (2007) 64 *The William and Mary Quarterly* 287
Edling M,'When Johnny Comes Marching Home ... from the Bank' (2008) 9 *Common Place* www.common-place-archives.org/vol-09/no-01/edling/
Edling M,'En historia om tva republiker: Finansieringen av det Mexikanska kriget' in Max Edling and Patrik Winton (eds) *Ett nödvändigt ont. Statsskuld och politik i Förenta Staterna och Sverige 1780–1870* (Opuscula Historica Upsaliensia 2009)
Edling M, *A Hercules in the Cradle: War, Money and the American State, 1783–1867* (University of Chicago Press 2014)
Einhorn R, 'Patrick Henry's case Against the Constitution: The Structural Problem with Slavery' (2002) 22 *Journal of the Early Republic* 549
Einhorn R, 'Tax Aversion and the Legacy of Slavery' (2006). www.press.uchicago.edu/Misc/Chicago/194876.html, accessed 24 August 2020
Elliott JH, 'A Europe of Composite Monarchies' (1992) 137 *Past and Present* 48
Epstein RA, *The Classical Liberal Constitution: The Uncertain Quest for Limited Government* (Harvard University Press 2014)
Eugster B and Strijbis O, 'The Swiss: A Political Nation?' (2011) 17 *Swiss Political Science Review* 397.
Finkelman P, 'Slavery and the Constitutional Convention: Making a Covenant with Death' in Richard Beeman, Stephen Botein, and Edward C. Carter II (eds), *Beyond Confederation: Origins of the Constitution and American National Identity* (University of North Carolina Press 1987)
Fitz C, *Our Sister Republics: The United States in an Age of American Revolutions* (Norton 2016)
Flanagan C, 'A Revolution for Empire: Ideas and the Making of the Constitution, 1787–8' (2018) 8 *Journal of Early American History* 153
Flores I, 'La Constitución de 1857 y sus reformas: a 150 años de su promulgación', in Diego Valadés and Miguel Carbonell (eds), *El proceso constituyente mexicano: a 150 años de la Constitución de 1857 y 90 de la Constitución de 1917* (Instituto de Investigaciones Jurídicas 2007)

Fowler W, *Santa Anna of Mexico* (University of Nebraska Press 2007)
Fowler W, *Malcontents, Rebels, and Pronunciados: The Politics of Insurrection in Nineteenth-Century Mexico* (University of Nebraska Press, 2012)
Fritzmaurice J, *The Politics of Belgium: A Unique Federalism* (Hurst and Company 1996)
Gargarella R, *Latin American Constitutionalism, 1810–2010: The Engine Room of the Constitution* (Oxford University Press 2013)
Graber M, Levinson S, and Tushnet M, (eds), *Constitutional Democracy in Crisis?* (Oxford University Press 2018)
Green J, *Peripheries and Center: Constitutional Development in the Extended Polities of the British Empire and the United States, 1607–1788* (Norton 1986)
Guardino P, *Peasants, Politics, and the Formation of Mexico's National State: Guerrero, 1800–1857* (Stanford University Press 1996)
Guardino P, *The Dead March: A History of the Mexican-American* War (Harvard University Press 2017)
Hale CA, *The Transformation of Liberalism in Late Nineteenth-Century Mexico* (Princeton University Press 1989)
Hamnett B, 'Early Liberalism, and the Regional Politics of Oaxaca, 1828–1853' (1991) 10 *Bulletin of Latin American Research* 3
Harding R, *Liberalism, Constitutionalism and Democracy* (Oxford University Press 1999)
Heaman EA, *Tax, Order, and Good Government: A New Political History of Canada, 1867–1917* (McGill Queen's University Press 2005)
Heaman EA, *A Short History of the State in Canada* (Toronto University Press 2015)
Henry S, 'Belgium's Survival at risk in French-Dutch Split' *Edmonton Journal* (Alberta, 23 April 2010)
Herring G, *From Colony to Superpower: U.S. Foreign Relations since 1776* (Oxford University Press 2008)
Hodgins B, 'The Canadian Political Elite Attitude's Towards the Nature of the Plan of Union' in W.H. Heick (ed), *Federalism in Canada and Australia: The Early Years* (Wilfrid Laurier University Press 1978)
Holmes S, 'Constitutions and Constitutionalism' in Michel Rosenfeld and András Sajó (eds), *The Oxford Handbook of Comparative Constitutional Law* (Oxford University Press 2012)
Hulsebosch D, 'Being Like a State: How Americans (and Britons Built the Constitutional Infrastructure of a Developing Nation' (2018) 59 *William and Mary Law Review* 1239.
Hutson J, *The Sister Republics: Switzerland and the United States from 1776 to the Present* (Library of Congress 1991)
Johnson C, 'Fixing the Constitutional Absurdity of the Apportionment of Direct Tax' (2004) 21 *Constitutional Commentary* 295
Judge J, *The United States of Belgium: The Story of the First Belgium Revolution* (Lueven University Press 2018)
Katz F', The Liberal Republic and the Porfiriato, 1867–1910' in Leslie Bethell (ed.), *Mexico since Independence* (Cambridge University Press 2012)
Kelly P, 'The European Revolutions of 1848 and the Transnational Turn in Civil War History' (2014) 4 *The Journal of the Civil War Era* 431
Labunski R, *James Madison and the Struggle for the Bill of Rights* (Oxford University Press 2006)
LaCroix A, *The Ideological Origins of American Federalism* (Cambridge University Press 2010)

Leibritz W, 'Fiscal Federalism in Belgium: Main Challenges and Considerations for Reform' (OECD Economics Department Working Papers 2009)
Lerner MH, *A Laboratory of Liberty: The Transformation of Political Culture in Republican Switzerland, 1750–1848* (Brill 2012)
Levinson S, 'Compromise and Constitutionalism' (2011) 38 *Pepperdine Law Review* 821
López-Alves F, *State Formation and Democracy in Latin America, 1810–1900* (Duke University Press 2000)
Loughlin M, 'The Contemporary Crisis of Constitutional Democracy' (2019) 29 *Oxford Journal of Legal Studies* 435
Krauel R, 'Prince Henry of Prussia and the Regency of the United States, 1786' (1911) 17 *The American Historical Review* 44
Madison J, 'Preface to Debates in the Convention of 1787' (1787) www.consource.org/document/james-madison-preface-to-debates-in-the-convention-of-1787/ accessed 24 August 2020
Matson CD and Onuf P, *A Union of Interests: Political Economic Thought in Revolutionary America* (University Press of Kansas 1990)
McCoy D, 'James Madison and Visions of American Nationality in the Confederation Period. A Regional Perspective' in Richard Beeman, Stephen Botein, and Edward C. Carter II (eds), *Beyond Confederation: Origins of the Constitution and American National Identity* (University of North Carolina Press 1987)
Morton W 'British North America and a Continent in Dissolution, 1861–71' (1962) 47 *History* 139
Muldoon J, *Empire and Order: The Concept of Empire, 800*–1800 (Macmillan 1999)
Murphy WF, *Constitutional Democracy: Creating and Maintaining a Just Political Order* (Johns Hopkins University Press 2007)
Neufeld S, 'Military and Nation in Mexico, 1821–1916' in William H. Beezley (ed.), A *Companion to Mexican History and Culture* (Blackwell 2011)
O'Brien P, 'Reflections on Fiscal Foundations and Contexts for the Formation of Economically Effective Eurasian States from the Rise of Venice to the Opium War' in Yun-Casalilla and Patrick K O'Brien (eds), *The Rise of Fiscal States: A Global History 1500–1914* (Cambridge University Press 2012)
Onuf P, *The Origins of the Federal Republic: Jurisdictional Controversies in the United States 1775–1787* (University of Pennsylvania Press 1983)
Pagden A, *Lords of all the World: Ideologies of Empire in Spain, Britain and France c.1500–c.1800* (Yale University Press 1995)
Palmer R, *The Age of Democratic Revolution* (first published 1959 Princeton University Press 2014)
Pantoja D, *Bases del constitucionalismo mexicano: La Constitución de 1824 y la teoría constitucional* (Fondo de Cultura Económica 2017)
Philippe Van Parijs, *Real Freedom for All: What (if Anything) Can Justify Capitalism?* (Oxford University Press 2003)
Pitts J, 'Political Theory of Empire and Imperialism' in Sankar Muthu (ed.), *Empire and Modern Political Thought* (Cambridge University Press 2012)
Planert U, (ed.), *Napoleon Empire: European Politics in Global Perspective* (Palgrave 2016)
Pocock JGA, *Virtue, Commerce and History* (Cambridge University Press 1985)
Rabasa E, *La Constitución y la Dictadura* (first published 1912 Porrúa 1976)
Rakove J, *Original Meanings: Politics and Ideas in the Making of the Constitution* (Vintage 1997)
Rodríguez JE, (ed), *The Divine Charter: Constitutionalism and Liberalism in Nineteenth-Century Mexico* (Rowman and Littlefield 2005)

Sartori G, *Comparative Constitutional Engineering: An Inquiry into Structures, Incentives and Outcomes* (Macmillan, 1994)
Sexton J, *Debtor Diplomacy: Finance and American Foreign Relations in the Civil War Era* (Oxford University Press 2005)
Scheppele K, 'Aspirational and Aversive Constitutionalism: The Case for Studying Cross-Constitutional Influence Through Negative Models' (2003) 1 *International Journal of Constitutional Law* 296
Schmid C, *Conflict and Consensus in Switzerland* (University of California Press 1981)
Shi D, 'Sward's Attempt to Annex British Columbia, 1865–1869' (1978) 47 *Pacific Historical Review* 217
Simon J, *The Ideology of Creole Revolution: Imperialism and Independence in American and Latin American Political Thought* (Cambridge University Press 2017)
Smith A, 'Continental Divided: The Canadian Banking and Currency Laws of 1871 in the Mirror of the United States' (2012) 13 *Entreprise and Society* 455.
Smith A, 'Toryism, Classical Liberalism and Capitalism: The Politics of Taxation and the Struggle for Canadian Confederation' (2008) 89 *The Canadian Historical Review* 1
Smith D, *The Invisible Crown: The First Principle of Canadian Government* (first published 1995, Toronto University Press 2013)
Tenenbaum B, *The Politics of Penury: Debts and Taxes in Mexico, 1821–1856* (University of New Mexico Press)
Thomson G, 'Bulwarks of Patriotic Liberalism: National Guard, Philharmonic Corps and Patriotic Juntas in Mexico, 1847–88' (1990) 22 *Journal of Latin American Studies* 31
Thomson G, 'Popular Aspects of Liberalism in Mexico, 1848–1888' (1991) 10 *Bulletin of Latin American Research* 265
Vaughan F, *The Canadian Federalist Experiment: From Defiant Monarchy to Reluctant Republic* (McGill Queen's University Press 2003)
Vazquéz J, 'Un viejo tema: el federalismo y el centralismo' (1993) 42 *Historia Mexicana* 621
Waldstreicher D, *Slavery's Constitution: From Revolution to Ratification* (Hill and Wang 2009)
Washington G, 'Officers of the Army' (Speech at Head Quarters Newburgh, 15 March 1783) https://founders.archives.gov/documents/Washington/99-01-02-10840
Wimmer A and Feinstein Y, 'The Rise of the Nation-State across the World, 1816 to 2001' (2010) 75 *American Sociological Review* 764
Witte E, Craeybeckx J, and Meyen A, *Political History of Belgium: From 1830 Onwards* (VUB University Press 2000)
Wood GS, *The Creation of the American Republic, 1776–1787* (University of North Carolina Press 1969)
Woolf S, *Napoleon's Integration of Europe* (Routledge 1991)
Zimmer O, *A Contested Nation: History, Memory and Nationalism in Switzerland* (Cambridge University Press 2003)
Zoraida Vázquez J, 'Reflexiones sobre el ejército mexicano y la fundación del estado mexicano', in Juan Ortiz Escamilla (ed.), *Fuerzas militares en Iberoamérica siglos XVIII y XIX* (El Colegio de México 2015)

7 Inequality and discontent

A comparative constitutional law inquiry on South Asia and Latin America

Pasquale Viola

1 Introduction. From the cultural to the legal field and the way back

The constitutional struggle against (formal and substantial) inequalities is marked by the revival of cultural and ethnic factors, leading to a sort of 'domestic ethnic implants', due to the necessary acknowledgment of culture-specific rules which prove stronger than state law, in opposition to mere positive law.[1] This trend becomes a revolutionary pathway towards contemporary forms of constitutionalism. In such cases, customs and traditions enhance endogenous elements of social identification, as well as hidden inequalities. Over the last decades, in Asia[2] and Latin America[3] this phenomenon has triggered new claims by minorities to preserve their traditions, as well as the struggle for legal recognition of non-legal factors.

Frequently, social groups are the actors that claim a peculiar ethnic identity,[4] with the aim to preserve their own traditions and social structures shaped

1 The ethnic implants in the legal systems are no longer a South-North migration result, but also an outcome of internal or domestic consciousness and concern about the cultural heritage and the socio-legal traditions developed within a community framework. However, both the external and the internal pressures pose 'new theoretical and practical challenges for accommodating plurality.' Cf Werner Menski, *Comparative Law in a Global Context. The Legal Systems of Asia and Africa* (Cambridge University Press 2006) 26. This chapter was elaborated within the framework of the PRIN 2017 'From legal pluralism to the intercultural state. Personal law, exceptions to general rules and imperative limits in the European legal space' (2017RYJAFW_001).

2 Asia and its regions are more likely a theoretical concept with no clearly defined geographical and social areas, than a fixed and strictly identified set of boundaries. For the purpose of this chapter, the analysis is based on some explanatory regional experiences, i.e. India and Nepal for South Asia, the Philippines for South-East Asia, and South Korea for East-Asia.

3 For this chapter's purposes, Latin America comprises Mexico, Central America, the Caribbean, and South America. A specific focus will be made on the constitutional experiences of Mexico, Peru, Colombia, Argentina, Bolivia, Ecuador and Chile. *See* Alexander Dawson, *Latin America Since Independence. A History with Primary Sources* (Routledge 2010); Marshall C. Eakin, 'Does Latin America have a common history?' (2014) 1 *Vanderbilt e-Journal of Luso-Hispanic Studies* 30; Edwin Williamson, *Historia de América Latina* (Fondo de Cultura Económica 2013).

4 The analysis is focused on the pivotal role of cultural and social groups, excluding the references to the individual legal status given by the recognition of citizenship and the issues related to the *locus standi*.

through experience, orality, and memory in contrast with – or as an evolution of – the chthonic tradition.[5] As well as for ethnic rules, also legal formants, necessary objects of study for any comparative law analysis, 'hortatory or not, may not be strictly legal'.[6] Thus, it becomes relevant to unveil how contemporary constitutions deal with minority groups in order to fulfil their obligations with the citizens and the people that live under the corresponding positive legal system. According to this perspective, there is a strong entanglement between tradition, customs, ethnic belonging and the concept of 'minority' within an inequality framework. Minorities are a sort of legacy given by a substratum made of traditions established through centuries of cultural layering, sharing the conceptual background with the notion of 'diversity'.[7] These fields of research are usually studied by legal scholars only with a formal approach that adopt a bottom-up or a top-down methodology according to the civil or common law traditions. However, research based on a pure case or doctrinal study does not suffice in providing a wide framework of the issues related to diversity. In fact, the study of diversity and minorities needs an interdisciplinary attitude, starting from historical, anthropological, and sociological analyses.[8] This assumption does not exclude the investigation on constitutional provisions, because the aforementioned process of cultural stratification is acknowledged by the transposition of customs and ethnic elements into constitutional texts.

However, a mere legalistic approach, even though analytical, would lack knowledge with respect to the genesis of a peculiar legal discipline. For this reason, several research projects on law 'in context' have been conducted in recent decades, illustrating the uncountable variables of social realities far from the Western idea of the nation-state.[9] This is more evident in the Asian scenario, where the cultural diversity within state boundaries is prominent and sometimes

5 Patrick H. Glenn, *Legal Traditions of the World: Sustainable Diversity in Law* (Oxford University Press 2004) 60. See also Pierre Legrand and Roderick Munday (eds), *Comparative Legal Studies: Traditions and Transitions* (Cambridge University Press 2003); Ann E. Black and Gary F. Bell, *Law and Legal Institutions of Asia. Traditions, Adaptations and Innovations* (Cambridge University Press 2011).

6 Rodolfo Sacco, 'Legal formants: a dynamic approach to comparative law (Installment I of II)' (1991) 39 *The American Journal of Comparative Law* 1.

7 Cf Raymond Boudon and Francois Bourricaud, *A Critical Dictionary of Sociology* (Routledge 1989); Gordon Marshall, *Oxford Dictionary of Sociology* (Oxford University Press 1998); Bryan S. Turner, *The Cambridge Dictionary of Sociology* (Cambridge University Press 2006); Steve Bruce and Steven Yearley, *The Sage Dictionary of Sociology* (Sage 2006); Anthony Giddens and Philip W. Sutton, *Essential Concepts in Sociology* (Polity 2014).

8 Domenico Amirante, 'Al di là dell'Occidente. Sfide epistemologiche e spunti euristici nella comparazione "verso Oriente"' (2015) 17 *Diritto Pubblico Comparato ed Europeo* 1; Lucio Pegoraro and Angelo Rinella, *Sistemas constitucionales comparados* (Vol. II, Astrea 2018).

9 Kim L. Scheppele, 'The agendas of comparative constitutionalism' (2003) 13 *Law and Courts* 5; Alfred Stepan, Juan J. Linz and Yogendra Yadav, *Crafting State-Nations. India and Other Multinational Democracies* (Johns Hopkins University Press 2011); Arun K. Thiruvengadam, *The Constitution of India. A Contextual Analysis* (Bloomsbury 2017). *See* also Martin Belov (ed.), *Global Constitutionalism and Its Challenges to Westphalian Constitutional Law* (Hart 2018).

has become the founding myth[10] of a country, according to the acceptance of a social state of facts. This assumption is confirmed by the permanence of many countries in which numerous ethnic, religious, and linguistic diversities coexist, without undermining the institutional stability of the state.[11]

Some remarkable examples in Asia (India, Nepal and the Philippines, while South Korea demonstrates the impossibility to approach Asia in a simplistic and 'orientalist' way) and in Latin America (Mexico, Peru, Bolivia, Colombia, Ecuador, and in a less perceptible way Argentina and Chile) made their own state arrangements based on pluralism. In these cases, the ethnic factor led to two different effects: 1) the acknowledgment of diversity with its customs and traditions, 2) the impact of customs and traditions not only on the legal system through constitutions and human rights, but also on the state-building patterns, with a special focus on the administration of local bodies and the rights of ethnic communities to self-determination (within the state legal system). In other words, there is a sort of convergence in recognising minor ethnic groups and their cultures as elements of integration, avoiding a nationalistic assimilation and trying to reduce inequalities. From this trend, the question is whether the cultural foundations revolutionise the state-building phase and/or the constitutional scheme.

In the light of the previous considerations, this chapter deals with the contemporary background of 'cultural discontent' and the constitutional protection of minorities in some significant Asian and Latin-American experiences. The analysis will be conducted through a multidisciplinary comparative law approach and the exploration of the relevant constitutional provisions, in order to focus on the dialogue between the 'ethnic factor' and the constitutional order.[12] The chapter deals, first, with an attempt to introduce concepts such as ethnicity and multiculturalism in Asia, then it examines the influence of minorities on the state organisation and their protection. In the following part, the analysis illustrates the importance of the ethnic factor in Latin-American constitutions, concluding with some remarks on the evolution of contemporary constitutionalism within a theoretical, legal and social framework.

2 Cases of subsidiary, hegemonic and liberal ethnic-based states in Asia

Ethnicity can be defined as 'a sense of group belonging, based on ideas of common origins, history, culture, language, experience and values'.[13] Post-colonial

10 On multiculturalism as funding myth of Nepal *see* Pasquale Viola, 'Lingua e diritto nella Costituzione nepalese del 15 settembre 2015: 'diversità non discordante' e Stato multiculturale' (2016) 28 *DPCE Online* 77.

11 Cf Domenico Amirante, *Lo Stato multiculturale. Contributo alla teoria dello Stato dalla prospettiva dell'Unione indiana* (BUP 2014).

12 See Pasquale Viola, 'The Nepalese path towards the constitutional protection of minorities: a comparative Asian perspective' (2019) 26 *Revista General de Derecho Público Comparado* 1.

13 Francesca Decimo and Alessandra Gribaldo, *Boundaries Within: Nation, Kinship and Identity Among Migrants and Minorities* (Springer 2017) 24. On ethnicity, cf Martín Hopenhayn and

studies highlighted the common cultural and sociological fate of Asia and Latin America during colonialism, especially concerning the clash between the imposition of Western law and the ancestral beliefs of existing social groups. Nowadays, the overlapping of pre- and post- legal structures is reversed in the contemporary concept of legal pluralism,[14] trying to consolidate domestic instances with international ones.

After many attempts to find common cultural roots in Asia, the thesis of the absence of a specific dominant philosophy could be the specific feature of this region. Indeed, simplistic ways to reduce Asia to a single definition just reveal an orientalist approach to its history. This assumption is more evident in the field of ethnic, linguistic, and anthropological studies, considering the immense cultural variety of this region.

In the political and legal fields of study, such degree of diversity challenged the doctrinal construction of Western dogmatic concepts like 'state' and 'nation',[15] obliging the adoption of different pragmatic approaches. Distinctive languages, customs, cultures are located inside the same boundaries, and constitutional texts dealt with these issues, elaborating suitable solutions for guaranteeing a stable and (not always) peaceful co-existence among different ethnic groups.[16]

This chapter rejects a reductionist and orientalist approach, but a macro-comparison always lacks the in-depth analysis of a specific phenomenon. For these reasons, a short outline is provided about ethnic minorities in India, Nepal, the Philippines and South Korea, considered as significant cases in South Asia, South-East Asia and East Asia.

Alvaro Bello, 'Discriminación étnico-racial y xenofobia en América Latina y el Caribe' (2001) 47 *CEPAL – SERIE Políticas Sociales* 7: 'Mientras la raza se asocia a distinciones biológicas atribuidas a genotipos y fenotipos, especialmente con relación al color de la piel, la etnicidad se vincula a factores de orden cultural, si bien con frecuencia ambas categorías son difícilmente separables'. In this essay, starting from the ideas pointed out by Edward W. Said, *Cultura e imperialismo* (Anagrama 1993), the authors state that: 'El colonialismo va a ser una fuente primordial para la constitución de las ideas sobre las diferencias raciales. La misma idea de la superioridad racial europea frente a la supuesta inferioridad y salvajismo de los nativos de América serán parte de los procesos históricos de construcción de imágenes culturales de conquistados y conquistadores'.

14 Werner Menski, 'Beyond Europe', in Esin Örücü and David Nelken (eds), *Comparative Law. A Handbook* (Hart 2007); Marc Galanter, 'Justice in many rooms: courts, private ordering and indigenous law' (1981) 19 *Journal of Legal Pluralism* 1; Masaji Chiba (ed.), *Asian Indigenous Law in Interaction with Received Law* (Routledge 1986); Masaji Chiba, *Legal Pluralism: Towards a General Theory through Japanese Legal Culture* (Tokai University Press 1989).

15 Domenico Amirante, 'Post-modern constitutionalism in Asia: perspectives from the Indian experience' 6 (2013) *NUJS Law Review* 213; Elisabetta Basile and Michelguglielmo Torri (eds), *Il subcontinente indiano verso il terzo millennio* (FrancoAngeli 2002). On the debate about legal classifications and models *see* Amirante (n 8); cf. Konrad Zweigert and Hein Kötz, *Introduzione al diritto comparato. I Principi fondamentali* (Giuffré 1992); René David and Camille Jauffret-Spinosi, *I grandi sistemi giuridici contemporanei* (CEDAM 2004); Antonio Gambaro and Rodolfo Sacco, *Sistemi giuridici comparati* (UTET 2008). On the nation-state and state-nation theory *see* Stepan, Linz and Yadav (n 9) 8. About the state-nation theory applied to Nepal's contemporary constitutional history: Viola (n 10).

16 On the effects of ethnicity issues on state-building: Yash Ghai (ed.), *Autonomy and Ethnicity: Negotiating Competing Claims in Multi-Ethnic States* (Cambridge University Press 2000).

India is a proper example of cultural and ethnic diversity in South Asia, and the constitutional protection of minorities plays a pivotal role in the legal system, with its extensive legacy related to affirmative actions.[17] For instance, the ethnic dimension had a pivotal role in the state-building process – as demonstrated by the first arrangement of the states on a linguistic base[18]– while the protection of minorities has always been at the core of the amending constitutional processes and judicial activism.[19] On this aspect, legal attention for Scheduled Tribes and Castes[20] is one of the most relevant examples of such constitutional interest. The Constitution of India contains provisions for the protection of these communities,[21] with the aim of safeguarding indigenous groups and their customs, providing them with extensive administrative autonomy. On the one hand, the Fifth Schedule of the Constitution refers to the whole country–except for the North-East states, that are administrated under the Sixth Schedule – and implicitly recognises, as part of India's legal system, customs and traditions of these communities. On the other hand, the Sixth Schedule, besides entrusting peculiar legislative, executive, and judicial powers to local bodies, expressly accepts into the legal system their customs and traditions.[22]

The Federal Democratic Republic of Nepal also challenges the classic conception of the nation-state. The social features of the country may give the idea of a state with substantial unitary features, especially after the so-called process of Hinduisation/Nepalisation.[23] Despite this unifying narrative, the Nepalese state has evolved on a substratum of diversities that influenced the state-building phase succeeding the Maoist Revolution and the transition from monarchy to the republic,[24] shifting from authoritarianism to a democratic and participatory

17 Cristophe Jaffrelot, 'The impact of affirmative action in India: more political than socioeconomic' (2006) 5 *India Review* 173; K.S. Chalam, *Caste-Based Reservations and Human Development in India* (Sage 2007); Satish Deshpande and Yogendra Yadav, 'Redesigning affirmative action, caste and benefits in higher education' (2006) 41 *Economic and Political Weekly* 2419; Marc Galanter, *Competing Equalities: Law and the Backward Classes in India* (Oxford University Press 1991); Thomas E. Weisskopf, *Affirmative Action in the United States and India. A Comparative Perspective* (Routledge 2004); Ashwini Deshpande, *Affirmative Actions in India* (Oxford University Press 2013).

18 Stepan, Linz and Yadav (n 9).

19 For an introductory framework: Hormasji M. Seervai, *Constitutional Law of India* (Universal Law Publishing 2015); M.P. Jain, *Indian Constitutional Law* (LexisNexis 2018); P.M. Bakshi, *Commentary on the Constitution of India* (Universal Law Publishing 2016); Mahendra P. Singh, *V.N. Shukla's Constitution of India* (EBC 2017).

20 Cf. some contemporary perspectives on scheduled tribes and castes in the light of an outline of India's Constitution: Madhav Khosla, *The Indian Constitution* (Oxford University Press 2012); Sujit Choudhry, Madhav Khosla and Pratap B. Mehta (eds), *The Oxford Handbook of the Indian Constitution* (Oxford University Press 2016); Thiruvengadam (n 9).

21 Articles 244, 244-A, 371-A to J, Fifth and Sixth Schedules, Constitution of India, 1950.

22 *See* Mahendra P. Singh, *The Indian Legal System: An Enquiry* (Oxford University Press 2019).

23 T. Louise Brown, *The Challenge to Democracy in Nepal. A Political History* (Routledge 1996).

24 Yash Ghai, 'The old order is dying, the new order is not yet born. Politics of constitution demolishing and constitution building in Nepal' in A.H.Y. Chen (ed.), *Constitutionalism in Asia in the Early Twenty-First Century* (Cambridge University Press 2014).

system of governance.[25] The socio-cultural context of the 'new' state is deeply plural, with many ethnic, religious and linguistic differences.[26] In this context, the contemporary Constitution of Nepal is trying to manage socio-economic issues in such a way to avoid political instability, secession, or dispersion of state power. The state-building phase aimed to introduce cooperative federalism inspired by the Indian federal scheme, as well as the parliamentary system of government.[27] The Nepalese state-building phase, in addition to considering the cultural and linguistic factors as crucial elements, clearly shows the close relationship between ethnicity and identity. In the past, the binomial Hindu religion/Muluki Ain inspired legal provisions, supported by the elites, aiming to exclude from the political agenda the demands of backward social groups (e.g. Madhesi, Janajati and women). According to some authors, the Madhesi versus Pahadi dichotomy is an example of 'democratic' exclusion.[28] This form of ethnic identity has an impact also on other ethnic groups in the Terai, i.e. on the Tharu people, who would be totally excluded from a political agenda investing only on the creation of 'one Madhesi' land, exacerbating the relationships among ethnic groups. Furthermore, also an opening to a more peaceful co-existence between Madhesi and Tharu in the Terai would not take into account further minor ethnic groups that live in the same region.

The Constitution of Nepal, in Art. 306, defines minorities as 'ethnic, linguistic and religious groups whose population is less than the percentage specified by the federal law, and includes groups that have their distinct ethnic, religious or linguistic characteristics, aspirations to protect such features and are subjected to discrimination and oppression'.[29] The establishment of a new state needs the

25 Ibid.

26 Yash Ghai (ed.), *Autonomy and Ethnicity: Negotiating Competing Claims in Multi-Ethnic States* (Cambridge University Press 2000).

27 Cf. P. Viola, *Costituzionalismo autoctono. Pluralismo culturale e trapianti giuridici nel subcontinente indiano* (Bononia University Press 2020).

28 The word Pahadi refers to Nepalese people that come from the Kathmandu valley, while the term Madeshi assumed a different meaning. In earlier times, the word Madhesi was used as a geographic marker for inhabitants of the Terai plain in southern Nepal (close to the Indian border). Over the decades, the term Madhesi acquired a specific definition: 'not just a Terai citizen, but a true ethnicity with caste structure, languages, names and religious rituals distinct from both Indians and Nepali Pahadis.' Jason Miklian, *Nepal's Terai: Constructing an Ethnic Conflict* (International Peace Research Institute 2008); Mahendra Lawoti, *Toward a Democratic Nepal: Inclusive Political Institutions for a Multicultural Society* (SAGE 2005); Kalpana Jha, *The Madhesi Upsurge and the Contested Idea of Nepal* (Springer 2017). The re-invention of the Madhesi identity added to the geography new ethnic, caste, and class attributes. This newly ethnic division impacts on many political and legal aspects. Along with an oppositional construction of the identity, they demand to be proportionally included in the social service and in the armed forces; they also demand recognition of their languages as official, as well to redefine the constituencies according to the Madhesi population. See also Mahendra Lawoti, *Looking Back, Looking Forward: Centralization, Multiple Conflicts, and Democratic State Building in Nepal* (East-West Center 2007).

29 Part 34, Definitions and Interpretations, Art. 306, Constitution of the Federal Democratic Republic of Nepal. All the articles mentioned in this paragraph with no further information are part of the Nepalese Constitution, 2015.

creation of an identity consistent with the social context. Article 3 deals with the definition of the Nepalese nation, highlighting the multicultural roots of a state that had been forced to be mono-cultural in the past. In fact, the different cultural heritages are collectively responsible and mutually inspired by a common aspiration to constitute a nation 'united in diversity'. In contrast, Art. 4 recognises inclusiveness as one of the keystones of the new Nepal. The definition of Art. 306 and the provisions contained in Articles 3 and 4 offer a clear idea of the new ideological foundation of Nepal, departing from the old conception of nation-state, and further pursuing the same contextual approach which had characterised the state-building phase. Moreover, the composition of local bodies is strongly influenced by minorities. As stated in Part 17 of the Constitution, the village executives must include women and Dalit or people belonging to minority communities elected by the members of the village assembly amongst themselves. The municipal executive must also include women and Dalit or people belonging to minority communities elected by the members of the Municipal Assembly.[30] As for the state structure, the impact of the existence of minorities and the demand for social and political inclusion led the Constituent Assembly to give a peculiar arrangement to the directive principles, policies and obligations of the state; in the same way, the Constitution aims to develop social and cultural values founded on national pride, democracy, pro-people, respect for labour, entrepreneurship, discipline, dignity and harmony, and to consolidate national unity by maintaining social cohesion, solidarity and harmony, recognising cultural diversity.[31]

The importance of minorities and the adoption of an inclusive policy in a socialist-oriented democracy is also demonstrated by the establishment of the National Inclusion Commission. The functions, duties, and powers of this Commission are quite wide, and include conducting research on the condition and the implementation of the policies related to minorities and other vulnerable communities (Khas Arya, Pichhada class, persons with disabilities, senior citizens, labourers, peasants, minorities and marginalised communities, backward classes, people of Karnali and the indigent class). Besides the National Inclusion Commission, the Constitution provides for the establishment, by the Federal Parliament, of several constitutional bodies, i.e. the Indigenous Nationalities Commission, the Madhesi Commission, the Tharu Commission, and the Muslim Commission.[32]

The Philippines is a suitable example of a multicultural state in South-East Asia, as per the presence of different ethnic groups.[33] On this regard, the Constitution

30 Articles 215, 216, 222 and 223, Constitution of the Federal Democratic Republic of Nepal, 2015.

31 Art. 50, Constitution of the Federal Democratic Republic of Nepal, 2015.

32 Art 261ff., Constitution of the Federal Democratic Republic of Nepal, 2015.

33 On a population of approx. 106 million people (July 2018 est.), there are seven main ethnic groups: Tagalog 28.1%, Bisaya/Binisaya 11.4%, Cebuano 9.9%, Ilocano 8.8%, Hiligaynon/Ilonggo 8.4%, Bikol/Bicol 6.8%, Waray 4%, other local ethnicities 26.1%, other foreign ethnicity 0.1% (2010 est.). Furthermore, the population speaks Filipino (based on Tagalog) and

of the Philippines provides indigenous groups with the right to self-governance, considered as a principle of the state policy,[34] and diversity is declared as 'national patrimony'.[35] About self-governance of indigenous communities, Article XVI 'General provisions', Sec 12 of the Constitution provides that: 'The Congress may create a consultative body to advise the President on policies affecting indigenous cultural communities, the majority of the members of which shall come from such communities.' This article sets the base for the legal formalisation of ethnic social structures and organs, specifying a consultative body with indigenous members.

The South Korean case is radically different from the previous ones.[36] In fact, the Constitution does not devote any provision to specific ethnic groups, nor defers to other legal bodies a specific duty for the protection of ethnic diversity. The reason for this choice is the cultural-homogenous population and the absence of relevant ethnic claims. However, the Constitution of South Korea provides indirect relevance and general protection to cultural diversity, in order to fulfil the universal obligation for the protection of human rights.[37] Nevertheless, the absence of endogenous cultural minorities does not prevent multicultural

---

English, and there are eight major dialects: Tagalog, Cebuano, Ilocano, Hiligaynon or Ilonggo, Bicol, Waray, Pampango, and Pangasinan. Data: www.cia.gov/library/publications/resources/the-world-factbook/ (accessed: 21 August 2020). Cf. Marc R. Thompson and Eric V.C. Batalla (eds), *Routledge Handbook of the Contemporary Philippines* (Routledge 2018) 1: 'The Philippines is a fascinating example of a "poor country democracy" where issues of economic development and poverty, political participation and stability, as well as ethnicity and migration are crucial'. *See* also Omar S. McDoom, 'Ethnic inequality, cultural distance, and social integration: evidence from a native-settler conflict in the Philippines' (2019) 45 *Journal of Ethnic and Migration Studies* 1532; Gregg Bankoff and Kathleen Weekley, *Post-Colonial National Identity in the Philippines: Celebrating the Centennial of Independence* (Routledge 2002).

34 The Constitution of Philippines establishes indigenous right to self-governance: 'Article II, Declaration of principles and State policies principles, Sec. 22: The State recognizes and promotes the rights of indigenous cultural communities within the framework of national unity and development'.

35 Cf. Article XII, National economy and patrimony, Sec. 5: 'The State, subject to the provisions of this Constitution and national development policies and programs, shall protect the rights of indigenous cultural communities to their ancestral lands to ensure their economic, social, and cultural well-being. The Congress may provide for the applicability of customary laws governing property rights or relations in determining the ownership and extent of ancestral domain'; and Article XIV, Education, science and technology, arts, culture, and sports, Sec. 2: 'The State shall [...] 4. Encourage non-formal, informal, and indigenous learning systems, as well as self-learning, independent, and out-of-school study programs particularly those that respond to community needs.'

36 www.cia.gov/library/publications/the-world-factbook/geos/ks.html (accessed: 21 August 2020).

37 Article 10, Constitution of South Korea, 1987: 'All citizens shall be assured of human worth and dignity and have the right to pursue happiness. It shall be the duty of the State to confirm and guarantee the fundamental and inviolable human rights of individuals.' Article 11 of the Constitution of South Korea: '1. All citizens shall be equal before the law, and there shall be no discrimination in political, economic, societal, or cultural life on account of sex, religion, or social status. 2. No privileged caste shall be recognized or ever established in any form. 3. The awarding of decorations or distinctions of honor in any form shall be effective only for recipients, and no privileges shall ensue therefrom.'

demands, in the light of the recent economic development of the country[38] and the subsequent arrival of numerous migrants from Asia, Europe, and North-America, which have determined similar conditions for 'ethnic implants' and demands of their legalisation.

In the abovementioned multicultural experiences, the consequence of the instrumental use of diversity was the introduction of culture-rooted elements in the constitutional system, in order to respond to the claim for participation and representation in public decision-making processes, with a clear intent to realise a democracy capable of guaranteeing social justice. In the light of these circumstances, as stated by Y. Ghai,[39] the relationship ethnicity/state architecture in multi-ethnic realities can ground the identification of two models: 1) the liberal state, which tends not to recognise diversity, considering people as citizens having the same rights and obligations; 2) ethnic-based state, i.e. states based on the political recognition of ethnic groups as bearers of rights. The second model is further sub-divided into two sets: i) the hegemonic state, in which a caste or ethnic group prevails over the others; ii) subsidiary state, characterised by consensual politics, power-sharing, and proportionality of representatives.

According to this scheme, India and the Philippines represent a mixture of subsidiary and hegemonic ethnic-based state, while Nepal, from being a hegemonic ethnicity-based state, is trying to shift towards the subsidiary model under the Constitution of 2015. Conversely, South Korea could be classified as a liberal state, where diversity plays no pivotal role in the set-up of the constitutional order and the state.

3 The constitutional acknowledgment of diversity in Latin America

The ethnic factor is one of the most pervasive elements of debate in Latin America, affecting the state-building options and the actual programmes of economic

38 An example of the Western-like development of Koreans is provided by the change in demographic: 'In less than half a century, the fertility and mortality regimes in the Republic of Korea have changed from the typical developing-country pattern to one characteristic of developed countries' Hanam S. Phang, 'Demographic dividend and labour force transformations in Asia: the case of the Republic of Korea', UN Department of Economic and Social Affairs, www.un.org/en/development/desa/population/publications/pdf/ageing/egm-mex-phang.pdf (accessed: 21 August 2020) 119. See also Giovanna M.D. Dore, Jae H. Ku and Karl D. Jackson (eds), *Incomplete Democracies in the Asia-Pacific. Evidence from Indonesia, Korea, the Philippines* (Palgrave 2014).

39 Yash Ghai, 'Ethnicity, identity, participation and social justice: a constitution for new Nepal' (2011) 3 *International Journal on Minority and Group Rights* 309, 311: 'In the ethnic-based state, ethnic groups are fundamental building blocks of the political system and many rights of citizenship can only be exercised through membership of an ethnic group. Citizenship rights are differentiated. Representation and participation are based on ethnic distinctions. Therefore, group rights are frequently more important than individual rights. There is often explicit recognition in the public sphere of cultural differences between communities, blurring the distinction between the public and private.'

development of this region.[40] The estimated number of indigenous peoples of the region is around 42 million, equal to the 8% of the entire population. In this scenario, the country-based presence of ethnic minorities is consistent. For instance, in Mexico there is an indigenous population of 16.83 million, equal to the 15% of the population, while in Peru indigenous groups represent the 26% of the entire population.[41] In Guatemala and Bolivia there is the highest coefficient of indigenous peoples according to the entire population: 41%. Colombia, Ecuador, Argentina and Chile also register a prominent presence of indigenous minorities.

Similarly to Asian constitutionalism, the existence of an ontological multicultural society affected the state-building phase. This influence is demonstrated by the interest that constitutions show for the preservation of cultural diversity and the recognition of indigenous and ethnic rights in order to guarantee their subsistence, self-determination, and integration within the state framework.

According to the ethnic composition of the society, constitutional provisions are evidence of the impact that diversity exercises at the highest level of the legal systems. For instance, the Mexican Constitution points out that 'The nation is multicultural, based originally on its indigenous peoples, described as descendants of those inhabiting the country before colonisation and that preserve their own social, economic, cultural and political institutions, or some of them' (Art. 1),[42] and Art. 2A states: 'This Constitution recognizes and protects the indigenous peoples' right to self-determination and, consequently, the right to autonomy'.[43] The multicultural concept of the society is well exemplified by the Constitution of Peru, in Art. 2 n. 19 ('The State recognizes and protects the ethnic and cultural diversity of the Nation')[44] and in the Colombian Constitution (Art. 7, recognition of ethnic and cultural diversity),[45] while the Argentinian Constitution indirectly acknowledges the existence of ethnic diversity inside the list of the legislative powers of the Congress.[46] The cases of Ecuador and Bolivia are particularly interesting, especially for their contribution to the debate on the

40 Cf. Monica C. DeHart, *Ethnic Entrepreneurs: Identity and Development Politics in Latin America* (SUP 2010); Kay B. Warren and Jean E. Jackson, *Indigenous Movements, Self-Representation, and the State in Latin America* (UTP 2002); Ferran Cabrero, 'Ejercer derechos, refundar el Estado', in Ferran Cabrero (ed.), *Ciudadanía intercultural: aportes desde la participación política de los pueblos indígenas de Latinoamérica* (PNUD 2013).

41 *Latinoamérica indígena en el siglo XXI. Primera década* (Banco Internacional de Reconstrucción y Fomento/Banco Mundial 2015).

42 Art. 1, Constitution of Mexico, 1917.

43 Art. 2, l. A, Constitution of Mexico, 1917.

44 Art. 2, n. 19, Constitution of Peru, 1993: 'Every person has the right: […] To his ethnic and cultural identity. The State recognizes and protects the ethnic and cultural diversity of the Nation.'

45 Art. 7, Constitution of Colombia, 1991: 'The State recognizes and protects the ethnic and cultural diversity of the Colombian Nation.'

46 Chapter IV: The powers of Congress, Art. 75, n. 17, Constitution of Argentina, 1994: 'The Congress shall have power: […] 17. To recognize the ethnic and cultural pre-existence of indigenous Argentine peoples.'

link between cultures and the state.[47] In Bolivia, indigenous people are the 41% of the population (4.12 million), and the Constitution defines the state as '[...] inter-cultural, decentralized and with autonomies', founding itself 'on plurality and on political, economic, juridical, cultural and linguistic pluralism in the integration process of the country' (Art 1).[48] Furthermore, in recognising ethnic diversity, the Constitution of Bolivia refers to the pre-colonial existence of social groups able to be conceptually assimilated to the modern hypothesis of nation.[49] In Ecuador, where the indigenous population is estimated as 1.02 million (7% of the entire population),[50] the rights of communities, peoples, and nations are recognised by the Constitution in Chapter 4, Art. 56: 'Indigenous communities, peoples and nations, the Afro-Ecuadorian people, the back-country people (Montubios) of the inland coastal region, and communes are part of the single and indivisible Ecuadorian State'.[51]

Differently, the Chilean state-building phase did not take into account an open recognition of the indigenous people, considering the concept of nation as the result of belonging to a defined institutional set, as per the concept of 'nation-state'. The Constitution indirectly recognises limitations to the exercise of sovereignty in order to respect 'the essential rights that emanate from the human nature'.[52] As a directive principle and duty of the state, institutions have to 'respect and promote those rights, guaranteed by this Constitution, as well as by international treaties which have been ratified by Chile and that are in force'.[53] In this way, the copious framework of international regimes for the recognition and the protection of ethnic minorities and their rights has become an integral part of the Chilean legal system.[54]

47 Silvia Bagni, *`Lo Stato interculturale: primi tentativi di costruzione prescrittiva della categoría', in Silvia Bagni, Giorgia Pavani and Giovanni Figueroa Mijía (coords), La ciencia del derecho constitucional comparado. Estudios en homenaje a Lucio Pegoraro (Tomo II, Tirant Lo Blanch 2017); Pegoraro* and Rinella (n 8)." with "Silvia Bagni, `Lo Stato interculturale: primi tentativi di costruzione prescrittiva della categoría', in Silvia Bagni, Giorgia Pavani and Giovanni Figueroa Mijía (coords), *La ciencia del derecho constitucional comparado. Estudios en homenaje a Lucio Pegoraro* (Tomo II, Tirant Lo Blanch 2017); Pegoraro and Rinella (n 8).

48 Art. 1, Constitution of Bolivia, 2009: 'Bolivia is constituted as a Unitary Social State of Pluri-National Communitarian Law (Estado Unitario Social de Derecho Plurinacional Comunitario) that is free, independent, sovereign, democratic, inter-cultural, decentralized and with autonomies. Bolivia is founded on plurality and on political, economic, juridical, cultural and linguistic pluralism in the integration process of the country.'

49 Art. 2, Constitution of Bolivia, 2009: 'Given the pre-colonial existence of nations and rural native indigenous peoples and their ancestral control of their territories, their free determination, consisting of the right to autonomy, self-government, their culture, recognition of their institutions, and the consolidation of their territorial entities [...]'. See also Bernd Marquardt, *Historia constitucional comparada de Iberoamérica. Las seis fases desde la revolución de 1810 hasta la transnacionalización del siglo XXI* (Editorial Ibáñez 2016).

50 *Latinoamérica indígena en el Siglo XXI. Primera década* (2015).

51 Cf the provisions related to Montubios: Articles 56, 59, 60, 257 and Sixth Transitory Provision Constitution of Ecuador, 1991.

52 Art. 1, Constitution of Chile, 1980.

53 Art. 5, Constitution of Chile, 1980.

54 *Derechos de las minorías: normas internacionales y orientaciones para su aplicación* (United Nations 2010).

The process and outcome of the ongoing constituent phase will prove to what extent such principles are intrinsically embedded within this system." Please add the following citation in a separate footnote 55 after this new sentence: "S. Ragone and J.I. Núñez Leiva, 'Algunas coordenadas esenciales sobre la Convención Constitucional' (2021) *DPCE Online*.

This outline of the constitutional protection of ethnic minorities in Latin America shows some recurrent topics. On the one hand, colonialism exacerbated the ethnic clash between indigenous peoples and colonialists, leaving a heritage of differences depending on (cultural, linguistic, historical, sociological, etc.) diversity; on the other, colonisers brought the concept of uniformity as the foundation of the political unity. As a result of this approach, the development of the idea of the liberal state encompassed the concept of 'one nation', hiding the deep diverse ethnic roots of the population. However, domestic cultures (indigenous, pre-Columbian, or pre-colonial) have been able to survive, at least partially, to the homologation pressures. Latin-American (as well as Asian) constitutions share the will to recognise ethnic groups, the protection and implementation of cultural rights, as well as the right to self-governance and representation.

If diversity has been considered a value in the contemporary idea of the (multicultural) state, the concept of 'integration' must be adapted to diversity as the main asset of the state, avoiding the risk of a mere assimilation or 'tolerance' in the dialectic integration/preservation.[55] From this perspective, the answer of the legal systems to ethnic phenomena (external or endogenous) designs a new pattern, which may determine a critical rethinking of the general theories of the state.

4 Conclusion

Diversity can be a stress factor or the funding myth of a state; it may inspire the adoption of new constitutional tools or determine a democratic crisis due to the efforts to establish a 'one-nation-one-people' state. The aforementioned experiences, however, show some common features: i) the historical and social background deeply influenced the constituent phases in taking into account diversity, as well as minorities, when drafting the constitutional orders; ii) an effect of this recognition is the acknowledgment of diversity with its customs and traditions; iii) cultural aspects permeate the core of the state from a territorial and administrative perspective, as well as the organisation of power-sharing; iv) customs and traditions impact not only on the legal system through constitutions and human rights, but also on the state-building patterns, drawing attention to the administration of local bodies, as well as the rights of ethnic communities to self-determination (within the state legal system). In other words, there is a converging interest in recognising minor ethnic groups and their cultures as elements of integration, avoiding a mere nationalistic assimilation which would stress the democratic setting. In doing so, the constitutional order guarantees

55 An example of the dialectic integration/preservation is Art. 89, Constitution of Peru, 1993: 'The State respects the cultural identity of the rural and native communities.'

the participation in political decision-making and territorial administration, while recognising – directly or indirectly – the legal facet of ethnic traditions worth being included in the formal legal system.

References

Amirante D., 'Post-modern constitutionalism in Asia: perspectives from the Indian experience' (2013) 6 *NUJS Law Review* 213.

Amirante D., *Lo Stato multiculturale. Contributo alla teoria dello Stato dalla prospettiva dell'Unione indiana* (BUP 2014).

Amirante D., 'Al di là dell'Occidente. Sfide epistemologiche e spunti euristici nella comparazione "verso Oriente"' (2015) 17 *Diritto Pubblico Comparato ed Europeo* 1.

Bagni, S., *'Lo Stato interculturale: primi tentativi di costruzione prescrittiva della categoría',* in Silvia Bagni, Giorgia Pavani and Giovanni Figueroa Mijía (coords), *La ciencia del derecho constitucional comparado. Estudios en homenaje a Lucio Pegoraro (Tomo II, Tirant Lo Blanch 2017).*" with "Bagni S., 'Lo Stato interculturale: primi tentativi di costruzione prescrittiva della categoría', in Silvia Bagni, Giorgia Pavani and Giovanni Figueroa Mijía (coords), *La ciencia del derecho constitucional comparado. Estudios en homenaje a Lucio Pegoraro* (Tomo II, Tirant Lo Blanch 2017).

Bakshi P.M., *Commentary on the Constitution of India* (Universal Law Publishing 2016).

Bankoff G. and Weekley K., *Post-Colonial National Identity in the Philippines: Celebrating the Centennial of Independence* (Routledge 2002).

Basile E. and Torri M. (eds), *Il subcontinente indiano verso il terzo millennio* (FrancoAngeli 2002).

Belov M. (ed.), *Global Constitutionalism and Its Challenges to Westphalian Constitutional Law* (Hart 2018).

Black E.A. and Bell G.F., *Law and Legal Institutions of Asia. Traditions, Adaptations and Innovations* (Cambridge University Press 2011).

Boudon R. and Bourricaud F., *A Critical Dictionary of Sociology* (Routledge 1989).

Bruce S. and Yearley S., *The Sage Dictionary of Sociology* (Sage 2006).

Cabrero F. (coord.), *Ciudadanía intercultural: aportes desde la participación política de los pueblos indígenas de Latinoamérica* (PNUD 2013).

Chalam K.S., *Caste-Based Reservations and Human Development in India* (Sage 2007).

Chiba M. (ed.), *Asian Indigenous Law in Interaction with Received Law* (Routledge 1986).

Chiba M., *Legal Pluralism: Towards a General Theory through Japanese Legal Culture* (Tokai University Press 1989).

Choudhry S., Khosla M., and Mehta P.B. (eds), *The Oxford Handbook of the Indian Constitution* (Oxford University Press 2016).

David R. and Jauffret-Spinosi C., *I grandi sistemi giuridici contemporanei* (CEDAM 2004).

Dawson A., *Latin America Since Independence. A History with Primary Sources* (Routledge 2010).

Decimo F. and Gribaldo A., *Boundaries Within: Nation, Kinship and Identity among Migrants and Minorities* (Springer 2017) 24.

DeHart M.C., *Ethnic Entrepreneurs: Identity and Development Politics in Latin America* (SUP 2010).

Deshpande A., *Affirmative Actions in India* (Oxford University Press 2013).

Deshpande S. and Yadav Y., 'Redesigning affirmative action, caste and benefits in higher education' (2006) 41 *Economic and Political Weekly* 2419.

Dore G.M.D., Ku J.H. and Jackson K.D. (eds), *Incomplete Democracies in the Asia-Pacific. Evidence from Indonesia, Korea, the Philippines* (Palgrave 2014).

Eakin M.C., 'Does Latin America have a common History?' (2014) 1 *Vanderbilt e-Journal of Luso-Hispanic Studies* 30.

Galanter M., 'Justice in many rooms: courts, private ordering and indigenous law' (1981) 19 *Journal of Legal Pluralism* 1.

Galanter M., *Competing Equalities: Law and the Backward Classes in India* (Oxford University Press 1991).

Gambaro A. and Sacco R., *Sistemi giuridici comparati* (UTET 2008).

Ghai Y. (ed.), *Autonomy and Ethnicity: Negotiating Competing Claims in Multi-Ethnic States* (Cambridge University Press 2000).

Ghai Y., 'Ethnicity, identity, participation and social justice: a constitution for new Nepal' (2011) 3 *International Journal on Minority and Group Rights* 309.

Ghai Y., 'The old order is dying, the new order is not yet born. Politics of constitution demolishing and constitution building in Nepal' in A.H.Y. Chen (ed.), *Constitutionalism in Asia in the Early Twenty-First Century* (Cambridge University Press 2014).

Giddens A. and Sutton P.W., *Essential Concepts in Sociology* (Polity 2014).

Glenn H.P., *Legal Traditions of the World: Sustainable Diversity in Law* (Oxford University Press 2004).

Hopenhayn M. and Bello A., 'Discriminación étnico-racial y xenofobia en América Latina y el Caribe' (2001) 47 *CEPAL – SERIE Políticas sociales.*

Jaffrelot C., 'The impact of affirmative action in India: more political than socioeconomic' (2006) 5 *India Review* 173.

Jain M.P., *Indian Constitutional Law* (LexisNexis 2018).

Jha K., *The Madhesi Upsurge and the Contested Idea of Nepal* (Springer 2017).

Khosla M., *The Indian Constitution* (Oxford University Press 2012).

Lawoti M., *Looking Back, Looking forward: Centralization, Multiple Conflicts, and Democratic State Building in Nepal* (East-West Center 2007).

Lawoti M., *Toward a Democratic Nepal: Inclusive Political Institutions for a Multicultural Society* (Sage 2005).

Legrand P. and Munday R. (eds), *Comparative Legal Studies: Traditions and Transitions* (Cambridge University Press 2003).

Louise Brown T., *The Challenge to Democracy in Nepal. A Political History* (Routledge 1996).

Marquardt B., *Historia constitucional comparada de Iberoamérica. Las seis fases desde la revolución de 1810 hasta la transnacionalización del siglo XXI* (Editorial Ibáñez 2016).

Marshall G., *Oxford Dictionary of Sociology* (Oxford University Press 1998).

McDoom O.S., 'Ethnic inequality, cultural distance, and social integration: evidence from a native-settler conflict in the Philippines' (2019) 45 *Journal of Ethnic and Migration Studies* 1532.

Menski W., *Comparative Law in a Global Context. The Legal Systems of Asia and Africa* (Cambridge University Press 2006).

Menski W., 'Beyond Europe', in E. Örücü and D. Nelken (eds), *Comparative Law. A Handbook* (Hart 2007).

Miklian J., *Nepal's Terai: Constructing an Ethnic Conflict* (International Peace Research Institute 2008).

Pegoraro L. and Rinella A., *Sistemas constitucionales comparados* (Vol. II, Astrea 2018).

Ragone S. and Núñez Leiva J.I., 'Algunas coordenadas esenciales sobre la Convención Constitucional' (2021) *DPCE Online*.
Sacco R., 'Legal formants: a dynamic approach to comparative law (Installment I of II)' (1991) 39 *The American Journal of Comparative Law* 1.
Said E.W., *Cultura e imperialismo* (Anagrama 1993).
Scheppele K.L., 'The agendas of comparative constitutionalism' (2003) 13 *Law and Courts* 5.
Seervai M., *Constitutional Law of India* (Universal Law Publishing 2015).
Singh M.P., *The Indian Legal System: An Enquiry* (Oxford University Press 2019).
Singh M.P., *V.N. Shukla's Constitution of India* (EBC 2017).
Stepan A., Linz J.J. and Yadav Y., *Crafting State-Nations. India and Other Multinational Democracies* (Johns Hopkins University Press 2011).
Thiruvengadam A.K., *The Constitution of India. A Contextual Analysis* (Bloomsbury 2017).
Thompson M.R. and Batalla E.V.C. (eds), *Routledge Handbook of the Contemporary Philippines* (Routledge 2018).
Turner B.S., *The Cambridge Dictionary of Sociology* (Cambridge University Press 2006).
Viola P., 'Lingua e diritto nella Costituzione nepalese del 15 settembre 2015: 'diversità non discordante' e Stato multiculturale' (2016) 28 *DPCE Online* 77.
Viola P., 'The Nepalese path towards the constitutional protection of minorities: a comparative Asian perspective' (2019) 26 *Revista General de Derecho Público Comparado* 1.
Viola P., *Costituzionalismo autoctono. Pluralismo culturale e trapianti giuridici nel subcontinente indiano* (Bononia University Press 2020).
Warren K.B. and Jackson J.E., *Indigenous Movements, Self-Representation, and the State in Latin America* (UTP 2002).
Weisskopf E.T., *Affirmative Action in the United States and India. A Comparative Perspective* (Routledge 2004).
Williamson E., *Historia de América Latina* (Fondo de Cultura Económica 2013).
Zweigert K. and Kötz H., *Introduzione al diritto comparato. I principi fondamentali* (Giuffré 1992).

8 A silent revolution

How Islamic religious law is paving its way to the European legal orders

Wojciech Brzozowski

1 Introduction

The dynamic growth of the Muslim population in Europe will inevitably intensify the challenges related to the accommodation of the needs and demands inspired by Islam. This process, engaging both the Muslim minority and the non-Muslim majority, is likely to bring mutual discontent and dissatisfaction, and generate tensions in social life. It will also profoundly transform the European legal space, affecting common standards as well as domestic legislation. Or, as I argue in this chapter, the future tense is no longer entirely appropriate here: this transformation has already begun.

The increasing influence of Islamic religious law (Sharia) on the European legal orders appears to be one of the most important dimensions of the current crisis of constitutional democracy in Europe, although it is often overlooked. I have taken the liberty of not discussing those other dimensions, as I believe that this book as a whole does justice to them. Instead, this chapter focuses attention on some developments which seem to have escaped the attention of many chroniclers of this crisis, or which tend to be examined only in a piecemeal manner.

The emergence of Islamic religious law in Europe is a *revolution* in the sense in which Harold J. Berman talks about revolutions in his inspiring book:

> they involved not only the creation of new forms of government but also new structures of social and economic relations, new structures of relations between church and state, and new structures of law, as well as new visions of the community, new perspectives on history, and new sets of universal values and beliefs.[1]

And this revolution is *silent*, because it is so multi-faceted and is arriving by so many paths that the change is likely to pass unnoticed, until the moment when it becomes irreversible.

1 Harold J Berman, *Law and Revolution: The Formation of the Western Legal Tradition* (Harvard University Press 1983) 19.

The question which is central to this chapter is whether Islamic religious law may be – or should be or must never be – recognised by the European states and accommodated within the domestic legal systems. The European response to this question is ambiguous, often self-contradictory, and inconsistent. I argue that there is an increasing need to take a clear and decisive stance on the issue of Sharia, possibly trying to agree on and adopt a common approach in Europe. It is quite an irony that the doctrine of sovereignty, which was developed as a result of the religious wars of the sixteenth century, arising from the need to rely on a political body which would be stronger than any of the competing religious factions,[2] is now under threat from the same old rival: religion.

I begin the present chapter by identifying what is so disturbing about Sharia from the European perspective. By this term – in the hope to avoid its misguided or unfortunate interpretations – I essentially understand the founding values of the European Convention on Human Rights, such as human dignity, respect for democracy and human rights, gender equality, tolerance, openness to dialogue, and peaceful resolution of conflicts. Then I proceed to explore in detail the three main paths by which Islamic law is entering the European legal orders. The subsequent section discusses the implications of these developments for the concept of state sovereignty. In the final considerations, I intend to map out the desired response to Sharia in Europe.

2 Is Sharia really a threat to human rights and democracy?

There is a great body of work concerning Sharia's deficiencies with regard to respecting human rights and the principles of democracy. Suggestions have been made that the moral intuition embodied in the language of international human rights law can never make peace with traditionalist Islamic law, as the two systems are so fundamental to their supporters that any move away from them would be unacceptable.[3] While depicting human rights law as a kind of secular faith is not a new idea,[4] seeing it equated with radical Islamic worldviews and labelled as one of the conflicting fundamentalisms may be disturbing or even shocking to a Western mind. No matter how accurate this vision is, it probably grasps the essence of the matter on a more general level: from the perspective of mainstream human rights orthodoxy, Islam is another world.

The Council of Europe's assessment of the political aspirations of Islam was established many years ago, in unambiguous terms, in the case of *Refah Partisi*

2 Michel Troper, 'Sovereignty and Laïcité' in Susanna Mancini and Michel Rosenfeld (eds), *Constitutional Secularism in an Age of Religious Revival* (Oxford University Press 2014) 150.

3 Neville Cox, 'The Clash of Unprovable Universalisms – International Human Rights and Islamic Law' (2013) 2 *Oxford Journal of Law and Religion* 307, 310.

4 Cf. Henri Féron, 'Human rights and faith: a "world-wide secular religion"?' (2014) 7 *Ethics & Global Politics* 181.

and Others v Turkey. The case, decided by the Grand Chamber of the European Court of Human Rights, gave the Court the opportunity to conclude that:

> Sharia, which faithfully reflects the dogmas and divine rules laid down by religion, is stable and invariable. Principles such as pluralism in the political sphere or the constant evolution of public freedoms have no place in it.... It is difficult to declare one's respect for democracy and human rights while at the same time supporting a regime based on sharia, which clearly diverges from Convention values, particularly with regard to its criminal law and criminal procedure, its rules on the legal status of women and the way it intervenes in all spheres of private and public life in accordance with religious precepts.[5]

This short passage captures the essence of Strasbourg's distrust of Sharia. The Court highlighted the general incompatibility of the Islamic ideal of political community with the Convention, at the same time highlighting some of the most problematic areas. Its reasoning is driven by a simple yet irresistible logic: recognising any system of values which unconditionally prioritises religious faith over democratic commitments will inevitably dismantle the rule of law. It is not hard to see why: 'religion presents God's invariable Will, whereas democracy portrays humankind's variable will; the variable should be guided by the criterion of the invariable and, whenever they conflict, the invariable Word of God always has priority'.[6]

Such a clear-cut rejection of Sharia in the Grand Chamber's judgment met with considerable criticism, voiced from positions which obviously do not sympathise with the somewhat utopian vision of building a European caliphate, but instead call for a more nuanced approach to the concept of Sharia. It was argued that the Court failed to define what it meant by Sharia,[7] a notion which cannot be reduced to a body of law in the Western sense, much less to a form of government. The word Sharia, literally meaning a road, a path, or a direction, refers not only to what is mandated or admissible in the legal sense, but provides broad guidelines on how to live a decent life.[8] Taking that into account, an official condemnation of Sharia as a whole could be counterproductive: it will neither help combat fundamentalism nor attract the non-radical followers of Islam to the European understanding of democracy and human rights.

5 *Refah Partisi and Others v Turkey* Apps nos 41340/98, 41342/98, 41343/98, 41344/98 (ECtHR, 13 February 2003) para 123.

6 Yaser Ellethy, *Islam, Context, Pluralism and Democracy: Classical and Modern Interpretations* (Routledge 2015) 245.

7 Christian Moe, '*Refah* revisited: Strasbourg's Construction of Islam' in W Cole Durham, Jr, Rik Torfs, David M Kirkham and Christine Scott (eds), *Islam, Europe and Emerging Legal Issues* (Ashgate 2012) 250; Maurits S Berger, 'Understanding Sharia in the West' (2018) 6 *Journal of Law, Religion and State* 236, 237.

8 Irene Oh, 'Islamic Conceptions of Human Rights' in Thomas Cushman (ed), *Handbook of Human Rights* (Routledge 2014) 258.

Yet, taking the Court's side in this dispute, it can be argued that the Grand Chamber was far from dismissing Sharia in its every aspect. While the central passage from *Refah Partisi* starts with exposing the features of Sharia which do not sit well with pluralism or the ever-changing public freedoms, it later proceeds to declare that what is unacceptable is not personal religiosity of some kind but 'a regime based on sharia'; this is due to the fact that such a regime would diverge from the values enshrined in the Convention. Similarly, a distinction has been drawn between Islam and Islamism, the former being a religion and the latter being 'a religiously disguised form of political extremism'.[9] It would be logical to think that rejecting a regime based on religious rules does not necessarily imply rejecting religious rules, at least as long as these are accepted on a voluntary basis and confined to the private sphere. Looking through the lenses of human rights law, political or religious fundamentalism – no matter how undesirable in public life – should not be deemed an issue as long as it does not have a direct impact on other people's lives and does not intend to undermine the legal order.

There is also another important question: should the Council of Europe bodies, notably the European Court of Human Rights, assume that there is one single version of Sharia which is representative for Islam in Europe or elsewhere? The global Muslim community has not developed commonly accepted views on most legal issues, because many Sharia rules do not come directly from God but stem from the Islamic tradition, and also because the interpretation of textual rules is not homogenous.[10] This goes contrary to the popular belief that the claims of Sharia are not open to (re)negotiation. Moreover, since there is no ultimate instance in the Islamic world which would pronounce final legal opinions, as the Holy See does in the Roman Catholic tradition, alternate views on many subjects are allowed.[11] Attempts are being made to reconcile Islam with modernity and secular values, with the aim of framing it as a reasonable comprehensive doctrine in Rawlsian terms.[12]

Re-examining Islamic teaching in relation to some particularly controversial issues and supporting non-radical opinions on the true content of religious rules may be a way for Islam to come to terms with the Western ideal of democracy. Nevertheless, for a few reasons this picture seems overly optimistic. First, there may be differing views on a range of issues in Islam, but with regard to many aspects of personal and social life, e.g. same-sex unions, an overwhelmingly prevailing interpretation exists, and it is far from the answers that the Council of Europe or the European Union would be ready to give. This is mostly because rules grounded on clear and unambiguous scripture are considered immutable in Islamic scholarship.[13] Second, it would be short-sighted to expect that

9 PACE Resolution 1743 (2010) of 23 June 2010 – 'Islam, Islamism and Islamophobia in Europe' para 20.

10 Cox (n 3) 311.

11 Oh (n 8) 260; see also Moe (n 7) 253.

12 Mohammed Hashas, *The Idea of European Islam: Religion, Ethics, Politics and Perpetual Modernity* (Routledge 2018).

13 Moe (n 7) 254.

intellectual projects could be immediately accepted and made part of people's lives, especially in closed traditional communities. Last, even a rapid shift in the prevailing Muslim attitudes to modernity does not imply the complete eradication of the most radical codes of conduct, and in the end, it is radical Islam that raises most concern in Europe. Western fears are inevitably shaped by stories such as the Charlie-Hebdo massacre or the controversy over *Jyllands-Posten* Muhammad cartoons rather than by the mere existence of halal shops or Islamic financial instruments.

The key issue in the debate on the compatibility of Islam with the European legal orders seems to be the nature of human rights. It is often argued that while the Muslim world has embraced the general concept of human rights, it has difficulty accepting Western-bias in human rights declarations.[14] In a much similar vein, Muslims are said to potentially endorse a broad view of human rights, but not necessarily the direction in which this concept has been developed in the Western legal discourse.[15] But how exactly would that work? How can the concept of human rights be embraced without accepting its content? Is it a real alternative to the Western perspective or merely a rhetorical device deliberately used to hide the fact that the Islamic version of this concept is in fact hollowed out and meaningless?

To approach a possible answer, it may prove useful to study the Islamic response to the Universal Declaration of Human Rights, namely the Cairo Declaration of Human Rights in Islam (CDHRI).[16] This remarkable document bears some resemblance to the original, yet it does not take much time to realise that the foundations of the Islamic vision of human rights are very different from the United Nations framework. Clues can be found in the preamble. The Cairo Declaration was not created to recognise the diversity and variety of value systems in a plural world; instead, its makers strive 'to guide all humanity which is confused because of different and conflicting beliefs and ideologies and to provide solutions for all chronic problems of this materialistic civilization'. Seeing the existence of conflicting beliefs as a problem and not as a natural feature of the modern world could not be more remote from the Western appraisal of pluralism, especially with respect to religious matters.[17] The language used to mention personal freedom is equally different from the universal standard – the recognition of freedom goes hand in hand with the 'right to a dignified life in accordance with the Islamic Shari'ah'. This, apparently, does not leave much room for different life choices. But how can anyone expect to have a choice under laws which have clearly been sent from heaven? Fundamental rights and

14 Oh (n 8) 256.
15 Cox (n 3) 310.
16 The Cairo Declaration of Human Rights in Islam, adopted and issued at the 19th Islamic Conference of Foreign Ministers in Cairo on 5 August 1990, www.fmreview.org/Human-Rights/cairo.html accessed 17 April 2020.
17 For an overview of the CoE findings concerning religious pluralism, see Dorota Anna Gozdecka, *Rights, Religious Pluralism and the Recognition of Difference: Off the Scales of Justice* (Routledge 2016) 13–24.

freedoms are not mere human concepts but 'binding divine commands'; safeguarding rights and freedoms, apart from being a legal obligation, constitutes 'an act of worship'; and a violation thereof is much more than just a breach of law, as it amounts to 'an abominable sin'.

As the reader goes deeper and deeper, it transpires from the text that although its wording, at least in some parts, was intended to match closely the UN language, the content is as distant from the universal standard as Cairo is from New York. The Islamic vision of human rights is definitely at odds with the idea of reproductive rights, since '[t]he preservation of human life throughout the term of time willed by Allah is a duty prescribed by Shari'ah'[18] and it even mentions the foetus as deserving to be 'safeguarded and accorded special care'.[19] It is also in conflict with gender equality: woman is equal to man in human dignity and enjoys financial independence, yet she has 'her own rights to enjoy as well as duties to perform', whereas it is the husband who is 'responsible for the maintenance and welfare of the family'.[20] As the last sentence makes clear, equal dignity does not translate into equal status in the family or social life. It is therefore plausible to assume that the Cairo Declaration, despite providing for women's access to some aspects of community life, does not ensure their recognition in roles other than wife and mother.[21] In addition, while marriage and family have been declared worthy of protection,[22] it is beyond question that the Islamic approach to human rights does not permit enacting laws to allow sexual relations outside of marriage, or allow same-sex marriage.[23]

The differences between the Western concept of human rights and its aspiring Islamic doppelganger are particularly sharp with regard to freedom of religion or belief. The well-known universal formula starting with 'everyone has the right to…' has been replaced with the assertion that 'Islam is the religion of true unspoiled nature', followed by a prohibition on forcing man to change his religion to another religion or to atheism.[24] The Cairo Declaration does not make any reference to the manifestations of religion to which protection needs to be afforded, such as teaching, practice, worship, and observance, as in the universal and European human rights legal frameworks.[25] In fact, all that it protects is the right to follow the teachings of Islam – a concept which hardly requires additional support in Muslim-majority countries. At the same time, abandoning these teachings seems to be particularly problematic. While the legitimacy of

18 Article 2(c) CDHRI.

19 Article 7(a) CDHRI.

20 Article 6(a,b) CDHRI.

21 Leila Hilal, 'The Cairo Declaration on Human Rights in Islam and International Women's Rights' (1997) 5 *Circles: Buffalo Women's Journal of Law and Social Policy* 85, 89.

22 Article 5(a,b) CDHRI.

23 Abdullah al-Ahsan, 'Law, Religion and Human Dignity in the Muslim World Today: An Examination of OIC's Cairo Declaration of Human Rights' (2008) 24 *Journal of Law and Religion* 569, 573.

24 Article 10 CDHRI.

25 Cf. Article 18(1) ICCPR, Article 9(1) ECHR, Article 10(1) CFREU.

conversion from one faith to another outside Islam is not disputed by Muslim scholars, traditional apostasy laws strictly prohibit conversion from Islam to another religion.[26] In both religious and legal perspectives, this is the line which must not be crossed.

The Cairo Declaration may not have great practical resonance in strictly legal terms, but it gives, without a doubt, an insight to the Islamic approach to the idea of human rights as compared with the Western tradition. It is the same concept only in name, with 'the most compelling difference being that it seems to reduce the rights of citizens to a level of subservience to the law rather than serving as a trump against that law'.[27] It should come as no surprise that at the end of this rather concise document, in which Sharia is nevertheless evoked as many as 15 times, it was stipulated that the only source of reference for the explanation or clarification of any of its articles is Sharia.[28]

Is Sharia really an enemy to democracy and human rights then? As I sought to demonstrate earlier in this section, it would be a natural reaction of a scholar to escape this question by multiplying doubts as to what exactly is meant by Sharia and displaying a variety of currents in Islamic legal thought. Notably, distinctions could be drawn between personal life choices and the constitutional design of a country, in a fashion somehow oblivious to the fact that in Muslim-majority countries these two factors are interdependent. Yet, I concur with the view of Dominic McGoldrick, who argued that despite all the efforts to reconcile Islam with human rights by reinterpreting Islamic governance – efforts which certainly deserve respect and support – it cannot be denied that Sharia has a long way to go before it will evolve to become compatible with modern human rights law, and that at present it remains incompatible.[29] The same could be said of Sharia vis-à-vis democracy: for the latter the idea of eliminating pluralism, or confining it to a range of opinions within one religious system, is intrinsically unacceptable.

3 Three paths of Sharia to the European legal space

This discrepancy between Sharia and the Western vision of human rights and democracy does not prevent Islamic law from leaking into the European legal orders. The Sharia-based concepts may be introduced and supported as an alternative to the traditional legal institutions or merely tolerated at the margin of the legal system; or they can be disguised as claims for accommodating diversity, using the human rights language to integrate religious institutions with that

26 Abdullah Saeed, 'Limitations on Religious Freedom in Islam: Rethinking through the *Maqasid*?' in Silvio Ferrari (ed), *Routledge Handbook of Law and Religion* (Routledge 2015) 377–378.

27 Cox (n 3) 325.

28 Article 25 CDHRI.

29 Dominic McGoldrick, 'The Compatibility of an Islamic/*Shari'a* Law System or *Shari'a* Rules with the European Convention on Human Rights' in Robin Griffith-Jones (ed), *Islam and English Law: Rights, Responsibilities and the Place of Shari'a* (Cambridge University Press 2013) 45–46.

system. In this section, I will outline and appraise three main paths by which Sharia is paving its way to the European legal space: (1) open endorsement, (2) recognising or tolerating extra-legal religious adjudication, and (3) accommodating Muslim identity claims. A similar, albeit not identical, classification was proposed by Dominic McGoldrick some years ago in a paper which offered an examination of how Muslims may – or must not – be accommodated in Europe.[30] Seen from today's perspective, McGoldrick's considerations might seem like a prophecy, and I believe that prophecies need to be revisited and assessed in light of real-life scenarios.

3.1 Open endorsement

Recognising Islam as the state religion and requiring the compatibility of legislation with divine laws would immediately render any discussion on the respect for European values impossible. It should go without saying that such extreme forms of the establishment of religion are rather rare to find, and non-existent in Europe.

Out of 47 member states of the Council of Europe, many have substantial Muslim communities, but only three have Muslim-majority populations, and these are Albania, Azerbaijan, and Turkey.[31] Obviously, none of them is a theocracy. In a recent study, it has been proposed to divide the constitutional systems of 49 Muslim-majority countries into three categories: those defining (explicitly or implicitly) their states as secular, those recognising Islam as the official religion, and those referring to Sharia as a (or the) legal source or compatibility requirement. All the three CoE Muslim member states have been classified as falling into the first category, with the constitutions of Azerbaijan and Turkey explicitly defining the state as secular, and Albania doing so in an implicit way.[32] This last observation is highly questionable. The Albanian Constitution openly declares that '[i]n the Republic of Albania there is no official religion'.[33] Such wording should be acknowledged as openly defining the state as secular. At the same time, of these three countries only Albania is considered to be truly democratic.[34]

While constitutional endorsement of Islam is not encountered anywhere in the European legal space, it needs to be noted that all the three Muslim-majority countries, which also happen to be members of the Organisation of Islamic

30 Dominic McGoldrick, 'Accommodating Muslims in Europe: From Adopting Sharia Law to Religiously Based Opt Outs from Generally Applicable Laws' (2009) 9 *Human Rights Law Review* 603.

31 www.globalreligiousfutures.org/countries accessed 17 April 2020.

32 Ahmed T Kuru, *Islam, Authoritarianism, and Underdevelopment: A Global and Historical Comparison* (Cambridge University Press 2019) 39.

33 Article 10(1) of the Constitution of Albania, see www.constituteproject.org/constitution/Albania_2016.pdf accessed 17 April 2020.

34 Kuru (n 32) 40.

Cooperation, are signatories to the Cairo Declaration. Just how being party to the European Convention on Human Rights can be reconciled with committing to the values of the Cairo Declaration remains a mystery. Arguably, supporting the Islamic vision of, or rather alternative to, democracy and human rights via international law instruments entails undermining the values on which the Council of Europe was founded.

The support for the Cairo Declaration was adamantly criticised by the Parliamentary Assembly of the Council of Europe, though the Assembly needed to come a long way to reach this point. The preparatory works on the report discussing the incompatibility of Sharia with human rights standards were conducted under pressure from Turkey and Azerbaijan, which intended to avoid any debate on the matter and even managed to remove some members of the Assembly who had been critical of Islam from the drafting of the report.[35] Yet, when the report was ready, the rapporteur had no alternative but to admit that the attempts to reconcile Sharia with human rights in the universal sense were at best imperfect. It was stated in the report that the Islamic international documents, notably the Cairo Declaration, were often 'more religious than legal texts' and that they had serious flaws – disguising limitations to the rights being declared by references to domestic legislation or to Sharia, or by providing vague definitions of the rights, as well as omitting certain aspects of the human rights legal framework.[36] The findings of the report were accepted by the Assembly in a resolution which stressed Islam's inability to be brought into harmony with human rights law and expressed the Assembly's great concern that Albania, Azerbaijan, and Turkey had endorsed the Cairo Declaration.[37]

The prospects of Sharia becoming a binding source of law outside Muslim-majority countries may at first seem somewhat remote from reality, but it should not be forgotten that Islamic law actually still is applied in some territories of such Council of Europe member states through official endorsement, or at least was until recently. This may happen if the Muslim-minority population is not distributed evenly across the country and dominates in a particular region.

This is notably the case of Western Thrace (Greece), where the questions of personal status and family law with regard to the members of Muslim minority are governed by Islamic law and subject to a mufti's jurisdiction.[38] Until 2018,

35 Nicolas Bauer, 'Confrontation of Islamic Sharia and Human Rights at the Council of Europe', https://eclj.org/religious-freedom/coe/confrontation-de-la-charia-islamique-et-des-droits-de-lhomme-au-conseil-de-leurope accessed 17 April 2020.

36 PACE Report of 3 January 2019 (Doc. 14787) – 'Compatibility of Sharia law with the European Convention on Human Rights: Can States Parties to the Convention be signatories to the "Cairo Declaration"?' para 26.

37 PACE Resolution 2253 (2019) of 22 January 2019 – 'Sharia, the Cairo Declaration and the European Convention on Human Rights' para 4.

38 See Konstantinos Tsitselikis, 'Applying Shari'a in Europe: Greece as an Ambivalent Legal Paradigm' (2010) 2 *Yearbook of Muslims in Europe* 663. This issue lay at the root of the case of *Molla Sali v Greece*, which was decided by the Grand Chamber of the European Court of Human Rights in 2018. I will discuss this case later in the chapter.

this legal framework was obligatory for any member of the Muslim minority of that region, without the right to opt out; now, it has become optional, with the religious authority exercising jurisdiction only if both parties subject their dispute to Sharia law.[39] The situation was similar in Mayotte, one of the French overseas departments, which until 2011 had a system of Islamic law in civil matters, automatically applicable to Muslim citizens, who nevertheless had the right to waive it in favour of ordinary civil law.[40] But even today Sharia law is being officially enforced in the Northern Caucasus, a Muslim-majority region in the Russian Federation; its rigid application, particularly in Chechnya, is reported to give rise to gross violations of human rights.[41] Although technically these regions are part of the Council of Europe, they can hardly be seen as complying with its standards.

3.2 *Recognising or tolerating extra-legal religious adjudication*

In countries where the Muslim population is far from becoming a majority, both on the national and regional levels, the state authorities are not likely to accept Sharia as an official source of state law. Nevertheless, Islamic law may pave its way to such jurisdictions by means of voluntary religious adjudication, officially recognised or at least tolerated by the state.

The term 'recognition' may be misleading, as it to some extent obscures the difference between open endorsement (in which, technically, the decisions of religious courts are *recognised* too) and some forms of accommodation of non-binding religious arbitration.[42] This difference may be explained by reference to the distinction between parallel legal systems with personal status laws (as in Mayotte or Western Thrace until recently, where the applicable legal order depended on the religious affiliation of the party) and plural systems (in which religious adjudication is supplementary to civil jurisdiction).[43] In this section, only the plural systems are discussed.

Little is known about the actual scale of this phenomenon across Europe. It would be most surprising though if non-official Islamic adjudicating or counselling bodies were not present in most countries with a substantial Muslim minority. Voluntary religious adjudication as such has remained out of sight of the European Court of Human Rights, which has had little to decide on such matters. In addition, as noted a few years ago, no consistent jurisprudence had

39 Apostolos Anthimos, 'Sharia law in Greece: Blending European Values with Islamic Tradition' (24 January 2018) https://conflictoflaws.net/2018/sharia-law-in-greece-blending-european-values-with-islamic-tradition accessed 17 April 2020.

40 PACE (n 36) paras 55–58.

41 Ibid., paras 59–61.

42 Cf. Ian Leigh, 'Religious Adjudication and the European Convention on Human Rights' (2019) 8 *Oxford Journal of Law and Religion* 1, 3–4.

43 Ibid., 3. The author draws this distinction on the earlier findings of Lorenzo Zucca.

been developed, and the judgments did not even contain cross-references to one another.[44]

Yet, in relation to Islam, the phenomenon has been widely discussed and examined with regard to the example of the United Kingdom, which has a long track record of dealing with Muslim arbitration tribunals and Sharia councils. These two types of institutions should not be confused. Muslim arbitration tribunals are recognised within the state law and they operate under the Arbitration Act 1996, just like any other arbitration institution, religious or not, whose aim is to provide the fair resolution of disputes. It is important that their decisions can be enforced by state courts, which implies that they need to be made known to the public authorities in the first place, and that they are subject to oversight. Should the decisions not conform to the state legal systems, they shall not be officially recognised nor enforced.[45]

Sharia councils, in turn, act beyond the province of the law. They are not considered to be part of the official legal system and their decisions are not enforceable by public agencies. Acting like courts, they provide a form of alternative dispute resolution to people who, at least in theory, voluntarily accept religious jurisdiction. The cases referred to these councils predominantly concern marital issues, but they also cover commercial law and inheritance disputes.[46] In short, the rulings of arbitration tribunals can be considered as *recognised* within the sense explained earlier in this section, whereas the decisions adopted by Sharia councils fall into the 'toleration' category.

The operation of non-binding Muslim adjudicative mechanisms in the United Kingdom has now for some time been one of the most popular topics in law and religious studies. The public interest in it rose suddenly after the famous lecture given by Rowan Williams, at that time Archbishop of Canterbury, at the Royal Courts of Justice in 2008. This lecture, proposing a 'transformative accommodation' of the new legal and religious reality, launched a stormy debate, and not just among university scholars.[47] The approach suggested by the Archbishop entailed 'a scheme in which individuals retain the liberty to choose the jurisdiction under which they will seek to resolve certain carefully specified matters', such as 'aspects of marital law, the regulation of financial transactions and authorised structures of mediation and conflict resolution'.[48]

There are a number of reasons why this picture did not meet with unanimous approval from the non-Muslim audience. The main reason for concern is not the

44 Cf. Michał Rynkowski, 'Religious Courts in the Jurisprudence of the European Court of Human Rights' (2016) 18 *Ecclesiastical Law Journal* 62, 65.

45 PACE (n 36) para 51.

46 Ibid., paras 46–47.

47 For a detailed discussion of the events shortly preceding and following this lecture, see Robin Griffith-Jones, 'The "Unavoidable" Adoption of Shari'a Law – The Generation of a Media Storm' in Griffith-Jones (n 29).

48 Rowan Williams, 'Civil and Religious Law in England: A Religious Perspective' in Griffith-Jones (n 29) 32.

operation of Islamic arbitration within the state legal framework, but the silent activity of Sharia councils in the field of marital law and family disputes, with a rather lengthy list of religiously motivated practices which should not be deemed worthy of respect in a democratic society.[49] The list of wrongdoings includes: 'discrimination against women, reactionary rulings prolonging marital captivity, lax approaches to domestic violence and informing victims of their rights, the absence of child safeguarding mechanisms, wilful blindness to English law and the steady corrosion of social cohesion'. Another big and unsolved problem is the existence of unregistered religious marriages, which potentially complicates issues such as custody of children, the financial consequences of a divorce, or inheritance disputes.

Many explanations are offered as to why Muslim people may prefer religious-only marriage of non-recognition. While some motivations clearly do not deserve accommodation, e.g. when the husband enters into a non-recognised marriage which is de facto polygamous with the intention of avoiding the risk of being prosecuted for bigamy,[50] other grounds for restricting oneself to a religious marriage ceremony may seem more legitimate.[51] The overall image may therefore be ambiguous, but the adverse legal effects of non-recognition are difficult to deny.

Lately, the disturbing activities of Sharia councils in the United Kingdom have been brought to the attention of the Parliamentary Assembly of the Council of Europe.[52] Although the resolution adopted by the Assembly was criticised for failing to adequately address the issue due to lack of precision, naivety, and moral panic,[53] it seems that the grounds for concern remain.

Again, this is not to say that *any* form of religious adjudication is essentially wrong or inherently dangerous. Let us go back to the distinction put forward earlier: there is an essential difference between Muslim arbitration tribunals and Sharia councils. Plenty of religions offer various forms of non-state arbitration to their members, and in many such cases there may be no grounds for public authorities to step in. The argument was made that in the absence of a moral consensus as to the fundamental values, religious arbitration can be a useful tool for allowing many different faith-based communities to flourish.[54] Also,

49 Patrick J Nash, 'Sharia in England: The Marriage Law Solution' (2017) 6 *Oxford Journal of Law and Religion* 523, 524.

50 See Rebecca Probert and Shabana Saleem, 'The Legal Treatment of Islamic Marriage Ceremonies' (2018) 7 *Oxford Journal of Law and Religion* 376, 377.

51 For an empirical data-based study, see Islam Uddin, '*Nikah*-only Marriages: Causes, Motivations, and Their Impact on Dispute Resolution and Islamic Divorce Proceedings in England and Wales' (2018) 7 *Oxford Journal of Law and Religion* 401, 407–416.

52 PACE (n 37) para 8.

53 Russell Sandberg and Frank Cranmer, 'The Council of Europe and Sharia: An Unsatisfactory Resolution?' (2019) 21 *Ecclesiastical Law Journal* 203.

54 Michael J Broyde, *Sharia Tribunals, Rabbinical Courts, and Christian Panels: Religious Arbitration in America and the West* (Oxford University Press 2017) 265; see also Farrah Ahmed and Senwung Luk, 'How Religious Arbitration Could Enhance Personal Autonomy' (2012) 1 *Oxford Journal of Law and Religion* 424.

in more pragmatic terms, religious arbitration may simply owe its popularity to the fact that it is often more effective in dispute resolution than state courts.[55] If we situate religious arbitration panels within the broader context of specialised ADR tribunals which provide expertise in construction or international trade, then perhaps – it was suggested – specific expertise in religious matters should be deemed no different.[56] This is acceptable as long as the state regulates such arbitration in three important ways, making sure that: (1) it is accepted on voluntary basis, (2) arbitrations are limited to monetary matters, and (3) procedural due process is followed in religious hearings.[57]

These conditions are not met in Sharia councils and there would be a fundamental misreading of the nature of these institutions in the claim that they are similar to Islamic arbitration. It has been reported that in many cases the parties do not voluntarily consent to bring their matters before these councils, and that especially women are pressured into accepting their jurisdiction.[58] The activity of Sharia councils is certainly not limited to financial matters, as they exercise jurisdiction in relation to a wide range of issues of personal status and marital law. Owing to the fact that they operate in the shadow of the law, state oversight cannot be exercised over their activity and procedural safeguards may not be guaranteed.

3.3 Accommodating Muslim identity claims

In a pluralist world, claims for accommodation of cultural and religious distinctiveness can only be on the rise. People seeking such accommodation come from a variety of social backgrounds and may be driven by different motivations: while for some of them identity-based claims bridge the gap between their own beliefs and the habits of the dominant culture, for others this may be a powerful political vehicle used to redefine the public sphere by importing ideas from the margins to the mainstream. Using the foot-in-the-door technique has proved useful in the history of the empowerment of minorities. There is nothing intrinsically wrong with it. Yet, this technique can also be used to seek recognition of codes of conduct which are backward, discriminatory, or incompatible with human dignity, and we know that this is how certain Sharia-based practices are assessed in Western societies.

For many years, there had been little support for Muslim identity claims in the European Court of Human Rights. Notably, the Court's case-law regarding the

55 Cf. Matthias Kötter, 'Non-State Justice Institutions: A Matter of Fact and a Matter of Legislation' in Matthias Kötter, Tilmann J Röder, Gunnar Folke Schuppert, Rüdiger Wolfrum (eds), *Non-State Justice Institutions and the Law: Decision-Making at the Interface of Tradition, Religion and the State* (Palgrave Macmillan 2015) 158–159.

56 Broyde (n 54) 244.

57 Ibid., 269.

58 See e.g. Jessie Brechin, 'A Study of the Use of Sharia Law in Religious Arbitration in the United Kingdom and the Concerns That This Raises for Human Rights' (2013) 15 *Ecclesiastical Law Journal* 293, 300.

right to wear religious symbols and clothing until 2017 would inevitably reveal an embarrassing truth – to put it bluntly, Muslims always lose.[59] The scope of this chapter does not allow for recalling the Court's arguments in all the cases in which claims based on Islamic identity proved to be largely unsuccessful, especially when the obligation to remove the full-face veil was at stake.[60] Typically, the Court would assert that the respondent state had not overstepped its margin of appreciation, or that the domestic authorities were in principle better placed to assess how to strike a fair balance between the competing values, or that acting to maintain the principle of secularism was consistent with the Convention – or all of the above. Perhaps this allegedly Muslim-unfriendly approach reached its apogee in a widely known case concerning a criminal ban on wearing in the public space an item of clothing intended to conceal the face, such as a niqab or a burqa.[61] The case was decided by the Court in favour of the ban, on the grounds that the state had been pursuing a legitimate aim, namely the right of others to live in a space of social interaction. The judgment met with heavy criticism, mostly because of the vagueness of the 'living together' principle, but some of the voices also highlighted the negative impact of the Court's decision on the empowerment of identities.[62]

Recently, however, there has been evidence that might suggest a shift in the Court's position vis-à-vis Muslim sensitivity. Three judgments need to be mentioned in this respect.

In 2017, the Court ruled in favour of a Muslim who had been punished for refusing to remove his *taqiyah* (skullcap) while giving evidence before a criminal court.[63] The applicant's wish to appear in the courtroom in a skullcap was said to be inspired by tradition, even though it did not represent a strong religious duty. The Court held that this behaviour had not jeopardised the proper conduct of the hearing and the integrity of the trial. The judgment went as far as to compliment the applicant for showing up at the hearing as summoned and standing up when requested. In light of the Court's earlier case-law, the ruling was so surprising that it made Eva Brems confess: 'Upon reading the press release, my first – admittedly cynical – reaction was: "so Muslims have rights after all"'.[64]

59 Or, to be more precise, almost always; cf. *Ahmet Arslan v Turkey* App no 41135/98 (ECtHR, 23 February 2010).

60 See *Leyla Şahin v Turkey* App no 44774/98 (ECtHR, 10 November 2005); *Dahlab v Switzerland* App no 42393/98 (ECtHR, 15 February 2001); *Kurtulmuş v Turkey* App no 65500/01 (ECtHR, 24 January 2006); *Dogru v France* App no 27058/05 (ECtHR, 4 December 2008); *Kervanci v France* App no 31645/04 (ECtHR, 4 December 2008); *Ebrahimian v France* App no 64846/11 (ECtHR, 26 November 2015); *El Morsli v France* App no 15585/06 (ECtHR, 4 March 2008).

61 *S.A.S. v France* App no 43835/11 (ECtHR, 1 July 2014); see also *Dakir v Belgium* App no 4619/12 (ECtHR, 11 July 2017); *Belcacemi and Oussar v Belgium* App no 37798/13 (ECtHR, 11 July 2017).

62 See Jill Marshall, '*S.A.S. v France*: *Burqa* Bans and the Control or Empowerment of Identities' (2015) 15 *Human Rights Law Review* 377.

63 *Hamidović v Bosnia and Herzegovina* App no 57792/15 (ECtHR, 5 December 2017).

64 Eva Brems, 'Skullcap in the Courtroom: A Rare Case of Mandatory Accommodation of Islamic Religious Practice' (*Strasbourg Observers*, 11 December 2017) www.strasbourgobservers.

This new approach to religious symbols in the courtroom was confirmed in another case. The applicant complained about not being able to attend the hearing as she would not be allowed to enter the courtroom unless she removed her hijab.[65] Her victory in Strasbourg was described as 'very significant' and representing 'a potentially important development' in the Court's case-law.[66]

Shortly afterwards, the Court declared unanimously that there had been no violation of the Convention in a case in which the applicant had been held criminally liable for making statements – during public seminars entitled 'Basic Information on Islam' – from which it could be understood that Muhammad had had paedophilic tendencies.[67] The applicant's incriminating statements referred to a marriage which the Prophet had concluded with Aisha, a six-year-old at that time, and consummated some years later, while she was still a little girl. The Chamber joined the domestic courts in the view that the applicant 'had failed to neutrally inform her audience of the historical background, which consequently had not allowed for a serious debate on that issue'.[68] By many, myself included, the judgment was received with shock and disbelief, as it was a clear departure from the Strasbourg's earlier views on blasphemy. It could be argued that, acting in defence of Muslim sensitivity, the adjudicating panel had 'eroded the freedom of speech while doing nothing meaningful for religious tolerance'.[69]

One swallow does not make a summer, but three judgments may indicate a new opening. The future will show whether the Court will continue this new attitude of deference to Muslim identity claims. At present, it is still able to stand for free speech, at least in the most extreme cases.[70]

4 Islamic religious law and state sovereignty

There can be little doubt that the traditional Westphalian concept of state sovereignty is largely outdated. The assumption that the supreme and uncompromised power lies within the state may remain central to constitutional studies,[71] but there is an evident lack of a fit between the conditions in which this idea was developed and the reality of the modern world. The state's exclusive powers are challenged by a variety of factors, such as human rights law, the settlement of conflicts by international courts, the economic leverage of foreign trade

com/2017/12/11/skullcap-in-the-courtroom-a-rare-case-of-mandatory-accommodation-of-islamic-religious-practice accessed 22 April 2020.

65 *Lachiri v Belgium* App no 3413/09 (ECtHR, 18 September 2018).

66 Kaushik Paul, '*Lachiri v Belgium* and Bans on Wearing Islamic Dress in the Courtroom: An Emerging Trend' (2019) 21 *Ecclesiastical Law Journal* 48, 52.

67 *E.S. v Austria* App no 38450/12 (ECtHR, 25 October 2018).

68 Ibid., para 54.

69 Marko Milanovic, 'Legitimizing Blasphemy Laws Through the Backdoor: The European Court's Judgment in *E.S. v. Austria*' (*EJIL:Talk!*, 29 October 2018) www.ejiltalk.org/legitimizing-blasphemy-laws-through-the-backdoor-the-european-courts-judgment-in-e-s-v-austria accessed 22 April 2020.

70 *Tagiyev and Huseynov v Azerbaijan* App no 13274/08 (ECtHR, 5 December 2019).

71 Cf. Michel Troper, 'Sovereignty' in Michel Rosenfeld and András Sajó (eds), *The Oxford Handbook of Comparative Constitutional Law* (Oxford University Press 2012) 350.

partners, or the operation of multinational companies. Global religions are too, undeniably, transnational actors challenging the role of the state.[72] Absolute sovereignty belongs to the past.

Should it be assumed that the steady entry of Islamic law into the European legal space is yet another manifestation of this simple truth? The answer depends to some extent on how we frame the discussion on legal pluralism – whether we believe that it is fundamentally misguided to fear threats to sovereignty as long as the state fully retains its potential power to revoke or freeze its recognition of non-state norms and regulatory bodies, or we demand active state interference in the operation of such institutions if the idea of sovereignty is to be saved. Ian Leigh clearly subscribes to the former view when he argues that there is no threat to the unity or sovereignty of state law posed by the recognition of religious law, for it is contractual in nature and does not involve any change to the rule of recognition.[73] Dieter Grimm, in turn, believes that legal pluralism 'seems to question the sovereignty of the state, which finds its most important expression in the sovereign's power to determine the laws of the land and in the monopoly of legitimate physical force to secure compliance with them'[74] and proceeds to declare that in order to satisfy the requirements of sovereignty, the state needs to be able to make the applicability of non-state regulations 'dependent on certain conditions such as its conformity with certain substantive or procedural principles of state law'.[75] Also, Grimm holds that the scope of religious law should be limited, leaving the state sufficient subject matter for regulation.[76]

I find Grimm's view more convincing, as I believe that the focus should be placed primarily on the state's actual control over the applicability of non-state regulations and not on its hypothetical ability to deny recognition thereof. Or, it may as well be that the notion of sovereignty is a red herring, whereas the real issue is the balance of regulatory power between the state and the non-state institutions of a religious nature.

No matter which perspective is to be adopted, it is clear that some of the advances of Islamic law in Europe considerably diminish the scope in which European states are still able to exercise authority. This is becoming increasingly noticeable on many levels. Open endorsement of Islamic international soft-law documents, such as the Cairo Declaration, does not per se result in adopting binding rules, but such commitments may be easily translated into interpretive guidelines used for law-making, law enforcement, and adjudication on rights.

72 Michele Saporiti, 'The Concept of Sovereignty and the Transnational Challenge of Global Religions. A Theoretical Framework' in Martin Belov (ed), *Global Governance and Its Effects on State and Law* (Peter Lang 2016).

73 Leigh (n 42) 6–7.

74 Dieter Grimm, 'Sovereignty and Religious Norms in the Secular Constitutional State', in Jean L Cohen, Cécile Laborde (eds), *Religion, Secularism, and Constitutional Democracy* (Columbia University Press 2016) 351.

75 Ibid., 352.

76 Ibid., 353.

Accepting or tolerating religious adjudication may weaken the regulatory power of the state and the protection of rights, although a distinction needs to be made between recognising arbitration (with a clearly defined legal framework within which it is authorised) and acknowledging the existence of parallel legal canons (which implies that legislation and jurisdiction are delegated);[77] also, it should be borne in mind that within the arbitration model there is a wide range of options to adopt, for the state may either treat the agreement to opt for arbitration as a contract within the meaning of state law, or it may use its power to enforce the performance of obligations resulting from the agreement, e.g. by compelling attendance at the hearing.[78] Accommodating Muslim identity claims, whether by adopting legislation which offers faith-based exemption from obligations of general applicability or recognising conscientious objections, or by affording higher protection to Muslim sensitivity in religious matters, lets the genie out of the bottle too.

One might be tempted to think that, in this respect, Islam is no different from any other religion – some European states openly endorse Christianity, religious arbitration is not confined to one single religious tradition, and conscience-based claims can be inspired by a variety of convictions. In actual fact, the way in which the Islamic law contests state sovereignty is *very* different, and the reasons for this are fourfold.

First, the very nature of Sharia makes it distinct from other religions which compete with the state in the realm of morality or which even demonstrate aspirations to redesign the public sphere. According to Sharia, sovereignty rests exclusively within God.[79] Second, as I sought to demonstrate, the disagreement between Islamic law and the values which underpin the European Convention on Human Rights is fundamental, and the scope of this disagreement is exceptionally wide. Third, assuming that global religions can be a powerful source of identity, as they are able 'to build up a thick sense of belonging out of sovereign states',[80] Islam in Muslim-minority countries – which is the most common situation in Europe – is at a particular advantage. Conversely, the growing popularity of claims for conscientious exemptions may be indicative of the decline of state power.[81] Fourth, while many religions are likely to generate social pressure on the unconcerned or simply less devout members of the population, this issue becomes even more problematic in the case of Islam, whose European adherents

77 Andrea Büchler, *Islamic Law in Europe? Legal Pluralism and its Limits in European Family Laws* (Ashgate 2011) 109.

78 Cf. Farrah Ahmed, 'Enforcing Religious Laws' in Rex Ahdar (ed), *Research Handbook on Law and Religion* (Edward Elgar Publishing 2018) 254.

79 Muhammad Khalid Masud, 'Clearing Ground: Commentary to "Shari'a and the Modern State"' in Anver M Emon, Mark S Ellis, Benjamin Glahn (eds), *Islamic Law and International Human Rights Law: Searching for Common Ground?* (Oxford University Press 2012) 109–110.

80 Saporiti (n 72) 105.

81 Cf Lorenzo Zucca, 'Is There a Right to Conscientious Objection?' in Susanna Mancini and Michel Rosenfeld (eds), *The Conscience Wars: Rethinking the Balance between Religion, Identity, and Equality* (Cambridge University Press 2018) 130–131.

often live in closed communities and their consent to religious rules may not be as voluntary as it appears from the outside. As Grégor Puppinck notes on Islam, 'there is reason to wonder about the true freedom to leave it, especially since Sharia punishes apostasy with death. There is great hypocrisy in believing that consent is enough to guarantee freedom and perhaps also some cowardice'.[82]

The recent evidence goes to show that in response to these developments Europe is stepping back. Puppinck's remarks were made in the context of the long-awaited Strasbourg judgment in the case concerning the application of Sharia law to an inheritance dispute contrary to the will of the testator, in Western Thrace.[83] While acknowledging a violation of the rights of the widow, who had been deprived of three-quarters of her inheritance, the Grand Chamber rushed to assure that 'freedom of religion does not require the Contracting States to create a particular legal framework in order to grant religious communities a special status entailing specific privileges'.[84] The negative assessment of Sharia's consistency with the Convention, as established in *Refah Partisi*, was not repeated. Should it be assumed from this silence that the Court is opening the door to the limited application of Islamic law in the European legal space?[85]

5 Conclusion

This contribution was written with the intention of addressing an issue which ought to receive greater public attention. Islamic religious law is slowly but steadily entering the European legal orders through many doors. The rapid advances of Sharia confront Europe with an entirely different legal tradition, which sets high demands for accommodation, many of them challenging the role of the state in an unprecedented manner, and in many cases diverges from the established standards of human rights protection, especially with regard to its rules on the legal status of women and minorities. Regrettably, the European Court of Human Rights has recently been reluctant, or less ready than before, to acknowledge the revolutionary impact of these developments.

'Muslims are at home in Europe', the Parliamentary Assembly of the Council of Europe has proudly announced in one of its resolutions,[86] recalling its earlier findings on the contribution of the Islamic civilisation to Europe. Indeed, they are, and this is by no means negotiable. Nor does it, however, justify the departure from upholding European values in the confrontation with a legal system which actively contests its very foundations.

82 Grégor Puppinck, 'Sharia: What Emerges From The *Molla Sali v. Greece Judgment*', www.eclj.org/religious-autonomy/echr/charia--ce-que-rvle-la-dcision-de-la-cedh accessed 22 April 2020.

83 *Molla Sali v Greece* App no 20452/14 (ECtHR, 19 December 2018).

84 Ibid., para 155.

85 Dominic McGoldrick, 'Sharia Law in Europe? Legacies of the Ottoman Empire and the European Convention of Human Rights' (2019) 8 *Oxford Journal of Law and Religion* 517, 564–565.

86 PACE (n 9) para 3.

My argument is that the practice of accommodating Muslim sensitivity should again be grounded in a stable and consistent value-based framework. The state must not fear rejecting claims which, if satisfied, would effectively deprive it of any supervision on the application of religious law in the most vulnerable spheres of life, thus leaving the weakest with no protection. The road to social peace is possible through establishing clear requirements – and that includes red lines – in relations with Islam, not through avoiding criticism, and certainly not by the accommodation of Muslim claims at all cost. Religious arbitration is compatible with European values as long as it meets the substantive and procedural standards set by the state, whereas personal legal systems and an overly indulging approach to religious sensitivities leave the door open to fundamentalism and injustice.

And there is one final point: self-confidence. As Saporiti observes, 'contemporary nation states should be able to reshape their identity. In this process, they can learn from global religions the best way to build up a successful and inclusive strategy'.[87] Similarly, in order to confront otherness without compromising its unique identity, Europe may need to restore faith in its own values first.

References

Ahmed F, 'Enforcing Religious Laws' in R Ahdar (ed), *Research Handbook on Law and Religion* (Edward Elgar Publishing 2018)

Ahmed F and Luk S, 'How Religious Arbitration Could Enhance Personal Autonomy' (2012) 1 *Oxford Journal of Law and Religion* 424

al-Ahsan A, 'Law, Religion and Human Dignity in the Muslim World Today: An Examination of OIC's Cairo Declaration of Human Rights' (2008) 24 *Journal of Law and Religion* 569

Anthimos A, 'Sharia Law in Greece: Blending European Values with Islamic Tradition' (24 January 2018) https://conflictoflaws.net/2018/sharia-law-in-greece-blending-european-values-with-islamic-tradition accessed 17 April 2020

Bauer N, 'Confrontation of Islamic Sharia and Human Rights at the Council of Europe', https://eclj.org/religious-freedom/coe/confrontation-de-la-charia-islamique-et-des-droits-de-lhomme-au-conseil-de-leurope accessed 17 April 2020

Berger MS, 'Understanding Sharia in the West' (2018) 6 *Journal of Law, Religion and State* 236

Berman HJ, *Law and Revolution: The Formation of the Western Legal Tradition* (Harvard University Press 1983)

Brechin J, 'A Study of the Use of Sharia Law in Religious Arbitration in the United Kingdom and the Concerns That This Raises for Human Rights' (2013) 15 *Ecclesiastical Law Journal* 293

Brems E, 'Skullcap in the Courtroom: A Rare Case of Mandatory Accommodation of Islamic Religious Practice' (*Strasbourg Observers*, 11 December 2017) www.strasbourgobservers.com/2017/12/11/skullcap-in-the-courtroom-a-rare-case-of-mandatory-accommodation-of-islamic-religious-practice accessed 22 April 2020

87 Saporiti (n 72) 109.

Broyde MJ, *Sharia Tribunals, Rabbinical Courts, and Christian Panels: Religious Arbitration in America and the West* (OUP 2017)
Büchler A, *Islamic Law in Europe? Legal Pluralism and its Limits in European Family Laws* (Ashgate 2011)
Cox N, 'The Clash of Unprovable Universalisms – International Human Rights and Islamic Law' (2013) 2 *Oxford Journal of Law and Religion* 307
Ellethy Y, *Islam, Context, Pluralism and Democracy: Classical and Modern Interpretations* (Routledge 2015)
Féron H, 'Human Rights and Faith: A "World-wide Secular Religion"?' (2014) 7 *Ethics & Global Politics* 181
Gozdecka DA, *Rights, Religious Pluralism and the Recognition of Difference: Off the Scales of Justice* (Routledge 2016)
Griffith-Jones R, 'The "Unavoidable" Adoption of Shari'a Law – The Generation of a Media Storm' in R Griffith-Jones (ed), *Islam and English Law: Rights, Responsibilities and the Place of Shari'a* (Cambridge University Press 2013)
Grimm D, 'Sovereignty and Religious Norms in the Secular Constitutional State', in JL Cohen, C Laborde (eds), *Religion, Secularism, & Constitutional Democracy* (Columbia University Press 2016)
Hashas M, *The Idea of European Islam: Religion, Ethics, Politics and Perpetual Modernity* (Routledge 2018)
Hilal L, 'The Cairo Declaration on Human Rights in Islam and International Women's Rights' (1997) 5 *Circles: Buffalo Women's Journal of Law and Social Policy* 85
Kötter M, 'Non-State Justice Institutions: A Matter of Fact and a Matter of Legislation' in M Kötter, TJ Röder, G Folke Schuppert, R Wolfrum (eds), *Non-State Justice Institutions and the Law: Decision-Making at the Interface of Tradition, Religion and the State* (Palgrave Macmillan 2015)
Kuru AT, *Islam, Authoritarianism, and Underdevelopment: A Global and Historical Comparison* (Cambridge University Press 2019)
Leigh I, 'Religious Adjudication and the European Convention on Human Rights' (2019) 8 *Oxford Journal of Law and Religion* 1
Marshall J, '*S.A.S. v France*: *Burqa* Bans and the Control or Empowerment of Identities' (2015) 15 *Human Rights Law Review* 377
Masud MK, 'Clearing Ground: Commentary to "Shari'a and the Modern State"' in AM Emon, MS Ellis, B Glahn (eds), *Islamic Law and International Human Rights Law: Searching for Common Ground?* (Oxford University Press 2012)
McGoldrick D, 'Accommodating Muslims in Europe: From Adopting Sharia Law to Religiously Based Opt Outs from Generally Applicable Laws' (2009) 9 *Human Rights Law Review* 603
McGoldrick D, 'The Compatibility of an Islamic/*Shari'a* Law System or *Shari'a* Rules with the European Convention on Human Rights' in R Griffith-Jones (ed), *Islam and English Law: Rights, Responsibilities and the Place of Shari'a* (Cambridge University Press 2013)
McGoldrick D, 'Sharia Law in Europe? Legacies of the Ottoman Empire and the European Convention of Human Rights' (2019) 8 *Oxford Journal of Law and Religion* 517
Milanovic M, 'Legitimizing Blasphemy Laws Through the Backdoor: The European Court's Judgment in *E.S. v. Austria*' (*EJIL:Talk!*, 29 October 2018) www.ejiltalk.org/legitimizing-blasphemy-laws-through-the-backdoor-the-european-courts-judgment-in-e-s-v-austria accessed 22 April 2020

Moe C, '*Refah* Revisited: Strasbourg's Construction of Islam' in WC Durham, Jr, R Torfs, DM Kirkham and C Scott (eds), *Islam, Europe and Emerging Legal Issues* (Ashgate 2012)

Nash PJ, 'Sharia in England: The Marriage Law Solution' (2017) 6 *Oxford Journal of Law and Religion* 523

Oh I, 'Islamic Conceptions of Human Rights' in T Cushman (ed), *Handbook of Human Rights* (Routledge 2014)

Paul K, '*Lachiri v Belgium* and Bans on Wearing Islamic Dress in the Courtroom: An Emerging Trend' (2019) 21 *Ecclesiastical Law Journal* 48

Probert R and Saleem S, 'The Legal Treatment of Islamic Marriage Ceremonies' (2018) 7 *Oxford Journal of Law and Religion* 376

Puppinck G, 'Sharia: What Emerges From the *Molla Sali v. Greece* Judgment', www.eclj.org/religious-autonomy/echr/charia--ce-que-rvle-la-dcision-de-la-cedh accessed 22 April 2020

Rynkowski M, 'Religious Courts in the Jurisprudence of the European Court of Human Rights' (2016) 18 *Ecclesiastical Law Journal* 62

Saeed A, 'Limitations on Religious Freedom in Islam: Rethinking through the *Maqasid*?' in S Ferrari (ed), *Routledge Handbook of Law and Religion* (Routledge 2015)

Sandberg R and Cranmer F, 'The Council of Europe and Sharia: An Unsatisfactory Resolution?' (2019) 21 *Ecclesiastical Law Journal* 203

Saporiti M, 'The Concept of Sovereignty and the Transnational Challenge of Global Religions. A Theoretical Framework' in M Belov (ed), *Global Governance and Its Effects on State and Law* (Peter Lang 2016)

Troper M, 'Sovereignty' in M Rosenfeld and A Sajó (eds), *The Oxford Handbook of Comparative Constitutional Law* (Oxford University Press 2012)

Troper M, 'Sovereignty and Laïcité' in S Mancini and M Rosenfeld (eds), *Constitutional Secularism in an Age of Religious Revival* (Oxford University Press 2014)

Tsitselikis K, 'Applying Shari'a in Europe: Greece as an Ambivalent Legal Paradigm' (2010) 2 *Yearbook of Muslims in Europe* 663

Uddin I, '*Nikah*-only Marriages: Causes, Motivations, and Their Impact on Dispute Resolution and Islamic Divorce Proceedings in England and Wales' (2018) 7 *Oxford Journal of Law and Religion* 401

Williams R, 'Civil and Religious Law in England: A Religious Perspective' in R Griffith-Jones (ed), *Islam and English Law: Rights, Responsibilities and the Place of Shari'a* (Cambridge University Press 2013)

Zucca L, 'Is There a Right to Conscientious Objection?' in S Mancini and M Rosenfeld (eds), *The Conscience Wars: Rethinking the Balance between Religion, Identity, and Equality* (Cambridge University Press 2018)

Part IV

Economic challenges to constitutional peace and order in times of crisis of neoliberalism

9 The transformative side of law

Reflections on the reconstruction of a radical democratic labour law[1]

Marie Diekmann

1 Normative crisis of democracy

Democracy and human rights promote the (formerly) revolutionary idea that people are equal. As normative projects, however, they are ambiguous. While in the liberal understanding only formal equality of rights is meant, more radical readings also understand democracy and human rights as a normative program that includes further democratisation and materialisation.[2] With the Enlightenment, for the first time, people recognised each other as equals.[3] Those in power are subject to democratic control and must justify therefore themselves. The relationship between individuals and the state is redefined by granting the individual indispensable rights qua humanity, which the state cannot dispose of freely, but which it must protect. Human rights thus establish a normative order, in which the state must give reasons when it restricts the freedom of subjects. The law is the central medium for sealing off against attacks on individuals and subalterns by the state and even powerful private actors. The French Revolution inseparably linked human rights and democracy, both of which follow on from the other.[4]

The normative idea of human equality is confronted with empirical inequalities concerning the status of citizenship and structural inequalities based on concepts such as class, race and gender.[5] Hannah Arendt declares the treatment of refugees a test case for human rights claiming that rights are worthless when it shows that the loss of political community leads to the de facto loss of human

1 I thank Brooke Perry and Nadine Rettenmaier for correcting my English.

2 In this sense I tend to use the terms of democracy and human rights as synonyms, as they are normatively, but also historically intertwined (cf. Wellmer (2005) 308 ff.).

3 See Rossanvallon (2013), 23 ff.

4 Menke (2011), p. 249.

5 The matrix of inequality is in reality more complex, as discrimination depends on the interrelation of categories. Moreover, these categories are more complex in themselves, as symbolic capital (see Bourdieu 2009) and psychological skills (see Illouz 2007) come into play.

rights.[6] But even if we look at the status of citizens within a political community, it is evident that the opportunity to enjoy liberal freedoms is very unequally distributed and depends largely on social status. Hence, we see a permanent tension between the idea of equality and the reality of inequality, and the idea of equality of humans in its emphatic understanding is in a permanent crisis.

Apart from that, democratic and human rights norms are indeed massively challenged by far right-wing propaganda. The current crisis of the democracies of the Global North can thus be understood not only as a political or economic crisis, but also as a normative crisis. The current rise and political success of the far right challenge the normative constitutions of liberal democracies and is to some extent attributed to economic inequalities.[7]

Although there is certainly no monocausal explanation for the current crisis, and I do not want to touch upon economism, economic and social inequality and neoliberal politics seem to be contributing significantly to the current crisis of democracy and human rights. It is therefore worth reconsidering the strategies used so far to address the problem of social and economic inequality, such as labour rights and economic democracy. It quickly becomes clear that not only democracy and the idea of human rights in general, but also democratic labour law is in crisis.

In the following, starting from the crisis of democratic equality, I will show how labour law conceptually responds to this crisis by adding a transformative logic to liberal law towards more social justice and democracy, while remaining in crisis itself. I will then present some reflections on how the crisis of labour law could be overcome and how labour law could regain its transformative power.

2 Transformation through immanent critique

The following section examines the transformative logic of labour law as promoted by the labour movement.

2.1 The paradox of liberal law

In his early work period, Karl Marx undertook a critique of human rights as provided by the French Revolution.[8] According to Marx, liberal human rights are free from feudal submission by assigning to every human being an equal status as a free citizen and therefore produce emancipation from former domination. His criticism, however, points to another side of law which can be called the paradox of liberal law: the freedom of law produces and veils illiberal power relations by assigning socially produced inequality to the sphere of the non-legal or prerogative, thus naturalising it. The autonomy that liberal law provides

6 Arendt (2011), p. 402.

7 Probably best known is the study of Thomas Piketty (Piketty 2013); cf. also Nachtwey (2016).

8 Marx (1844/2006).

is therefore flawed as it covers true heteronomy, because people are in reality much less free in their (legal) choices than the law assumes. And – this is the paradox – it goes even further: the freedom created by the law comes with costs for the subjects, as their inability to fully enjoy their legal freedom appears as the result of a personal failure.

The law thus transfers societal responsibility to the individual. It is therefore no coincidence that the idea of human rights goes hand in hand with a whole range of theories about why black people, women, children, etc., are less able to perform or make decisions because of their biology and should therefore enjoy fewer rights.[9] Hence, the liberal concept of human rights, paradoxically, undermines its own normative suppositions as the liberal notion of freedom leads to heteronomy.

But even though Marx admits the emancipatory progress modern law brings compared to feudalism, he neglects its transformative potentials. Modern Law[10] establishes a new standard of critique that enables subalterns to address the law with their demands by contesting biologistic assumptions and demanding to be treated equally. The law thus comprises a subversive dynamic of emancipation.[11] The project of human rights, as it emphasises (despite all historical exclusions) freedom and equality for all, consequently makes the law susceptible for immanent, i.e. transformative critique.[12] Just as the emergence of new forms of chauvinism can be seen as a kind of implication of the Enlightenment and human rights, the expansion and integration of those formerly excluded is already laid down in the law.

The law thus contains a logic of subversive self-critique allowing subalterns to address the law with emancipatory projects and thus transform it towards social

9 Marx does not draw attention to structural exclusion of various kinds, but focuses exclusively on economic status. A broader perspective has been established by feminist and postcolonial authors who show how the Enlightenment was accompanied by a variety of biologistic theories (see, e.g. Klinger (2003); Maihofer 2001). Pierre Rossanvallon traces the emergence of a liberal-conservative ideology, particularly for the justification of social inequalities (Rossanvallon, note 3 above, 108 ff.). Accordingly, once equality had become the central norm in societies, only differences based on virtue or talent were considered justified. Differences were thus attributed to the behaviour of individuals and on nature. At the same time, natural differences were emphasised and extended, and the individual's sphere of responsibility was enlarged. The effect of the Enlightenment and modern law is thus a paradoxical constitution of the subject in which equality is inverted into inequality. Rossanvallon also points to effective counter-strategies of opponents of the ideal of equality (while Maihofer and Klinger instead refer to the intrinsic normative dynamics of modern rights). Thus, the enormous social inequalities that worsened in the course of capitalist development in the nineteenth century could be seen as morally justified. Massive poverty was thus not generated by certain social and economic structures but was the result of a reprehensible lifestyle.

10 I am using the term 'modern law' in a broad sense, comprising the form of subjective rights (cf. Menke 2015), but mainly pointing to law that comprises the idea of human rights.

11 Raimondi (2011), p. 100.

12 Immanent critique is the main project of different forms of critical theory aiming at transformation by addressing normative contradictions in well-established social practices (see Stahl 2013).

justice. The idea of human equality as a normative reference for subalterns therefore gives the law a self-transforming dynamic, as evidenced by the extension of the law to those who were previously excluded like women and blacks. To a certain extent, this also applies to social status.

Christoph Menke criticises Marx for solely focusing on private law in the strict sense and neglecting, what he calls, 'the other side' of law.[13] Accordingly, modern law comprises norms of inclusion and therefore opposes the strict individualist logic of civil law by integrating norms that reflect social inequality such as labour law and social rights.

But there is also a downside to the legal project of labour law, which can be illustrated by a critique of the labour contract. Hugh Collins reformulates the Marxian paradox[14] of law for labour law, saying that '[…] the contract of employment embraces an authoritarian structure that appears to be at odds with the commitment in liberal societies to values such as liberty, equal respect, and respect for privacy'.[15] According to Collins, the liberal employment contract contradicts liberal values as it establishes a relationship of subordination. It does so by establishing an authority of the employer that goes beyond a simple contractual obligation. With the employment contract, the employer acquires the right to instruct the employee to use his time as the employer sees fit. The employee undertakes to follow the instructions. What exactly is covered by the employer's instruction is to some extent unclear and only becomes concrete at the moment the instructions are given. These may include appearance, language, and manners. As a rule, the employer can even change the place of work. If the employee then takes longer to get to work or even has to move to another city, this is basically his private problem.

The problem of labour law is therefore that, despite its proclamations of (constructed) equality and autonomy of the contractual parties, it embraces an authoritarian organisation of labour. Considering how much decision power the law refers to the employer over the employee, we see that in the field of labour we accept a much lower level of freedom than in the political sphere. For Collin, this is indeed contrary to liberal norms, since these norms do not provide for different levels of liberty, but the same for everyone. The normative justification for this is, of course, that everyone is free not to work or to seek a working environment that suits their personal preferences. But as soon as we recognise factual economic needs to work,[16] this justification no longer applies.

13 Menke (2013), 282 ff.

14 He does so without explicitly referring to Marx by formulating his argument in a similar logic. Unlike Marx, however, he refers positively to liberal freedoms.

15 Collins (2018), p. 48.

16 Despite the fact that we have to consider the crucial importance work has for our identity and societal integration (Déjours et al. 2018, 69 ff.), and even if there is a choice to work or not to work or to find another job, we must, as soon as we accept work being part of the public sphere, from a democratic point of view reject this argument as we also would not accept arguments that people who do not like their freedom to be infringed by the state should go find another social community or state.

Some are even more drastic in their critique of the labour contract. David Ellerman links employment to the temporary legal first rule on objects, saying that 'hiring' is close, if not the same as 'renting' – only that the notion is used for people, whereas the second is reserved for objects. But according to Ellerman, the legal relationship established by rent/hire is very similar.[17] And only recently Elisabeth Anderson's anthology *Private Government* received some attention discussing the thesis, that the labour contract in fact establishes a private government of the employer over the employee, which is in some ways comparable to a dictatorship, since it creates an asymmetrical power relation in which the powerful party is able to exercise arbitrary control over the other party.[18]

Although this might seem somewhat exaggerated or rather one-sided, these assumptions allude to a normative problem of the labour relation and labour law which is banal and evident as well as being widely ignored at the same time: the labour contract, even if previously concluded by equal parties, is based on an unequal social status and establishes an asymmetrical relationship with large decision powers of one party over the other. If one takes a sophisticated concept of democracy as a basis, the power relationship that determines the working relationship is problematic in that an important part of life is organised in an undemocratic way.

2.2 *Labour law and labour movement*

Nowadays, even strong critiques of the labour contract would not be directed against labour law and the labour contract as such. As Ellerman puts it:

> Of all rental contracts, the employment contract has been the most modified and attenuated by social constraints. Labor legislation and the countervailing power of unions have both worked to mitigate the commodity nature of labor services and to insure that people are rented in a manner as 'human' as possible. But all of these socially mitigating circumstances should not be taken as an excuse to obfuscate the basic fact that the employment contract to buy labor by the day, the week, or the year is the contract to hire or rent the person by the day, the week, or the year.[19]

As indicated above, the law nevertheless reflects to some extent the power asymmetry that underlies and structures the labour relation. Historically, and from a subaltern perspective, the labour contract is a huge progress as it imposes rules on both contractual parties and therefore limits the power of the employer. This is particularly true because the historical and dogmatic alternative was usually a

17 Ellerman (1992), 60 f.
18 Anderson (2017).
19 Ellerman, note 17 above, p. 61.

simple service contract or no explicit contract at all.[20] The alternative to labour law is therefore business or corporate law. The labour contract recognises an imbalance of power between the contractual parties and therefore implies specific rules that modify the legal relation – mostly to protect the employee from power abuse by the employer. Modern labour law includes a range of protective standards, from dismissal regulations to rules on non-discrimination, which transforms civil law from a rather formal to a more materialistic logic.

Regular civil law assumes a strictly formal autonomy. It is therefore permissible under civil law, for example, to conclude contracts that are unilaterally disadvantageous to the weaker party, even if one of the parties actually had little choice but to conclude the contract. It is formally a free decision to enter into a contract with an Internet provider, to rent an apartment, or to conclude an employment contract. However, these decisions are only really free to a limited extent. And to say that one is free to have no apartment, no Internet provider, and no work may be true in the strict sense of private autonomy, but it is at the same time cynical. The law takes into account the market asymmetry which structures these contractual relationships in the form of special protective rights for tenants and consumers – and also for employees. These protective forms of law alter the formal concept of autonomy of civil law.[21] They add a normative logic that is alien to strictly liberal law, which aims at material justice. Labour law extends this logic to the point that it includes collective actions and collective contracts, which disrupt the individualist account of civil law and to a certain level the border between public law and civil law.

The collective side of labour law enables social actors, who are different from the state, to set up rules for the enterprise or even entire industries. State law thus takes a step back in favour of social self-determination. In my opinion, the importance of the collective side is radically underestimated. For we are actually dealing here with a different logic of generating law than we otherwise find. There is a direct opening of the law – albeit very limited in its scope – to subaltern legislation, integrated into state law. Subalterns are not obliged to go to court and convince them, but they are legally legitimised to fight for their interests and reach an agreement with the employers' side that lays down new rules for work.

However, this legal-theoretical formulation is not intended to hide the fact that the state does not simply withdraw voluntarily but was forced to do so by the labour movement. Labour law has historically been fought for by the labour movement – partly in physical and bloody struggles. The fight for more humane working conditions has always been a major part of the labour movement. The collective strike has been one of the most powerful weapons of the subaltern classes to force social progress or to fight against the lowering of social standards. And it is the social actors, such as the labour unions, who have pushed the

20 Which does of course not necessarily mean that there is no contractual relation from a dogmatic point of view.

21 Cf. Auer (2016).

law beyond its narrow liberal concepts of contract and autonomy. To a certain extent, therefore, the law reflects the power relations underlying and structuring the labour relation, not only by introducing protective standards, but also by acknowledging collective social actors.

Collective rights, such as the right to strike, are of twofold importance in the field of labour: on the one hand, they are more instrumental in enforcing and protecting individual rights. On the other hand, they are traditionally an originally collective right in the sense of a common situation of the working class.[22]

Moreover, labour law implies a radical democratic perspective that goes beyond liberal human rights and formal democracy, as it promotes participation of employees on decisions concerning the workplace. It does so by establishing three different and intertwined strategies for establishing more symmetrical power relations between employers and employees: (1) introducing standards of legal protection that limit the power of the employer, (2) enabling collective action to pursue collective interests and conclude collective agreements in order to organise industrial relations, (3) limiting the power of the owner over his company by promoting democratic decision-making in the companies.

The collective legal institutions of labour law refer to much more radical democratic concepts than today's labour discourses suggest. For instance, the German model of co-determination goes back to the Council Communist Movement at the beginning of the twentieth century and the German Revolution of 1918/19. The Weimar Constitution created – with Article 165 WRV – the basis for the establishment of democratic institutions within companies as well as outside as a supplement to parliamentarianism. These included, on the one hand, workers' councils at company level and at the level of the industry and the state to represent the interests of workers. On the other hand, workers and entrepreneurs as well as other groups were to join together in economic councils 'for the fulfilment of all economic tasks and for participation in the execution of socialization laws' (156 WRV).

An important task of the economic councils was thus the socialisation of the economy. As we know, the Weimar Republic did not develop into an economic democracy, but into a fascist dictatorship. In the Federal Republic the old council tradition was continued – under changed political circumstances – but in its radicalism it fell far short of its model, and the labour movement did not manage to build up sufficient pressure to achieve further reforms. Nevertheless, German co-determination is still comparatively well-developed today, but is currently threatening to erode, as we will now see.

3 New freedoms and neoliberal backlash

Although it is worth looking at the revolutionary beginnings of co-determination in order to explore its normative and transformative potential, obviously not

22 Ingram (2011), 281 f.

much has remained of that beginning. The rights of works councils are subject to strict limits, and the employer's right of property imposes limits wherever business decisions have to be made. This system is far from an economic democracy in which economic councils complement parliamentary democracy.

And even these democratic structures, whose competences are limited, are under massive pressure. In Germany, the erosion of the regional collective bargaining system and – somewhat later – company co-determination is well observed and has been diagnosed since the 1990s at the latest.[23] The situation is even more dramatic when we look at international or transnational industrial relations. Even though the idea of economic rights and democracy is not a pure project of the labour movement but is fed by various ideological sources, including religious ones, and at times it looked a little as if this project could have great success, an almost contradictory reality arose.[24]

The European Union has a distinctly pro-economic orientation, in which collective industrial action by trade unions would in fact be seen primarily as a restriction on the free movement of services and goods.[25] While entrepreneurial rights are at the heart of economic integration, the wage-earning perspective remains structurally unimportant. The recent attempts by the European Commission to establish a social pillar seem more like a rhetorical strategy than a serious reorientation of the EU.[26]

In *The Spirit of Philadelphia*, Alain Supiot traces how reorientation of the International Labour Organisation (ILO) in 1944 with the aim of a fair global economic and labour order was followed by an 'ultraliberal doctrine' that became dominant and made economic and labour policy correspondingly authoritarian.[27] Supiot describes a shift in the teleology of law through its neoliberalisation. Law is then no longer primarily committed to social justice and democracy but is instead oriented towards the preservation and promotion of the economy, which is understood as natural law in the sense of social scientific scientism. This orientation towards the natural science paradigm, the question of whether and how the economy can be shaped politically, is always at stake. This question is crucial for labour law. For if politics takes precedence over business, employment relationships can be legally structured. However, if the economy is determined by its own invariant logic, there is actually no scope for shaping employment relationships and thus no scope for labour law.

23 Ellguth and Trinczek (2016).

24 Beyer (2011), 292 f.

25 This has at ghe latest become evident since the European Court of Justice ruled to the detriment of labour unions in Laval and Wiking. In both cases, the Court recognised in principle a right to strike, but subordinated it to the employer's liberties (cf. Resolution of the Executive Committee of the ETUC 2008).

26 The naming is striking, which is based on the pillar structure of the EU before the Lisbon Treaty – albeit purely rhetorical. There is no cooperation comparable to the former pillars in this area.

27 Supiot (2011).

Grégoire Chamayou argues in a similar direction. He describes the active autonomisation of the economy as a neoliberal strategy since the 1970s. Thus, the political project of neoliberalism consists primarily in politically arranging the sphere of the economy in such a way that it is removed from the democratic power of government.[28] This policy is directed against trade unions and workers' rights.[29] In contrast, labour law holds the view that society and the economy are political projects and must therefore be organised fairly. The controversy about the autonomy of the economy or the relationship between economics and politics is currently re-emerging in legal discourses with regard to the digitalisation of work. Jeremias Prassl shows how actors of the gig economy successfully create positive narratives about innovation, sharing, and overall progress of digital work to avoid labour regulation.[30] Precarious work is thus reshaped as pure innovation, suggesting that legal concepts such as labour protection or collective bargaining are old-fashioned and hostile to innovation and therefore need to be limited:

> Rebranding old-school labour intermediation as an exciting new technological innovation thus poses a fundamental challenge to existing regulatory structures: if the gig economy is a radically new way of organizing work, old-fashioned employment law should no longer apply. [...] In these accounts, the on-demand economy is a key to transforming work for the future [...]'[31]

This understanding of labour law is 'based on tales of entrepreneurship and innovation',[32] avoids concepts of justice and democracy and shifts the economic risks from enterprises to workers.[33] International ultraliberalisation (as Supiot calls it) or authoritarian liberalism (as Chamayou calls it) is primarily organised at the level of nation states and does not run solely through labour law. Rather, the decisive factor is that flexibility within and outside companies is increasingly synchronised.[34] The neoliberal reorientation of industrial relations is accompanied by an increasingly authoritarian welfare state whose norms are only conditionally oriented towards social justice, but all the more towards individual performance and responsibility.[35]

28 Chamayou (2018), 236 f.
29 *Ibid.*, 31 ff.
30 Prassl (2018), 31 ff.
31 Ibid., p. 45.
32 Ibid., p. 46.
33 Ibid., p. 86.
34 Dörre (2007), p. 30.
35 This is again well illustrated by the example of Germany and the Hartz IV reforms. The complex intertwining of labour and social law norms contributes to the disciplining of wage earners. Thus, employees are also required by the social law regulations to remain in bad employment relationships. Those who quit their job themselves or are dismissed due to their behaviour, do not receive unemployment benefit immediately – even though this is based on unemployment

The normative reorientation is not limited to the law, but has effects on and within the subjects, their normative orientations and their self-concepts. Numerous studies examine in particular the changed autonomy spaces within industrial relations, which include gains in freedom, but also place higher demands on the subjects' self-government.[36] The gains in freedom of the new post-Fordist forms of work are ambivalent and in part associated with high costs for the individuals. For while, on the one hand, the stabilising integration into the company social organisation is becoming more precarious, at the same time the sometimes paradoxical and burdensome demands on the creativity, self-control and self-organisation of the subjects are simultaneously gaining in importance.[37]

This goes hand in hand with a decollectivisation of industrial relations, which manifests itself, among other things, in the aforementioned erosion of the national collective bargaining system and company co-determination and also attacks the preconditions for collective action under labour law asymmetrically to the detriment of the employees.[38] This is basically, because collectively organising interests is becoming increasingly difficult due to socio-structural processes of differentiation and individualisation.[39] However, Robert Castel emphasises that this is strictly speaking a collective process of decollectivisation, in which social inequalities are reproduced.[40] The inequality structure of class society thus remains intact. But the political perspective of class struggle is lost.

A much more positive assessment of the change in industrial relations could be made by emphasising the gains in greater individualisation and freedom. Nevertheless, the following observations seem to me to be inevitable: the side of labour law that aims to democratise labour relations and protect wage earners is becoming visibly precarious. This applies in particular to the collective orientation that characterises labour law, so that there is a further shift of power to the disadvantage of the employee side. What a reorientation of labour law could look like is the decisive question which we will pursue in the following section.

4 Reconstructing a democratic labour law

A successful approach would strategically probably have to 'convince critics that economic rights are not socialist'.[41] The problem is that if the disintegration of labour law is to be effectively counteracted, a collective perspective that limits ownership and business decisions is essential. The establishment of individual

insurance contributions. The state employment agencies have extensive powers to put the unemployed under pressure. In fact, the reforms extended sanctions to claim periods that had previously been largely unconditional. Measures that come across as "support" for the unemployed can actually be used to impose sanctions.

36 Diekmann (2020), 58 f.

37 Voswinkel (2002), 74 ff.

38 With more details on German labour law, Diekmann, see note 35 above.

39 Castel (2003), 7 ff.

40 Ibid., 12 ff.

41 Beyer, note 23 above, p. 306.

legal positions and welfare state benefits may defuse the situation but remains in a logic in which the employee side always remains precarious. Without claiming that this is a realistic perspective under given circumstances, it would be decent to strengthen the transformational side of collective labour law, which aims at overcoming economic inequality. In my view, the most interesting aspect of labour law is precisely the integration of a socialist perspective in the liberal system of rights. To refute the suspicion of socialism may therefore indeed be an important strategic concern and, separation from authoritarian socialism is necessary. But anyone who wants more than cosmetic changes and takes economic inequality seriously as a democratic and human rights problem cannot avoid it insofar as socialism historically represents the attempt to overcome economic inequality in the first place. But this does not necessarily mean a rigid insistence on historical concepts and terms. The socialist perspective here functions more as a social and collective orientation of liberalism.

4.1 Labour rights as human rights

An obvious approach is the normative foundation of labour law in human rights as the 'alignment of labour law and human rights is intuitively appealing'.[42] However, there seems to be a gap between human rights and labour rights. The latter do not play an important role in human rights regimes as these regimes usually follow a liberal agenda and put more emphasis on property rights than on labour rights. From this perspective labour rights tend to appear even as an infringement of human rights as they put into question the absolute sovereignty of the employer.

However, the right to strike is protected by international and national law. For example, Article 11 of the European Convention on Human Rights protects the right to 'freedom of peaceful assembly and to freedom of association with others, including the right to form and to join trade unions for the protection of his interest'. The German Basic Law protects the right to strike in Article 9 Paragraph 3. Yet, the codification of the right to strike is in both examples vague and the right to strike itself is not explicitly mentioned. Furthermore, international law leaves decisive aspects of the right to strike to the national legislation. As the right to strike has been recognised by international and national courts, there is no doubt it exists in terms of dogmatics. However, the right to strike's normative justification stays obscure and contested.[43] In the case of the German Basic Law, the Federal Labour Court had long shied away from recognising the right to strike.[44] It was much more activist, however, in the construction of owners' positions that opposed the strike and, in any case, made it liable for

42 Atkinson (2018), p. 124.

43 Bogg and Estlund (2018), p. 229.

44 Cf. especially the decision of 28 January 1955 (BAGE 1, 291). As the Court could not deny the right to strike without risking outrageous reactions, it recognised the customary practice of strike as being part of the legal system.

damages.[45] While the rights of workers were hardly discussed at all, the right to property was normatively extremely charged.

This is particularly remarkable as the German constitution historically contains a compromise between capitalist and socialist economic forms.[46] The unambiguous interpretation of the Federal Labour Court steered the economic constitution in a different direction from the one envisaged in the Basic Law. It was only the development of a modern fundamental rights dogmatics by the Federal Constitutional Court that established the right to strike as a fundamental right in German constitutional dogmatics beyond doubt. This was done not least by relativising the normatively charged right to property by emphasising its social implications and distinguishing between those areas in which property is of primary importance for one's own way of life and those in which derived property rights and the freedom of others collide.[47]

What this should make clear is that the relationship of human rights and labour law depends crucially on the respective rights architecture. Understanding human rights as abstract moral concepts that provide essentially individualist rights might help to justify some labour rights such as a right to decent work conditions.[48] But an individualist rights concept will not provide more than individualist rights, whereas the more interesting part of labour law is – as I have tried to make clear – its collective side. Reservations against a stronger foundation of labour law in human rights are fed precisely by the fear that this would further weaken the collective side of labour law.[49]

But it is not only the individualistic conception of human rights that makes them useless for a foundation of labour law, as Kevin Kolben shows as he shows that the collective side of labour law implies a process-orientation that is alien to most human rights concepts:

> Central to this procedural conceptualization of labor rights is the role of collective voice: a fundamental and constitutive aspect of labor rights is their quality of what I call process-oriented mobilization rights. Mobilization rights are facilitative and procedural in the sense that they provide a legal right for workers to form a collective that, through the power of law, can force the firm to negotiate work conditions against a backdrop of state-prescribed minimal standards.[50]

What Kolben correctly sees as an obstacle to align labour rights with human rights, could also be a chance for human rights to improve their own normative foundation and scope. I do not want to play down the concerns Kolben

45 Critical on this jurisdiction: Wiethölter (1970).
46 Günther (2006), 86 ff.
47 Decision of the German Federal Constitutional Court, 1 March 1979 (BVerfGE 50, 290, 347 ff.).
48 Atkinson, note 41 above, p. 135.
49 Davies (2013) p. 45.
50 Kolben (2010), p. 472.

expresses, especially since he justifies them both theoretically and based on empirical knowledge. And I do not want to consider how realistic and enforceable the concept of rights proposed here is. But – although this is a purely academic consideration for the time being – it seems to me to be beneficial to reflect on how human rights themselves could incorporate a collective, more process-oriented, bottom-up perspective. This is tantamount to abandoning the strictly liberal concept of human rights and above all to relativising the right of property and its spin-offs.[51] It would be limited by the workers' collective right of self-determination and the entrepreneurial freedom of decision derived from ownership would be further limited by a legally secured democratic decision-making process.

The decisive point here is that a rights-foundation for labour law crucially depends on the concept of human rights. As long as human rights remain in a strict individualist logic, the junction of human rights and labour rights carries serious perils. A widely understood right to strike seems to be indispensable in any case. In this sense, Alan Bogg and Cynthia Estlund propose a 'dynamic normative interaction' of various basic liberties as normative foundation for the right to strike.[52] In their conception of fundamental liberties, they explicitly invoke democratic norms by referring to Philip Pettit's thoughts on republicanism and the idea that democratic societies normatively seek relations of non-domination. In my view, this approach is particularly attractive because it reflects the relationship between fundamental rights and democracy and, on this basis, seeks normative grounds that lead to a stronger focus on human equality[53] as a common normative core.

4.2 Democratic teleology of law

As we have seen above, the central concern of the labour movement and the historical project of labour law was also the expansion of democratic standards into the field of industrial relations. One approach to realign labour law could therefore consist of strengthening its democratic foundations by establishing a democratic teleology of labour law. The democratic interpretation of labour law can go hand in hand with its rights-foundation if this rights-foundation implies a collective perspective. In the dogmatic beginnings of labour law, its democratic purpose was

51 Innumerable legal positions are derived from the right of property, which on closer inspection can hardly be justified in terms of human rights. For example, legal persons enjoy the basic right to property, and social inequality is consolidated over generations through protected inheritance rights. A particularly odd and poorly justified example is the so-called 'Recht am eingerichteten und ausgeübten Gewerbebetrieb' in German labour law which has been invented by the Federal Labour Court and criminalises general strikes (cf. note 45 above).

52 Bogg and Estlund, note 42 above, p. 230.

53 The strong link between fundamental rights and democracy reveals the obvious problem of human rights, which is that they are in reality (as indicated by Hannah Arendt) mostly rights of national citizens. Therefore we have reason to talk about citizens' rights. However, I voluntarily stick to the notion of human rights as I do not want to give up the universal approach.

very present in labour law discourses, and it is astonishing from an academic perspective that these discourses have almost completely disappeared from academic discourse. Instead, narratives of neoliberal economics serve as a reference.

The enterprise of a democratic teleology would be to normatively re-frame labour law in the sense of emphasising its potentials for the democratisation of society. For this purpose it may be helpful to recall earlier concepts of labour law. Different authors can be considered for this. For example Hugo Sinzheimer, who was in charge of codifying the structure of the Councils in the Weimar Constitution influenced thinkers such as Otto Kahn-Freund and Wolfgang Abendroth.

The democratic significance of the labour and economic constitution was at the centre of Abendroth's thinking which was engaged in the post-war debates in Germany on how to re-install a democracy in the aftermath of fascism. In addition to considerations of equality in the field of economics, he also made considerations for labour law that we could call subject-theoretical today.[54] Accordingly, democratic subjectivities can only arise in democratic practices. Wage earners learn democratic participation in their struggle for better working conditions and co-determination. They do this in the field of economics, i.e. in a field of experienced heteronomy. In this way, trade unions increase the integrative power of democracy and enable the development of collective and individual autonomy simply by organising democratic practices.

What Abendroth describes is basically a democratic teleology of law. The purpose of law is therefore to enable and promote democratic practices and life forms – including the area of economic and industrial relations. In his argumentation Abendroth referred often to the alliances of industry and employers with the fascists in the Weimar Republic. Trade unions and the labour movement, on the other hand, were important opponents of the Nazis.

Similar arguments are nowadays brought forward by Martin O'Neil and Stuart White who point to the empirical connection of labour organisation and democratisation.[55] They also see an empirical connection between democracy and organised labour and, in addition to theoretical arguments, present a whole series of empirical evidence for this connection. Accordingly, trade unions can for example increase political equality by promoting the interests of those who are structurally underrepresented in political institutions.[56] By way of shorthand, there is a whole range of not just theoretical, but also historical and empirical evidence linking organised labour and unions to the stabilisation of democracies.

There are also more abstract approaches that are suitable for formulating a democratic teleology of law. Daniel Loick promotes a critique of human rights that allows a perspective on rights beyond methodological individualism.[57] This

54 Cf., e.g. Abendroth (2008b), p. 124; Abendroth (2008a), p. 242.

55 O'Neill & White (2018), p. 256 ff.

56 Ibid., 261 f.

57 Loick is himself not significantly referring to labour law and is coming from a strictly philosophical perspective that is far from dogmatics. In my opinion, however, his thoughts can be transferred very well to labour law.

means that law can also be measured according to whether it can conceive of human beings as beings related to sociality and community and whether it enables or damages these relationships.[58] This means on the one hand that freedom of contract and private property, insofar as they establish private spheres of rule, are relativised to a certain extent.[59] On the other hand, this means that social rights, participation rights, and collective rights are being upgraded within the human rights architecture. It also means, and this makes Loick's explicitly (in a philosophical sense) anarchist approach particularly interesting from the perspective of labour law, a partial withdrawal of the law that leaves regulation to social actors and introduces a kind of democratic process in the area of human rights.[60]

It is therefore also adequate to understand labour rights as a juridical practice to reflect the blind spots of liberal human rights or, to put it in Marx's theoretical framework, an attempt to deal with the paradox of human rights. Labour rights can hence be interpreted as being part of the project of immanent critique of modern law.

At the same time we have to acknowledge, taking the concepts of liberty and equality that form the normative core of human rights and democracy seriously, that labour rights and more generally, social rights, must necessarily be part of the normative project of human rights. In this sense, we can understand collective labour rights as a democratic blank space secured by human rights allowing a democratic process in a defined area.

This idea of law is peculiarly intriguing in terms of the relationship between human rights and democratic processes. While the legal form of rights, despite its iterative dynamics, tends to close off spaces of political action, the collective form of rights integrates a defined political process into the system of rights. This allows for the integration of democratic principles of justice that cannot be represented in subjective rights without weakening them to an extent where they do not really show effect. This is regularly the case for social rights which seem to be hard to translate to dogmatics.[61]

Using the example of the German welfare state principle, Cara Röhner explores how social rights, if they are not conceived as subjective rights, only develop a 'weak normativity' and therefore only have a limited effect in practice.[62] A teleological approach runs the risk of falling into the same trap of inefficiency as we know it from the welfare state principle, since a teleological principle serves as an interpretive guideline, but is itself not enforceable. In combination with a stronger collective rights-foundation of labour law this could, however, help the law to de-neoliberalise. What is attractive about this approach is that it can be dogmatically justified because it refers to the dogmatic beginnings of labour law

58 Loick (2017), 300 ff.
59 Loick (2013), 316 ff.
60 Cf. Ibid., p. 318.
61 Röhner (2019), p. 64.
62 Ibid., 43 ff.

and also, that it allows the integration of what O'Neil/White call a 'promotive stance' towards labour organisations:

> In short, if strong unions are a feature of robust democracy, and if a democratic state should take action to sustain the conditions for its own health as a democracy, then surely the state should be supportive of trade unionism.[63]

So the democratic interpretation of law allows differentiation between associations according to the role they play in a democratic society. At the same time, democratic teleology is not necessarily exclusive to the benefit of well-established trade unions, but serves as a broader perspective aiming at allowing symmetrical relations in social life. For labour law, this means that those subalterns who do not benefit from standards of legal protection, such as those who are not integrated into the labour market or who work as freelancers, must also be included in some way. In the context of the digitalisation of work, there is currently increased discussion about the reorientation of labour law concepts in order to include excluded workers. This rather broad approach must be specified for the respective law context. In any case, such a teleological reorientation would call into question many established dogmas of labour law and thus mean a radical normative reorientation of labour law. However, especially from a subaltern perspective, the approach must also take into account considerations of legal certainty. This puts us in a bit of a dilemma: on the one hand, a radical reorientation of labour law seems to be indicated, on the other, it would be negligent, especially in view of the shifts in the balance of power between employers and trade unions, to soften established legal positions. The best way to manage this dilemma seems to me to be the 'promotive stance' as postulated by O'Neil and White. In more abstract terms, Loick's idea of a democratic law that is measured according to its social effects, leads in the same direction: the law (and those who interpret and apply it) should take sides in order to enable symmetrical social relations.

5 Conclusion

Even if there is no simple causal relationship here, the crisis of democracy must also be understood as a crisis of equality – and especially as a crisis of economic equality. This goes hand in hand with a weakening of the position of wage earners and trade unions, which also shows itself as a crisis of labour law. Labour law, which is in keeping with Fordism, hardly seems to fit modern industrial relations. It has thus also lost its transformative power. In many cases, neoliberal paradigms seem to have taken the place of the perspective of democratising the economy. Even in view of the danger of a loss of legal security, the radical reorientation of labour law seems to me to be indicated. This project implies

63 O'Neill and White, note 54 above, p. 264.

strengthening of collective human rights, partisanship of the law for subalterns, and a radical deconstruction of central dogmatic concepts such as property and the right to strike. The reorientation of labour law along a democratic teleology is aimed at establishing symmetrical relations in the economic sphere and therefore allows the less powerful greater scope for action than those who have economic power. In particular, means of industrial action that have so far been prohibited in most legal systems, such as plant blockades, but possibly also the extension of freedom of association to hitherto barely organised subalterns, should be discussed.

References

Abendroth, Wolfgang (2008a) 'Die Berechtigung gewerkschaftlicher Demonstration für die Mitbestimmung der Arbeitnehmer in der Wirtschaft', in M. Buckmiller, J. Perels, and U. Schöler, eds., *Gesammelte Schriften: 1949–1955*, Hannover: Offizin Verlag.

Abendroth, Wolfgang (2008b) 'Verfassungsrechtliche Grenzen des Streikrechts', in M. Buckmiller, J. Perels and U. Schöler, eds., *Gesammelte Schriften: 1949–1955*, Hannover: Offizin Verlag.

Anderson, Elizabeth (2017) *Private Government: How Employers Rule our Lives (and Why We Don't Talk About It)*, Princeton: Princeton University Press.

Arendt, Hannah (2011) 'Es gibt nur ein einziges Menschenrecht', in C. Menke and F. Raimondi, eds., *Die Revolution der Menschenrechte: Grundlegende Texte zu einem neuen Begriff des Politischen*, Berlin: Suhrkamp, 394–410.

Atkinson, Joe (2018) 'Human Rights as Foundations for Labour Law', in H. Collins, G. Lester and V. Mantouvalou, eds., *Philosophical Foundations of Labour Law*, Oxford: Oxford University Press, 122–138.

Auer, Marietta (2016) 'Eigentum, Familie, Erbrecht: Drei Lehrstücke zur Bedeutung der Rechtsphilosophie im Privatrecht'. *AcP (Archiv für die civilistische Praxis)*, 239–276.

Beyer, Gerald J. (2011) 'Economic Rights: Past, Present, and Future', in T. Cushman, ed., *Handbook of Human Rights*, New York: Routledge, 291–310.

Bogg, Alan and Cynthia Estlund (2018) 'The Right to Strike and Contestatory Citizenship', in H. Collins, G. Lester, and V. Mantouvalou, eds., *Philosophical Foundations of Labour Law*, Oxford: Oxford University Press, 229–251.

Bourdieu, Pierre (2009) 'Ökonomisches Kapital, kulturelles Kapital, soziales Kapital', in H. Solga, ed., *Soziale Ungleichheit: Klassische Texte zur Sozialstrukturanalyse*, Frankfurt am Main: Campus, 111–125.

Castel, Robert (2003) 'Das Verschwimmen der sozialen Klassen', in J. Bischoff, P. Boccara, R. Castel, and K. Dörre, eds., *Klassen und soziale Bewegungen: Strukturen im modernen Kapitalismus*, Hamburg: VSA, 7–17.

Chamayou, Grégoire (2018) *La société ingouvernable: une généalogie du libéralisme autoritaire*, Paris: La fabrique.

Collins, Hough (2018) 'Is the Contract of Employment Illiberal?', in H. Collins, G. Lester, and V. Mantouvalou, eds., *Philosophical Foundations of Labour Law*, Oxford: Oxford University Press, 48–67.

Davies, A. C. L. (2013) 'The "Constitutionalisation" of Labour Law: Possibilities and Problems', in K. S. Ziegler and P. M. Huber, eds., *Current Problems in the Protection of Human Rights: Perspectives from Germany and the UK*, Oxford: Hart Publishing, 45–68.

Déjours, Christophe, Jean-Philippe Deranty, Emmanuel Renault, and Nicholas H. Smith (2018) *The Return of Work in Critical Theory: Self, Society, Politics*, New York: Columbia University Press.

Diekmann, Marie (2020) 'Soziale Beziehungen und kollektives Handeln in der Plattformökonomie: Überlegungen zum arbeitsrechtlichen Umgang mit dem Problem betrieblicher Isolation von Crowdworker*innen', in S. Klawitter et al. eds., *Arbeitsrecht im Zeitalter der Digitalisierung: Dokumentation der 9. Assistentinnenund Assistententagung im Arbeitsrecht vom 25.–27.07.2019*, Baden-Baden: Nomos, 53–71.

Dörre, Klaus (2007) 'Prekäre Klassengesellschaft? Zur Strukturierung und Verbreitung sozialer Ungleichheit im Finanzmarkt-Kapitalismus', in C. Kaindl, ed., *Subjekte im Neoliberalismus*, Marburg, 19–47.

Ellerman, David P. (1992) *Property and Contract in Economics: The Case for Economic Democracy*, Oxford: Blackwell.

Ellguth, Peter and Rainer Trinczek (2016) 'Erosion der betrieblichen Mitbestimmung – Welche Rolle spielt der Strukturwandel?' *WSI Mitteilungen*, 172–182.

Günther, Klaus (2006) *Politik des Kompromisses: Dissensmanagement in pluralistischen Demokratien*, Wiesbaden: VS Verlag für Sozialwissenschaften.

Illouz, Eva (2007) *Gefühle in Zeiten des Kapitalismus: Frankfurter Adorno-Vorlesungen 2004, Institut für Sozialforschung an der Johann Wolfgang Goethe-Universität, Frankfurt am Main*, Frankfurt am Main: Suhrkamp.

Ingram, David (2011) 'Group rights. A Defense', in T. Cushman, ed., *Handbook of Human Rights*, New York: Routledge, 277–290.

Klinger, Cornelia (2003) 'Die Dialektik der Aufklärung im Geschlechterverhältnis', in S. Asal & J. Rohbeck, eds., *Aufklärung und Aufklärungskritik in Frankreich: Selbstdeutungen des 18. Jahrhunderts im Spiegel der Zeitgenossen*, Berlin: BWV, Berliner Wiss.-Verl.

Kolben, Kevin (2010) 'Labor Rights as Human Rights?' *Virginia Journal of International Law*. 449–484.

Loick, Daniel (2013) 'Abhängigkeitserklärung. Recht und Subjektivität', in R. Jaeggi and D. Loick, eds., *Nach Marx: Philosophie, Kritik, Praxis*, Berlin: Suhrkamp.

Loick, Daniel (2017) *Juridismus: Konturen einer kritischen Theorie des Rechts*, Berlin.

Maihofer, Andrea (2001) 'Dialektik der Aufklärung – Die Entstehung der modernen Gleichheitsidee, des Diskurses der qualitativen Geschlechterdifferenz und der Rassentheorie im 18. Jahrhundert', in S. Hobuß, C. Zimnik, B. Hartmann, and J. Pătruţ, eds., *Die andere Hälfte der Globalisierung: Menschenrechte, Ökonomie und Medialität aus feministischer Sicht*, Frankfurt: Campus–Verl.

Marx, Karl (1844/2006) *Zur Judenfrage*, Berlin: Karl Dietz Verlag.

Menke, Christoph (2011) 'Einleitung' in C. Menke and F. Raimondi, eds., *Die Revolution der Menschenrechte: Grundlegende Texte zu einem neuen Begriff des Politischen*, Berlin: Suhrkamp, 247–252.

Menke, Christoph (2013) 'Die "andre Form" der Herrschaft: Marx "Kritik des Rechts"', in R. Jaeggi and D. Loick, eds., *Nach Marx: Philosophie, Kritik, Praxis*, Berlin: Suhrkamp, 273–295.

Menke, Christoph (2015) *Kritik der Rechte*, Berlin: Suhrkamp.

Nachtwey, Oliver (2016) *Die Abstiegsgesellschaft: Über das Aufbegehren in der regressiven Moderne*, Berlin: Suhrkamp.

O'Neill, Martin and Stuart White (2018) 'Trade Unions and Political Equality', in H. Collins, G. Lester, and V. Mantouvalou, eds., *Philosophical Foundations of Labour Law*, Oxford: Oxford University Press, 252–270.

Piketty, Thomas (2013) *Le Capital au XXIe siècle*, Paris: Éditions du Seuil.
Prassl, Jeremias (2018) *Humans as a Service: The Promise and Perils of Work in the Gig Economy*, Oxford: Oxford University Press.
Raimondi, Francesca (2011) 'Einleitung', in C. Menke and F. Raimondi, eds., *Die Revolution der Menschenrechte: Grundlegende Texte zu einem neuen Begriff des Politischen*, Berlin: Suhrkamp, 95–101, 373–380.
Resolution of the Executive Committee of the ETUC (2008) Response to ECJ Judgments Viking and Laval, 3 July.
Röhner, Cara (2019) *Ungleichheit und Verfassung: Vorschlag für eine relationale Rechtsanalyse*, Weilerswist: Velbrück.
Rossanvallon, Pierre (2013) *Die Gesellschaft der Gleichen*, Hamburg: Hamburger Edition HIS.
Stahl, Titus (2013) What is Immanent Critique? *SSRN Electronic Journal* SSRN Working Paper http://ssrn.com/abstract=2357957.
Supiot, Alain (2011) *Der Geist von Philadelphia: Soziale Gerechtigkeit in Zeiten entgrenzter Märkte*, Hamburg: Hamburger Ed.
Voswinkel, Stephan (2002) 'Bewunderung ohne Würdigung? Paradoxien der Anerkennung doppelt subjektiver Arbeit', in A. Honneth, ed., *Befreiung aus der Mündigkeit: Paradoxien des gegenwärtigen Kapitalismus*, Frankfurt am Main: Campus.
Wellmer, Albrecht (2005) 'Menschenrechte und Demokratie', in S. Gosepath and G. Lohmann, eds., *Philosophie der Menschenrechte*, Frankfurt am Main: Suhrkamp, 265–291.
Wiethölter, Rudolf (1970) 'Zur politischen Funktion des Rechts am eingerichteten und ausgeübten Gewerbebetrieb'. *Kritische Justiz* (3) 121–139.

10 The 'quiet' revolutions in pension insurance and the constitutional safeguards in Eastern Europe

The cases of Bulgaria, Slovenia, and Latvia

Teodora Petrova

1 Introduction

Social protection could be seen as one of the pillars of democracy.[1] It provides collective solutions that enable individuals to lead full and free lives,[2] by addressing the potential social risks which one could experience during his or her lifetime. Apart from providing solutions to social dangers, however, social protection could also present numerous challenges to the democratic society. To elaborate, social protection systems are constantly modified due to their inherent connection to a nation's social and economic foundations. Some reforms could lead to far-reaching changes to and limitations of respective social rights, which alone could significantly hamper the ability of a social protection system to live up to its promises, i.e. to be capable of supporting beneficiaries' continued exercise of their freedom in the face of realised social risk.

The economic and demographic challenges could be especially pressing upon the long-term social protection branches, due to their considerable budgets and longer benefit-payment periods. Public pension systems represent the most notable example in this regard. The financing challenges that they pose are often related to the flow and balance of pension funds' incomes and expenses. At the same time, the systems are particularly susceptible to factors such as population decline and aging. Consequently, insufficient funding can have considerable impact on states' budgets.

1 P Schoukens and D Pieters (eds), *Social Security Quo Vadis? Interviews with Western European Social Security Administrators* (2007) 85.

2 U Becker, 'Sozialrecht und Sozialrechtswissenschaft' (2010) 65 *Zeitschrift für öffentliches Recht* 607, 611.

Nine out of the ten countries with the fastest population decline worldwide belong to Eastern Europe,[3] with Bulgaria leading the ranking and Latvia following this troubling trend.[4] Slovenia, like other countries in the region, is home to an aging population coupled with low-birth rates that will likely give it one of the highest old-age dependency ratios in the world.[5]

In response to these social processes and their economic pressures, Eastern European pension systems react with various degrees of action and reform attempts. Some of the proposed changes could be characterised as 'quiet revolutions'. They are 'quiet' because they occur via established legislative mechanisms. Yet, they can engender revolutionary consequences. On the one hand, such revolutions might lead to significant transformation, limitation or even negation of planned or acquired pension rights. On the other hand, due to the reforms' retrenchment character, revolutions can erode trust in the pension system and skew the democratic balance in a society.

Public pension systems are often based on the so-called 'contract between generations' where the younger population provides for retirees' benefits.[6] The mandatory participation in the system entails a limitation of individuals' freedom with the promise that one day, when the given social risk occurs, the system will provide for financial security in old age. In this way, through the pension system, people retain their freedom and ability to actively participate in society.

One might wonder how constitutional democracies can prevent such revolutions, or at least mitigate their potentially detrimental effects on pension rights. The question is even more relevant for Eastern European states, given the demographic and economic challenges in the region. Specifically, given pension insurance's considerable importance in maintaining democratic equilibrium, constitutional safeguards in Eastern Europe are crucially important for beneficiaries' rights in the face of these 'quiet revolutions'. The research hypothesis is that constitutional safeguards can prove instrumental in preserving the essence of pension rights against quiet revolutions. These safeguards can play crucial roles in the Eastern European context, supporting pension insurance's role as a pillar of democratic balance in society.

In order to address the research question, this chapter will focus on the constitutional jurisprudence of Bulgaria, Latvia, and Slovenia. Generally, Eastern European pension matters represent an under-researched field in legal scholarship.

3 The Economist, 'If Hell is Other People, Bulgaria is Paradise' (2018). www.economist.com/europe/2018/01/11/if-hell-is-other-people-bulgaria-is-paradise (accessed 5 April 2020).

4 EUROSTAT, 'People in the EU – Population Projections' (2017) https://ec.europa.eu/eurostat/statistics-explained/index.php/People_in_the_EU_-_population_projections#Population_projections (accessed 5 April 2020).

5 United Nations Department of Economic and Social Affairs, Population Division, 'World Population Ageing 2019: Highlights' (New York 2019) 17.

6 Veall MR, 'Public Pensions as Optimal Social Contracts' (1986) 31 *Journal of Public Economics* 237, 237.

At the same time, the region faces numerous issues influencing its pension systems' development. To address the relevant legal questions at hand, this chapter focuses on a given pension system's normative foundations and traces the constitutional guarantees for insurees.

In concentrating on Eastern Europe, it needs to be emphasised that the region does not represent a homogenous subject. Rather, various internal differences characterise the Eastern European region. Thus, to better understand some of the nuances in constitutional protection, one has to engage with analyses of constitutional solutions in different Eastern European states. The three proposed countries represent a similar but also quite diverging choice of case studies. Namely, they share comparable, but also deviating historical backgrounds.[7] The countries' varying economic development might also presuppose interesting differences in the responses of their pension systems to financial hardships.[8] Finally, the Bulgarian, Latvian, and Slovenian pension systems are comparable since pay-as-you-go (PAYG) financed public funds fund the largest part of national mandatory pension insurance schemes.[9]

2 Theoretical starting point: democracies and revolutions in pension insurance

It could be argued that due to the 'intimate connection' between democracy and freedom, one of the democratic state's fundamental obligations is to enable the exercise of freedom.[10] Therefore, the democratic state has to ensure that the exercise of freedom is possible for all members of society and alternatively should support all those restricted in exercising freedoms. In this sense, social protection could be seen as a tool through which the state ensures that

7 All of the three countries share a socialist past. However, Slovenia used to be part of Yugoslavia and Latvia was a republic of the Soviet Union.

8 For instance, in economic terms the three countries vary distinctly. While the GDP per inhabitant in euros is 6,800 in Bulgaria, it is 12,490 in Latvia and 20,490 in Slovenia. EUROSTAT, 'Economic Indicators: GDP per Inhabitant' https://ec.europa.eu/eurostat/cache/infographs/economy/desktop/index.html (accessed 4 April 2020). A further fact which could potentially be reflected in the results of the study is the fact that Latvia was seriously impacted by the European debt crisis and lost approximately 25% of its GDP between 2008 and 2010. However, it already returned to economic growth in the second half of 2010. For more on the topic, see A Åslund and V Dombrovskis, *How Latvia Came through the Financial Crisis* (Institute for International Economics 2011) 1–4.

9 See Mutual Information System on Social Protection, 'Bulgaria: VI. Old-age' (2019) www.missoc.org/missoc-database/comparative-tables/results/ (accessed 5 April 2020); Mutual Information System on Social Protection, 'Latvia: VI. Old-age' (2019) www.missoc.org/missoc-database/comparative-tables/results/ (accessed 5 April 2020); Mutual Information System on Social Protection, 'Slovenia: VI. Old-age' (2019) www.missoc.org/missoc-database/comparative-tables/results/ (accessed 5 April 2020). A small part of the pension insurance contributions in the countries are directed to capital-funded schemes.

10 J Brennan, 'Democracy and Freedom' in Carmen E Pavel (ed.), *The Oxford Handbook of Freedom* (Oxford University Press 2018) 335, 357–348.

individuals can benefit from one of the fundamental virtues of democracy.[11] Social protection measures can also promote greater equality by supporting those who are vulnerable and enabling their participation in society and democratic processes.[12]

However, social protection does not imply that the state should unconditionally distribute social benefits to all. On the contrary – the focus on the value of freedom stresses the importance of one's own care for him- or herself. Such are the foundations of the basic social premise stating that everyone should provide for their own personal wellbeing and that of their families.[13] The state should then address deficits in this basic social premise through supporting or risk-mitigating measures, in particular by establishing social protection schemes.

As a particularly vulnerable group, the elderly's protection from financial risks is historically one of the oldest forms of social protection. Pension insurance systems are an expression of the states' responsibilities toward elderly members of society, providing for their continuous exercise of freedom through measures for financial security in old age. The exact design of pension insurance measures, as well as their coverage, benefit amount and qualifying conditions, are open and broad questions.[14] Domestic political views often influence the answers to these conundrums and the concrete design of the systems.[15]

Designing a pension system is a delicate task, especially given the long-term and mandatory character of public pension insurance. Today's contributors paying retirees' pensions need to be certain that once they retire, they will also receive benefits. Further, the qualifying conditions for these benefits need to be shaped in a manner that corresponds to the effort and contribution of different individuals. Additionally, conditions must reflect the normative base at the time of the making of the contributions.

Pensions' long-term character and the lengthy qualifying insurance periods make the pension system susceptible to a wider range of threats, including but not limited to financial and demographic unsustainability. Such obstacles require pension systems to constantly adapt to new social situations. This hallmark of the pension insurance opens it to 'quiet revolutions', i.e. attempted pension system optimisations that might result in serious curbing of pension rights.

Such 'revolutions' maybe quiet, as they occur via the established legislative mechanisms and are prima facie just attempts to supporting a given system. However, these revolutions might be detrimental in two main regards. First, the legislator might be inclined to drastically revise some of the qualifying conditions or even the granted benefits prompted by different pressures. Attempts to

11 S Ringen, *What Democracy is for* (Princeton University Press 2009) 236–237.

12 U Becker, 'Verfassungsrechtliche Vorgaben für Sozialversicherungsreformen' (2010) *99 Zeitschrift für die gesamte Versicherungswissenschaft* 585, 588.

13 HF Zacher, 'Zur Anatomie des Sozialrechts' in Walter Bogs, Wolfgang Gitter and Georg Wannagat (eds), *Die Sozialgerichtsbarkeit* (1982) 329, 330.

14 Becker (n 12) 588.

15 Ibid.

revolutionise pension rights might take many shapes, such as introducing abrupt reforms, cutting pension benefits by more than half, and suddenly changing pension calculation rights that leave some beneficiaries with considerably lower pensions. The 'quiet' revolutions could then result in the installing of the doubt that the system is not capable of upholding its promises.

Beyond engendering discontent and mistrust in the public pension system, revolutions in pension insurance can have further detrimental consequences in the context of a democratic society that reach outside of the realm of social protection. For the sake of the pension insurance system's continuing existence, individuals' freedom is limited, and they are mandatorily included in different pension schemes. This compulsory enrolment permits the system to function continuously and fulfil its purpose of taking care of at-risk members of society. However, it can be argued that the limitation of the freedom entailed in the mandatory participation requires that the built system is efficient and able to provide sufficient protection when needed. If this is not the case, then individuals' freedom was infringed upon for the sake of no proportionate gains. A systemic failure to provide the required protection because of a component's revolution and the curbing of the rights of the beneficiaries can thus deteriorate not only trust in the law, but also the democratic foundations of a given society.

The constitutional safeguards for pension insurance are then potential tools through which stability and peace could be re-established in the given society. The protection of pension rights ensures that people cannot only realise their social rights, but also continue to also exercise their civil and political rights as members of democratic societies, despite risks accompanying old age. Hence, by setting limits to legislators' actions and providing clear interpretation on the substance of pension rights, constitutional protection can help preserve some of the fundamentals of the democratic order.

3 Constitutional foundations of the right to pension in Bulgaria, Slovenia, and Latvia

An examination of the constitutional safeguards and their potential to mitigate revolutions in pension insurance should begin with an overview of the respective normative foundations. In a constitutional democracy, the constitution limits the scope of legislators' actions. Generally, if relevant constitutional requirements exist, states should adhere to constitutional provisions in the design and reform of pension systems.[16] The pertinent constitutional provisions and their interpretations by the constitutional courts in Bulgaria, Slovenia, and Latvia are quite similar.

16 U Becker, 'Security from a Legal Perspective' (2015) 3 *Rivista del Diritto della Sicurezza Sociale* 515, 517.

3.1 The right to pension

The Latvian, Bulgarian, and Slovenian constitutions each contain the right to social security. The Latvian Constitution (or *Satversme* as it is referred to in Latvian) provides a specific reference to social security in old age[17] and the Slovenian Constitution explicitly states that the right to a pension is a form of the right to social security.[18] The Bulgarian Constitution does not explicitly enumerate the right to pensions, but the Constitutional Court has explicitly stated that pension rights are part of the right to social security stated in Article 51.[19] The constitutional courts in each of the three countries recognise the complicated character of the right to social security. This right involves 'a very complex system of possible substance and relationships dictated by various circumstances'.[20] The right, while difficult to realise,[21] still needs to guarantee 'a stable and predictable, as well as effective, fair and sustainable system of social protection that ensures a proportional social security'.[22] Furthermore, the elaboration of the right to social security is congruent with the democratic state's above-mentioned task of ensuring that individuals can exercise their freedoms. Namely, constitutional interpretations have stressed that the realisation of the right to social security needs to mitigate the effects of potential social risks.[23]

3.2 Relevant principles and the right to property

In addition to the right of social security, other important constitutional rights and principles define the scope of the right to social security, and hence the right to a pension. One such example of a guide for legislative action is the welfare state principle, entailing that the protection of social rights should be a leading concern for the country.[24] Constitutional review and interpretation of this

17 Article 109 of the Latvian Constitution. Also see K Dupate, 'The Constitutional Social Security Rights in the Republic of Latvia' in Alexandre Egorov and Marcin Wujczyk (eds), *The Right to Social Security in the Constitutions of the World: Broadening the Moral and Legal Space for Social Justice* (ILO Global Study Volume 1: Europe. International Labour Organisation 2016) 151.

18 Article 50 of the Slovenian Constitution.

19 For instance, see Decision No 10 of 13 September 2012 (Bulgarian Constitutional Court).

20 U-I-135/92 of 30 June 1994 para 5 (Slovenian Constitutional Court).

21 Decision No 2 of 22 February 2007 (Bulgarian Constitutional Court).

22 Decision in case No 2010-17-01 of 29 October 2010 para 7 (Latvian Constitutional Court).

23 Ibid. para 1; Decision No 10 of 13 September 2012 (Increase of Retirement Age Case, Bulgarian Constitutional Court). Also see E Drumeva, *Constitutional Law/Конституционно право* (5th edn, Ciela 2018) 786.

24 G Strban, 'Country Report on Slovenia' in Ulrich Becker (ed.), *Security: A General Principle of Social Security Law in Europe* (Europa Law Publishing 2010) 399, 402. V Mrachkov, 'Конституционализиране на осигурителното право/Constitutionalisation of the Social Security Law' in Krassimira Sredkova (ed.), *Актуални проблеми на трудовото и осигурителното право/Current Issues of Labor and Social Security Law: Осигурителна ли е българската осигурителна система?/Does the Bulgarian social Security System have an Insurance Character?* (VIII. 'St. Kliment Ohridski' University Publishing 2016) 37.

principle in both Slovenia and Bulgaria has been very cautious and reserved.[25] In contrast, the Latvian constitutional case-law relies on the principle of a socially responsible state, which entails the state's obligation to develop a regulatory framework contributing to a 'balanced and sustainable policy' for the sake of the society's wellbeing.[26]

Apart from the legislator's obligation to protect the welfare state, insurees have legitimate expectations regarding the realisation of their pension rights. Hence, by participating in pension insurance schemes, they benefit from the protection of the principle of trust in the law[27] that their acquired rights will be respected. The aspects of legal expectations and trust in the law are both building blocks of the rule of law in Latvia, Slovenia and Bulgaria.[28] The principle of the rule of law requires that legislators' actions must be consequent and foreseeable,[29] and, when required, reforms are to be introduced in a manner which provides beneficiaries the necessary possibility to adapt to new regulations.[30] However, this principle does not obstruct pension system alterations. On the contrary, reforming the system when necessary is one of the state's fundamental tasks, so as to support its proper functioning.[31]

Pension rights also benefit from the safeguards of the principle of equality,[32] and, to a certain extent, from the consequences stemming from the right to property. The principle of equality is usually examined not on its own, but in relation to a given pension right,[33] and could be potentially compatible with dissimilar treatment when it is aimed at establishing 'substantive (material) equality between genders'.[34] The right to property has been interpreted in different ways in all three constitutional jurisdictions. The Slovenian Constitutional Court

25 Still, the interpretation of the principle in Bulgaria has acquired more influential standing in the last years. In Mrachkov (n 24) 28–49.

26 Decision in case No 2011-03-01 of 19 December 2011 para 22 (Latvian Constitutional Court).

27 U-I-29/96-39 of 8 May 1997 para 15 (Pension Calculation Case, Slovenian Constitutional Court).

28 Ibid. para 15; the Latvian Constitutional Court rather refers to the term 'judicial state', see Decision in case No 2009-43-01 of 12 December 2009 para 32 (Pension Reduction Case, Latvian Constitutional Court).

29 Decision No 8 of 10 October 2013 on case No 6/2013 (Bulgarian Constitutional Court).

30 Pension Calculation Case (n 27) para 26. On the controversial character of the lack of transitionary measures, see U-I-86/96 of 12 December 1996 para 18 (Slovenian Constitutional Court). The Bulgarian Constituional Court also considers that the forseeability of the legal regulation is a hallmark of the legal certainty and the rule of law, but this does not represent an absolute requirement. See Increase of Retirement Age Case (n 23).

31 Pension Calculation Case (n 27) para 26; Decision No 21 of 15 July 1998 (Pension Ceiling Case, Bulgarian Constitutional Court).

32 Pension Ceiling Case (n 31); U-I-298/96 of 11 November 1999 (Slovenian Constitutional Court).

33 Pension Reduction Case (n 28) para 20.

34 Strban G, 'Constitutional Protection of the Right to Social Security in Slovenia' in Alexandre Egorov and Marcin Wujczyk (eds), *The Right to Social Security in the Constitutions of the World: Broadening the Moral and Legal Space for Social Justice* (ILO Global Study Volume 1: Europe. International Labour Organisation 2016) 243, 255.

declared that the right to a pension, resulting from social insurance, benefits from the safeguards of both the right to social security and the right to property.[35] The Latvian constitutional jurisprudence also holds that pensions, regardless of the date of their granting or source of funding, 'pertain to the content of the notion "property"[36] even if the pension rights could not be understood as property rights in the classic sense'.[37] Thus far, Bulgaria has adopted a more restricted approach. Namely, the right to property has been explicitly stated to yield protection to the pension insurance rights in capital-funded schemes, as these rights have a concrete numeral expression, i.e. the balance in the individual account.[38] The process of pension insurance in the public pension system, however, does not benefit from the protection of the right to property. Still, in all three countries, the right to a pension is not constitutionally tied to a particular benefit amount.

3.3 Constitutional complaint

Despite some very slight differences in relations to the extent of the interpretation of the right to property, it seems that in general the right to a pension has similar constitutional dimensions in Latvia, Slovenia, and Bulgaria. However, there are considerable differences pertaining to the sphere of the possibility for one to seek protection of their constitutional rights. While the constitutions of both Latvia and Slovenia establish the possibility of individual constitutional complaints,[39] the Bulgarian Constitution does not envisage this option.[40] Furthermore, while both Slovenian and Latvian courts of lower instance can request the initiation of proceedings for the constitutional review of legal acts,[41] only the Bulgarian

35 Up-770/06-18 of 27 May 2009 para 3 (Slovenian Constitutional Court).

36 Decision in case No 2007-01-01 of 8 June 2007 para 20 (Latvian Constitutional Court).

37 Pension Reduction Case (n 28) para 20.

38 Decision No 7 of 31 May 2011 on case No 21/2010 (Bulgarian Constitutional Court).

39 In Slovenia, Art. 160 of the Constitution and in Latvia: 'Section 17. Rights to Submit an Application Regarding Initiation of a Matter' of the Constitutional Court Law. In both Slovenia and Latvia, the constitutional complaint can be submitted in relation to violations of fundamental rights and freedoms. Before the submission of such complaint, the ordinary legal remedies need to be exhausted. However, there are exceptions to this rule in both cases, for instance, when implementation of the challenged legal act will result in 'irreparable consequences' (Art. 51 (2) of the Slovenian Constitutional Court Act) or when it is established that no ordinary legal remedies exist (Decision in case No 2012-23-01 of 24 October 2012 para 14, Latvian Constitutional Court). For more on the constitutional complaint in Slovenia, see Mavčič AM, 'The Slovenian Constitutional Review' (2009) 94. On Latvia, see Badovskis M and others, 'Public Law: Latvia' in Tanel Kerikmäe and others (eds), *The Law of the Baltic States* (Springer 2017) 191, 203.

40 Some authors in Bulgaria argue for the establishing of the constitutional complaint in the country. See Penev P, 'Bulgarian Constitutional Justice and Fundamental Rights Safeguards/Българското конституционно правосъдие и защитата на основните права' (2013) 12 *Адвокатски преглед* 18, 24–27.

41 In Slovenia, Article 156 of the Constitution and Article 23 of the Constitutional Court Act. In Latvia, 'Section 17. Rights to Submit an Application Regarding Initiation of a Matter' in the Constitutional Court Law.

Supreme Court of Cassation and the Supreme Administrative Court can ask for these reviews.[42] When faced with a potentially unconstitutional law, Bulgarian courts of lower instance must inform the supreme courts in the country on the matter; they cannot request constitutional review themselves.[43] The eventual consequences of these diverging mechanisms for the constitutional safeguards will be extrapolated below.

4 Comparative analyse: constitutional safeguards in Bulgaria, Latvia, and Slovenia

Because of the inherent relationship between social benefits and economics, authorities in all of the three countries enjoy considerable freedom when designing the systems that function in order to realise social rights.[44] The state needs to have leeway in order to adapt pension systems to contemporary challenges.[45] What is more, individuals cannot expect pension systems to remain static.[46] Nonetheless, constitutional safeguards curb the freedom to alter pension systems. The following will examine how constitutional jurisdictions applied to these safeguards in practice when the pension systems were subjected to retrenchment reforms. In doing so, this section discusses differences in the respective constitutional courts' approaches. The review will analyse both acquired and planned rights, as well as the transitional requirements for the reforms, which allow those impacted by the changes to adapt to the new situations. This section further examines which pension rights can and cannot be limited on the basis of constitutional safeguards.

4.1 Adjusting pension benefits

In terms of the question of acquired pension rights, each of the three case-study countries strictly limits interfering with realised rights.[47] This, however, does not infer that such acquired rights cannot be progressively modified. Alterations,

42 Article 150 of the Bulgarian Constitution.

43 Article 15 of the Law on the Judicial Power.

Some consider this to be an indirect mechanism for the citizens to initiate a constitutional review. See OK Yankov, 'Перспективи за възприемане на индивидуалната конституционна жалба в българската правна система. Други способи за защита на конституционните права на отделния гражданин в Република България/Prospects for the Perception of the Individual Constitutional Complaint in the Bulgarian Legal System. Other Ways of Protecting the Constitutional Rights of the Citizens in the Republic of Bulgaria.' (2016) http://gramada.org/перспективи-възприемане-индиви/#_ftnref41 (accessed 5 April 2020).

44 Pension Calculation Case (n 27); Pension Reduction Case (n 28) para 24.

45 Decision in case No 2009-08-01 of 26 November 2009 para 22.3 (Pension Indexation Case, Latvian Constitutional Court); Pension Ceiling Case (n 31).

46 Pension Calculation Case (n 27) para 26.

47 U-I-150/94-16 of 15 June 1995 para 6 (Slovenian Constitutional Court); Decision No 12 of 25 September 1997 (Working Pensioners Case, Bulgarian Constitutional Court); Pension Reduction Case (n 28) para 24.

though, must conform with constitutional principles,[48] such as legal certainty. In relation to a case concerning the halting of pension indexation due to serious economic pressures, the Latvian Constitutional Court has argued that the principle of legal certainty protected both acquired rights and planned rights yet to be conferred.[49] Legal certainty concerns rights that are foreseen in the legislature though all of the preconditions for the rights' occurrence are still not met. Even so, the protection of planned rights is less extensive when compared to the safeguards of already acquired rights. The main goal behind the constitutional safeguard of the principle of legal certainty is to enable people to plan their future.

Since a reform halting planned indexation entered into force on the date when the initially envisaged indexation was supposed to take place, the Latvian Constitutional Court claimed that insurees had reasonable legal certainty that the indexation would have occurred.[50] However, given that considerable economic deterioration in the state caused the contested reform, budget optimisations represented part of the state's efforts to maintain the functioning of the whole social protection system. Such reforms serve 'substantial social interests' and ultimately cannot violate the principle of legal certainty of the concerned individuals as the indexation has not occurred.[51] Furthermore, the right to indexation did not have a predetermined fixed amount and thus it could not be viewed as a substantial component of individuals' abilities to plan for the future. Serious contemporary economic concerns in Latvia, coupled with the fact that pension indexation was halted before it occurred (i.e. there was no interference with an already acquired right), arguably led the Court to conclude the legislator committed no constitutional violation.

In a case before the Slovenian Constitutional Court which likewise concerned adjustment of pension benefits, a reform which was challenged as being unconstitutional introduced slower pension increases based on goal of costs reduction.[52] Similarly to the Latvian example, the Slovenian Constitutional Court stated that expected rights also benefit, to a certain extent, from constitutional safeguards due to the legislator's obligations to act in a consistent manner by adopting reforms proportionate to the intended outcome. In assessing the constitutional balance, lawmakers must weigh the alternations' impacts on beneficiaries' lives given the gravity of the reform against the foreseeability of the given reform. Because the field of pension benefit adjustment experiences numerous changes, reforms are foreseeable possibilities. Thus, even if the change interfered with the principle of legal certainty, the measure may not be excessive.

48 U-II-1/11-46 of 10 March 2011 (Slovenian Constitutional Court); Working Pensioners Case (n 47).

49 Pension Indexation Case (n 45) para 24.

50 Ibid. para 24.

51 Ibid., para 25.

52 U-I-31/96 of 26 November 1998 (Slovenian Constitutional Court).

The constitutional safeguards provided to the legitimate expectations should not obstruct economic development.[53]

The introduction of pension ceilings in Bulgaria also arguably challenged insurees' legitimate expectations.[54] The reform was challenged on the grounds that pension ceilings allegedly curb the right to social security. The Constitutional Court rejected this argument. It reasoned that since the Constitution does not provide concrete guidance on the pension system's design, this task is left to the legislator. Thus, if it was necessary for floors and ceilings to be introduced in order to support the pension system's functioning, and if no acquired pension rights were harmed in the process, then there was no constitutional infringement. The same idea can be inferred from the Slovenian Constitutional Court reasoning that minimum and maximum pension calculation bases stem from the principle of solidarity and are not incompatible with the right to social security.[55]

4.2 Interfering with pension benefit's core

Each constitutional court in Latvia, Slovenia, and Bulgaria, however, took a different approach to reforms interfering with the core of the pension benefit amount. For instance, during the 2009 economic crisis, a Latvian pension reform measure instituted varying benefit cuts, reaching up to a 70% reduction of the benefits of some groups, such as employed pensioners.[56] The retrenchment measures were an expression of the dire economic situation, and resulted in the restriction of fundamental rights.[57] The Court stipulated that the right to a pension could be restricted if the retrenchment was 'established by the law, justified by a legitimate end and conforms to the principle of proportionality'.[58] The limitation of budget spending is considered a legitimate goal when it aims to maintain the sustainability and future existence of the given pension fund.[59] Still, even an economically dire situation cannot serve as comprehensive justification for the curbing of already acquired rights.[60] The Court's proportionality test[61] concluded that the reform could achieve the intended aim of balancing revenue and expenditures.[62] Nevertheless, due to the reforms' hasty passing, legislators have not complied with the requirement to assess alternate solutions and attempt to find a less restrictive approach.[63] Turning to the question of the principle of

53 Strban (n 34) 251.
54 Pension Ceiling Case (n 31).
55 Strban (n 34) 247.
56 Pension Reduction Case (n 28) para 32.
57 Ibid., para 25.
58 Ibid., para 26.
59 Ibid., para 27.2.
60 Ibid., para 27.2.
61 Ibid., para 28.
62 Ibid., para 29.2.
63 Ibid., para 30.

individuals' legitimate expectations stemming from Article 1 of the Satversme,[64] the Court again underlined that the principle does not preclude any reforms in general. But legislators must ensure that reasonable confidence in the legal order is maintained. Hence, if the pension rights are temporarily altered for the greater benefit of the society, the legislator must ensure that smooth transitional periods or future compensatory mechanisms are also foreseen.[65] Because the legislators established neither of these options, there was also a violation of Article 1 of the Satversme.[66] Similarly, the Slovenian Constitutional Court declared that a Slovenian reform that changed the basis for pension calculation and thus affected the self-employed in an unequal fashion by threatening to substantially lower some of their pension benefits omitted necessary introductions of smooth transitory periods.[67] The Court explicitly underlined that a social protection system, such as the pension scheme, does not tolerate rapid alterations, and authorities must introduce gradual changes, if necessary, only *ex nunc*.[68]

Analogously to the other two constitutional courts, the Bulgarian Constitutional Court also declared unconstitutional attempts to considerably curb the amounts of both acquired and planned pension benefits.[69] In a case concerning the limitation of working pensioners' pension benefits based on acquired pension rights, the defendants argued that given the pension system's PAYG character, those who are engaged in economic activity contribute to benefits for current retirees. Thus, those who continue to work should not be entitled to full pension amounts. However, the Court considered that the right to a pension which has already been acquired could be curbed only on the basis of constitutional provisions. The Court did not consider arguments based on pension system financing to be of constitutional character.

4.3 *Transitionary periods in pension reforms*

Nevertheless, the Bulgarian Constitutional Court's approach differs from Latvian and Slovenian case-law in its assessment of the compatibility of rapid pension insurance reforms with the rights of the beneficiaries. A case of the Bulgarian Constitutional Court concerned a retirement age increase that began nine years earlier than what was originally stated in the law.[70] The Court argued

64 Ibid., para 30.2.2.
65 Ibid., para 32.
66 In its case-law, the Latvian Constitutional Court has derived the principle of legal expectations from Article 1 of the Satversme. See K Krūma and S Statkus, 'The Constitution of Latvia – A Bridge Between Traditions and Modernity' in Anneli Albi and Samo Bardutzky (eds), *National Constitutions in European and Global Governance: Democracy, Rights, the Rule of Law* (TMC Asser Press 2019) 951, 963.
67 Pension Calculation Case (n 27) para 32.
68 Ibid., para 27.
69 Decision No 11 of 29 July 1992 (Bulgarian Constitutional Court); Working Pensioners Case (n 47).
70 Increase of Retirement Age Case (n 23).

that the legislator's requirement to act in a foreseeable manner is not an absolute one and could be overstepped in cases when the social protection system is in need of optimising measures. Given the demographic challenges the system faced, the sudden retirement age increase was compatible with the constitutional right to pension. In its reasoning, the Court only mentioned that retirement age increase reforms must be accompanied by further measures ensuring people thus required to work longer are indeed able to do so. The approach contrasts strongly with the Latvian example, where the Court examined the authorities' rash decisions in detail to assess their proportionality and considered the sufficiency of transitional periods and compensatory mechanisms. Furthermore, the Bulgarian approach to transitionary period requirements differs from the Slovenian Constitutional Court's conclusion that pension insurance reforms should be of a gradual nature with corresponding transitional periods since the pension system cannot withstand abrupt alterations.

5 Constitutional safeguards' potential to mitigate quiet revolutions in pension insurance

Pension insurance is above all income insurance.[71] The level of financial security provided by pension systems is closely related to the systems' efficiency and participants' mandatory inclusion[72] in the state's pension system. On one hand, such mandatory participation is a prerequisite for the functioning and existence of the pension system. On the other hand, it limits the freedom of the insurees.[73] Therefore, mandatory pension insurance simultaneously hampers and facilitates individual freedom by protecting against social risks associated with old age, thereby enabling diverse groups' democratic participation in society.

Arguably, restraining personal freedom imposes certain requirements on pension system efficiency. Namely, in a democratic society, where individual freedom is a celebrated and fundamental virtue, the limitation of certain freedoms is tolerated to enrol individuals in the system and thus enable the community's ability to mitigate social risk. Nevertheless, intrusion into one's freedom of choice could hardly be justified if the pension system cannot provide promised financial security in old age. If a pension system is unable to guarantee old-age financial security or is suddenly reformed in a manner that significantly affects pension rights, then it would seem that mandatory participation only maintains current benefit payments. In that case, the inter-generational contract of pension insurance, whose balance is essential also in economic terms in maintaining Paretho-efficiency,[74] could be violated. Such a scenario also undermines individual freedom as a core

71 HJ Zacher, 'Ziele der Alterssicherung und Formen ihrer Verwiklichung' in Hans F Zacher (ed.), *Alterssicherung im Rechtsvergleich* (Studien aus dem Max-Planck-Institut für Ausländisches und Internationales Sozialrecht Bd. 11, 1. Aufl. Nomos 1991) 25, 32.

72 Becker (n 12) 592–593.

73 Ibid.

74 Veall (n 6) 237.

virtue of democracy[75] by mandatorily including citizens in a pension system that would not provide them with sufficient financial security in old age and would therefore limit their possibilities for the exercise of freedom. Thus, the result of quiet revolutions in pension insurance can harm not only one's trust in the law, but also unbalance the democratic foundations in a given society.

5.1 *Limits to constitutional safeguards and extent of protection for pension rights*

To what extent do constitutional safeguards in Eastern Europe prevent such crises in pension insurance and contribute to pension system efficiency? As evidenced above, constitutions guarantee no fixed level of pension benefit. The right to property, even when interpreted as protecting pension rights, cannot specify a concrete amount.[76] The pension system remains free to adjust benefit amounts in accordance with the economic and social challenges it encounters. In terms of amount, the Slovenian constitutional interpretation calls for pension benefits that enable continuity of the standard of living.[77] In economic crises, the Latvian Constitutional Court argued that the right to social security includes a pension of minimum level, which must provide for a life 'worthy of a human being'.[78] It underlined that pensioners, especially those who have income falling below the established minimum levels, are a vulnerable social group that should be particularly protected.[79] In terms of the pension amount, the Bulgarian constitutional jurisprudence states that the question is left to the legislator, but that the social state principle imposes the objective of securing moderate levels of benefits for all members of the society.[80]

Apart from being unable provide for fixed benefit amounts, the case-law further demonstrates that constitutional safeguards fall short of effectively protecting further aspects of the pension rights, such as indexation freezing. It seems that pension amount adjustment cannot benefit from the principle of legal certainty since the sphere of pension indexation is frequently subject to alterations. In addition, benefit adjustments could not conclusively help beneficiaries plan their future since indexations do not feature a fixed amount, and do not concern

75 Ringen (n 11) 5.

76 As the Constitutional Court of Latvia puts it, 'The Constitutional Court acknowledges that wide freedom of action should be granted to the State in respect of property rights in the area of social rights, for the rights provided by Article 105 of the Constitution do not guarantee a specific pension amount, and they may be subject to restriction' (see Pension Reduction Case (n 28) para 20). The situation could be different in cases of capital-funded pension insurance based on private law contracts, since, as the Bulgarian Constitutional Court states, then the pension rights are related to a concrete financial amount, even during the insurance process, visible in the individual account.

77 U-II-1/11-46 of 10 March 2011 (n 48).

78 Pension Reduction Case (n 28) para 31.2.

79 Ibid.

80 Increase of Retirement Age Case (n 23).

the core of the pension benefit. Rather, they supplement the already granted amount. Still, the significance of indexation measures has grown during the last years in terms of their impact on pension adequacy and, consequently, on pension system efficiency.[81] Studies have shown that indexation measures are often sacrificed in attempts to boost pension funds' financial sustainability.[82] Nevertheless, indexation measures are essential, especially when cumulatively accounting for the rest of the contemporary factors affecting pension levels, such as non-standard and shorter working-life patterns that affect contributions and resulting pension amounts.

In contrast to the adjustment of benefits' amounts, a common and observable denominator in Latvia, Slovenia, and Bulgaria is that the core of the pension benefit is constitutionally safeguarded against the 'quiet revolutions' threatening to curb its amount. This remains the case even in times of severe financial duress and holds true even if the benefit has not yet been granted.[83] Legislators cannot easily interfere with the main granted benefit amount because, as a core benefit, it might be foundational to individuals' abilities to plan their futures. The possibility of organising one's life and future as one deems suitable is inextricably linked to the exercise of freedom.[84] The constitutional courts' approach in this regard is congruent with European Court of Human Rights case-law, which also weighs on the curbing of social protection benefits against the ability of the concerned individual to adjust to the reform.[85] Of course, constitutional protection in this regard is not unlimited. Planned pension rights are more open to reform measurements. Even so, alterations must feature sufficient transitional periods sensitive to the impact of the pension rights change on beneficiaries' lives.

5.2 Varying depth of constitutional scrutiny

In terms of the requirements stemming from pension rights during transitional periods, Bulgarian constitutional jurisprudence has been admittedly the most modest of the three jurisdictions, in addition to being reluctant to establish constitutional obligations for the legislator. While all three constitutional courts indicate the modifiable nature of pension insurance, Slovenian and Latvian case-law explicitly states that regardless of whether rights are realised or not, pension systems should not be subjected to abrupt pension reforms. Thus, the most striking difference in the constitutional safeguards evidenced in the Bulgarian,

81 EM Hohnerlein, 'Pension Indexation for Retirees Revisited – Normative Patterns and Legal Standards' (2019) 19(3) *Global Social Policy* 246.

82 Ibid.

83 Pension Calculation Case (n 27).

84 Ringen (n 11) 5.

85 For more on the topic, refer to P Popelier, 'Legal Certainty and the European Courts: Accessibility and Legitimate Expectations as Standards of Reasonableness' in Mark Fenwick, Mathias M Siems and Stefan Wrbka (eds), *The Shifting Meaning of Legal Certainty in Comparative and Transnational Law* (Hart Publishing 2017) 29, 40–41.

Latvian, and Slovenian case-law is the response to reforms motivated by serious pressures on the pension system. Bulgarian constitutional jurisprudence established that, in turbulent times, pension insurance systems may be subject to unforeseeable or inconsistent alterations.[86] In contrast, even in times of serious financial obstacles to the entire state, the Latvian constitutional reasoning argued for the necessity of either transitional periods or compensatory mechanisms that take care of the infringed rights of the beneficiaries.

The varying degrees of constitutional reform scrutiny impacts constitutional safeguards' abilities to respond to quiet pension revolutions. Arguments based on serious pressures and need for budget optimisations are often brought to the fore, especially given the overall tendency and advocacy for retrenchment of pension rights. Yet, even when considerable financial and social challenges confront a system, it will need to consider insurees' rights. Abrupt reforms coupled with the lack of requirements for comprehensive transitory or compensatory measures could erode the public trust and basic social foundation upon which pension systems are built.

5.3 Constitutional safeguards in the Eastern European climate of public authority mistrust

Differences in the extent of the constitutional requirements for legislators might be further exacerbated by limited mechanisms for requesting constitutional review in Bulgaria. To clarify, individuals' constitutional complaints could enable the constitutional court to review a greater range of reforms and thus could provide more opportunities to develop constitutional requirements for alterations affecting people's ability to plan their future. Some legal scholars claim that the ability of individuals to file constitutional complaints has enabled constitutional courts to review and act more in regard to fundamental rights protection.[87] Furthermore, the possibility of constitutional complaints could strengthen beneficiaries' beliefs that constitutional rights are more than mere words declared on paper. The constitutional complaint is a way through which those who are most affected by a given reform can independently contest it, without and solely relying on authorities' actions.[88] Even states with stable and long-standing rule of law traditions tend to experience issues due to a faltering of societal confidence in respective institutions' timely and reliable actions.[89]

The diminishing confidence in institutions' work, however, holds true with even greater force in the Eastern European region where individuals tend to

86 Increase of Retirement Age Case (n 23).
87 M de Visser, *Constitutional Review in Europe* (Hart Publishing 2014) 153.
88 Ibid.
89 Ibid.

distrust public authorities as well as the ordinary judicial system.[90] In this climate of general doubt towards state action, constitutional courts number among the few institutions that still enjoy the trust of the society.[91] Given this particular context, the constitutional complaint mechanism might release some of the accumulating societal pressure for pension insurance retrenchment reforms while simultaneously contributing to constitutional dialogue in a given state.[92]

Finally, individuals' rights to constitutional complaint raise the constitutional awareness of the society as a whole, which could be of particular importance for states suffering from rule of law insufficiencies. For instance, in the context of Latvia, constitutional complaints have been instrumental in the development of constitutionalism as 'a remedy against the public power' which 'emphasizes the importance of the person in the state and also allows rights to be developed based on constitutionalism'.[93]

Naturally, the constitutional complaint is not a panacea. For instance, even if the possibility for requesting a constitutional review in a state exists, not all citizens would be able to equally benefit from it due to personal factors, such as socioeconomic status.[94] Still, examining the applicants' sections of the cases discussed here demonstrates that some of the cases that contributed to the unveiling of constitutional safeguards against the quiet revolutions in pension insurance were related to individuals' complaints. By providing an opportunity for the insurees to challenge reforms on constitutional grounds, constitutional complaints can bolster individuals' trust in the effectiveness of the constitutional safeguards in place and the law in general.[95]

90 B Bugarič, 'A Crisis of Constitutional Democracy in Post-Communist Europe: 'Lands in-between' Democracy and Authoritarianism' (2015) 13(1) *International Journal of Constitutional Law* 219, 228.

91 For more on the low trust in public institutions in Slovenia as well as on the different perception of the Constitutional Court and its journey towards establishing itself as legal authority in the country, see M Cerar, 'Slovenia's Constitutional Court within the Separation of Powers' in Wojciech Sadurski (ed.), *Constitutional Justice, East and West: Democratic Legitimacy and Constitutional Courts in Post-communist Europe in a Comparative Perspective* (Law and Philosophy Library. *Kluwer Law International* 2010) 213, 237–238. On the difficult path of the building of post-communist constitutionalism in Bulgaria, see V Ganev, 'The Rise of Constitutional Adjudication in Bulgaria' in Wojciech Sadurski (ed.), *Constitutional Justice, East and West: Democratic Legitimacy and Constitutional Courts in Post-communist Europe in a Comparative Perspective* (Law and Philosophy Library. Kluwer Law International 2010) 247.

92 Penev (n 40) 24.

93 A Endziņš and V Sinkevičius, 'Constitutional Review in Latvia and Lithuania: A Comparative Analysis' (2017) 3(2) *International Comparative Jurisprudence* 161, 172.

94 For instance, in the context of Slovenia, where a constitutional complaint mechanism is available, the recipients of social assistance were supposedly less empowered to constitutionally enforce their rights at a time when their pension social assistance rights were limited. Strban (n 34) 252.

95 On the importance of constitutional courts for the building of democracy in Eastern Europe and that it is up to the constitutional courts to solidify the features of constitutional democracies, see I Epstein, J Knight, and O Shvetsova, 'The Role of Constitutional Courts in the Establishment and Maintenance of Democratic Systems of Government' (2001) 35(1) *Law & Society Review* 117.

5 Conclusion

Today, European pension systems face multifaceted obstacles. On the one hand, in many countries aging populations and the low-birth rates pose the threat that fewer insurees will have to finance the pensions paid out in the future. On the other hand, the spread of digitalisation and the new forms of atypical work fundamentally challenge many pension schemes' financing mechanisms, due to the different earnings patterns affecting social protection contributions.

All of these impediments potentially lead to fewer pension fund contributions and thus pose financing sustainability threats. Eastern European states suffering from severe population decline and aging processes feel the reverberations of the challenges outline quite strongly. Naturally, these countries attempt to mitigate the pressures on their pension systems through reforms. Some of the changes even attempt to quietly revolutionise pension insurance by significantly and abruptly altering the main aspects of pension rights.

In such instances, constitutional safeguards are crucial in limiting legislators' actions and preserving beneficiaries' pension rights. Constitutional protections not only safeguard pension rights, but they also, in a broader sense contribute to the democratic balance in a given society. By protecting pension rights and individuals' respective benefits, constitutional safeguards mitigate attempted quiet revolutions in pension systems and thus contribute to people's continued ability to exercise their freedom as members of society, even in old age. However, if such constitutional safeguards fail to preserve pension rights, the results could erode trust in the law, violate the contract between generations, which is foundational for most pension systems in Eastern Europe, and undermine the virtue of freedom as a cornerstone of democracy.

The Latvian, Slovenian, and Bulgarian case studies demonstrate that constitutional safeguards can protect the core of pension benefits in these Eastern European states. Constitutional protection, therefore, strives to ensure that, despite reforms, beneficiaries can retain their freedom to shape their lives as they will. However, constitutions could not provide for a concrete pension amount and do not yield safeguards for certain pension amount alterations, such as halting indexation measures. Although such reforms could be perceived as unimportant for ones' ability to plan their future, their impact on individuals' lives could be much further reaching than originally thought given the increasing relevance of indexation measures for adequate old-age benefits.

The impact of constitutional safeguards in the face of quiet attempts to revolutionise pension rights is especially valuable in the Eastern European context. Constitutions' effectiveness in protecting individual rights depends on the constitutional courts.[96] Given the general climate of mistrust in the actions of

96 S Bartole, 'Conclusions: Legitimacy of Constitutional Courts: Between Policy Making and Legal Science' in Wojciech Sadurski (ed.), *Constitutional Justice, East and West: Democratic Legitimacy and Constitutional Courts in Post-communist Europe in a Comparative Perspective* (Law and Philosophy Library. Kluwer Law International 2010) 409, 431.

the public authorities, constitutional courts remain some of the few institutions that still enjoy the trust of most of society.[97] By providing clear signals on the limits upon which retrenchment reforms cannot trespass, Eastern Europe constitutional courts reinforce individuals' trust that pension systems will live up to their promises, and thus strengthen the democratic balance in society. In this regard, the mechanism of constitutional complaint empowers people to claim their rights and could contribute to the social equilibrium required for the sustainable functioning of the public pension system.

References

Åslund A and Dombrovskis V, *How Latvia Came through the Financial Crisis* (Institute for International Economics 2011).

Badovskis M and others, 'Public Law: Latvia' in Tanel Kerikmäe and others (eds), *The Law of the Baltic States* (Springer 2017) 191, DOI: 10.1007/978-3-319–54478-6.

Bartole S, 'Conclusions: Legitimacy of Constitutional Courts: Between Policy Making and Legal Science' in Wojciech Sadurski (ed.), *Constitutional Justice, East and West: Democratic Legitimacy and Constitutional Courts in Post-communist Europe in a Comparative Perspective* (Law and Philosophy Library. Kluwer Law International 2010) 409.

Becker U, 'Sozialrecht und Sozialrechtswissenschaft' (2010) 65 *Zeitschrift für öffentliches Recht* 607, DOI: 10.1007/s00708-010-0078-7.

Becker U, 'Verfassungsrechtliche Vorgaben für Sozialversicherungsreformen' (2010) 99 *Zeitschrift für die gesamte Versicherungswissenschaft* 585, DOI: 10.1007/s12297-010-0128–9.

Becker U, 'Security from a Legal Perspective' (2015) 3 *Rivista del Diritto della Sicurezza Sociale* 515, DOI: 10.3241/80434.

Becker U and others (eds), *Security: A General Principle of Social Security Law in Europe* (Europa Law Publishing 2010).

Brennan J, 'Democracy and Freedom' in Carmen E Pavel (ed.), *The Oxford Handbook of Freedom* (Oxford University Press 2018) 335, DOI: 10.1093/oxfordhb/9780199989423.013.15.

Bugarič B, 'A Crisis of Constitutional Democracy in Post-Communist Europe: "Lands in-between" Democracy and Authoritarianism' (2015) 13(1) *International Journal of Constitutional Law* 219, DOI: 10.1093/icon/mov010.

Cerar M, 'Slovenia's Constitutional Court within the Separation of Powers' in Wojciech Sadurski (ed.), *Constitutional Justice, East and West: Democratic Legitimacy and Constitutional Courts in Post-communist Europe in a Comparative Perspective* (Law and Philosophy Library. Kluwer Law International 2010) 213.

Drumeva E, *Constitutional Law/Конституционно право* (5th edn, Ciela 2018).

Dupate K, 'The Constitutional Social Security Rights in the Republic of Latvia' in Alexandre Egorov and Marcin Wujczyk (eds), *The Right to Social Security in the Constitutions of the World: Broadening the Moral and Legal Space for Social Justice* (ILO Global Study Volume 1: Europe. International Labour Organisation 2016) 151.

97 Cerar (n 91) 228.

Egorov A and Wujczyk M (eds), *The Right to Social Security in the Constitutions of the World: Broadening the Moral and Legal Space for Social Justice* (ILO Global Study Volume 1: Europe, International Labour Organisation 2016).

Endziņš A and Sinkevičius V, 'Constitutional Review in Latvia and Lithuania: A Comparative Analysis' (2017) 3(2) *International Comparative Jurisprudence* 161, DOI: 10.13165/10.13165/j.icj.2017.12.004.

Epstein L, Knight J, and Shvetsova O, 'The Role of Constitutional Courts in the Establishment and Maintenance of Democratic Systems of Government' (2001) 35(1) *Law & Society Review* 117, DOI: 10.2307/3185388.

EUROSTAT, 'Economic Indicators: GDP per Inhabitant' https://ec.europa.eu/eurostat/cache/infographs/economy/desktop/index.html (accessed 4 April 2020).

Ganev V, 'The Rise of Constitutional Adjudication in Bulgaria' in Wojciech Sadurski (ed), *Constitutional Justice, East and West: Democratic Legitimacy and Constitutional Courts in Post-communist Europe in a Comparative Perspective* (Law and Philosophy Library. Kluwer Law International 2010) 247.

Hohnerlein EM, 'Pension Indexation for Retirees Revisited – Normative Patterns and Legal Standards' (2019) 19(3) *Global Social Policy* 246, DOI: 10.1177/1468018119842028.

Kerikmäe T and others (eds), *The Law of the Baltic States* (Springer 2017) DOI: 10.1007/978-3-319–54478-6.

Krūma K and Statkus S, 'The Constitution of Latvia – A Bridge Between Traditions and Modernity' in Anneli Albi and Samo Bardutzky (eds), *National Constitutions in European and Global Governance: Democracy, Rights, the Rule of Law* (TMC Asser Press 2019) 951, DOI: 10.1007/978–94–6265–273–6_20.

Mavčič AM, 'The Slovenian Constitutional Review' (2009).

Mrachkov V, 'Конституционализиране на осигурителното право/Constitutionalisation of the Social Security Law' in Krassimira Sredkova (ed.), *Актуални проблеми на трудовото и осигурителното право/Current Issues of Labor and Social Security Law: Осигурителна ли е българската осигурителна система?/Does the Bulgarian social Security System have an Insurance Character?* (VIII. 'St. Kliment Ohridski' University Publishing 2016).

Mutual Information System on Social Protection, 'Bulgaria: VI. Old-age' (2019) www.missoc.org/missoc-database/comparative-tables/results/ (accessed 5 April 2020).

Mutual Information System on Social Protection, 'Latvia: VI. Old-age' (2019) www.missoc.org/missoc-database/comparative-tables/results/ (accessed 5 April 2020).

Mutual Information System on Social Protection, 'Slovenia: VI. Old-age' (2019) www.missoc.org/missoc-database/comparative-tables/results/ (accessed 5 April 2020).

Pavel CE (ed.), *The Oxford Handbook of Freedom* (Oxford University Press 2018) DOI: 10.1093/oxfordhb/9780199989423.001.0001.

Penev P, 'Bulgarian Constitutional Justice and Fundamental Rights Safeguards/Българското конституционно правосъдие и защитата на основните права' (2013) 12 *Адвокатски преглед* 18.

Popelier P, 'Legal Certainty and the European Courts: Accessibility and Legitimate Expectations as Standards of Reasonableness' in Mark Fenwick, Mathias M Siems, and Stefan Wrbka (eds), *The Shifting Meaning of Legal Certainty in Comparative and Transnational Law* (Hart Publishing 2017) 29, DOI 10.5040/9781509911288.

Ringen S, *What Democracy is for* (Princeton University Press 2009), DOI: 10.1515/9781400831678.

Sadurski W (ed.), *Constitutional Justice, East and West: Democratic Legitimacy and Constitutional Courts in Post-communist Europe in a Comparative Perspective* (Law and philosophy library, Kluwer Law International 2010).

Schoukens P and Pieters D (eds), *Social Security Quo Vadis? Interviews with Western European Social Security Administrators* (2007).

Strban G, 'Country Report on Slovenia' in Ulrich Becker and others (eds), *Security: A General Principle of Social Security Law in Europe* (Europa Law Publishing 2010) 399.

Strban G, 'Constitutional Protection of the Right to Social Security in Slovenia' in Alexandre Egorov and Marcin Wujczyk (eds), *The Right to Social Security in the Constitutions of the World: Broadening the Moral and Legal Space for Social Justice* (ILO Global Study Volume 1: Europe. International Labour Organisation 2016) 243.

The Economist, 'If Hell is Other People, Bulgaria is Paradise' (2018)www.economist.com/europe/2018/01/11/if-hell-is-other-people-bulgaria-is-paradise (accessed 5 April 2020).

United Nations Department of Economic and Social Affairs, Population Division, 'World Population Ageing 2019: Highlights' (New York 2019).

Veall MR, 'Public Pensions as Optimal Social Contracts' (1986) 31 *Journal of Public Economics*237, DOI: 10.1016/0047–2727(86)90020-4.

Visser M de, *Constitutional Review in Europe* (Hart Publishing 2014).

Yankov OK, 'Перспективи за възприемане на индивидуалната конституционна жалба в българската правна система. Други способи за защита на конституционните права на отделния гражданин в Република България/Prospects for the Perception of the Individual Constitutional Complaint in the Bulgarian Legal System. Other Ways of Protecting the Constitutional Rights of the Citizens in the Republic of Bulgaria' (2016) http://gramada.org/перспективи-възприемане-индиви/#_ftnref41 (accessed 5 April 2020).

Zacher HF, 'Zur Anatomie des Sozialrechts' in Walter Bogs, Wolfgang Gitter and Georg Wannagat (eds), *Die Sozialgerichtsbarkeit* (1982) 329.

Zacher HF, 'Ziele der Alterssicherung und Formen ihrer Verwiklichung' in Hans F Zacher (ed.), *Alterssicherung im Rechtsvergleich* (Studien aus dem Max-Planck-Institut für Ausländisches und Internationales Sozialrecht Bd. 11, 1. Aufl. Nomos 1991) 25, DOI: 10.5282/ubm/epub.10149.

11 Constitutional change in Greece as a result of the financial crisis

Privatisations and the silent (r)evolution of the economic constitution

Apostolos Vlachogiannis

1 Introduction

In the past few years, Greece has experienced in a very intense way the turmoil of the financial crisis. As a result, the Greek Constitution has also found itself lying at the epicentre of the storm. The democratic institutions and the constitutional system were put to a great test. Although the Constitution proved amply its resilience,[1] we should not ignore the fact that major constitutional change has been produced all these years. The factual and political pressure exerted on all three branches of government, along with the all-encompassing engagements contained in the three bailout agreements (Memoranda)[2] were the driving forces of reforms that have significantly altered the country's legal landscape and affected the course of the country for many decades to come.

During this period, new landmark statutes were passed. The body of constitutional doctrine has been adapted to the changed circumstances. Settled precedents were overruled. Old concepts have been reshaped and new ones have been invented. In addition to these, basic assumptions about the Constitution have been overthrown and shared conceptions of how the Greek Fundamental Law works and evolves through time have been modified. In fact, the Greek Constitution went through a series of substantial changes, which have not been integrated into the written text, but form part of what could be called the 'unwritten' or the 'living Constitution' or the 'Constitution-in-practice', as US

1 This has been pointed out by Antonis Manitakis, 'The Impressive Resilience of the Greek Constitution in the Current Financial crisis' in Lina Papadopoulou and others (eds), *Legitimacy Issues of the European Union in the Face of Crisis: Dimitris Tsatsos In Memoriam* (Nomos Verlag 2017) 217 and Evangelos Venizelos, 'Resilience, Adaptability and Amendment of the Constitution. Thoughts on a Comprehensive Evaluation of the 2009–2019 period' [in Greek] (2019) *Journal of Administrative Law* 682.

2 The first Memorandum was signed in May 2010 (bilateral Greek Loan Facility – GLF) and the second one in March 2012 (EFSF loan to Greece). The third and last Memorandum was signed in July 2015 (ESM loan to Greece) and expired in August 2018.

constitutional scholars such as Akhil Reed Amar,[3] Jack Balkin,[4] or Bruce Ackerman[5] have described it. All this happened of course within the formal structure of an extremely hard to amend Constitution.[6]

Through this chapter I will try to explain by which means and in what respect the Greek living Constitution has changed in the aftermath of the crisis, in the particular field of privatisations, and what the effects are of this change on the legitimacy of the constitutional system as a whole. It follows that my approach is mainly descriptive. In the same way that Balkin and Levinson have studied the emergence of the surveillance state in the US,[7] we probably need to start by studying the adjustment of the Greek Constitution to the crisis as well as to the post-crisis era and by describing these processes of constitutional decision-making. Only then, will we be able to evaluate, at a second stage, their results from a democratic legitimacy point of view.[8]

The general aim of this chapter is to apply Balkin's theory of living constitutionalism, as developed in the US legal order, to the Greek Constitution and thus contribute to understanding the processes of constitutional change during the crisis. By providing a broad and strictly descriptive legal outline of the privatisation process taking place in Greece, it will become possible to show how the Greek Constitution has profoundly, though silently, changed as a result of the pressure exerted by the European economic Constitution and the new European economic governance.[9]

3 '[T]he written Constitution itself invites recourse to certain things outside the text – things that form America's unwritten Constitution. When viewed properly, America's unwritten Constitution supports and supplements the written Constitution without supplanting it.' Amar Akhil Reed, *America's Unwritten Constitution: The Precedents and Principles We Live By* (Basic Books 2012).

4 'What we call a "living Constitution" is really the product of constitutional construction and changes in constitutional construction over time.' Jack Balkin, *Living Originalism* (HUP 2011) 320. Balkin also states that '[t]ogether, all of the various constructions, institutions, laws, and practices that have grown up around the text over time form what we might call the 'Constitution-in-practice'. Jack Balkin, 'Nine Perspectives on Living Originalism' (2012) 3 *University of Illinois L. Rev.* 101, 102.

5 'The living Constitution is a product of these eight cycles of popular sovereignty…' Bruce Ackerman, 'The Living Constitution' (2007) 120 HLR 1737, 1758.

6 Article 110 of the Constitution regulating the amendment procedure sets considerable substantive as well as procedural limits. In para 1, it contains the so-called eternity clause of the Greek Constitution and in the following paragraphs, it determines the supermajorities needed for the amendment, after the intervention of a general election creating a two consecutive Parliaments system.

7 Jack Balkin and Sanford Levinson, 'The Processes of Constitutional Change: From Partisan Entrenchment to the National Surveillance State' (2006) 75 *Fordham L. Rev* 489; Jack Balkin, 'The Constitution in the National Surveillance State' (2008) 93 *Minn. L. Rev.* 1.

8 Balkin, *Living Originalism* (n 4) 130 and 278.

9 The notion of 'new European economic governance' is briefly discussed in Kaarlo Tuori, 'The European Financial Crisis – Constitutional Aspects and Implications' (2012) EUI Working Papers LAW 2012/28, 17 ff. https://papers.ssrn.com/sol3/papers.cfm?abstract_id=2171824 (accessed 18 April 2020).

By adopting a functionalist and sectorial approach it will be made clear that the 'European Constitution' shapes national Constitutions and affects national constitutionalism without however having created beforehand the necessary democratic preconditions. This marked 'empowerment' of the European economic Constitution, which creates a similar national counterpart, seemingly leads to an exacerbation of the well-known democratic deficit of the European Union and reproduces it at the national level within the context of the economic crisis as well as the post-crisis landscape.[10] The (r)evolution of the economic Constitution thus represents a fracture in the constitutional system, allowing EU goals of market liberalisation combined with the institutional lenders' demands to penetrate it widely. This is exactly the point that needs to be brought into surface and then evaluated. How does this process take place and in which ways can it be consequently considered legitimate from a constitutional and democratic angle?

Within this context, the Greek Constitution is presented here as a flexible framework of government, a living document capable of adapting to changing circumstances and accommodating change. The case of privatisations and the subsequent evolution of the economic Constitution will be used as an example that best illustrates the process of constitutional change. This chapter focuses on this particular sector of the Constitution[11] because it is highly revelatory not only of the cataclysmic change endured by the Greek Constitution during the crisis, but also of the interrelatedness between the current national policy on privatisations, on the one hand, and European Union law and the institutional lenders' demands, on the other. This particular sector of the economic Constitution has been subject to drastic changes that have earmarked it and in a sense, driven it apart from the other corpus of constitutional doctrine. In other words, it highlights a fragmentation of the Constitution, resulting from the pressure of the crisis along with the pressure of EU political imperatives and law.

Unavoidably, we have to admit that an interdisciplinary approach, combining law and economics, would be indispensable in order to fully evaluate the effectiveness, impact, and externalities of this process of grand scale privatisations. That said, the aim here is not to exhaust the knowledge on this particular object, but to use privatisations as a case study, a tool to unveil a larger blueprint. Having these remarks in mind, it will be argued that law 3986/2011 and law 4389/2016 creating respectively the Hellenic Republic Asset Development Fund (HRADF) and the Hellenic Corporation of Assets and Participations (HCAP), also called the 'super-Fund', are deeply entrenched, legally and politically, in the

10 The post-crisis landscape in Greece is defined by the formal exit from the Memoranda era in August 2018 and the beginning of the enhanced surveillance framework pursuant to Regulation (EU) 472/2013 of the European Parliament and of the Council of 21 May 2013 on the strengthening of economic and budgetary surveillance of Member States in the euro area experiencing or threatened with serious difficulties with respect to their financial stability [2013] OJ L140/1.

11 The notion of 'sector' refers to the 'sectoral Constitution' described by Kaarlo Tuori with regard to the European Constitution. See Kaarlo Tuori, ***European Constitutionalism*** (Cambridge University Press 2015) 22–23.

Greek legal order. In this sense, they form part of the Greek living Constitution. They also represent a paradigm shift in the Greek economic Constitution, which has undoubtedly moved to a more (neo-)liberal direction in this realm. The dilemma to privatise or not seems utterly irrelevant now. In fact, several institutional mechanisms that allow massive privatisation schemes have already been put into place and all legal and political barriers that could block privatisations have been lifted.

The first part of this chapter will attempt to show how the privatisation programme has been implemented so far in Greece through the media of the HRADF and the HCAP, without omitting to highlight the reactions that they have created. The second part examines the subsequent evolution of the Greek economic Constitution in the field of privatisations in order to explain, in the third part, in which way this change fits the description of what Balkin calls a 'constitutional construction' and how its constitutional and democratic legitimacy is produced.

2 Privatising in action

The era of the Memoranda has been marked by ambitious privatisation schemes. They have certainly not been carried out in full, but they haunted nonetheless political controversies and, yet more, public discourse for a long period of time. The issue of privatisation in Greece lent itself in the past few years to a widespread socio-political debate and unfortunately led in some cases in exasperated terms over the role of the state, the limits of private initiative and the perspectives of the Greek economy in general. This debate concerned above all the constitutional limits to privatisation and the (lack of) democratic legitimacy of the measures taken within the context of the economic crisis. It is important therefore to describe how the policy on privatisations has been set out and shaped in order to be able then to study the relation between democracy and economic crisis under the aegis of the Constitution.

2.1 The HRADF[12]

In light of these preliminary remarks, it is important to state beforehand that the HRADF experience in Greece seems so far to have been unprecedented[13]

12 This part draws much of the information about the HRADF from the article by Apostolos Vlachogiannis, 'The Greek Experience of Privatisation through the Hellenic Republic Asset Development Fund' (2019) 15 *Int. J. Public Policy* 78.

13 Johannes Masing, 'Droits fondamentaux et privatisations: Une perspective allemande' (2013) 9 Jus Politicum http://juspoliticum.com/article/Droits-fondamentaux-etprivatisations-une-perspective-allemande-648.html (accessed 6 April 2020); Ugo Mattei, 'Rendre inaliénable les biens communs', *Le Monde Diplomatique* (Paris, 11 December 2011) www.monde-diplomatique.fr/2011/12/MATTEI/47058 (accessed 6 April 2020).

in Europe.[14] The only historical precedent for this operation is the creation of the *Treuhandanstalt* after the fall of the German Democratic Republic and the reunification of Germany.[15] In no other European country that we know of has such a large-scale privatisation been carried out in such terms and in such a compressed period of time. This of course only points to the complex issue of democratic legitimacy of this grandiose project. But first, we need to know how things happened at the first place.

Seen from a historical perspective, the development of public assets has steadily been used by the Greek state in order to boost economic growth and contribute to overcoming financial hardships in turbulent periods.[16] However, no historical precedent is comparable to what has happened during the past few years. It is not only the scale of the programme that has been devised and put to practice since 2011, but also the instrument for its implementation which has contributed to the uniqueness of the current situation. The establishment of the HRADF has altered Greek understanding of the process of privatisation. It has also significantly affected, for better or for worse, the way that it is run. The programme is massive, employs a technocratic structure that hinders political accountability as well as judicial review. Moreover, it touches sensitive areas of state sovereignty. That said, it promises to deliver faster and better results, hence more efficiency.

In order to understand the unique nature of the HRADF and evaluate its functioning, we have to examine its genealogy, namely the conditions that led to its creation. The specific privatisation program has not in fact stemmed from a national political debate, as was the case in the early 1990s, nor was it part of an electoral campaign of any party at that time. It came out as a pure necessity imposed by Greece's lenders and as a condition, among others, for cashing out the requisite loans in order to avert the country's bankruptcy.[17]

The HRADF was established on 1 July 2011 by virtue of law 3986/2011, which has been subsequently modified by a series of other laws, as a corporation (*société anonyme*) whose sole shareholder was the Greek state. Its primary goal, as described in the Medium-term Fiscal Strategy Framework 2012–2015, has

14 There seems to be a striking analogy with the Chilean experience as described by Patricio Meller, 'A Review of Chilean Privatization Experience' (1993) 33 *The Quarterly Review of Economics and Finance* 95 and Eduardo Bitran and Pablo Serra, 'Regulatory Issues in the Privatization of Public Utilities: The Chilean Experience' (1994) 34 *The Quarterly Review of Economics and Finance* 179.

15 For the Treuhandanstalt see Peter Badura, 'Constitutional and Legal Problems of Privatization in Germany' (1991) 5 *Direito e justiça* 31, 41 ff.

16 Manolis Velegrakis, *The Notion of Public Property in Greek Law* [in Greek] (Nomiki Vivliothiki 2012) 60; Kostas Kostis, *History's Spoiled Children: The Building of the New Greek State 18th–21st century* [in Greek] (Polis 2013) 313 ff.

17 The first Memorandum of Economic and Financial Policies annexed to law 3845/2010 sketched out explicitly the preparation of a forthcoming privatisations programme. Law 3985/2011, which preceded the law creating the HRADF and through which the Medium-Term Fiscal Strategy for 2012–2015 was approved, contained in Chapter B II a specific privatisations programme in order to boost public revenue. Since then, privatisations have been a constant of all bailout and post-bailout agreements.

been to serve the national debt by reorganising the management of assets owned by the state and generating revenues. At the same time, the portfolio of the HRADF, containing not only real estate but also infrastructure and corporate assets, could be regarded as a means of securing the lenders' claims in Greece.[18] By contrast, the HRADF also appears to fulfil another goal of a completely different nature: attracting foreign investment and contributing to the liberalisation of markets previously controlled by state monopolies. The list of the assets transferred illustrates this mission quite clearly: ports, airports, national highways, the railway company, part of the electricity and energy network and other infrastructure are all included in its portfolio.

This confusion about the goals promoted by the activity of the HRADF – leading one to think that it would be more correct to speak of an evolution of goals – is inherent in the operation of the HRADF. It is sufficient to translate its name literally from Greek, 'Fund for the Development of Private Property of the State'. However, the name of the HRADF does not fully correspond to its portfolio and its operation. Given the classic distinction in French administrative law, which has been also adopted by Greek doctrine,[19] between private and public property of the state, many of the items contained in the HRADF's portfolio typically belong to the public property of the state. These items extend far beyond the notion of commons and envelop public entities that cannot be legally sold nor be stripped of their public character. They include ports, airports, national highways, and land plots extending to the seashore.[20] This proves, beyond doubt, the point that the HRADF, far from selling exclusively private property, is actually managing public property of the state. When items cannot be sold, their use is conceded to private entities for a period of up to 99 years. As a consequence, by assigning the privatisation of these assets to the HRADF, the settled fundamental distinction between private and public is completely blurred.

The creation and subsequent operation of the HRADF aroused, especially at an early stage, many reactions from all sides of the political spectrum. Following the initial reactions, several movements attempted to translate them into legal terms.[21] In its turn, this led to the rise of many constitutional grievances, which were articulated as constitutional claims challenged by the courts. These grievances were basically directed towards the creation itself as well as the way that the HRADF fulfils its mission. First of all, the issue of the violation of the democratic principle and the principle of national and popular sovereignty,

18 This is a point that we should hold on for now to and which will be further elaborated in section 2.2.

19 Velegrakis (n 16) 51 ff.

20 See official site www.hradf.com/en/portfolio (accessed 6 April 2020).

21 Balkin describes in his *Living Constitutionalism* (n 4) 332–334 this process of translating constitutional politics into constitutional law, in which lawyers and judges alike engage, as a horizontal translation as opposed to the notion of (vertical) translation proposed by Lawrence Lessig. See his monumental article 'Fidelity in Translation' (1993) 71 *Texas L. Rev.* 1165.

enshrined in art. 1 of the Constitution[22] has been raised. Concretely, the terms of the deal leading to its creation have been described as 'colonial-style'[23] and stripping the country of its 'family silver';[24] in other words, the country is considered to have been thus alienated from most of its valuable resources and infrastructure.

This has also given rise to more specific issues of democratic legitimacy and accountability. On the one hand, the primacy of the executive over the legislature is seen as a democratic downturn denounced for its repeated occurrence. Referring to the German theory of '*Wesentlichkeit*', all important decisions affecting the general course of the country should be taken in Parliament through the voting of a law.[25] However, the founding statute of the HRADF contains a delegation clause to an administrative organ, the Inter-ministerial Restructuration and Privatisation Committee, to which has been assigned the power to transfer to the HRADF any other asset than those specifically mentioned by the founding statute. On the other hand, the creation of a limited liability company governed entirely by private law but also serving public interest goals of the utmost importance is considered to blur the exact nature of the HRADF and block any form of accountability. It is not easy to understand to what extent the HRADF is still governed by public law. As a consequence, it is impossible to affirm if the state is still entirely in charge of this operation.[26]

As for the process of privatisation itself, there have been objections over conflict of interest in some cases, most importantly in the case of the lease-back of 28 government buildings.[27] Moreover, in the case of Elliniko, the sale of the biggest land plot in Europe, complaints about favouritism and sudden modification of the terms of the tender process have put into question the transparency of the privatisation procedure.[28] The same complaints have been repeated on the

22 Para 2. Popular sovereignty is the foundation of government.
Para 3. All powers derive from the People and exist for the People and the Nation; they shall be exercised as specified by the Constitution.

23 Akritas Kaidatzis, 'To Whom do the State's Assets Belong? Who is permitted to sell them and how?' [in Greek] in Iro Sagounidou-Daskalaki (ed.), *TAIPED: An Instrument for the 'Sell-Off' of Public Property and for the Abolition of the National Sovereignty of Greece* (2nd edn, Andy's Publishers 2012).

24 Tom Bawden and Charlie Cooper, 'Everything Must Go! The Great European Fire Sale', *The Independent* (London, 18 February 2012) www.independent.co.uk/news/world/europe/everything-must-go-the-great-european-fire-sale-7079815.html (accessed 6 April 2020); Sagounidou-Daskalaki (ed.) (n 23).

25 Jürgen Staupe, *Parlamentsvorbehalt und Delegationsbefugnis. Zur „Wesentlichkeitstheorie' und zur Reichweite legislativer Regelungskompetenz, insbesondere im Schulrecht* (Duncker und Humblot 1986)103 ff.

26 This point will be further discussed in the following section about the HCAP.

27 Judgment 275/2013 of the 7th Sub-Chamber of the Court of Audit, which was later reversed by judgment 1204/2014 of the 6th Chamber, highlighted a conflict of interest in this transaction and annulled it.

28 Judgment 197/2014 of the 7th Sub-Chamber of the Court of Audit, which was later reversed by judgment 3800/2014 of the 6th Chamber, had initially struck down the transfer of Ellinikon.

occasion of the public tender organised for the casino included in the Elliniko area.[29]

Last but not least, it has been argued that the privatisation scheme, implemented through the means of a limited liability company governed by private law, leads to an evasion of efficient judicial control by exploiting the gaps in the Greek system of dual jurisdiction. In fact, due to the organisation of the system of justice, administrative tribunals and most importantly the Supreme Administrative Court, the Council of State (CoS), do not have jurisdiction to control the acts of a corporation, except at the very premature stage of the transfer of the asset to the HRADF. All the while, civil tribunals lack the legal tools needed in order to provide an efficient check on these forms of transactions. Moreover, the CoS has adopted a strict interpretation of the rules of standing limiting the right of citizens groups and trade unions to challenge privatisation. This has been criticised as generally restricting the right to effective judicial protection.[30] The overall result is that the political decision concerning privatisations can only be attacked at a relatively premature stage, when its consequences are not yet obvious, and by very few actors. This means that the planned privatisation can go mostly unchallenged as to its substance.

However, it has to be emphasised that all these grievances, though they have mobilised an array of politicians, activists, and citizens groups, especially until 2015, have been recognised as unfounded by the Council of State, which has blocked just one privatisation, and this under very special circumstances. The only case where a claim was found valid, was the transfer to the HRADF of the majority shares of the Athens Water and Sewage Company.[31] As will be explained in the next part, this shows that the CoS could indeed have blocked other privatisations as well, even at their early development. It also shows, in a marked way, the discrepancy between alleged and confirmed violations of the law and the Constitution. Several scholars, political movements, and citizen groups, are convinced, from their point of view, of the illegality and unconstitutionality of the transfers and are therefore prone to consider them illegitimate, whereas, law-makers, the administration, and the courts share a completely different approach on this matter. The courts especially have mostly allowed the process to unfold without hindrance. Taking into consideration the political will to proceed with privatisations and the substantial economic and financial stakes at hand they have adopted a largely deferential and probably consequentialist approach.

29 The case is pending before the CoS, where an action for annulment has been filed against decision 10/2020 of the Authority for the Examination of Preliminary Appeals (Remedies Review Body).

30 Eleni Lappa, 'Circumventing judicial control with regard to privatisations of public enterprises' [in Greek] (2015) *The Constitution* 23, 31–32.

31 CoS Plen 1906/2014 (declaring unconstitutional the transfer from the State to Hellenic Republic Asset Development Fund of shares corresponding to 34,033% of the share capital of Athens Water Supply and Sewerage Company).

2.2 The super-fund

The HCAP (also known as the super-Fund), was established in May 2016 by virtue of law 4389/2016, which has been modified by numerous subsequent laws. The HCAP owns a portfolio which comprises almost anything of value owned by the Greek state: shares of all public utility companies still controlled by the state (electricity, natural gas, water and sewage); more than 70,000 real estate items across Greece including infrastructure left from the Olympic Games of 2004; small islands, marinas and tourist facilities; all the main ports and regional airports; large portions of the banks' share capital; public transports; postal services; shares in an oil company and others.[32]

What is intriguing is the fact that all these assets are virtually controlled by the European Commission and the European Stability Mechanism (ESM). According to articles 191 and 192 of law 4389/2016, the Supervisory Board (SB) of the HCAP holds some very important powers. It is responsible for nominating the board of directors of the corporation, among whom are the chairman and chief executive officer; it supervises and evaluates their actions and decisions and can also revoke them. In a more or less similar way, the SB controls the governing boards of the subsidiary companies of the HCAP. Furthermore, the transfer back to the Greek state of any item contained in the portfolio of the company rests upon its agreement.

The SB consists of five members only nominally appointed by the general assembly of the sole shareholder, i.e. the Greek state. In reality, only three members are selected by the Greek state, with the agreement of the European Commission and the ESM which act jointly; whereas two members, one of whom is the chairman, are selected by the Commission and the ESM, acting jointly, with the agreement of the Minister for Finance. At this point, it must be added that every decision needs four votes (art. 191 para 6). The conclusion is that the members selected by the European Commission and the ESM enjoy the power of veto. Based on the above, especially taking into consideration the way that the organ is legally constituted and the very important powers that have been granted to it, some authors have been led to argue that the creation of the HCAP is unconstitutional; for it violates the principle of national sovereignty.[33]

Compared to the HRADF, certainly, the goal of revenue collection is still on the table. For a period of 99 years – the duration of the super-fund – state assets shall be mainly used in order to pay off national debt. In fact, according to article

32 As a whole, the super-Fund is the owner of the totality of shares of the HRADF, the Public Properties Company (ETAD) and the Hellenic Financial Stability Fund (HFSF). Its portfolio also contains participations in several State-Owned Enterprises (SOEs) operating in core sectors of the Greek economy (energy, water and sewerage, infrastructure, transportation, services etc.), such as the Public Power Corporation (DEI), the Post (ELTA), the Athens Public Transport Organisation (OASA).

33 Sotiris Lytras, 'Public Entities and the "Hellenic Corporation of Assets and Participations (HCAP)"', (2019) *Journal of Administrative Law* 173, 186.

199, all privatisation revenues coming from HRADF are still channelled 100% towards the paying off of the debt (the same goes for the revenues from the Hellenic Financial Stability Fund); whereas all other forms of revenue shall be split, so that half will be used to pay off the national debt and half will be used for investments either by the Greek state or by the HCAP, based on the super-fund's investment policy. It is therefore evident that the creation of the new fund has just accrued the range of sources of revenue destined to pay off the debt by leaving intact the existing ones.

However, the new scheme should also be examined in a new light. All state assets have been placed under the lender's supervision as collateral for the loans provided. It is worth noting that the original plan for the creation of the super-Fund was part of the Grexit scenario, which unfolded in July 2015, as recorded by the *Guardian*.[34] It should be pointed out here that the HRADF was also partially designed to fulfil this task, but in a very superficial and inefficient way, because it was still controlled by Greek authorities. This is no more the case. The lenders have finally got hold of the management of the assets through the creation of the HCAP and succeeded in using it as collateral. To illustrate this point, law 4549/2018 has ratified the June 2018 Amendment Agreement relating to the accession of HCAP to the agreement signed between the ESM and Greece in 2015 – i.e. the third bailout agreement. The purpose of this accession, as stated in the new clause 14.2A of the agreement,[35] is, also to guarantee that in case of non-performance by the Greek state of its obligations under the initial agreement the HCAP will act as guarantor and pay the amount due or indemnify the ESM accordingly.

In addition to that, the previously defective form of democratic accountability (the decision of the Inter-ministerial Restructuration and Privatisation Committee and transfer to the state-controlled HRADF) is abolished. Most of the state assets have already been transferred to the HCAP through law 4389/2016, which was voted in order to implement the loan agreement of 2015 and is therefore a direct offspring of the third financial aid agreement signed by Greece. Some other subsequent laws followed soon thereafter – mainly 4425/2016. From that point on, the umbilical cord with the state is cut once and for all. Every previous remark about the defaults of the function of the HRADF is thus not only reaffirmed but also exacerbated.

To sum up, the creation of the new super-Fund seems to add some qualitatively new elements into the experience that we have had so far, proving further the point that the policy on privatisation is not a passing choice but a permanent feature of our constitutional structure.

34 Ian Traynor, 'Three Days that Saved the Euro' *The Guardian* (London, 22 October 2015) www.theguardian.com/world/2015/oct/22/three-days-to-save-the-euro-greece (accessed 18 April 2020).

35 For the full text of the amended Agreement see: www.esm.europa.eu/sites/default/files/greece_ffa_consolidated_june_2018.pdf (accessed 26 April 2020).

3 The subsequent evolution of the economic constitution

In this part, drawing on the description of the creation and the ensuing role of the HRADF and the HCAP in the implementation of the privatisations programme, the effects which it has had on constitutional doctrine will be analysed. The activity in which these two companies have been engaged will be contextualised within the greater framework of the evolution of the Greek Constitution, in order to defend afterwards the thesis that they form part of a durable constitutional construction.

The notion of the economic Constitution stems from the German interwar theoretic discussion and is usually associated with the ordoliberal school of thought. According to ordoliberals, the (Weimar) Constitution incorporated and should have incorporated a 'total decision' (*Gesamtentscheidung*) in favour of the free market.[36] Since then, the notion of economic Constitution has become a term of art and is now mainly used to describe the set of rules and principles regulating the national economy and shaping the relations between the state and the free market. Analysis will be based on this more generally accepted latter version.

The Greek Constitution has always been read as being economically neutral, as actually most of the constitutions tend to be read.[37] It does not choose between private initiative and market economy (art. 5 para 1[38] and art. 17 para 1[39]), on the one hand, and state intervention and regulation on the other (art 106);[40] nor does it favour the maintenance or inauguration of a particular economic system.[41] It more or less allows every government to freely shape its policy within the boundaries of the Constitution.[42] Just as the 1980s was the era of nationalisations and interventionist policy, the 1990s was the era of (rather timid) efforts of market liberalisation.

36 Tuori, 'The European Financial Crisis – Constitutional Aspects and Implications' (n 9) 2.

37 Tuori, *European Constitutionalism* (n 11) 183.

38 All persons shall have the right to develop freely their personality and to participate in the social, economic and political life of the country, insofar as they do not infringe the rights of others or violate the Constitution and the good usages.

39 Property is under the protection of the State; rights deriving there from, however, may not be exercised contrary to the public interest.

40 Para 2. Private economic initiative shall not be permitted to develop at the expense of freedom and human dignity, or to the detriment of the national economy.

Para 3. With the reservation of the protection provided in article 107 in connection with the re-export of foreign capital, the law may regulate the acquisition by purchase of enterprises or the compulsory participation therein of the State or other public agencies, in the event these enterprises are of the nature of a monopoly or are of vital importance to the development of sources of national wealth or are primarily intended to offer services to the community as a whole.

41 Giorgos Gerapetritis, 'Constitution and European Union Law Regarding the Privatisation of Ports' [in Greek] (2009) *Business and Company Law* 269, 270.

42 Art 82 para 1 of the Constitution states accordingly that '[t]he Government shall define and direct the general policy of the Country, in accordance with the provisions of the Constitution and the laws'.

Several leading decisions by the CoS regarding the functional[43] privatisation of telecommunications and the energy sector had defined during the 1990s the constitutional framework within which privatisations must take place in order that the balance between state intervention and the free market is preserved, in conformity with the Constitution.[44] That said, a leading precedent at the end of this period set, for the first time, specific constitutional limits on the concession to private individuals of a power reserved for the state.[45] At the same time, the prevalent approach in scholarship was to construe the Constitution mostly as a barrier, forbidding a wide spectre of transactions transferring to the private sector goods and services that are under the control of the state.[46] This means that the debate was still open. Constitutional doctrine produced by the courts seemed more eager to accept privatisations in principle, but also provided for the basic legal arsenal to scholars defending the conception of the Constitution as a barrier to privatisations.

In light of this, it only appears natural that when the HRADF was created in 2011 many tried to interpret and evaluate it, from a constitutional point of view, by using the previous tools and doctrines. It hardly seems as a surprise that the initial reaction was to consider the creation of the HRADF as transgressing the boundaries imposed by the Constitution.[47] What remained however to be found was if the current privatisation program could be seen in continuity with previous privatisation efforts, hence subject to the same rules and limits; or if it constituted a rupture, hence a radical paradigm shift, which pushed for a reconceptualisation of the process and the reestablishment of the rules and principles that govern it.

It is without doubt that the establishment of the HRADF and subsequently of the Super-fund has definitely changed not only the way of thinking about privatisations but also what is believed about the existence of constitutional barriers to privatisations. The first mark of this rupture was the persistent will of the legislator to go forward with the plan despite the reactions. It should be remembered here, that the government is first and foremost responsible for shaping

43 As functional – and therefore not proprietary – privatisation is qualified any delegation of a public task or service to private individuals. Akritas Kaidatzis, 'A Typology of the Constitutional Limitations on Privatization' (2009) 10 *Hellenic Review of European Law* 79.

44 In a series of legal opinions (PE) controlling the legality of the relevant presidential decrees, the CoS elaborated on the constitutional principles governing the privatisation of public utility companies, such as the universality and equality of the services provided, as well as the principle of continuity (see CoS PE 158/1992, para 3; Cos PE 385/1995; CoS PE 33/1998).

45 CoS Plen 1934/1998 (declaring unconstitutional the granting to a private company of the power to impose parking fines).

46 The most prominent effort was the book by Akritas Kaidatzis, *Constitutional Limits of Privatizations* [in Greek] (Sakkoulas 2006). In a similar vein, we could also note Maria Karamanov, *The Limits of Privatizations, Sustainable State and Public Property* [in Greek] (Kyriakidis 2011).

47 The creation of the HRADF was indeed not welcomed by many scholars and was further deemed unconstitutional, for a number of reasons, as explained in the collective volume by Sagounidou-Daskalaki (ed) (n 23).

general policy and in particular the economic policy of the country, according to article 82 of the Constitution. Following this, the courts have, as a general rule, refrained from blocking privatisations completed through the medium of the HRADF. They have thus showed deference to political decision-making. The Council of State especially, acting as the Supreme Administrative Court and a de facto Constitutional Court has refused to annul transfers of public assets to the HRADF and consequently block privatisations. The only exception to the rule was the case of the Athens water and sewage company;[48] a case which has been emblematic but has also been criticised for its apparent inconsistency with previous case-law.[49] By contrast, in a series of judgments (more than 100) the CoS has rejected complaints about the privatisations' procedure and substance. These include cases regarding the privatisation of ports, airports, as well as land plots of great value.[50] All these decisions lead us to conclude that the once perceived barriers to privatisation by elements of the academic community and even previous constitutional doctrine are in reality parchment barriers according to the famous expression by James Madison.[51]

Subsequently, the way in which the HRADF and the super-Fund have operated so far combined with their mission to pursue privatisations on such a massive scale in the future are factors which push towards extensive market liberalisation. This can now be achieved even without additional political support, since all the necessary parts of the mechanism have been assembled allowing it henceforth to function in a quasi-autonomous mode. It could also be viewed as an attempt to transform the old social-democrat model to a new (neo-)liberal one. In this sense, the founding laws of the HRADF and the super-Fund should be treated as landmark statutes that signal a shift in the constitutional regime or the paradigm governing the economic Constitution. What still remains to be seen is how exactly this process has taken place and how it affects the overall democratic legitimacy of the system.

4 The policy of privatisations as a constitutional construction

The cataclysmic effects of the crisis, traceable in the whole spectre of the legal landscape (legislation, case-law, administrative practice, understandings shared by legal actors) have incited constitutional scholars to revise their assumptions

48 CoS Plen 1906/2014.

49 Georgios Karavokyris, The constitutional limits of privatisations of public utility companies: Commentary on judgment 1906/2014 of the Council of State (Plen.)' [in Greek] (2015) 63 *Hellenic Review of Human Rights* 161, 173.

50 See e.g. CoS Plen 1129 and 1144/2016 (Kos and Mykonos ports); CoS 506-510/2016 (Piraeus port); CoS Plen 1985–1986/2016 (14 regional airports); CoS Plen 1761/2019 (Elliniko area).

51 In Federalist Letter No 48, Madison writes: 'Will it be sufficient to mark, with precision, the boundaries of these departments, in the constitution of the government, and to trust to these parchment barriers against the encroaching spirit of power? This is the security which appears to have been principally relied on by the compilers of most of the American constitutions.'

about the relationship between the Constitution and reality. To what extent has a constitution, which is very hard to amend and indeed has not been amended during the past years,[52] been able to withstand the factual pressure of the crisis and evolve within its context so as to avoid that the constitutional system breaks as a whole?

The most notable theory developed in order to explain this discrepancy has been the theory of constitutional resilience offered by Contiades-Fotiadou. According to them, the term 'resilience' means the ability to adapt while fulfilling fundamental goals. It follows that 'a resilient constitution, when faced by a severe crisis, can adapt without losing its normativity and allows democracy and the rule of law to also demonstrate resilience'.[53] In order to preserve the basic functions of the Constitution intact, a degree of elasticity and flexibility to its provisions should first be accorded, necessary to accommodate the effects of reality until the Constitution bounces back and constitutional normality is restored (recovery phase). Accordingly, four types of reaction to the crisis appear: adjustment, breakdown, submission, and stamina.[54] The writers argue that the Greek case has been mainly a case of submission: the constitutional system survived by wholly surrendering to the caveats of the crisis, without however suffering a breakdown of its most vital functions.[55] This latter point of view is further reinforced by other authors supporting the idea that the Greek Constitution proved itself during the crisis and managed to preserve intact its most essential features.[56]

This interpretation of the Constitution's reaction to the crisis has the advantage of reconciling smoothly the inamendability of the Constitution with the undeniable subtle (or not so subtle) changes which it has endured. It offers moreover a very persuasive account of the crisis case-law, covering an initial phase of submission and a subsequent phase of recovery through reaction.[57] However, this approach is limited to certain aspects of the crisis and cannot be applied in every field. More profoundly, it completely eludes the question of change: not everything was meant to be the same after the crisis. On the contrary, some things were there to stay.

52 The Constitution was amended only in November 2019. However, no amendment bears a relation to privatisations. As a further remark, it must be noticed that the crisis experience appears to have had little impact on the 2019 amendments, which have mostly dealt with pre-crisis issues. See Venizelos (n 1) 682, 688.

53 Xenophon Contiades and Alkmene Fotiadou, 'On Resilience of Constitutions. What Makes Constitutions Resistant to External Shocks?' (2015) *9 International Constitutional Law Journal* 3.

54 Xenophon Contiades and Alkmene Fotiadou, 'How Constitutions Reacted to the Financial Crisis' in Xenophon Contiades (ed), *Constitutions in the Global Financial Crisis. A Comparative Analysis* (Routledge 2013) 47–52.

55 Contiades and Fotiadou, 'On Resilience of Constitutions. What Makes Constitutions Resistant to External Shocks?' (n 53) 3, 16.

56 See (n 1).

57 See Apostolos Vlachogiannis, 'From Submission to Reaction: The Greek Courts' Stance on the Financial Crisis' in Zoltán Szente and Fruszina Orosz (eds), *New Challenges to Constitutional Adjudication in Europe: A Comparative Perspective* (Routledge 2018) 72.

Following this last remark, it is necessary to provide an account of the constitutional changes brought about by the crisis. These changes are substantial, enduring, and discernible especially in the field of the economic Constitution. They represent fractures in the dominant, until the crisis, understandings of the constitutional canon and form part of new constitutional narratives[58] that need to be brought to light.

Critical for this understanding is the notion of constitutional constructions and the subsequent distinction between interpretation and construction in constitutional law. This theme has been a main topic of recent US constitutional scholarship.[59] It can also serve as a guide for exploring processes of constitutional change in different legal orders. As Balkin explains, when the constitutional text is vague or ambiguous, or offers an abstract standard or principle, or is mute, there can be no talk of 'constitutional interpretation'. Instead, doctrines created by courts, as well as institutions and practices created by the political branches are examples of constitutional constructions that flesh out and implement the constitutional text and its underlying principles.[60] Living constitutionalism, thus redefined, concerns the process of constitutional construction and can be understood as 'the process by which some durable or canonical constructions become embedded, extended, and supplemented in constitutional culture, while others are slowly limited, expunged, or made practically irrelevant'.[61]

This way of understanding the processes of constitutional change could also be applied in the Greek case. The difference would be that in Greece the driving forces of mobilisation were not, as in the theory proposed by Balkin, citizens' and movements' mobilisation, but top-down pressure from the EU institutions charged with the surveillance of the Greek economy and the implementation of the financial agreements signed. This pressure has led to structural reforms in several fields, such as market regulation, the social security system, labour law and budgetary rules. The ensuing reforms represent significant and lasting changes which have repercussions on the understanding of the Constitution and take the form of constitutional constructions.

Following these remarks and in order to prove that a constitutional construction regarding privatisations has indeed occurred, we have to examine if and how the laws governing the HRADF and the HCAP and the administrative and judicial practices surrounding them are entrenched in the Greek constitutional order. HRADF and its successor, the super-Fund, are first and foremost an offspring of the biggest crisis which Greece has undergone in its most recent

58 On the notion of 'constitutional narrative' see the exemplary article by Robert Cover, 'The Supreme Court 1982 Term – Foreword: Nomos and Narrative' (1983) 97 HLR 4, 4–5.

59 Keith Whittington, *Constitutional Construction: Divided Powers and Constitutional Meaning* (Harvard University Press 1999); Randy Barnett, *Restoring the Lost Constitution: The Presumption of Liberty* (Princeton University Press 2003); Laurence B. Solum, 'The Interpretation-Construction Distinction' (2010) 27 *Constitutional Commentary* 95.

60 Balkin, *Living Originalism* (n 4) 14–15.

61 Ibid., 315–316.

history. Only this fact is able to explain politically and financially their creation. The privatisation projects carried out have indeed been a constant feature of the crisis period. Given however the structure and portfolio of the new Fund especially, it is highly likely that privatisation will still continue to be a basic policy of the Greek state for the decades to come.

In fact, the current policy on privatisation has not only been an integral part of the fiscal adjustment programs implemented in Greece and therefore a passing corollary of the crisis. More importantly, it is further considered to be a central element of the post-Memoranda period. It has accordingly been incorporated into the enhanced surveillance status that the country has enjoyed since the summer of 2018 (eventually through the following decades). With respect to this, the annex to the Eurogroup statement on Greece of 22 June 2018 regarding the completion of the ESM programme[62] – a statement of high political importance sealing officially the era of the Memoranda – contains the commitments necessary to ensure the continuity and completion of reforms adopted under this programme.[63] In other words, it sets the political agenda of the decades to come, as well as the legal framework within which the enhanced surveillance of Greece, according to Regulation 473/2013 (part of the Two-pack), will take place. It should not come as a surprise that the fifth point out of six states that 'the Asset Development Plan and the Strategic Plan of HCAP will be implemented on a continuous basis' and further mentions specific privatisation projects to be completed during 2019 basically through the medium of the HRADF.

It is now possible to understand in which way the current policy on privatisation is deeply entrenched, legally and politically. First of all, it is based on a large political consensus. The HRADF was created by the PASOK (centre-left) and ND (centre-right) government, whereas the super-Fund was established by the SYRIZA one (left). Second, the official lenders of Greece have insisted all these years that such privatisation schemes should be implemented and have succeeded in gaining access to the management of the super-Fund. This means that the founding laws of the HRADF or the HCAP are not likely to be abolished or even essentially modified without the lender's acquiescence.[64] Third, courts, acting as independent agents, have not proved so far that they could – or wished to for that matter – set a barrier to privatisations. Last but not least, the privatisation goals set by the HRADF and the super-Fund are inextricably linked to

62 www.consilium.europa.eu/fr/press/press-releases/2018/06/22/eurogroup-statement-on-greece-22-june-2018/ (accessed 14 April 2020).

63 Annex: Specific commitments to ensure the continuity and completion of reforms adopted under the ESM programme www.consilium.europa.eu/media/35749/specific-commitments-to-ensure-the-continuity-and-completion-of-reforms-adopted-under-the-esm-programme.pdf (accessed 14 April 2020).

64 To prove this point, the amended Agreement signed between the ESM and Greece explicitly enounces the obligation of the beneficiary Member State (i.e. Greece) 'to promptly notify ESM upon becoming aware of any proposal to amend the HCAP Law or the HCAP Internal Regulation in a material respect and of the details of such amendment, and to provide to ESM such further information as ESM may reasonably require in connection with such amendment' [clause 3.7 i (i)].

the fiscal targets set by the European institutions and the commitments which the country must honour in order to be able to pay off its debt. The policy on privatisations is significantly reinforced by its compatibility with two of the most fundamental goals of the 'European Constitution': fiscal discipline and market liberalisation in sectors such as energy and transports. In the case of Greece, the two are inseparably linked together. All these elements taken into consideration, privatisations conceived as a general set of ideas, landmark statutes, administrative practice and judicial doctrine have formed a durable constitutional construction. They are therefore crucial to the proper understanding of Greece's Constitution-in-action after the crisis.

The legitimacy of this privatisation policy bears, nevertheless, a very complex question. The program has been approved by all governing parties as a means to avert economic catastrophe and the country's bankruptcy. It has also been silently approved by most of the important actors in the constitutional system and especially the courts exercising their power of judicial review. At the same time, the programme is directly linked to the fundamental EU goals of market liberalisation and fiscal discipline; goals that according to theory, are transubstantiated into national constitutional goals.[65]

But again, this analysis seems to beg the question of the legitimacy of these EU goals themselves from a European internal point of view. Whence exactly is democratic legitimacy to be drawn and where is it to be sought – at the national or the European level?[66] That said, examining here the question of EU's democratic deficit would lead us far astray. Suffice to say, regarding this case, that as long as the European goals themselves are legitimate and provided that the approval of this policy by all leading actors of the national constitutional system is taken into consideration, the constitutional construction of privatisation in Greece does enjoy democratic legitimacy, although of a different and more complex nature than common constitutional objectives.

5 Epilogue

The Greek Constitution has experienced during the years of the economic crisis a silent revolution – though not at all a 'velvet' one– that has reshaped some of

65 Article 28 of the Constitution, along with its interpretative declaration, form the legal basis of the country's accession to the European Union. Many scholars qualify this article as a 'portal' through which EU goals are integrated into the national legal order, thus provoking informal constitutional change. Lina Papadopoulou, *National Constitution and Community Law: The Question of Primacy* (A.N. Sakkoulas 2009) 443–446, where also all relevant citations can be found. This idea strikes an analogy with the principle of '*Europafreundlichkeit*' of the German Constitution, enshrined in the *Bundesfassungsgericht* Lisbon judgment (BVerfG, Judgment of the Second Senate of 30 June 2009 – 2 BvE 2/08, para 240).

66 Miguel Poiares Maduro and others, 'The Euro Crisis and the Democratic Governance of the Euro: Legal and Political Issues of a Fiscal Crisis' in Miguel Poiares Maduro and others, *The Democratic Governance of the Euro* (2012) *RSCAS Policy Paper* 2012/08 3 https://cadmus.eui.eu/handle/1814/23981 accessed 18 April 2020.

its core tenets, such as the equilibrium between state intervention and market economy. As a result, several new constitutional constructions have emerged that have replaced others. Privatisations are indeed one of them, since they are inscribed in the new 'normality' succeeding the crisis and signal a wholly new approach of the economic Constitution. Thus, a new era of privatisations comes into light forming part of the Greek living Constitution post-crisis. Understanding the place of these new constructions in the post-Memoranda constitutional structure is the key to understanding the role of the Greek Constitution and more generally of national constitutionalism within the gears of the new European economic governance.

In light of this comprehension of facts, Greece appears only as the tip of the iceberg – some would venture to qualify it as a guinea pig – conveying a larger blueprint which concerns processes that have already been set in action Europe wide (or to be more precise, within the whole of the Eurozone). For instance, France is also moving in this direction, which reinforces the idea that a more general tendency is at hand.[67] The true question that comes next of course is if the notion of construction serves as a guarantee of democratic legitimacy. In Balkin's theory the answer is easier to grasp, provided that the construction is the result of citizens' participation in constitutional decision-making processes and it does not stand in open contrast to fundamental constitutional principles.

In the Greek case, the answer is far harder to sketch. On a first level, this new construction is legitimate because it has passed political and judicial muster. It has been repeatedly called into question, but has withstood the blows and has survived all challenges, electoral ones included. It begets however, on a more profound level, the question of the legitimacy of the European project itself, severely tampered with through the crisis and often obfuscated in what is called multi-level constitutionalism.[68] While national constitutions that have endured the economic crisis maintain a shell of legitimacy, it is not at all certain that they enjoy substantive legitimacy when coming out of this trial. In fact, the exact same could be said about the cardinal notions of national and popular sovereignty which, as of late, have shared the same fate. This is why, all things considered, the evolution of the economic Constitution seems at the bottom to take the shape more of a silent revolution testing the democratic foundations and legitimacy of the national constitutional system as a whole.

67 Law no 2019-486 regarding growth and the transformation of companies, also known as Loi PACTE, provides in articles 130–136 for the privatisation of the three Paris airports. This move has caused much popular reaction and instigated a (failed) initiative to hold a referendum in order to avert it. In addition, article 137 of the same law provides for the privatisation of the national lottery company (*Française des jeux*).

68 For an overview of the issues see European Parliament, Constitutional Affairs Committee (Policy Department C), *Challenges of multi-tier governance in the European Union: Effectiveness, efficiency and legitimacy* (2012) https://espas.secure.europarl.europa.eu/orbis/sites/default/files/generated/document/en/BA0313053ENC_002.pdf (accessed 18 April 2020).

References

Ackerman Bruce, 'The Living Constitution' (2007) 120 *HLR* 1737

Amar Akhil Reed, *America's Unwritten Constitution: The Precedents and Principles We Live By* (Basic Books 2012)

Badura Peter, 'Constitutional and Legal Problems of Privatization in Germany' (1991) 5 *Direito e justiça* 31

Balkin Jack, 'The Constitution in the National Surveillance State' (2008) 93 *Minn. L. Rev.* 1

Balkin Jack, *Living Originalism* (Harvard University Press 2011)

Balkin Jack, 'Nine Perspectives on Living Originalism' (2012) 3 *University of Illinois L. Rev.* 101

Balkin Jack and Levinson Sanford, 'The Processes of Constitutional Change: From Partisan Entrenchment to the National Surveillance State' (2006) 75 *Fordham L. Rev* 489

Barnett Randy, *Restoring the Lost Constitution: The Presumption of Liberty* (Princeton University Press 2003)

Bawden Tom and Cooper Charlie, 'Everything Must Go! The Great European Fire Sale' *The Independent* (London, 18 February 2012) www.independent.co.uk/news/world/europe/everything-must-go-the-great-european-fire-sale-7079815.html (accessed 6 April 2020)

Bitran Eduardo and Serra Pablo, 'Regulatory Issues in the Privatization of Public Utilities: The Chilean Experience' (1994) 34 *The Quarterly Review of Economics and Finance* 179

Contiades Xenophon and Fotiadou Alkmene, 'How Constitutions Reacted to the Financial Crisis' in Xenophon Contiades (ed), *Constitutions in the Global Financial Crisis. A Comparative Analysis* (Routledge 2013)

Contiades Xenophon and Fotiadou Alkmene, 'On Resilience of Constitutions. What Makes Constitutions Resistant to External Shocks?' (2015) 9 *International Constitutional Law Journal* 3

Cover Robert, 'The Supreme Court 1982 Term – Foreword: Nomos and Narrative' (1983) 97 HLR 4

European Parliament, Constitutional Affairs Committee (Policy Department C), *Challenges of Multi-tier Governance in the European Union: Effectiveness, Efficiency and Legitimacy* (2012) https://espas.secure.europarl.europa.eu/orbis/sites/default/files/generated/document/en/BA0313053ENC_002.pdf (accessed 18 April 2020)

Gerapetritis Giorgos, 'Constitution and European Union Law Regarding the Privatization of Ports' [in Greek] (2009) *Business and Company Law* 269

Kaidatzis Akritas, *Constitutional Limits of Privatizations* [in Greek] (Sakkoulas 2006)

Kaidatzis Akritas, 'A Typology of the Constitutional Limitations on Privatization' (2009) 10 *Hellenic Review of European* Law 79

Kaidatzis Akritas, 'To Whom do the State's Assets Belong? Who is Permitted to Sell Them and How?' [in Greek] in Iro Sagounidou-Daskalaki (ed.) *TAIPED: An Instrument for the 'Sell-Off' of Public Property and for the Abolition of the National Sovereignty of Greece* (2nd edn, Andy's Publishers 2012)

Karamanov Maria, *The Limits of Privatizations, Sustainable State and Public Property* [in Greek] (Kyriakidis 2011)

Karavokyris Georgios, The Constitutional Limits of Privatizations of Public Utility Companies: Commentary on Judgment 1906/2014 of the Council of State (Plen.)' [in Greek] (2015) 63 *Hellenic Review of Human Rights* 161

Kostis Kostas, *History's Spoiled Children: The Building of the New Greek State 18th–21st Century* [in Greek] (Polis 2013)

Lappa Eleni, 'Circumventing Judicial Control with Regard to Privatizations of Public Enterprises' [in Greek] (2015) *The Constitution* 23

Lessig Lawrence, 'Fidelity in Translation' (1993) 71 *Texas L. Rev.* 1165

Lytras Sotiris, 'Public Entities and the "Hellenic Corporation of Assets and Participations (HCAP)"', (2019) *Journal of Administrative Law* 173

Maduro Miguel Poiares and others, 'The Euro Crisis and the Democratic Governance of the Euro: Legal and Political Issues of a Fiscal Crisis' in Miguel Poiares Maduro and others, *The Democratic Governance of the Euro* (2012) *RSCAS Policy Paper* 2012/08 3 https://cadmus.eui.eu/handle/1814/23981 (accessed 18 April 2020)

Manitakis Antonis, 'The Impressive Resilience of the Greek Constitution in the Current Financial Crisis' in Lina Papadopoulou and others (eds), *Legitimacy Issues of the European Union in the Face of Crisis: Dimitris Tsatsos in Memoriam* (Nomos Verlag 2017)

Masing Johannes, 'Droits fondamentaux et privatisations: une perspective allemande' (2013) 9 *Jus Politicum* http://juspoliticum.com/article/Droits-fondamentaux-etprivatisations-une-perspective-allemande-648.html (accessed 6 April 2020)

Mattei Ugo, 'Rendre inaliénable les biens communs', *Le Monde Diplomatique* (Paris, 11 December 2011) www.monde-diplomatique.fr/2011/12/MATTEI/47058 (accessed 6 April 2020)

Meller Patricio, 'A Review of Chilean Privatization Experience' (1993) 33 *The Quarterly Review of Economics and Finance* 95

Papadopoulou Lina, *National Constitution and Community Law: The Question of Primacy* (A.N. Sakkoulas 2009)

Sagounidou-Daskalaki Iro (ed), *TAIPED: An Instrument for the 'Sell-Off' of Public Property and for the Abolition of the National Sovereignty of Greece* (2nd edn, Andy's Publishers 2012)

Solum Laurence B., 'The Interpretation-Construction Distinction' (2010) 27 *Constitutional Commentary* 95

Staupe Jürgen, *Parlamentsvorbehalt und Delegationsbefugnis. Zur 'Wesentlichkeitstheorie' und zur Reichweite legislativer Regelungskompetenz, insbesondere im Schulrecht* (Duncker und Humblot 1986)

Traynor Ian, 'Three Days that Saved the Euro' *The Guardian* (London, 22 October 2015) www.theguardian.com/world/2015/oct/22/three-days-to-save-the-euro-greece (accessed 18 April 2020)

Tuori Kaarlo, *European Constitutionalism* (Cambridge University Press 2015)

Tuori Kaarlo, 'The European Financial Crisis – Constitutional Aspects and Implications' (2012) EUI Working Papers LAW 2012/28, 17 ff. https://papers.ssrn.com/sol3/papers.cfm?abstract_id=2171824 (accessed 18 April 2020)

Velegrakis Manolis, *The Notion of Public Property in Greek Law* [in Greek] (Nomiki Vivliothiki 2012)

Venizelos Evangelos, 'Resilience, Adaptability and Amendment of the Constitution. Thoughts on a Comprehensive Evaluation of the 2009–2019 period' [in Greek] (2019) *Journal of Administrative Law* 682

Vlachogiannis Apostolos, 'From Submission to Reaction: The Greek Courts' Stance on the Financial Crisis' in Zoltán Szente and Fruszina Orosz (eds), *New Challenges to Constitutional Adjudication in Europe: A Comparative Perspective* (Routledge 2018)

Vlachogiannis Apostolos, 'The Greek Experience of Privatisation through the Hellenic Republic Asset Development Fund' (2019) 15 *Int. J. Public Policy* 78

Whittington Keith, *Constitutional Construction: Divided Powers and Constitutional Meaning* (Harvard University Press 1999)

Conclusion

Peace and discontent are phenomena that predetermine constitutional dynamics. Constitutional dynamics relates to the constitutional law in action. It conceptualises constitutionalism conceived as a process of permanent adjustment of the 'law in books' as provided by the constitution and the other sources of law to the socio-political reality on the basis of the activity of the constitutional players. Thus, several factors shape constitutional dynamics – the implementation of the constitution and the constitutional law by the office holders and the citizen, the jurisprudence of the courts, the patterns of constitutional adjustment of the people complying with the constitutional requirements or disagreeing and dissenting with them in a more or less intense manner.

Peace and discontent offer important angles for the proper understanding (deconstruction, reconstruction and construction) of constitutional law perceived as a complex, multi-layered phenomenon deeply embedded in the socio-legal context and dependent upon constitutional imaginaries and normative ideologies and ideas. They massively influence the socio-legal shapes of constitutional law and master the human comprehension of the constitutional frameworks of legitimate and legal social and political conflict. This framework is itself permanently questioned by the challenges to constitutional order and disorder stemming from the realm of economy, politics, and religion and having deep psychological and anthropological implications.

Peace and discontent have an impact on the legitimacy and efficiency of the constitution and the constitutional order. They have projections in all three dimensions of constitutionalism – ideal, normative-institutional and socio-legal. Peace and discontent are reflected in the perception of constitutional order or disorder in symbolic-imaginary constitutionalism, in the constitutional imagination and anthropology of the socio-political community. They master the institutional design for peaceful coexistence and for maintaining of order and disorder via positive law and the legal institutions. And they influence the outcome of the functioning of the constitutional system in the light of the dominant normative ideologies and ideas. This outcome results in important socio-legal imprints of order and disorder producing factual peace and discontent or at least general impressions of peace and discontent.

Peace and discontent are shaped by the interplay between constitutional conflict and constitutional consensus. Constitutional conflict and constitutional consensus are the dynamic forces which move forward the constitutional order. They are of pivotal importance for liberal-democratic constitutionalism. And they rest upon the assumption that vivid constitutional democracy is built upon the interaction between constitutional statics and constitutional dynamics, constitutional order and constitutional disorder, constitutional conflict and constitutional consensus.

Hence, peace and discontent as socio-political categories are transformed into constitutionally relevant phenomena by virtue of the way the constitution and the constitutional system engages and works with them producing constitutional order, constitutional disorder, or both. Thus, peace and discontent offer specific viewpoints on some of the conceptual issues of constitutionalism related to constitutional ontology, constitutional teleology, and constitutional axiology.

In that regard, peace and discontent have multiple reflections on constitutionalism and constitutional law. Peace and discontent, order and disorder, conflict and consensus impact constitutional theory, constitutional design, constitutional politics and constitutional pragmatics. They have not only a range of important manifestations with philosophical, positivist, realist, and socio-legal aspects, but also a multitude of determinants and implications stretched between politics, economy, anthropology, and law.

This is the mission of the current edited volume. It unites a range of approaches to peace and discontent. It questions not only the impact of peace and discontent, but also the ways peace and discontent are resulting from the functioning of the constitution and the constitutional order. Thus, the task of the book is twofold. First, it aims at discussing the influence of the social dynamics triggered by the spread, clash, and competition between socio-political forces on the constitution, constitutional law, and constitutional order. Second, it seeks to explore how constitution and constitutional law produce and maintain order or lead to disorder as a result of the impact of socio-political conflict and conflictual or consensual constitutional dynamics.

All chapters of the book are unified by their focus on peace, discontent, order, and disorder and their constitutional manifestations and implications. Here the concept of the 'constitutional' is conceptualised in a broad sense encompassing the constitutional projections of the political, economic and religious relations, exploring the formal, ideal, and material constitution on the national and supranational level, in contemporary, historic, and comparative perspective.

An advantage of this edited volume is the fact that it offers a multidiscursive perspective on peace and discontent and their constitutional determinants, foundations, and implications. The multidiscursive approach of the devotes special attention to the political implications of conflict and consensus. It discusses issues and deficiencies of contemporary democracies with regard to legitimacy, efficiency, authority, identity, and inclusiveness. In this regard, the constitutional foundations of democratic peace and democratic discontent in times of crisis and transition are explored. Moreover, the book provides for critical assessment of the socio-economic determinants of peace and discontent related to both conceptual issues such as the 'material constitution' and different sector-specific reforms of the welfare state having important constitutional implications.

Last but not least, the religious foundations of peace and discontent are also discussed with regard to their impact on shaping contemporary constitutionalism in general and religious constitutionalism in particular. One of the highlights of the volume is the discussion of important historic, comparative, and contemporary issues of peace, order, and disorder in composite societies and the related national, ethnocentric, and religious factors for peace or discontent.

Thus, the book explores the pivotal role of peace and discontent in their socio-political embeddedness and in their relation to the key challenges to constitutionalism and constitutional law at the beginning of the twenty-first century. The book frames the discussion within a sound critical approach that is directed towards the two most important levels of power – the national and the EU level. Special attention is devoted to peace and discontent in the EU constitutional order. The problems of peace and discontent are researched not only with a view to the EU level, with regard to which the material constitution of the EU is explored. Peace and discontent are researched also as conceptual problems impacting the interaction and the interrelation between the constitutional orders of the EU and the EU Member States with a view to the issues of judicial dialogue, competence delimitation, and constitutional identity.

The book brings the reader to several implicit conclusions. These conclusions are the result of the intellectual dialogue between the chapters and their contributors. They stem from the collective intellectual effort to conceptually frame, deconstruct, reconstruct, and expose the most important features of peace and discontent, order and disorder, conflict and consensus, to define their constitutional implications and to explore the responses given by the contemporary constitutional orders to topical political, economic, and socio-cultural challenges.

The book demonstrates that constitutional orders are deeply shaken by the simultaneous work of several factors that are the joint concern of the contributors to this volume although viewed from different prisms.

The first main concern is the rising democratic discontent. It consists in the increasing dissatisfaction of the citizen with the performance of constitutional democracies due to their decreasing ability to deliver authoritative, just, democratic, and efficient solutions to the challenges of our time. The democratic discontent is challenging the borderline between legality and legitimacy. It questions traditional distinctions of the conceptual, normative, and practical varieties of democracies. It blurs the line between peaceful deliberation and participation and radical forms of discontent such as civil disobedience, protest behaviour and revolution.

The book shows that there are conceptual and pragmatic underpinnings of contemporary constitutional conflict. They concern the cracks in the conceptual design (e.g. related to the material constitution), the outdatedness of the decisions provided by constitutional orders incapable of delivering adequate responses to topical issues, the rise of conflict potential between the EU and domestic constitutional orders (as demonstrated by the analysis of the Weiss decision of the German Federal Constitutional Court or by the critical assessment of constitutional identity), the crisis of neoliberalism and multiculturalism, and the problems related to important reforms in the sphere of labour and social security law, pension law, and privatisation impacting the constitutional principles of democracy and the welfare state.

Thus, the book demonstrates the huge potential for implosion of constitutional democracies under the current legal and socio-legal circumstances. In fact, this is a book that problematises the cracks in constitutional democracy which make it not only prone to external risks but may soon produce its internal implosion. The contributors to the book critically assess some of the most important and topical cracks in normative ideology, constitutional design, and socio-political performance and eventually try to give some predictions for the future development of peaceful and democratic coexistence, for the foreseeable aspects of democratic improvement or demise and for the future of constitutional order and disorder in the light of their exposure to the challenges at the beginning of the twenty-first century.

Index

For Product Safety Concerns and Information please contact our EU
representative GPSR@taylorandfrancis.com
Taylor & Francis Verlag GmbH, Kaufingerstraße 24, 80331 München, Germany

www.ingramcontent.com/pod-product-compliance
Ingram Content Group UK Ltd.
Pitfield, Milton Keynes, MK11 3LW, UK
UKHW022018230926
475702UK00029B/1841
* 9 7 8 0 3 6 7 5 3 9 7 2 6 *